The Charlton
Standard Catalogue of

First World War
Canadian
Infantry Badges

2ND EDITION

PUBLISHER
W. K. CROSS

PRICING EDITOR
AL ROSEN

The Charlton Press

TORONTO, ONTARIO • BIRMINGHAM, MICHIGAN

COPYRIGHT AND TRADEMARK NOTICE

Copyright © 1994 Charlton International Inc. All rights reserved.

The terms Charlton, Charlton's, The Charlton Press, the Charlton Cataloguing System, Charlton Numbers and abbreviations thereof, are trademarks of Charlton International Inc. and shall not be used without written consent from Charlton International Inc.

While every care has been taken to ensure accuracy in the compilation of the data in this catalogue, the publisher cannot accept responsibility for typographical errors.

No part of this publication may be reproduced, stored in a retrieval system, or transmitted in any form or by any means, electronic, mechanical, photocopying, recording, or otherwise without the prior written permission of the copyright owner.

No copyright material may be used without written permission in each instance from Charlton International Inc. Permission will be liberally given for the use of the CHARLTON CATALOGUE NUMBERING SYSTEM by anyone wishing to do so, including its uses in advertisements of items for sale provided Charlton receives proper acknowledgement in each instance.

Permission is hereby given for brief excerpts to be used for the purpose of reviewing this publication in newspapers, magazines, periodicals and bulletins, other than in the advertising of items for sale, provided the source of the material so used is acknowledged in each instance.

Canadian Cataloguing in Publication Data
Main entry under title:
The Charlton standard catalogue of First
World War Canadian Infantry badges
1991-
Biennial.
Description based on: 2nd. ed.
ISSN 0706-0424
ISBN 0-8968-156-2 (2nd ed.)
1. Canada. Canadian Army--Infantry--Insignia--
Catalogs. 2. Badges--Canada--Catalogs.

UC535.C3C42   355.1'4   C94-900410-3

**Printed in Canada
in the Province of Ontario**

The Charlton Press

**Editorial Office
2010 Yonge Street
Toronto, Ontario M4S 1Z9
Telephone (416) 488-4653 Fax: (416) 488-4656**

EDITORIAL

Editor	W. K. Cross
Pricing Editor	Al Rosen
Editorial Assistant	Jean Dale
Editorial Assistant	Davina Rowan
Layout	Frank van Lieshout
Cover Photography	David MacFadyen

ACKNOWLEDGEMENTS

The Charlton Press wishes to thank all those who have assisted in this Second Edition of The Charlton Standard Catalogue of First World War Canadian Infantry Badges. In particular we would like to recognize:

John Anderton, C. G. Brooker, Edward Denby, J. R. G. Edwards, Jeffrey Hoare, Hugh King, Stephen M. Pallas, Robert I. Rolleg, Robert J. Russell and L. T. Wood.

We offer special thanks to John Anderton for his assistance with the C.E.F. collar information, Hugh King for reviewing these listings against his extensive collection of C.E.F. insignia and Chris Brooker for sending us his work on C.E.F. badges.

ABOUT THE PRICING IN THIS CATALOGUE

The purpose of this catalogue is to give the most accurate, up-to-date retail prices for all First World War Canadian Infantry badges. These prices are drawn from both dealer and collector activity, recent auction results and are averaged to reflect the current marketplace for Infantry badges.

A necessary word of caution. No catalogue can or should propose to be a fixed price list. Collector interest, badge rarity factors and other vagaries of the hobby itself invariably dictate time of transaction retail values.

This catalogue then, should be considered as a guide, showing the most accurate current retail prices possible for the collector and dealer alike.

Our pricing editor, Al Rosen, invites correspondence with collectors and dealers on pricing information for the 3rd edition. Please write to him at: 211 Yonge Street, Suite 200A, Toronto, Ontario, M5B 1M4.

CANADIAN MILITARY BADGES

We have made more Badges for the Canadian Expeditionary Force than any other firm in England, having cut over 700 different dies since August, 1914.

The average prices for battalion orders of 1,000 upwards are :—

Cap Badges	...	...	... 6d. each (12 cents).
Collar Badges	...	...	... 7½d. per pair (15 cents).
Shoulder Titles	...	...	... 7½d. per pair (15 cents).

Special designs cost slightly more, while ordinary maple leaves and plain titles are considerably less.

Officers' badges, when ordered in conjunction with men's, come out at special rates.

Our factory is self-contained, thus enabling us to guarantee rapid deliveries at low prices.

We also make up artistic reproductions of any badge in gold and silver as souvenirs.

Whatever you want in these goods, WRITE US.

TIPTAFT LTD.

Northampton Street

BIRMINGHAM : : England

'PHONE : CENTRAL 6661.
Telegraphic Address :
"TIPTAFT, BIRMINGHAM."

Contractors to the Canadian Government

TABLE OF CONTENTS

INTRODUCTORY NOTE

We have expanded material in the individual listings by a factor of five in this Second Edition. This expansion covers minor varieties (mainly in the makers) and compositional differences of the badges. These listings may be difficult to follow at first but but as soon as one understands the different characteristics of the makers the listings will add a new dimension to the collecting of CEF badges.

As with all new catalogues there will be errors and omissions. We do welcome your comments and insight on how we can improve future editions. If you have new information we would appreciate hearing from you.

CONDITION

A discussion on condition flows against the concept of something that by order was meant to be cleaned and polished. Is it correct to classify, in this case, by price for quality? It certainly is for officers versus other ranks as in most cases there is a major quality difference in design and manufacture and this must be indicated by a price difference. If a collection is built around the desire to have a series of original mint badges then it is only fair that the value must be placed on condition, for as with anything else there are fewer high quality items than low quality. In the First Edition we priced in two grades. In the Second we have listed one insignia in (E. F.) extremely fine condition leaving out mint. We are leaving the definitions in the Second Edition for we still feel that the collector may be willing to pay a slight premium for a mint badge but not sufficiently and often to merit a mint pricing category.

MINT: As the word implies, straight from the makers. The badge will have full factory finish, original lugs and no part or section of the badge will be missing or replaced.

EXTREMELY FINE: The badge will have 50 to 75% of the original finish. No part or section of the badge will be missing or replaced. One or two of the original lugs may be replaced. The replacement, however, must not alter the original design concept of the badge.

MAJOR VARIETIES

The following criteria were used to define major varieties of a C.E.F. badge.

> **1.** A new or completely different rendition of a major device used on the cap, collar or shoulder title.

> **2.** Any change in the legend carried on the cap badge.

The maple leaf is one device that varies between makers, but we have considered that difference to be only minor and not to be classified within a major catagory.

MINOR VARIETIES

The following criteria were used to define major varieties of a C.E.F. badge.

1. Small variations in design bewteen makers
2. Small variations between dies of the same maker
3. Different finishes
4. Different metal composition.

We have attempted to record all the minor varieties that exist in the badges of the Canadian Infantry of World War One, however, it is probable that we have missed some and hope that future editions will capture those missed.

MANUFACTURERS

The following list of makers will illustrate how extensive the manufacturing of C.E.F. Insignia was during 1914-1918 period.

CANADIAN MANUFACTURERS

O. B. Allen	Jacoby
J. D. Bailey	Jackson
Birks	Kinnear & Desterre
D. E. Black	Geo. H. Lees
Caron Bros.	Maybees
Chauncey Maybees	McDougall
F. W. Coates	Patterson Bros.
Cook	D. A. Reesor
Creighton's	Reynolds
Dingley	Roden Bros.
Dingwall	Rosenthal
Ellis Bros.	Wm. Scully
J R. Gaunt & Son Ltd. (Montreal)	Stanley & Aylward
G. F. Hemsleys	Wellings
Inglis	Wheatley

UNITED STATES MANUFACTURERS

Service Supply Company

GREAT BRITAIN MANUFACTURERS

Brown	Hicks
Firmin & Son	Reiche
J. R. Gaunt Son Ltd.	Tiptaft Ltd.
Goldsmiths & Silversmiths Company Ltd.	

It is not clear whether all the makers listed above actually manufactured badges. In some cases a cap badge may appear with two raised or incused names on the back, such as "INGLIS/BLACK". Did this mean that Inglis struck the badges for Black? Further research is definitely required on makers.

FASTENERS

The method by which the metal insignia was attached to the clothing.

Different styles used: Lugs, tangs, slide and pin

FINISHES

Badge finishes: The coating applied over the raw metal of the badge.

This seems to be a matter of personal preference by the commanding officer of the battalion when ordering badges. So far we have been unable to determine if there was a set of criteria by which the choice of finish could be selected.

The following finishes could be used:

Pickled (khaki):	Greenish-brown coating of enamel
Browning:	Light brown coating of enamel to give the appearance of bronze to match the uniform colour (sometimes referred to as bronze)
Black:	Black coating of enamel
Antique:	Brown/black coating of enamel
Nickel Plating:	Nickel over copper, brass, etc.
Silver Plating:	Silver over copper, brass, etc.
Gilt:	Gold over silver, copper, etc.

COMPOSITION

The composition of the C.E.F. insignia is straight foward for the only requirement was to produce a clean, clear impression of the chosen design in metal.

Metals compositions most used were:

Other Ranks:	Copper, brass, white metal
Officers:	Bronze, silver, gold, silver-plate on copper or brass, on copper or brass

"C" OVER NUMERAL COLLARS

The following illustrations will assist in the identification of the various manufacturers.

OTHER RANK COLLARS

J. R. GAUNT, LONDON
"C" OVER NUMERAL

Height: 30 mm
Composition: Brass
Oval "C" with serif. No bar on collars 1 to 9. Numerals joined top and bottom on collars 10 and over.

TIPTAFT, BIRMINGHAM
"C" BAR NUMERAL - LARGE

Height: 32 mm
Composition: Brass; White metal
Oval "C" with serif. The "C" and numeral separated by a bar. Numerals open at the bottom on collars 10 and over.

TIPTAFT, BIRMINGHAM
"C" BAR NUMERAL - LARGE

Height: 32 mm
Composition: Brass
Round "C" without serif; "C" and numerals separated by a bar. Numerals open at bottom on collars 10 and over.

TIPTAFT, BIRMINGHAM
"C" BAR NUMERAL - SMALL

Height: 26 mm
Composition: Brass
Round "C" without serif; "C" and numerals separated by a bar. Open at bottom on collars 10 and over.

NCO COLLARS

We have been unable to identify the makers of these collars. At least three different makers exist, however, at present, our listings are unable to attribute specific makers to specific collar types.

GAUNT TYPE
"C" OVER NUMERAL - LARGE

Height: 28 mm
Composition: Brass; White metal
Round "C", bar at top and bottom of numeral.

TIPTAFT TYPE
"C" BAR NUMERAL - LARGE

Height: 28 mm
Composition: Brass
Round "C", bar at top only.
Numeral with serif

TIPTAFT TYPE
"C" BAR NUMERAL - SMALL

Height: 25 mm
Composition: Brass
Round "C" almost closed.
Bar at top only

NUMBERING SYSTEM

In this Second Edition we have continued the development of a numbering system that will be useful in cataloguing the numerous varieties of C.E.F. badges.

The Charlton numbering system is based on cap badge designs and assigning the battlion number to that badge. When there is more than one major variety for a battalion we have listed the authorized variety first, followed by the remaining major varieties. Interim badges are listed last as they are home-made spur of the moment designs used for very short periods. In some cases either the information authorizing the design has yet to be located or possibly the design was never authorized. In these instances the badge listed first can be assumed to be the badge most frequently used.

The system is designed as follows:

1. A number which indicates the (battalion) badge number.

2. When the badge number is followed by a letter A, B, C, etc., this signifies that the battalion has more than one badge design or that the badge design will be found with two or more major varieties.

3. Following the badge variety number is a two digit number relating to the different insignia broken down as follows:

01 - 19 OR's Cap (Glengarry)

20 - 39 Officers' Cap Badges

40 - 59 OR's Collar Badges

60 - 79 Officers' Collar Badges

80 - 90 OR's and NCO "C" over numberal Collar Badges

91 - 99 OR's Shoulder Numerals and Titles

Within these groups the catalogue listings are jump numbered 02, 04, 06, etc. This system will allow for new findings that will undoubtedly occur. They then can be entered into the listings without disturbing the numbers already in place.

MECHANICS OF BADGE AUTHORIZATION

Authorization for each cap, collar or shoulder title went through the same procedure as the one illustrated in the reproduction letter for the 257th Battalion badge.

ONTO.
BAY STREET
Ap. 1227

Essay

STANLEY QUALITY GOLD
FILLED LINES, STERLING
ENAMELED SOUVENIRS,
SWISS WATCHES, ETC.

New Address
Richmond St. East
Phone M. 5577
Office and Factory

CABLE ADDRESS: *Essay, Toronto*
DO NOT INSURE GOODS FOR US

Stanley & Aylward

WHOLESALE JEWELERS

MONTREAL.
416 LINDSAY BUILD
PHONE, Up 2275

14K. RINGS AND JEWELRY
ENGLISH GOLD LINES.
COMMUNITY SILVER,
NOVELTIES, ETC.
ESSEX WATCHES.

JAN 11 1917
682-493-1.

Toronto, January 10th, 1917.

Colonel J. F. McDonald,

Director General Clothing Dep't.,

Military Dep't.,

Ottawa, Ont.

Sir:

Pursuant to instructions from Colonel Martin of the 257th Construction Battalion, C. E. F., we herein beg to enclose you sketch of cap badge for his battalion, corrected as desired by him.

We have the honour to be Sir,

FJA/ AH   Respectfully yours

257th Battalion, C E. F.

This design is made up on an oval shield supported by a
small cartouche, bearing the word Over-seas and a beaver, with
figures 257 in relief in the centre of the badge, supported by
crossed hammer and gauge and also maple leaves. This forms a
support for the vignette, which consists of a Derrick and the
fore-part of a railroad engine, descriptive of Railway Construction and Garter will be a high relief and contain the words
"Canadian Railway Construction Battalion", the whole is surmounted
by a crown.

ADDRESS REPLY TO
THE SECRETARY, MILITIA COUNCIL.
HEADQUARTERS,
OTTAWA, CANADA

AND QUOTE NO. H. Q. 683-493-1

DEPARTMENT OF MILITIA AND DEFENCE

OTTAWA, January 20th, 1917.

34-4-7

From-
     The Quartermaster-General,
          Canadian Militia.

To- The General Officer Commanding,
          Military District No.2,
               Exhibition Grounds,
                    Toronto.

Design of Badge,
257 Construction Battalion,
     C.E.F.

Sir,-

I have the honour, by direction, to state that
the Officer Commanding the marginally noted Unit has
forwarded to Militia Headquarters design of Cap Badge
for his Unit, which design has been approved by the
Hon. the Minister; provision of the badge to be without
expense to the Public.

Will you be kind enough to notify the Officer
Commanding 257th Railway Construction Battalion
accordingly.

The original design is being retained at
Headquarters as a record, the prints are being made and
will be forwarded in the course of a few days.

I have the honour to be,

Sir,

Your Obedient Servant.

Major-General
Quartermaster-General

M. F. A. 162.
500 Rms.—10-16.
2773-30-276.

FHC

2 M.D. 34-4-7

Toronto, Ontario, January 23,   7

The D.A.A. & Q.M.G., M.D.,No. 2,

Exhibition Camp.

The Officer Commanding,

257th Construction Battn.,C.E.F.,

105 Queen St.,W., Toronto.

Design of Badge
257th Construction
Battalion, C.E.F.

I beg to inform you that a letter, dated

20th January H.Q. 683-493-1, is the authority for

the adoption of the badge marginally noted, by the

Battalion under your command. The original design

is being retained at Headquarters as a record, but

prints are being made, and will be forwarded in the

course of a few days. Please note that the provision

of this badge is to be without expense to the Public.

Lieut-Colonel,

D.A.A. & Q.M.G., M.D. No. 2.

M. F. B. 239.
1 million—10-16.
H.Q. 1772-39-194.

In any further
correspondence on
this subject please
quote Number and
Date of this Com-
munication.

No. 24-4-7

Ottawa, Ont. Jan. 29th, 1917. 191___

From O.C. 257th. B'n.C.E.F.

Ottawa, Ont.

To The D.A.A.&.Q.M.G. M.D. No. 2.,

Toronto, Ont.

Design of Badge.
257th. O-S.B'n.C.E.F.

Sir:-

I have the honor to acknowledge receipt
of your 2 MD 34-4-7 of 23rd.inst. relative to the
subject marginally noted.

It is noted that the provision of the
badge is to be without expense to the public.

I have the honor to be,

Sir,

Your obedient Servant,

Lt-Col.
O.C.257th. B'n.C.E.F.

ADDRESS REPLY TO
THE SECRETARY, MILITIA COUNCIL,
HEADQUARTERS,
OTTAWA, CANADA

AND QUOTE NO. H.Q.683-493-1

DEPARTMENT OF MILITIA AND DEFENCE

OTTAWA,...............Feb. 3, 1917.................

From-
　　The Quartermaster-General,
　　　　Canadian Militia.

To-
　　The General Officer Commanding,
　　　　Military District No. 2,
　　　　　　Exhibition Grounds,
　　　　　　　　Toronto.

Badges,
257th Construction Battn.,
C.E.F.
_____

　　Sir,-

　　　　Adverting to H.Q. letter under above number
of the 20th ultimo, on the marginally noted subject,
I have the honour to forward herewith prints of
design therein referred to.

　　　　　　　　I have the honour to be,

　　　　　　　　　　Sir,

　　　　　　　　Your obedient Servant,

　　　　　　　　　　Major-General,
　　　　　　　　Quartermaster-General.

HCO/C

2 M.D. 34-4-7

Headquarters,

Exhibition Camp,

Toronto, Ontario,

February 6, 1917.

From -
   The D.A.A. & Q.M.G.,
      M.D. No. 2.

To -
   The Officer Commanding,
      257th O.S.Battn.,C.R.T.,
         105 Queen Street West,
            Toronto, Ontario.

Design of badge

      With reference to my letter of the
23rd January, and to your reply of the 29th
ultimo, on the marginally noted subject, I beg
to forward herewith prints of the design of badge
authorized for the Unit under your command.

          Lieut-Colonel,

    D.A.A. & Q.M.G., M.D. No. 2.

EHC.

GENERAL LIST

BADGE NUMBER: —

CANADA

Makers: Lees, Roden,
Scully, Tiptaft
Fasteners: Lugs, Tangs, Slide
Composition:
Other Ranks: Pickled copper
or brass; Browning
copper or brass
Officers: Gilt
Ref.: Not previously Listed

Note: Numerous makers exist and all are not listed.

Badge No.	Insignia	Rank	Description	Extremely Fine
- 2	Cap	ORs	Pickled copper	5.00
- 4		ORs	Pickled brass	5.00
- 6		ORs	Browning copper	5.00
- 8		ORs	Browning brass	5.00
- 21		Officers	Gilt	6.00
- 41	Collars	ORs	Pickled copper	2.00
- 43		ORs	Pickled brass	2.00
- 45		ORs	Browning copper	2.00
- 47		ORs	Browning brass	2.00
- 61		Officers	Gilt	3.00
- 91	Shoulders	ORs	Title: "CANADA"	2.00

PRINCESS PATRICIA'S CANADIAN
LIGHT INFANTRY

The headquarters on mobilization was Valcartier, Quebec. The Battalion sailed October 3rd, 1914 with a strength of thirty-three officers and one thousand and eighty three men under the command of Lieutenant-Colonel F. D. Farquhar, DSO.

BADGE NUMBER: —

PRINCESS PATRICIA'S CANADIAN LIGHT INFANTRY

Makers: Birks, Firmin, Tiptaft
Fasteners: Lugs, Slide, Pin
Composition:
Other Ranks: Browning copper or brass
Officers: Gilt with silver centre
Ref.: Not previously listed

"PPCLI" Straight

"PPCLI" Curved Upward

Note: Numerous makers exist and all are not listed.

Badge No.	Insignia	Rank	Description	Extremely Fine
- 2	Cap	ORs	Browning copper	28.00
- 4		ORs	Browning brass	75.00
- 21		Officers	Gilt with silver centre; Firmin	120.00
- 41	Collars	ORs	Browning copper	20.00
- 43		ORs	Browning brass	40.00
- 61		Officers	Gilt with silver centre; Firmin	50.00
- 91	Shoulders	ORs	Title: "PPCLI", Straight	5.00
- 93			Title: "PPCLI", Curved upward	5.00

ROYAL CANADIAN REGIMENT

The headquarters on mobilization was Halifax, Nova Scotia. The Battalion sailed August 26th, 1915 under the command of Lieutenant-Colonel A. E. Carpenter with a strength of thirty-four officers and one thousand and fifty-two men.

BADGE NUMBER: —

CYPHER "GVR"

Makers: Gaunt, Tiptaft, Scully
Fasteners: Lugs
Composition:
Other Ranks: White metal with browning brass overlay on design
Officers: Silver with gilt on brass overlay on design
Ref.: Not previously listed

Note: Numerous makers of this badge exist but all are not listed here.

Badge No.	Insignia	Rank	Description	Extremely Fine
- 2	Cap	ORs	White metal, Browning brass overlay on design; Gaunt	35.00
- 4		ORs	White metal, Browning brass overlay on design; Tiptaft	35.00
- 21		Officers	Silver, Gilt on brass overlay on design	50.00
- 41	Collars	ORs	Brass	10.00
- 61		Officers	Silver	25.00
- 91	Shoulders	ORs	Title: "RCR"	5.00

1ST INFANTRY BATTALION

"ONTARIO REGIMENT"

The Battalion was raised in Southwestern Ontario with mobilization headquarters at Camp Valcartier, Quebec under the authority P.C.O. 2067 August 6th, 1914. The Battalion sailed October 3rd, 1914 under the command of Lieutenant-Colonel F. W. Hill with a strength of forty-seven officers and one thousand one hundred and six other ranks. The Battalion served in France with the 1st Infantry Brigade, 1st Canadian Division. It was disbanded September 15th, 1920.

BADGE NUMBER: 1

No. - 1A   **ONT/1/CANADA**

                      NOT AUTHORIZED

Makers: Caron, Gaunt, Hicks, Tiptaft
Fasteners: Lugs
Composition:
Other Ranks: Browning copper with white metal overlay on design
Officers: Unknown
Ref.: Babin, Meek, Stewart, Cox,

Note: Three makers of this cap badge exist.
1. Gaunt; Fine veined leaf design with small type for "Canada". The Ontario ribbon curves downward. There is no line behind the "1".
2. Hicks; Fine veined leaf design with small type for "Canada". The Ontario ribbon curves downward with an outlining depth line just behind the "1". *(Illustrated)*
3. Tiptaft; Heavey veined leaf design with large type for "Canada". The Ontario ribbon is straight.

Badge No.	Insignia	Rank	Description	Extremely Fine
1A-2	Cap	ORs	Browning copper, Wm. overlay on design; Gaunt	30.00
1A-4		ORs	Browning copper, Wm. overlay on design; Hicks	30.00
1A-6		ORs	Browning copper, Wm. overlay on design; Tiptaft	30.00
1A-21		Officers	Unknown	- -

Badge No.	Insignia	Rank	Description	Extremely Fine
			Maple Leaf with Overlay of Design	
1A-41	Collars	ORs	Browning copper, Wm. overlay on design; Gaunt	50.00
1A-43		ORs	Browning copper, Wm. overlay on design; Hicks	50.00
1A-61		Officers	Unknown	- -
			Maple Leaf Embossed with Design	
1A-45	Collars	ORs	Browning copper; Tiptaft	40.00
1A-63		Officers	Unknown	- -
			"C" Over Numbers	
1A-81	Collars	ORs	"C" over "1"; Gaunt	15.00
1A-83		ORs	"C" Bar "1", Large "C"; Tiptaft	10.00
1A-85		NCO	"C" Bar "1"; Unknown	15.00
1A-91	Shoulders	ORs	Numeral: "1" ; Caron	15.00
1A-93		ORs	Numeral: "1"; Unknown	15.00
1A-95		ORs	Title: "1st over CANADIAN"; Unknown	15.00

No. - 1B   WESTERN/1/ONTARIO

Makers: Tiptaft
Fasteners: Lugs
Composition:
Other Ranks: Browning brass with white metal overlay on design
Officers: Gilt on brass with silver overlay on design. Superior construction
Ref.: Babin, Cox

Badge No.	Insignia	Rank	Description	Extremely Fine
1B-2	Cap	ORs	Browning brass, Wm. overlay on design; Tiptaft	30.00
1B-21		Officers	Gilt on brass, Silver overlay on design; Tiptaft	50.00
			Overlay Design	
1B-41	Collars	ORs	Browning brass; Tiptaft	25.00
1B-61		Officers	Gilt on brass; Tiptaft	50.00

No. - 1C   WESTERN/1/ONT

"ONTARIO" ABBREVIATED VARIETY

Makers: Unknown
Fasteners: Pin
Composition:
Other Ranks: Bronze copper with
white metal overlay
on design
Officers: Unknown
Ref.: Not previously listed

Badge No.	Insignia	Rank	Description	Extremely Fine
1C-2	Cap	ORs	Bronze copper, Wm. overlay on design; Unknown	250.00
1C-21		Officers	Unknown	- -
1C-41	Collars	ORs	Unknown	- -
1C-61		Officers	Unknown	- -

No. - 1D   1/CANADA

INTERIM BADGE

Makers: As General List
Fasteners: Lugs, Slide
Composition:
Other Ranks: Unofficial, "1"
overlay on General
List
Officers: Not known
Ref.: Not previously Listed

Badge No.	Insignia	Rank	Description	Extremely Fine
1D-2	Cap	ORs	General list, "1" overlay	150.00
1D-21		Officers	Unknown	- -
1D-41	Collars	ORs	General list, "1" overlay	30.00
1D-61		Officers	Unknown	- -

2ND INFANTRY BATTALION

"EASTERN ONTARIO REGIMENT"

The Battalion was raised in Eastern Ontario with mobilization headquarters at Camp Valcartier, Quebec under the authority of P.C.O. 2067 August 6th, 1914. The Battalion sailed October 3rd, 1914 with a strength of forty-five officers and one thousand and ninety-eight other ranks under the command of Lieutenant-Colonel D. Watson. The Battalion served in France and Belgium with the 1st Infantry Brigade, Ist Canadian Division. It was disbanded September 15th, 1920.

BADGE NUMBER: 2

No. - 2A   EASTERN/2/ONTARIO

NOT AUTHORIZED

Maple Leaf Design

Makers: Gaunt, Tiptaft
Fasteners: Lugs
Composition:
Other Ranks: Browning copper with white metal overlay on design
Officers: Unknown
Ref: Babin, Cox

Overlay Design

Note: Two makers of this cap badge exist.
1. Gaunt; Fine veined leaf design with small type for "Ontario". The "Eastern" ribbon curves downward.
2. Tiptaft; Heavy veined leaf design with large type for "Ontario". The "Eastern" ribbon is straight. *(Illustrated)*

Badge No.	Insignia	Rank	Description	Extremely Fine
2A-2	Cap	ORs	Browning copper, Wm. overlay on design; Gaunt	30.00
2A-4		ORs	Browning copper, Wm. overlay on design; Tiptaft	30.00
2A-21		Officers	Unknown	- -

Badge No.	Insignia	Rank	Description	Fine
		Maple Leaf Design		
2A-41	Collars	ORs	Browning copper, Wm. overlay on design; Gaunt	30.00
2A-43		ORs	Browning copper, Wm. overlay on design; Tiptaft	30.00
2A-61		Officers	Unknown	- -
		Overlay Design		
2A-45	Collars	ORs	Browning copper; Tiptaft	25.00
2A-47		ORs	Browning copper; Gaunt	25.00
2A-63		Officers	Unknown	- -
		"C" Over Numbers		
2A-81	Collars	ORs	"C" over "2"; Gaunt	10.00
2A-83		ORs	"C" bar "2", Large C, Brass; Tiptaft	12.00
2A-85		NCO	"C" over "2", Wm.; Unknown	12.00
2A-91	Shoulders	ORs	Numeral: "2"; Unknown	10.00
2A-93		ORs	Title: "E/ONT/R.over CANADA."	15.00

No. - 2B   2/BATTALION/SEMPER PARATUS

These cap and collar badges previously attributed to the 2nd Battalion were not issued to that Battalion. The badge design was submitted for authorization in January 1919 for the 2nd Battalion Canadian Garrison Regiment.

Makers: G & S Co.
Fasteners: Lugs
Composition:
Other Ranks: Browning copper; White metal
Offiers: Sterling silver with enamelling on "2" and legend
Ref.: Babin, Cox

Badge No.	Insignia	Rank	Description	Extremely Fine
2B-2	Cap	ORs	Browning copper; G & S Co.	40.00
2B-4		ORs	White metal; G & S Co.	25.00
2B-21		Officers	Sterling silver, with enamelling on "2" and legend; G & S Co.	120.00
2B-41	Collars	ORs	Browning copper; G & S Co.	20.00
2B-61		Officers	Sterling silver with enamelling on "2" and legend; G & S Co.	50.00

No. - 2C   **EAST ONTARIO REGT/2/BATTALION**
                        /SEMPER PARATUS

This cap, as with the similar types of the 2nd (2B), 47th and 48th Battalion badges, (with the legend "Semper Paratus",) possibly belongs to the militia period of 1920-1936.

Makers: Unknown
Fasteners: Lugs
Composition:
  Other Ranks: White metal
  Officers: White metal
Ref.: Babin, Meek, Stewart, Cox

Note: Matching collars are not known.

Badge No.	Insignia	Rank	Description	Extremely Fine
2C-2	Cap	ORs	White metal; Unknown	25.00
2C-21		Officers	White metal	100.00

No. - 2D   **2/CANADA**

                        INTERIM BADGE

Makers: As General List
Fasteners: Lugs
Composition:
  Other Ranks: Unofficial, "2" overlay on General List
  Officers: Not known
Ref.: Not previously listed

Badge No.	Insignia	Rank	Description	Extremely Fine
2D-2	Cap	ORs	General list, "2" overlay	50.00
2D-21		Officers	Unknown	- -
2D-41	Collars	ORs	General list, "2" overlay	20.00
2D-61		Officers	Unknown	- -

3RD INFANTRY BATTALION

"TORONTO REGIMENT"

The Battalion was raised in Toronto with mobilization headquarters at Camp Valcartier, Quebec under the authority of P.C.O. 2067 August 6th, 1914. The Battalion sailed October 3rd, 1914 under the command of Lieutenant-Colonel R. Rennie with a strength of forty-three officers and one thousand one hundred and one other ranks. The Battalion served in France and Belgium with the 1st Infantry Brigade, 1st Canadian Division. It was disbanded September 15th, 1920.

BADGE NUMBER: 3

No. - 3A   **TORONTO/3/REGIMENT**

NOT AUTHORIZED

Makers: Caron, Gaunt, Tiptaft, Unknown
Fasteners: Lugs
Composition:
Other Ranks: Browning brass with white metal overlay on design
Officers: Browning brass with silver overlay on design
Ref.: Babin

Note: This is a rare cap badge and prices are indications only. The maker of the cap badge is not known.

Badge No.	Insignia	Rank	Description	Extremely Fine
3A-2	Cap	ORs	Browning brass, Wm. overlay on design; Unknown	1,250.00
3A-21		Officers	Browning brass, Silver overlay on design; Unknown	1,750.00
3A-41	Collars	ORs	Unknown	- -
3A-61		Officers	Unknown	- -
"C" Over Numbers				
3A-81	Collars	ORs	"C" over "3"; Gaunt	10.00
3A-83		ORs	"C" bar "3", Large C; Tiptaft	14.00
3A-85		ORs	"C" bar "3", Small C; Tiptaft	14.00
3A-87		NCO	"C" bar "3", Brass; Unknown	8.00
3A-89		NCO	"C" bar "3", Wm.; Unknown	8.00
3A-91	Shoulders	ORs	Numeral: "3"; Caron	8.00
3A-93		ORs	Numeral: "3"; Unknown	8.00

No. - 3B

TORONTO/III/REGIMENT

Makers: Gaunt, Rosenthal, Tiptaft, Unknown
Fasteners: Lugs, Tangs
Composition:
Other Ranks: Browning copper or brass
Officers: Sterling silver with gilt numerals
Ref.: Babin, Meek, Cox, Stewart

Note: Three makers of this cap badge exist.
1. "Toronto" in large type, is a full part of the wreath of maple leaves. The Roman numeral "ones" are joined or separated; Gaunt. Thus there are two Gaunt makes. *(Illustrated)*
2. "Toronto" in small type, is only just fastened to the wreath of maple leaves. The Roman numeral "ones" are joined.
3. "Toronto" in small type, is half fastened to the wreath of maple leaves. The Roman numeral "ones" are separated; Tiptaft. This badge comes with a solid or void crown.

Badge No.	Insignia	Rank	Description	Extremely Fine
3B-2	Cap	ORs	Brownign copper, Joined; Gaunt	18.00
3B-4		ORs	Browning copper, Separate; Gaunt	18.00
3B-6		ORs	Browning copper; Rosenthal	18.00
3B-8		ORs	Browning brass, Solid; Tiptaft	18.00
3B-10		ORs	Browning brass, Void; Tiptaft	18.00
3B-21		Officers	Sterling silver, Gilt Numeral "III"; Unknown	100.00
3B-41	Collars	ORs	Browning copper; Gaunt	10.00
3B-43		ORs	Browning copper; Rosenthal	10.00
3B-45		ORs	Browning copper; Tiptaft	10.00
3B-61		Officers	Sterling silver, Gilt Numeral "III"; Unknown	50.00

No. - 3C   **3/CANADA**

INTERIM BADGE

Makers: As General List
Fasteners: Lugs
Composition:
Other Ranks: Unofficial, "3"
overlay on General
List
Officers: Unknown
Ref.: Not previously listed

Badge No.	Insignia	Rank	Description	Extremely Fine
3C-2	Cap	ORs	General list, "3" overlay	50.00
3C-21		Officers	Unknown	- -
3C-41	Collars	ORs	General list, "3" overlay	20.00
3C-61		Officers	Unknown	- -

4TH INFANTRY BATTALION

The Battalion was raised in Central Ontario with mobilization headquarters at Camp Valcartier, Quebec under the authority of P.C.O. 2067 August 6th, 1914. The Battalion sailed October 3rd, 1914 under the command of Lieutenant-Colonel R. H. Labatt, with a strength of forty-two officers and one thousand and eighty-four other ranks. The Battalion served in France and Belgium with the 1st Infantry Brigade, 1st Canadian Division. It was disbanded September 15th, 1920.

BADGE NUMBER: 4

No. - 4A   **CENTRAL/4/ONTARIO**

NOT AUTHORIZED

Makers: Gaunt, Tiptaft, Unknown
Fasteners: Lugs
Composition:
Other Ranks: Browning copper with white metal overlay on design
Officers: Gilt on copper, silver overlay on design
Ref.: Babin, Cox

Note: Three makers of this cap badge exist.
1. Tiptaft; large type for "Ontario"; the "4" is centered to the right of the "A" in Ontario. *(Illustrated)*
2. Gaunt; small type for "Ontario"; the "4" is centered directly over the "A" in Ontario
3. Unknown; small type for "Ontario"; the "4" is slightly to the right of the "A" in Ontario.

Badge No.	Insignia	Rank	Description	Extremely Fine
4A-2	Cap	ORs	Browning copper, Wm. Overlay on design; Tiptaft	37.50
4A-4		ORs	Browning copper, Wm. overlay on design; Gaunt	37.50
4A-21		Officers	Gilt on copper, Silver overlay on design; Unknown	375.00
4A-41	Collars	ORs	Browning copper; Tiptaft	20.00
4A-43		ORs	Browning copper; Gaunt	20.00
4A-61		Officers	Gilt on copper, Silver overlay on design; Unknown	100.00

Badge No.	Insignia	Rank	Description	Extremely Fine
		"C" Over Numbers		
4A-81	Collars	ORs	"C" over "4"; Gaunt	10.00
4A-83		ORs	"C" bar "4",Large C; Tiptaft	14.00
4A-85		NCO	"C" bar "4", Plain "4"; Unknown	20.00
4A-87		NCO	"C" bar "4", Serif "4"; Unknown	20.00
4A-91	Shoulders	ORs	Numeral: "4"; Unknown	5.00

No. - 4B   **4/CANADA**

Makers: G & S Co., Tiptaft, Unknown
Fasteners: Lugs
Composition:
Other Ranks: Browning brass with embossed "4"; Browning brass with white metal overlay on "4"; White metal
Officers: Sterling silver
Ref.: Babin, Meek, Stewart, Cox

Note: Three makers of this cap badge exist.
  1. Pointed leaf design with embossed "4"; G & S Co. *(Illustrated)*
  2. Blunt leaf design with embossed "4"; Tiptaft
  3. Blunt leaf design with overlay "4"; Unknown

Badge No.	Insignia	Rank	Description	Extremely Fine
4B-2	Cap	ORs	Browning brass; G & S Co.	55.00
4B-4		ORs	Browning brass; Tiptaft	55.00
4B-6		ORs	Browning brass, Wm. overlay on "4"; Unknown	95.00
4B-8		ORs	White metal; Unknown	50.00
4B-21		Officers	Sterling silver; Unknown	250.00
4B-41	Collars	ORs	Browning brass; G & S Co.	25.00
4B-43		ORs	Browning brass; Tiptaft	25.00
4B-45		ORs	Browning brass, Wm. overlay on "4"; Unknown	20.00
4B-47		ORs	White metal; Unknown	22.00
4B-61		Officers	Sterling silver; Unknown	65.00

5TH INFANTRY BATTALION

"WESTERN CANADIAN CAVALRY"

The Battalion was raised in Western Canada with mobilization headquarters at Camp Valcartier, Quebec under the authority of P.C.O. 2067 August 6th, 1914. The Battalion sailed October 3rd, 1914, with a strength of forty-five officers and one thousand and ninety-five other ranks under the command of Lieutenant-Colonel G. S. Tuxford. The Battalion served in France and Belgium with the 2nd Infantry Brigade, 1st Canadian Division. It was disbanded September 15th, 1920.

BADGE NUMBER: 5A

CANADA/5/WESTERN CAVALRY

NOT AUTHORIZED

Makers: G & S Co., Gaunt, Tiptaft, Unknown
Fasteners: Lugs
Composition:
Other Ranks: Browning copper
Officers: As above; Superior construction
Ref.: Babin, Meek, Stewart, Cox

Note: Three makers of this cap badge exist.
1. Badge with a void crown; Crossed stems are apart; Tiptaft
2. Badge with a solid crown; Crossed stems are apart; G & S Co. *(Illustrated)*
3. Badge with a solid crown; Crossed stems close together; Gaunt

Badge No.	Insignia	Rank	Description	Extremely Fine
5A-2	Cap	ORs	Browning copper; Tiptaft	30.00
5A-4		ORs	Browning copper; G & S Co.	30.00
5A-6		ORs	Browning copper; Gaunt	30.00
5A-21		Officers	Browning copper; G & S Co.	65.00
5A-41	Collars	ORs	Browning copper; Tiptaft	15.00
5A-43		ORs	Browning copper; G & S Co.	15.00
5A-45		ORs	Browning copper; Gaunt	15.00
5A-61		Officers	Browning copper; G & S Co.	25.00
			"C" Over Numbers	
5A-81	Collars	ORs	"C" over "5"; Gaunt	12.00
5A-83		ORs	"C" bar "5", Large C; Tiptaft	14.00
5A-85		NCO	"C" bar "5", Unknown	12.00
5A-91	Shoulders	ORs	Numeral: "5"; Unknown	8.00
5A-93		ORs	Title: "CANADA/5TH/WESTERN CAVALRY"	18.00

No. - 5B

5/CANADA
INTERIM BADGE

Photograph
Not Available
At Press Time

Makers: As General list
Fasteners: Lugs
Composition:
Other Ranks: Unofficial "5"
in brass overlay
on General list
Officers: Unknown
Ref.: Not previously listed

Badge No.	Insignia	Rank	Description	Extremely Fine
5B-2	Cap	ORs	General list, Brass "5" overlay	100.00
5B-21		Officers	Unknown	- -
5B-41	Collars	ORs	Unknown	- -
5B-61		Officers	Unknown	- -

6TH INFANTRY BATTALION

"FORT GARRY HORSE"

The Battalion was raised in Winnipeg Manitoba and mobilized at Camp Valcartier, Quebec under the authority of P.C.O. 2067 August 6th, 1914. The Battalion sailed from Canada on October 3rd, 1914 under the command of Lieutenant-Colonel R. W. Patterson with a strength of forty officers and one thousand one hundred and fifteen other ranks. On arrival in England the Battalion was reorganized as the Canadian Cavalry Depot. On January 21st, 1916 the Battalion organized the Fort Garry Horse of the Canadian Cavalry Brigade. The Battalion was disbanded September 15th, 1920.

BADGE NUMBER: 6

WESTERN/6/CANADA

NOT AUTHORIZED

Makers: Dingley, Hicks, Tiptaft, Unknown
Fasteners: Lugs
Composition:
Other Ranks: Browning copper with white metal overlay on design
Officers: Unknown
Ref.: Babin, Meek, Stewart, Cox

Note: Three makers of this cap badge exist.
1. A thick stemmed leaf with very fine veins running through the leaf; Dingley *(Illustrated)*
2. A thin stemmed leaf with heavy veins running through the leaf; Tiptaft
3. A thin stemmed leaf with fine veins running through leaf; Hicks

Badge No.	Insignia	Rank	Description	Extremely Fine
6-2	Cap	ORs	Browning copper, Wm. overlay on design, Solid; Dingley	22.00
6-4		ORs	Browning copper, Wm. overlay on design, Solid; Tiptaft	22.00
6-6		ORs	Browning copper, Wm. overlay on design, Void; Dingley	22.00
6-8		ORs	Browning copper, Wm. overlay on design, Void; Tiptaft	25.00
6-10		ORs	Browning copper, Wm. overlay on design, Void; Hicks	25.00
6-21		Officers	Unknown	- -

Badge No.	Insignia	Rank	Description	Extremely Fine
			Maple Leaf Design	
6-41	Collars	ORs	Browning copper, Wm. overlay on design, Void; Dingley	22.00
6-43		ORs	Browning copper, Wm. overlay on design, Void; Hicks	22.00
6-61		Officers	Unknown	- -
			Fort and Ribbon Design	
6-45	Collars	ORs	Browning copper; Tiptaft	24.00
6-63		Officers	Unknown	- -
			"C" Over Numbers	
6-81	Collars	ORs	"C" bar "6", Large C; Tiptaft	16.00
6-83		NCO	"C" bar "6", Brass; Unknown	14.00
6-85		NCO	"C" bar "6", White metal; Unknown	14.00
6-91	Shoulders	ORs	Numeral: "6"; Unknown	10.00

7TH INFANTRY BATTALION
"1ST BRITISH COLUMBIA REGIMENT"

The Battalion was raised in British Columbia and mobilized at Camp Valcartier, Quebec under the authority of P.C.O. 2067 August 6th, 1914. The Battalion sailed October 3rd, 1914 with a strength of forty-seven officers and one thousand one hundred and seventy-six other ranks under the command of Lieutenant-Colonel W. Hart-McHarg. The Battalion served in France and Belgium with the 2nd Infantry Brigade, 1st Canadian Division. It was disbanded September 15th, 1920.

BADGE NUMBER: 7

No. - 7A   **1/BRITISH COLUMBIA**

NOT AUTHORIZED

Makers: Caron, Gaunt, Hicks, Tiptaft
Fasteners: Lugs
Composition:
Other Ranks: Browning copper with white metal overlay on design
Officers: Gilt on brass with silver overlay
Ref.: Babin, Meek, Stewart, Cox

Note: It is yet to be confirmed whether the matching ORs collars are of the CEF period. Two makers of this cap badge exist.
1. A heavy veined leaf design having a large "1" with a blunt serif; Tiptaft *(Illustrated)*
2. A fine veined leaf design having a large "1" with a rounded serif; Hicks

Badge No.	Insignia	Rank	Description	Extremely Fine
7A-2	Cap	ORs	Browning copper, Wm. overlay on design; Hicks	18.00
7A-4		ORs	Browning copper, Wm. overlay on design; Tiptaft	20.00
7A-21		Officers	Gilt on brass, Silver overlay on design	200.00
7A-41	Collars	ORs	Browning copper; Hicks	15.00
7A-43		ORs	Browning copper; Tiptaft	15.00
7A-61		Officers	Brass, Wm. overlay on "CROWN/CREST/C/7"	100.00

Badge No.	Insignia	Rank	Description	Extremely Fine
		"C" Over Numbers		
7A-81	Collars	ORs	"C" over "7"; Gaunt	12.00
7A-83		ORs	"C" bar "7", Large "C"; Tiptaft	12.00
7A-85		NCO	"C" bar "7"; Unknown	12.00
7A-91	Shoulders	ORs	Numeral: "7"; Caron	15.00
7A-93		ORs	Title: "BRITISH/COLUMBIA"	15.00

No. - 7B   BC/VII/CANADA

Makers: G & S Co.
Fasteners: Lugs
Composition:
Other Ranks: Browning copper
Officers: Browning copper
with white metal
overlay on design
Ref.: Not previously listed

Note: This may be a Militia badge of the 1920-1936 period.

Badge No.	Insignia	Rank	Description	Extremely Fine
7B-2	Cap	ORs	Browning copper	Extremely Rare
7B-21		Officers	Browning copper, Wm. overlay on design	900.00
7B-41	Collars	ORs	Unknown	- -
7B-61		Officers	Unknown	- -

8TH INFANTRY BATTALION

"THE BLACK DEVILS"/"90TH WINNIPEG RIFLES"

The Battalion was raised in Brandon and Winnipeg, Manitoba, and Port Arthur and Kenora, Ontario with mobilization headquarters at Camp Valcartier, Quebec under the authority of P.C.O. 2067 August 6th, 1914. The Battalion sailed October 3rd, 1914 under the command of Lieutenant-Colonel L. J. Lipsett with a strength of forty-five officers and one thousand and eighty-five other ranks. The Battalion served in France and Belgium with the 2nd Infantry Brigade, 1st Canadian Division. It was disbanded December 15th, 1920.

BADGE NUMBER: 8

No. - 8A   **HOSTI ACIE NOMINATI**

NOT AUTHORIZED

Makers: Birks, Hemsley, Hicks, Inglis, Tiptaft
Fasteners: Lugs
Composition:
Other Ranks: Pickled copper; Browning copper; Blackened brass; or white metal
Officers:
A: Blackened copper with white metal overlay on ribbon
B: Sterling silver
Ref.: Babin, Meek, Stewart, Cox

Note: Four makers of this cap badge exist. Shoulder numerals are not known.
1. Devil holding cup tilting to the left; Three pronged pointed spear with voided tines; Hicks *(Illustrated)*
2. Devil holding basically a flat top cup straight up; Three pronged pointed spear with solid tines; Tiptaft
3. Devil holding a rounded top cup straight up; three pronged pointed spear with solid tines; Birks
4. Hemsley, Inglis not available.

Badge No.	Insignia	Rank	Description	Extremely Fine
8A-2	Cap	ORs	Pickled copper; Hemsley, Inglis	45.00
8A-4		ORs	Browning copper; Hemsley, Inglis	20.00
8A-6		ORs	Browning copper; Hicks	20.00
8A-8		ORs	Browning copper; Tiptaft	20.00
8A-10		ORs	Blackened brass; Birks	30.00
8A-12		ORs	Blackened Wm.; Birks	18.00
8A-14		ORs	Blackened Wm.; Tiptaft	18.00

Badge No.	Insignia	Rank	Description	Extremely Fine
8A-21	Cap	Officers	Browning copper, Wm. overlay on ribbon; Hicks	27.50
8A-23		Officers	Blackened copper, Wm. overlay on ribbon; Hicks	40.00
8A-25		Officers	Sterling silver; Tiptaft	65.00
8A-41	Collars	ORs	Pickled copper; Hemsley, Inglis	15.00
8A-43		ORs	Browning copper; Hicks	35.00
8A-45		ORs	Browning copper; Tiptaft	35.00
8A-47		ORs	Blackened Wm. Tiptaft	30.00
8A-61		Officers	Browning copper, Wm. overlay on ribbon; Hicks	40.00
8A-63		Officers	Blackened copper, Wm. overlay on ribbon; Hicks	40.00
8A-65		Officers	Sterling silver	30.00
		"C" Over Numbers		
8A-81	Collars	ORs	"C" bar "8", Large "C"; Tiptaft	14.00
8A-83		ORs	"C" bar "8", Small "C"; Unknown	14.00
8A-91	Shoulders	ORs	Numeral: "8"	Unknown

No. - 8B 1/HOSTI ACIE NOMINATI

Makers: Unknown
Fasteners: Lugs
Composition:
Other Ranks: Pickled copper
Officers: Unknown
Ref.: Not previously listed

Note: Matching collars are not known.

Badge No.	Insignia	Rank	Description	Extremely Fine
8B-2	Cap	ORs	Pickled copper	750.00
8B-21		Officers	Unknown	- -
8B-41	Collars	ORs	Unknown	- -
8B-61		Officers	Unknown	- -

9TH INFANTRY BATTALION

The Battalion was raised in Edmonton, Alberta and Ottawa, Ontario and mobilized at Camp Valcartier, Quebec under the authority of P.C.O. 2067 August 6th, 1914. The Battalion sailed October 3rd, 1914 with a strength of forty-four officers and one thousand one hundred and one other ranks under the command of Lieutenant-Colonel S. M. Rogers. In England the Battalion was redesignated the 9th Reserve Battalion and formed part of the Canadian Training Depot, located at Tidworth. It was disbanded September 15th, 1920.

BADGE NUMBER: 9

No. - 9A   **9/CANADA**

NOT AUTHORIZED

The white metal or silver overlay (CROWN/9/CANADA) is attached to the maple leaf by two wires soldered to the back of the overlay. These wires pass through two hand drilled holes and are bent onto the reverse of the maple leaf to secure the overlay. As the two holes were hand drilled the overlay position will vary slightly between badges. Matching collars are unknown. Beware of imitations.

Makers: Reiche, Tiptaft, Unknown
Fasteners: Lugs
Composition:
Other Ranks: Browning copper with white metal overlay on "Crown and Canada"
Officers: Browning copper with silver overlay on "Crown and Canada"
Ref.: Babin, Meek, Stewart, Cox

Badge No.	Insignia	Rank	Description	Extremely Fine
9A-2	Cap	ORs	Browning copper, Wm. overlay on "Crown and Canada"; Reiche	4,500.00
9A-21		Officers	Browning copper, Silver overlay on "Crown and Canada"; Reiche	5,000.00
Overlay Design				
9A-41	Collars	ORs	Brass, overlay design only	50.00
9A-61		Officers	Unknown	- -
"C" Over Numbers				
9A-81	Collars	ORs	"C" bar "9", Large "C"; Tiptaft	22.00
9A-83		ORs	"C" bar "9", Small "C"; Unknown	22.00
9A-91	Shoulders	ORs	Numeral: "9"; Unknown	15.00
9A-93		ORs	Title: "9"over "CANADA"	125.00

No. - 9B   **9/CANADA**

INTERIM BADGE

Makers: As General List
Fasteners: Lugs
Composition:
Other Ranks: Unofficial, "9"
overlay on General
List
Officers: Not known
Ref.: Not previously listed

Badge No.	Insignia	Rank	Description	Extremely Fine
9B-2	Cap	ORs	General list, "9" overlay	65.00
9B-21		Officers	Unknown	- -
9B-41	Collars	ORs	General list, "9" overlay	20.00
9B-61		Officers	Unknown	- -

10TH INFANTRY BATTALION

"10th CANADIANS"

The Battalion was raised in Calgary, Alberta and Winnipeg, Manitoba with mobilization headquarters at Camp Valcartier, Quebec under the authority of P.C.O. 2067 August 6th, 1914. The Battalion sailed October 3rd, 1914 under the command of Lieutenant-Colonel R. L. Boyle with a strength of forty-one officers and one thousand and sixty-five other ranks. The Battalion served in France and Belgium with the 2nd Infantry Brigade, 1st Canadian Division. It was disbanded September 15th, 1920.

BADGE NUMBER: 10

No. - 10A　　　　　　　**10TH/CANADIANS**

NOT AUTHORIZED

Makers: Caron, Gaunt, Hicks, Tiptaft, Unknown
Fasteners: Lugs
Composition:
Other Ranks: Browning copper or brass; White metal
Officers: Browning copper with white metal overlay on beaver and ribbon
Ref.: Babin, Meek, Stewart, Cox

Note: Three makers of this cap badge exist.
1. A small beaver with no water lines below the beaver; Tiptaft *(Illustrated)*
2. A large beaver with water lines below the beaver; Hicks
3. A small beaver with water lines below the beaver; Gaunt.

Badge No.	Insignia	Rank	Description	Extremely Fine
10A-2	Cap	ORs	Browning copper; Tiptaft	18.00
10A-4		ORs	Browning copper; Hicks	18.00
10A-6		ORs	Browning brass; Gaunt	18.00
10A-8		ORs	White metal; Unknown	- -

Badge No.	Insignia	Rank	Description	Extremely Fine
10A-21		Officers	Browning copper, Wm. overlay on beaver and ribbon; Hicks	55.00
10A-41	Collars	ORs	Unknown	- -
10A-61		Officers	Browning copper, Wm. overlay on beaver and ribbon; Hicks	55.00
		"C" Over Numbers		
10A-81	Collars	ORs	"C" over "10"; Gaunt	16.00
10A-83		ORs	"C" bar "10", Small C; Tiptaft	16.00
10A-85		ORs	"C" bar "10", Large C; Tiptaft	15.00
10A-87		NCO	"C" bar "10", Serifs; Unknown	16.00
10A-89		NCO	"C" bar "10", Serifs; Unknown	16.00
10A-91	Shoulders	ORs	Numeral: "10"; Caron	14.00

No. - 10B   **10/CANADA**

Makers: Tiptaft
Fasteners: Lugs
Composition:
Other Ranks: Browning copper with white metal overlay on design
Officers: Browning copper with silver overlay on design
Ref.: Not previously listed

Note: The overlay on this cap does not carry the "crown" as seen on all other caps of this design. The overlay is "10/CANADA" only. Matching Collar badges are unknown.

Badge No.	Insignia	Rank	Description	Extremely Fine
10B-2	Cap	ORs	Browning copper, Wm. overlay on design	1,400.00
10B-21		Officers	Browning copper, Silver overlay on design	Extremely Rare
10B-41	Collars	ORs	Unknown	- -
10B-61		Officers	Unknown	- -

11TH INFANTRY BATTALION

The Battalion was raised in Saskatchewan with mobilization headquarters at Camp Valcartier, Quebec under the authority of P.C.O. 2067 August 6th, 1914. The Battalion sailed October 3rd, 1914 under the command of Lieutenant-Colonel R. Burritt with a strength of forty-five officers and one thousand one hundred and nineteen other ranks. In England the Battalion was redesignated the 11th Reserve Battalion forming part of the Canadian Training Depot. The Battalion was disbanded September 15th, 1920.

BADGE NUMBER: 11

XI/BATTN/CANADA

NOT AUTHORIZED

Makers: Gaunt, Reiche, Tiptaft, Unknown
Fasteners: Lugs
Composition:
Other Ranks: Browning copper or brass
Officers: Bronze; Browning copper
Ref.: Babin, Meek, Stewart, Cox

Note: Three makers of this cap badge exist.
1. Framed ribbon with a wreath of 15 raised leaves; Gaunt
2. Plain ribbon with a wreath of 15 shallow leaves; Reiche
3. Plain ribbon with a wreath of 14 shallow leaves; Tiptaft *(Illustrated)*

Badge No.	Insignia	Rank	Description	Extremely Fine
11-2	Cap	ORs	Browning copper; Gaunt	20.00
11-4		ORs	Browning copper; Reiche	20.00
11-6		ORs	Browning copper; Tiptaft	20.00
11-8		ORs	Browning brass; Tiptaft	20.00
11-21		Officers	Bronze; Unknown	65.00
11-23		Officers	Browning copper; Gaunt	12.50
11-25		Officers	Browning copper; Reiche	12.50
11-41	Collars	ORs	Browning copper; Tiptaft	12.50
11-43		ORs	Browning brass; Tiptaft	12.50
11-61		Officers	Bronze; Unknown	35.00
"C" Over Numbers				
11-81	Collars	ORs	"C" bar "11", Small "C"; Tiptaft	16.00
11-83		NCO	"C" bar "11"; Unknown	14.00
11-91	Shoulders	ORs	Numeral: "11"; Unknown	16.00
		ORs	Title: "11BN"; Unknown	20.00

12TH INFANTRY BATTALION

The Battalion was raised in Quebec, New Brunswick and Prince Edward Island with mobilization headquarters at Camp Valcartier, Quebec under the authority of P.C.O. 2067, August 6th, 1914. The Battalion sailed October 3rd, 1914 under the command of Lieutenant-Colonel H. F. McLeod with a strength of forty-five officers and one thousand and twenty-eight other ranks. In England the 12th Battalion was redesignated the 12th Reserve Battalion forming part of the Canadian Training Depot. It was disbanded September 15th, 1920.

BADGE NUMER: 12

No. - 12A   **12/CANADA**

NOT AUTHORIZED

Makers: Dingley, Ellis
Tiptaft, Unknown
Fasteners: Lugs, Slide
Composition:
Other Ranks: Pickled brass;
Browning copper;
Blackened white
metal
Officers:
A: Sterling silver
B: Browning copper
with white metal
overlay on design
Ref.: Babin, Meek, Stewart, Cox

Note: Three makers of this cap badge exist.
1. Pointed leaf design with a large number "2"; Plain Canada ribbon; Dingley
2. Blunt leaf design with a small number "2"; Framed Canada ribbon; Tiptaft
   (Illustrated)
3. Pointed leaf design with a large number "2"; Plain Canada ribbon; Unknown

Badge No.	Insignia	Rank	Description	Extremely Fine
12A-2	Cap	ORs	Pickled brass; Unknown	40.00
12A-4		ORs	Browning copper; Tiptaft	22.00
12A-6		ORs	Blackened white metal; Dingley	45.00
12A-21	Cap	Officers	Sterling silver (2 pcs); Unknown	90.00
12A-23		Officers	Browning copper, Wm. overlay on design	35.00
12A-41	Collars	ORs	Pickled brass	20.00
12A-43		ORs	Browning copper	15.00
12A-45		ORs	Blackened White metal; Dingley	10.00
12A-61		Officers	Sterling silver	30.00
12A-63		Officers	Browning copper, Wm. overlay on design	20.00

Badge No.	Insignia	Rank	Description	Extremely Fine
		"C" Over Numbers		
12A-81	Collars	ORs	"C" bar "12", Small "C"; Tiptaft	15.00
12A-83		NCO	"C" bar "12"; Unknown	16.00
12A-91	Shoulders	ORs	Numeral: "12"; Ellis	12.00

No. - 12B   **OVERSEAS/12/BATTALION/CANADA**

Makers: Tiptaft, Unknown
Fasteners: Lugs
Composition:
Other Ranks: Browning copper
Officers: Unknown
Ref.: Babin

Note: Two makers of this cap badge exist.
1. Pointed leaf design with a small, plain "12"; Unknown *(Illustrated)*
2. Blunt leaf design with a large, framed "12"; Tiptaft.

Badge No.	Insignia	Rank	Description	Extremely Fine
12B-2	Cap	ORs	Browning copper; Unknown	100.00
12B-4		ORs	Browning copper;Tiptaft	400.00
12B-21		Officers	Unknown	- -
12B-41	Collars	ORs	Browning copper; Unknown	100.00
12B-43		ORs	Browning copper; Tiptaft	20.00
12B-61		Officers	Unknown	- -

13TH INFANTRY BATTALION

"ROYAL HIGHLANDERS OF CANADA"

The Battalion was raised in Quebec and Nova Scotia with mobilization headquarters at Camp Valcartier, Quebec under the authority of P.C.O. 2067 August 6th, 1914. The Battalion sailed October 3rd, 1914 under command of Lieutenant-Colonel F. O. W. Loomis with a strength of forty-five officers and one thousand one hundred and twelve other ranks. The Battalion served in France and Belgium with the 3rd Infantry Brigade, 1st Canadian Division. It was disbanded September 15th, 1920.

BADGE NUMER: 13

THE ROYAL HIGHLANDERS OF CANADA
/NEMO ME IMPUNE LACESSIT/
13TH BATT, 1ST CANADIAN DIVISION

NOT AUTHORIZED

Makers: Caron, Ellis, Gaunt, Tiptaft
Fasteners: Lugs
Composition:
Other Ranks: Browning copper; White metal
NCO: Brass and white metal
Officers:
   A. Silver and copper gilt
   B. Silver gilt
   C. Sterling silver
Ref.: Babin, Meek, Stewart, Cox

Note: Two makers of the ORs cap badge exist.
1. St. Andrew holding a wide bar cross; Tiptaft *(Illustrated)*
2. St. Andrew holding a narrow bar cross; Gaunt

Badge No.	Insignia	Rank	Description	Extremely Fine
13-2	Glengarry	ORs	Browning copper; Tiptaft	38.00
13-4		ORs	White metal; Tiptaft	50.00
13-6		ORs	White metal; Gaunt	50.00
13-21		NCO	Brass and Wm. (6 pc const)	400.00
13-23		Officers	Silver and copper gilt (6 pc const)	600.00
13-25		Officers	Silver, gilt (2 pc const)	150.00
13-27		Officers	Sterling Silver; Unknown	150.00

Badge No.	Insignia	Rank	Description	Extremely Fine
13-41	Collars	ORs	Browning copper; Tiptaft	20.00
13-43		ORs	Browning copper; Gaunt	20.00
13-61		Officers	Silver and copper, gilt	100.00
13-63		Officers	Silver, gilt; Unknown	80.00
13-65		Officers	Sterling silver; Unknown	65.00

"C" Over Numbers

Badge No.	Insignia	Rank	Description	Extremely Fine
13-81	Collars	ORs	"C" over "13"; Gaunt	24.00
13-83		ORs	"C" bar "13", Large "C"; Tiptaft	24.00
13-85		NCO	"C" bar "13"; Unknown	35.00
13-87		NCO	"C" bar "13", Silver and gilt; Unknown	150.00
13-91	Shoulders	ORs	Numeral: "13"; Caron	10.00
13-93		ORs	Numeral: "13"; Ellis	10.00

14TH INFANTRY BATTALION

"ROYAL MONTREAL REGIMENT"

The Battalion was raised from the Royal Montreal Regiment and mobilized at Camp Valcartier, Quebec under the authority of P.C.O. 2067 August 6th, 1914. The Battalion sailed with a strength of forty-six officers and one thousand and ninety-seven other ranks under the command of Lieutenant-Colonel F. J. Meighen on October 3rd, 1914. The Battalion served in France and Belgium with the 3rd Infantry Brigade, 1st Canadian Division. The Battalion was disbanded September 15th, 1920.

BADGE NUMBER: 14

HONI SOIT QUI MAL Y PENSE/
ROYAL MONTREAL REGT/CANADA

AUTHORIZED OCTOBER 15, 1915

Makers: Birks, Gaunt,
Scully, Tiptaft
Fasteners: Lugs
Composition:
Other Ranks: Browning copper
or brass
Officers: Unknown
Ref.: Babin, Meek, Stewart, Cox

Note: Three makers of this cap badge exist.
1. The motto has periods and the "Canada" ribbon is framed; Scully
2. The motto has no periods and the "Canada" ribbon is plain; Gaunt
3. The motto has no periods and the "Canada" ribbon is framed; Tiptaft *(Illustrated)*

Badge No.	Insignia	Rank	Description	Extremely Fine
14-2	Cap	ORs	Browning copper; Gaunt	18.00
14-4		ORs	Browning brass; Scully	55.00
14-6		ORs	Browning brass; Tiptaft	40.00
14-21		Officers	Unknown	- -
14-41	Collars	ORs	Browning copper; Gaunt	14.00
14-43		ORs	Browning brass; Scully	14.00
14-45		ORs	Browning brass; Tiptaft	14.00
14-61		Officers	Unknown	- -
		"C" Over Numbers		
14-81	Collars	ORs	"C" over "14"; Gaunt	30.00
14-83		ORs	"C" bar "14", Large C; Tiptaft	30.00
14-85		ORs	"C" bar "14", Small C; Tiptaft	25.00
14-87		NCO	"C" bar "14"; Unknown	25.00
14-91	Shoulders	ORs	Numeral: "14"; Birks	20.00

15TH INFANTRY BATTALION

"48TH HIGHLANDERS OF CANADA"

The Battalion was raised in Ontario and Quebec and mobilized at Camp Valcartier, Quebec under the authority of P.C.O. 2067 August 6th, 1914. The Battalion sailed October 3rd, 1914 with a compliment of forty-four officers and one thousand one hundred and nine other ranks under the command of Lieutenant-Colonel J. A. Currie. The Battalion served in France and Belgium with the 3rd Infantry Brigade, 1st Canadian Division. The Battalion was disbanded September 15th, 1920.

BADGE NUMER: 15

No. - 15A   **DILEAS GU BRATH/48 HIGHLANDERS/ 15TH CANADIAN BATTN**

NOT AUTHORIZED

Makers: Birks, Gaunt, Tiptaft, Unknown
Fasteners: Lugs

Ref.: Babin, Meek, Stewart, Cox

Composition:
Other Ranks: Browning copper or brass
Officers: As above; Superior condition

| Large "48" | Small "48" |

Note: The small "48" variety was issued in England to the 34th Draft. Matching collars are not known. Two makers exist but the differences are unknown.

Badge No.	Insignia	Rank	Description	Extremely Fine
		Small Number "48"; Large badge		
15A-2	Glengarry	ORs	Browning copper; Gaunt	75.00
15A-4		ORs	Blackened copper; Tiptaft	75.00
15A-6		ORs	Browning copper; Unknown	180.00
15A-21		Officers	Silverplate on copper; Unknown	700.00
		Large Number "48"; Small badge		
15A-8	Cap	ORs	Browning copper; Gaunt	40.00
15A-8		ORs	Blackened copper; Tiptaft	40.00
15A-23		Officers	Silverplate on copper; Tiptaft	450.00
		"C" Over Numbers		
15A-81	Collars	ORs	"C" bar "15"; Large "C"; Tiptaft	22.00
15A-83		NCO	"C" bar "15"; Unknown	25.00
15A-91	Shoulders	ORs	Numeral: "15"; Birks	22.00
15A-93		ORs	Title: "48" over "H of C"; Small "of"	30.00
15A-95		ORs	Title: "48" over "H of C"; Large "of"	30.00

No. - 15B

DILEAS GU BRATH
/48 HIGHLANDERS/CANADA

Makers: Tiptaft, Unknown
Fasteners: Lugs
Composition:
Other Ranks: Browning copper
Officers: White metal
Ref.: Babin, Stewart

Note: Three makers of this cap badge exist.
1. Design with two periods in the motto and a plain "48"; Tiptaft *(Illustrated)*
2. Design with three periods in the motto and a framed "48"; Unknown
3. Details are not known.

Badge No.	Insignia	Rank	Description	Extremely Fine
15B-2	Cap	ORs	Browning copper; Tiptaft	75.00
15B-4		ORs	Browning copper; Unknown	75.00
15B-6		ORs	Browning copper; Unknown	75.00
15B-21		Officers	White metal; Unknown	90.00
15B-41	Collars	ORs	Browning copper; Tiptaft	30.00
15B-43		ORs	Browning copper; Unknown	30.00
15B-45		ORs	Browning copper; Unknown	30.00
15B-61		Officers	White metal; Unknown	60.00

No. - 15C

DILEAS GU BRATH
/48 HIGHLANDERS OF CANADA

Photograph
Not Available
At Press Time

Makers: Unknown
Fasteners: Lugs
Composition:
Other Ranks: Copper
Officers: Unknown
Ref.: Babin

Note: Matching collars are not known.

Badge No.	Insignia	Rank	Description	Extremely Fine
15C-2	Cap	ORs	Browning copper; Unknown	250.00
15C-21		Officers	Silverplate on copper; Unknown	450.00
15C-23		Officers	White metal (Cast); Unknown	1,000.00
15C-41	Collars	ORs	Unknown	- -
15C-61		Officers	Unknown	- -

16TH INFANTRY BATTALION

"CANADIAN SCOTTISH"

The Battalion was raised in British Columbia, Manitoba and Ontario and mobilized at Camp Valcartier, Quebec under the authority of P.C.O. 2067 August 6th, 1914. The Battalion sailed October 3rd, 1914 with a strength of forty-seven officers and one thousand and ninety-six other ranks under the command of Lieutenant-Colonel R. G. Edwards Leckie. The Battalion served in France and Belgium with the 3rd Infantry Brigade, 1st Canadian Division. It was disbanded September 15th, 1920.

BADGE NUMBER: 16

16/DEAS GU CATH

NOT AUTHORIZED

Makers: Gaunt, Tiptaft, Unknown
Fasteners: Lugs
Composition:
Other Ranks: White metal
Officers: White metal;
Superior
construction
Ref.: Babin, Meek, Stewart, Cox

Note: Two makers of this cap badge exist.
1. Small type for motto with a narrow "1", 45 mm; Gaunt *(Illustrated)*
2. Large type for motto with a wide "1", 45 mm; Tiptaft
3. The officers browning copper badge with lugs is 37 mm high while both the white metal ORs badges are 45 mm.

Note: The ORs wore only the "C" over "16" collars.

Badge No.	Insignia	Rank	Description	Extremely Fine
16-2	Glengarry	ORs	White metal; Gaunt	20.00
16-4		ORs	White metal; Tiptaft	20.00
16-21		Officers	Sterling silver; Unknown	125.00
16-23		Officers	Browning copper; Unknown	125.00
16-61	Collars	Officers	Browning copper, 3 pcs; Unknown	60.00
16-63		Officers	Browning copper; Unknown	100.00

Badge No.	Insignia	Rank	Description	Extremely Fine
		"C" Over Numbers		
16-81	Collars	ORs	"C" over "16"; Gaunt	15.00
16-83		ORs	"C" bar "16"; Small "C"; Tiptaft	14.00
16-85		NCO	"C" bar "16"; Serifs; Unknown	15.00
16-87		NCO	"C" bar "16"; Without serifs; Unknown	15.00
16-91	Shoulders	ORs	Numeral: "16"; Caron	12.00
16-93		ORs	Title: "CANADIAN SCOTTISH"; Large version (Straight Canadian)	25.00
16-95		ORs	Title: 16/CANADIAN/SCOTTISH	25.00
16-97		Officers	Title: "CANADIAN SCOTTISH"; Small version (Curved Canadian)	15.00
16-99		Officers	Title: "CANADIAN/SCOTTISH"; Medium version (Curved Canadian)	15.00

17TH INFANTRY BATTALION

"NOVA SCOTIA HIGHLANDERS"
"SEAFORTH HIGHLANDERS OF CANADA"

The Battalion was raised in Nova Scotia with mobilization headquarters at Camp Valcartier, Quebec under the authority of P.C.O. 2067 August 6th, 1914. On September 21st, when the decision to proceed to England was finalized, the surplus infantry was consigned to this battalion. It sailed October 3rd, 1914 with a strength of thirty-nine officers and seven hundred and seventeen other ranks under the command of Lieutenant Colonel S. G. Robertson. On arrival in England the battalion was redesignated as the 17th Reserve Battalion and formed part of the Canadian Training Depot located at Tidworth Barracks. The battalion was disbanded September 15th, 1920.

BADGE NUMBER: 17

SEAFORTH HIGHLANDERS OF CANADA
/17/CUIDICH'N RIGH

NOT AUTHORIZED

Makers: Birks, Tiptaft, Unknown
Fasteners: Lugs
Composition:
Other Ranks: White metal
Officers:
    A. Gilt on white metal
    B. Sterling silver
Ref.: Babin, Meek, Stewart, Cox

Badge No.	Insignia	Rank	Description	Extremely Fine
17-2	Glengarry	ORs	White Metal; Tiptaft	45.00
17-21		Officers	Gilt on white metal; Unknown	400.00
17-23		Officers	Sterling silver; Unknown	400.00
17-41	Collars	ORs	White metal; Tiptaft	20.00
17-61		Officers	Gilt on white metal; Unknown	25.00
17-63		Officers	Sterling silver; Unknown	25.00
		"C" Over Numbers		
17-81	Collars	ORs	"C" bar "17", Small "C"; Tiptaft	15.00
17-83		NCO	"C" bar "17"; Unknown	15.00
17-85		NCO	"C" bar "17"; Unknown	15.00
17-91	Shoulders	ORs	Numeral: "17"; Birks	25.00

18TH INFANTRY BATTALION

"WESTERN ONTARIO REGIMENT"

The Battalion was raised and mobilized in London, Ontario under the authority of G.O. 36 March 15th, 1915. The Battalion sailed April 18th, 1915 under the command of Lieutenant-Colonal E. S. Wigle, with a strength of thirty-six officers and one thousand and eighty-one other ranks. The Battalion served in France and Belgium with the 4th Infantry Brigade, 2nd Canadian Division. It was disbanded September 15th, 1920.

BADGE NUMBER: 18

No. - 18A   **18/WESTERN ONTARIO/CANADA**

NOT AUTHORIZED

Makers: Birks, Tiptaft, Unknown
Fasteners: Lugs, Slide
Composition:
  Other Ranks: Browning copper
    Officers: As above; Superior construction
Ref.: Babin, Cox

Note: Two makers of this cap badge exist.
1. Pointed leaf design with plain numbers; Unknown *(Illustrated)*
2. Blunt leaf design with framed numbers; Tiptaft

Badge No.	Insignia	Rank	Description	Extremely Fine
18A-2	Cap	ORs	Browning copper; Unknown	18.00
18A-4		ORs	Browning copper; Tiptaft	20.00
18A-21		Officers	Browning copper; Unknown	45.00
18A-41	Collars	ORs	Browning copper; Unknown	16.00
18A-43		ORs	Browning copper; Tiptaft	16.00
18A-61		Officers	Browning copper; Unknown	24.00
			"C" Over Numbers	
18A-81	Collars	ORs	"C" over "18", Small "C"; Tiptaft	15.00
18A-91	Shoulders	ORs	Numeral: "18"; Birks	12.00

No. - 18B   18/CANADA

Makers: Lees, Tiptaft
Fasteners: Lugs
Composition:
Other Ranks: Browning copper
Officers: As above; Superior
construction
Ref.: Babin, Meek, Stewart, Cox

Note: Two makers of this cap badge exist.
1. Narrow band around "18" with a wide "8" type style; Lees
2. Wide band around "18" with a narrow "8" type style; Tiptaft *(Illustrated)*

Badge No.	Insignia	Rank	Description	Extremely Fine
18B-2	Cap	ORs	Browning copper, Solid; Lees	30.00
18B-4		ORs	Browning copper, Voided; Lees	240.00
18B-6		ORs	Browning copper, Solid; Tiptaft	30.00
18B-21		Officers	Browning copper, Solid; Lees	50.00
18B-41	Collars	ORs	Browning copper; Lees	15.00
18B-43		ORs	Browning copper; Tiptaft	15.00
18B-61		Officers	Browning copper; Lees	20.00

19TH INFANTRY BATTALION

The Battalion was raised and mobilized in Toronto, Ontario under the authority of G.O. 36 March 15th, 1915. Sailing was on May 13th, 1915 with a strength of forty-one officers and one thousand and seventy-three other ranks under the command of Lieutenant-Colonel J. J. McLaren. The Battalion served in France and Belgium with the 4th Infantry Brigade, 2nd Canadian Division. It was disbanded September 15th, 1920.

BADGE NUMBER: 19

No. - 19A   **19/CANADA**

NOT AUTHORIZED

Makers: Caron, Ellis, Gaunt,
Tiptaft, Unknown
Fasteners: Lugs
Composition:
Other Ranks: Browning brass
Officers: As above; superior
construction
Ref.: Babin, Cox

Note: Two makers of this cap badge exist, Gaunt and an unknown. They are very difficult to distinguish.

Badge No.	Insignia	Rank	Description	Extremely Fine
19A-2	Cap	ORs	Browning brass; Unknown	20.00
19A-4		ORs	Browning brass; Gaunt	20.00
19A-21		Officers	Browning brass; Unknown	60.00
19A-81	Collars	ORs	"C" over "19"; Gaunt	18.00
19A-83		ORs	"C" bar "19", Small "C"; Tiptaft	18.00
19A-85		NCO	"C" bar "19", White metal; Unknown	30.00
19A-91	Shoulders	ORs	Numeral: "19"; Caron	16.00
19A-93		ORs	Numeral: "19"; Ellis	16.00

No. - 19B   **19/CANADA**

Makers: Lees, Tiptaft, Unknown
Fasteners: Lugs
Composition:
Other Ranks: Browning copper or
brass
Officers: Unknown
Ref.: Babin, Meek, Stewart, Cox

Note: Two makers of this cap badge exist.
1. Large "19"; thin stemmed leaf; Lees
2. Small "19"; Large stemmed leaf; Tiptaft *(Illustrated)*

Badge No.	Insignia	Rank	Description	Extremely Fine
19B-2	Cap	ORs	Browning copper; Lees	18.00
19B-4		ORs	Browning copper; Tiptaft	18.00
19B-6		ORs	Browning brass; Tiptaft	20.00
19B-21		Officers	Browning brass; Unknown	20.00
19B-41	Collars	ORs	Browning copper; Lees	8.00
19B-43		ORs	Browning copper; Tiptaft	8.00
19B-61		Officers	Unknown	- -

No. - 19C   **19/CANADA**

The construction of this cap is identical to the 9th Battalion badge. The other ranks cap has a brass overlay (CROWN/19/CANADA) and the officers cap is silver. Matching collars are unknown. In regard to the brass overlay, since all others (9th, 10th, and 20th Battalions) are white metal, it is possible that constant polishing has removed the white metal plating.

Makers: Reiche
Fasteners: Lugs
Composition:
Other Ranks: Browning copper with brass overlay on design
Officers: Browning copper with silver overlay on design
Ref.: Babin

Badge No.	Insignia	Rank	Description	Extremely Fine
19C-2	Cap	ORs	Browning copper, Brass overlay on design	1,400.00
19C-21		Officers	Browning copper, Silver overlay on design	1,400.00
19C-41	Collars	ORs	Unknown	- -
19C-61		Officers	Unknown	- -

No. - 19D   **OVERSEAS BATTALION**
CANADA/19/DUTY FIRST

Photograph Not Available At Press Time

Makers: Unknown
Fasteners: Lugs
Composition:
Other Ranks: Brass
Officers: Unknown
Ref.: Not previously listed

Badge No.	Insignia	Rank	Description	Extremely Fine
19D-2	Cap	ORs	Brass; Unknown	Rare
19D-21		Officers	Unknown	- -
19D-41	Collars	ORs	Unknown	- -
19D-61		Officers	Unknown	- -

20TH INFANTRY BATTALION

"1ST CENTRAL ONTARIO REGIMENT"

The Battalion was raised in Central and Northern Ontario and mobilized in Toronto, Ontario under the authority of G.O. 36 March 15th, 1915. On May 15th, 1915 the Battalion sailed with a strength of thirty-five officers and eleven hundred other ranks under the command of Lieutenant-Colonel J. A. W. Allen. The Battalion served in France and Belgium with the 4th Infantry Brigade, 2nd Canadian Division. It was disbanded September 15th, 1920.

BADGE NUMBER: 20A　　　　**20**

NOT AUTHORIZED

Makers: Ellis, Lees, Tiptaft, Unknown
Fasteners: Lugs, Pin
Composition:
Other Ranks: Browning copper
Officers: Unknown
Ref.: Babin, Meek, Stewart, Cox

Note: Two makers of this cap badge exist.
　　1. Pointed maple leaf design with a small crown and large stem; Tiptaft *(Illustrated)*
　　2. Blunt maple leaf design with a large crown and a small stem; Lees

Badge No.	Insignia	Rank	Description	Extremely Fine
20A-2	Cap	ORs	Browning copper; Lees	25.00
20A-4		ORs	Browning copper; Tiptaft	30.00
20A-21		Officers	Unknown	- -
20A-41	Collars	ORs	Browning copper; Lees	15.00
20A-43		ORs	Browning copper; Tiptaft	20.00
20A-61		Officers	Unknown	- -
	"C" Over Numbers			
20A-81	Collars	ORs	"C" bar "20", Small "C"; Tiptaft	18.00
20A-91	Shoulders	ORs	Numeral: "20"; Ellis	14.00

No. - 20B

CANADA
/FIRST CENTRAL ONTARIO REGIMENT
/XX/CE LER ET FORTIS

Makers: Gaunt
Fasteners: Lugs
Composition:
 Other Ranks: Browning copper
 Officers: Gilt brass
Ref.: Babin, Cox

Badge No.	Insignia	Rank	Description	Extremely Fine
20B-2	Cap	ORs	Browning copper; Gaunt	30.00
20B-21		Officers	Gilt brass; Gaunt	100.00
20B-41	Collars	ORs	Browning copper; Gaunt	20.00
20B-61		Officers	Gilt brass; Gaunt	30.00

No. - 20C   **20/CANADA**

The construction of this badge is the same as the 9th and 19th Battalion badges. The overlay is white metal (CROWN/20/CANADA). The Officer's cap will have a silver overlay.

Makers: Reiche
Fasteners: Lugs
Composition:
 Other Ranks: Browning copper
with brass overlay
on design
 Officers: Browning copper
with silver overlay
on design
Ref.: Babin, Cox

Badge No.	Insignia	Rank	Description	Extremely Fine
20C-2	Cap	ORs	Browning copper, brass overlay on design; Reiche	1,200.00
20C-21		Officers	Browning copper, Silver overlay on design; Reiche	1,500.00
20C-41	Collars	ORs	Browning copper, brass overlay; Reiche	Rare
20C-61		Officers	Unknown	- -

21ST INFANTRY BATTALION

The Battalion was raised in Eastern Ontario and mobilized in Kingston, Ontario under the authority of G.O. 36 March 15th, 1915. The Battalion sailed May 4th, 1915 with a strength of forty-two officers and one thousand and fifty-seven other ranks under the command of Lieutenant-Colonel W. St. P. Hughes. The Battalion served in France and Belgium with the 4th Infantry Brigade, 2nd Canadian Division. It was disbanded September 15th, 1920.

BADGE NUMBER: 21

21/CANADA

NOT AUTHORIZED

Makers: Birks, Gaunt,
Tiptaft, Unknown
Fasteners: Lugs
Composition:
Other Ranks: Browning copper
Officers:
    A. Silverplate
    B. Gilt on brass
    C. Browning brass
    with white metal
    overlay on "21"
Ref.: Babin, Meek, Stewart, Cox

Note: Two makers of this cap badge exist.
1. Wide numbers with wide type for the lettering; Gaunt *(Illustrated)*
2. Narrow numbers with narrow type for the lettering; Tiptaft

Badge No.	Insignia	Rank	Description	Extremely Fine
21-2	Cap	ORs	Browning copper; Gaunt	20.00
21-4		ORs	Browning copper; Tiptaft	18.00
21-21		Officers	Silverplate; Unknown	40.00
21-23		Officers	Gilt on brass; Unknown	45.00
21-25		Officers	Browning brass, Wm. overlay on "21"; Unknown	120.00
21-41	Collars	ORs	Browning copper; Gaunt	10.00
21-43		ORs	Browning copper; Tiptaft	10.00
21-61		Officers	Gilt on brass; Unknown	10.00
21-63		Officers	Browning brass, Wm. overlay on "21"; Unknown	25.00
"C" Over Numbers				
21-81	Collars	ORs	"C" over "21", Small C; Tiptaft	25.00
21-83		NCO	"C" bar "21"; Unknown	30.00
21-85		NCO	"C" bar "21"; Unknown	20.00
21-91	Shoulders	ORs	Numeral: "21"; Birks	24.00

22ND INFANTRY BATTALION

"CANADIENS FRANCAIS"

The Battalion was raised in Quebec and mobilized in St. Jean, Quebec under the authority of G.O. 36 March 15th, 1915. The Battalion sailed May 20th, 1915 with a strength of thirty-six officers and one thousand and ninety-seven other ranks under the command of Lieutenant-Colonel F. M. Gaudet. The Battalion served in France and Belgium with the 5th Infantry Brigade, 2nd Canadian Division. It was disbanded September 15th, 1920.

BADGE NUMBER: 22

No. - 22A　　　　REGIMENT CANADIENS FRANCAIS
　　　　　　　　　　　　/JE ME SOUVIENS

NOT AUTHORIZED

Makers: Caron, Tiptaft, Unknown
Fasteners: Lugs
Composition:
　Other Ranks: Browning copper
　Officers: Browning copper
　　　　　　　with white metal
　　　　　　　overlay on design
Ref.: Babin, Meek, Stewart, Cox

Note: Two makers of this cap badge exist.
　　1. Large head beaver with a short crown; Caron. The badge is 38" mm. *(Illustrated)*
　　2. Small head beaver with a tall crown; Tiptaft. The badge is "41" mm.

Badge No.	Insignia	Rank	Description	Extremely Fine
22A-2	Cap	ORs	Browning copper; Caron	20.00
22A-4		ORs	Browning copper; Tiptaft	20.00
22A-21		Officers	Browning copper, Wm. overlay on design; Tiptaft	100.00
22A-41	Collars	ORs	Browning copper; Caron	15.00
22A-61		Officers	Browning copper;Tiptaft	20.00
	"C" Over Numbers			
22A-81	Collars	ORs	"C" over "22", Large "C"; Tiptaft	15.00
22A-83		ORs	"C" bar "22", Small "C"; Tiptaft	15.00
22A-85		NCO	"C" bar "22", White metal	15.00
22A-91	Shoulders	ORs	Numeral: "22"; Unknown	- -

No. - 22B   **REGIMENT CANADIEN FRANCAIS**
/22/JE ME SOUVIENS

Makers: Tiptaft, Unknown
Fasteners: Lugs
Composition:
Other Ranks: Browning copper
or brass
Officers:
A. Browning copper
with white metal
overlay on design
B. Sterling silver
Ref.: Babin, Cox

Note: Two makers of this cap badge exist.
1. Narrow crown with solid pattern; Unknown *(Illustrated)*
2. Wide crown with void pattern: Tiptaft

Badge No.	Insignia	Rank	Description	Extremely Fine
22B-2	Cap	ORs	Browning copper; Unknown	25.00
22B-4		ORs	Browning brass; Tiptaft	50.00
22B-21		Officers	Browning copper, Wm. overlay on design; Unknown	100.00
22B-23		Officers	Sterling silver; Tiptaft	100.00
22B-41	Collars	ORs	Browning copper; Unknown	10.00
22B-43		ORs	Browning brass; Tiptaft	10.00
22B-61		Officers	Browning copper, Wm. overlay on design	50.00
22B-63		Officers	Sterling silver; Tiptaft	50.00

23RD INFANTRY BATTALION

"MONTREAL BATTALION"

The Battalion was raised in British Columbia, Alberta, Manitoba and Quebec with mobilization headquarters at Quebec City under the authority of G.O. 26 March 15th, 1915. The Battalion sailed May 23rd, 1915, with a strength of thirty-five officers and nine hundred and forty-two other ranks under the command of Lieutenant-Colonel F. W. Fisher. In England the 23rd Battalion was redesignated the 23rd Reserve Battalion. It was disbanded September 15th, 1920.

BADGE NUMBER: 23

CANADA/CONCORDIA SALUS /MONTREAL/23/BATTALION

NOT AUTHORIZED

Makers: Birks, Caron, Ellis, Tiptaft, Unknown
Fasteners: Lugs
Composition:
Other Ranks: Browning copper or brass
Officers:
  A: Browning copper with silver overlay on "23"
  B: Silverplate on copper
  C: White metal
Ref.: Babin, Meek, Stewart, Cox

Badge No.	Insignia	Rank	Description	Extremely Fine
23-2	Cap	ORs	Browning copper; Tiptaft	20.00
23-4		ORs	Browning brass; Tiptaft	20.00
23-21		Officers	Browning copper, silver overlay on "23"; Tiptaft	50.00
23-23		Officers	Silverplate on copper; Unknown	100.00
23-25		Officers	White metal; Unknown	150.00
23-27		Officers	Gilt on copper; Tiptaft	50.00
23-41	Collars	ORs	Browning copper; Tiptaft	10.00
23-43		ORs	Browning brass; Tiptaft	10.00
23-61		Officers	Browning copper, silver overlay on "23"; Tiptaft	25.00

Badge No.	Insignia	Rank	Description	Extremely Fine
			"C" Over Numbers	
23-81	Collars	ORs	"C" bar "23"; Tiptaft	16.00
23-83		NCO	"C" over "23"; Unknown	18.00
23-91	Shoulders	ORs	Numeral: "23"; Caron	12.00
23-93		ORs	Numeral: "23"; Ellis	12.00
23-95		ORs	Numeral: "23"; Birks	12.00

24TH INFANTRY BATTALION

"VICTORIA RIFLES"

The Battalion was raised and mobilized in Montreal, Quebec under the authority of G.O. 36 March 15th, 1915. The Battalion sailed September 15th, 1915 with a strength of forty-two officers and one thousand and eighty-two other ranks under the command of Lieutenant-Colonel J. A. Gunn. The Battalion served in France and Belgium with the 5th Infantry Brigade, 2nd Canadian Division. It was disbanded September 15th, 1920.

BADGE NUMBER: 24

24/PRO ARIS ET FOCIS
/VICTORIA RIFLES/CANADA

NOT AUTHORIZED

Makers: Caron, Hemsley, Inglis, Tiptaft, Unknown
Fasteners: Lugs, Slide, Pin
Composition:
Other Ranks: Pickled copper; Browning copper; Blackened copper
Officers: Gilt on copper
Ref.: Babin, Meek, Stewart, Cox

Note: Two makers of this cap badge exist.
　　1. Pointed leaf design with plain ribbons; Hemsley, Inglis *(Illustrated)*
　　2. Blunt leaf design with framed ribbons; Tiptaft.

Badge No.	Insignia	Rank	Description	Extremely Fine
24-2	Cap	ORs	Pickled copper; Hemsley, Inglis	18.00
24-4		ORs	Browning copper; Tiptaft	18.00
24-6		ORs	Blackened copper; Tiptaft	18.00
24-21		Officers	Gilt on copper; Hemsley, Inglis	30.00
24-41	Collars	ORs	Pickled copper; Hemsley, Inglis	15.00
24-43		ORs	Browning copper; Tiptaft	15.00
24-61		Officers	Gilt on copper; Hemsley, Inglis	20.00
	"C" Over Numbers			
24-81	Collars	ORs	"C" bar "24", Small "C", Tiptaft	14.00
24-83		NCO	"C" bar "24"; Unknown	15.00
24-91	Shoulders	ORs	Numeral: "24"; Caron	12.00
24-93		ORs	Title: "24" over "CANADA"	24.00

25TH INFANTRY BATTALION

"VICTORIA RIFLES"

The Battalion was raised in Nova Scotia and mobilized in Halifax under the authority of G.O. 36 March 15th, 1915. The Battalion sailed May 20th, 1915 under the command of Lieutenant-Colonel G. A. LeCain with a strength of forty-two officers and one thousand and eighty-one other ranks. The Battalion served in France and Belgium with the 5th Infantry Brigade, 2nd Canadian Division. It was disbanded September 15th, 1920.

Badge Number: 25

OVERSEAS/NOVA 25 SCOTIA/CANADA

AUTHORIZED JUNE 1, 1915

Makers: Gaunt, Tiptaft, Unknown
Fasteners: Lugs, Pin
Ref.: Babin, Meek, Stewart, Cox

Composition:
Other Ranks: Browning copper or brass
Officers: White metal overlay on brass

Other Ranks Badge   Officer's Badge

Note: Two different die makers of this badge exist.
1. Large "25" with large type on the legend; Gaunt
2. Small "25" with small type on the legend; Tiptaft *(Illustrated)*
   A small overlay collar badge exists but it is not known if it is an officers dress badge or a sweetheart pin, even though it is seen sometimes with lugs.

Badge No.	Insignia	Rank	Description	Extremely Fine
25-2	Cap	ORs	Browning copper; Gaunt	20.00
25-4		ORs	Browning brass; Tiptaft	25.00
25-21		Officers	Browning copper, Gilt overlay of design; Gaunt	150.00
25-23		Officers	Browning brass, Wm. overlay of design; Tiptaft	150.00

Badge No.	Insignia	Rank	Description	Extremely Fine
25-41	Collars	ORs	Browning copper; Gaunt	8.00
25-43		ORs	Browning brass; Tiptaft	10.00
25-61		Officers	Browning copper, Gilt overlay of design; Gaunt	40.00
25-63		Officers	Browning brass, Wm. overlay of design; Tiptaft	40.00

"C" Over Numbers

Badge No.	Insignia	Rank	Description	Extremely Fine
25-81	Collars	ORs	"C" bar "25", Small "C"; Tiptaft	16.00
25-83		NCO	"C" bar "25"; Unknown	20.00
25-91	Shoulders	ORs	Numeral: "25"; Unknown	15.00
25-93		ORs	Title: "NOVA SCOTIA/25TH/CANADA"	25.00

26TH INFANTRY BATTALION

"NEW BRUNSWICK BATTALION"

The Battalion was raised in New Brunswick with mobilization headquarters at Saint John under the authority of G.O. 36 March 15th, 1915. The Battalion sailed June 13th, 1915 with a strength of forty-two officers and one thousand one hundred and eight other ranks under the command of Lieutenant-Colonel J. L. McAvity. The Battalion served in France and Belgium with the 5th Infantry Brigade, 2nd Canadian Division. It was disbanded September 15th, 1920.

BADGE NUMBER: 26

CANADA/26/NEW BRUNSWICK BATTALION

NOT AUTHORIZED

Makers: Caron, Ellis, Hemsley, Inglis, Tiptaft
Fasteners: Lugs, Tangs
Composition:
Other Ranks: Pickled copper or brass; Browning copper
Officers: As above; Superior construction
Ref.: Babin, Meek, Stewart, Cox

Note: Two different die makers of this badge exist.
  1. The numbers "2" and "6" are joined by the use of large size type for the lettering; Hemsley, Inglis *(Illustrated)*
  2. The numbers "2" and "6" are separated by the use of small type size for the lettering; Tiptaft

Badge No.	Insignia	Rank	Description	Extremely Fine
26-2	Cap	ORs	Pickled copper; Hemsley, Inglis	18.00
26-4		ORs	Pickled brass; Hemsley, Inglis	20.00
26-6		ORs	Browning copper;Tiptaft	30.00
26-21		Officers	Unknown	- -
26-41	Collars	ORs	Pickled copper; Hemsley, Inglis	12.00
26-43		ORs	Pickled brass; Hemsley, Inglis	15.00
26-45		ORs	Browning copper; Tiptaft	15.00
26-61		Officers	Unknown	- -
26-91	Shoulders	ORs	Numeral: "26"; Ellis	16.00
26-93		ORs	Numeral: "26"; Caron	16.00

27TH INFANTRY BATTALION

"CITY OF WINNIPEG REGIMENT"

The Battalion was raised in Ontario and Manitoba, with mobilization headquarters at Winnipeg, Manitoba under the authority of G.O. 36 March 15th, 1915. The Battalion sailed May 17th, 1915 under the command of Lieutenant-Colonel J. R. Snider with a strength of thirty-three officers and one thousand and thirty-nine other ranks. The Battalion served in France and Belgium with the 5th Infantry Brigade, 2nd Canadian Division. It was disbanded September 15th, 1920.

BADGE NUMBER: 27

CITY OF WINNIPEG/XXVII BATTN

NOT AUTHORIZED

Makers: Dingwall, Gaunt, Tiptaft
Fasteners: Lugs, Tangs
Composition:
Other Ranks: Pickled copper; Browning copper or brass
Officers: Browning copper or brass; Superior construction
Ref.: Babin, Meek, Stewart, Cox

Note: Three different makers of this cap badge exist.
1. Plain ribbons; Large and small engine; Dingwall*(Illustrated)*
2. Framed ribbons; Tiptaft
3. Insufficient data available.

Badge No.	Insignia	Rank	Description	Extremely Fine
27-2	Cap	ORs	Pickled copper; Dingwall	18.00
27-4		ORs	Pickled brass; Tiptaft	18.00
27-6		ORs	Browning copper; Tiptaft	18.00
27-8		ORs	Browning brass; Tiptaft	18.00
27-21		Officers	Browning copper; Tiptaft	50.00
27-23		Officers	Browning brass; Tiptaft	50.00
27-41	Collars	ORs	Pickled copper;Dingwall	16.00
27-43		ORs	Pickled brass; Tiptaft	18.00
27-45		ORs	Browning copper; Tiptaft	16.00
27-47		ORs	Browning brass; Tiptaft	16.00
27-61		Officers	Unknown	- -
	"C" Over Numbers			
27-81	Collars	ORs	"C" over "27"; Gaunt	16.00
27-83		ORs	"C" bar "27", Small "C"; Tiptaft	16.00
27-91	Shoulders	ORs	Numeral: "27"	10.00

28TH INFANTRY BATTALION

"NORTH WEST REGIMENT"

The Battalion was raised in Saskatchewan and Ontario with mobilization headquarters at Winnipeg, Manitoba under the authority of G.O. 36 March 15th, 1915. The Battalion sailed May 29th, 1915 under the command of Lieutnenant-Colonel J. F. L. Embury with a strength of thirty-six officers and one thousand and seventy-eight other ranks. The Battalion served in France and Belgium with the 6th Infantry Brigade, 2nd Canadian Division. It was disbanded September 15th, 1920.

BADGE NUMBER: 28

No. - 28A

NORTH WEST BATTALION/28/
OVERSEAS/CANADA

"OVERSEAS" VARIETY

Makers: Caron, Hemsley, Inglis, Scully, Tiptaft, Unknown
Fasteners: Lugs
Composition:
Other Ranks: Pickled copper; or brass; Browning copper; Blackened brass; Silverplate
Officers:
    A: Gilt on copper
    B: Sterling silver
Ref.: Babin, Meek, Stewart, Cox

Note: Three different makers exist for this cap badge.
1. Small "Overseas"; Hemsley, Inglis *(Illustrated)*
2. Medium "Overseas"; Scully
3. Large "Overseas"; Tiptaft

Badge No.	Insignia	Rank	Description	Extremely Fine
28A-2	Cap	ORs	Pickled copper; Hemsley, Inglis	20.00
28A-4		ORs	Pickled brass; Hemsley, Inglis	20.00
28A-6		ORs	Browning copper; Tiptaft	20.00
28A-8		ORs	Blackened brass; Scully	20.00
28A-10		ORs	Silverplate; Scully	25.00
28A-21		Officers	Gilt on copper, Void; Unknown	165.00
28A-23		Officers	Sterling silver, Solid; Unknown	240.00

Badge No.	Insignia	Rank	Description	Extremely Fine
28A-41	Collars	ORs	Pickled copper; Hemsley, Inglis	10.00
28A-43		ORs	Pickled brass; Hemsley, Inglis	10.00
28A-45		ORs	Browning copper; Tiptaft	10.00
28A-47		ORs	Blackened brass; Scully	10.00
28A-61		Officers	Gilt on copper; Unknown	30.00
28A-63		Officers	Sterling silver; Unknown	50.00
		"C" Over Numbers		
28A-81	Collars	ORs	"C" bar "28", Small "C"; Tiptaft	16.00
28A-91	Shoulders	ORs	Numeral: "28"; Caron	12.00
28A-93		ORs	Numeral: "28"; Ellis	12.00

No. - 28B   NORTH WEST BATTALION/28/CANADA

"NO OVERSEAS" VARIETY

NOT AUTHORIZED

Makers: Hemsley, Inglis, Tiptaft, Unknown
Fasteners: Lugs
Composition:
Other Ranks: Pickled copper; Browning copper
Officers: Gilt on copper
Ref.: Babin

Note: Two different makers exist. They are extremely difficult to distinguish. This badge was not authorized.

Badge No.	Insignia	Rank	Description	Extremely Fine
28B-2	Cap	ORs	Pickled copper; Hemsley, Inglis	20.00
28B-4		ORs	Browning copper; Tiptaft	20.00
28B-21		Officers	Gilt on copper; Unknown	150.00
28B-41	Collars	ORs	Pickled copper; Hemsley, Inglis	20.00
28B-43		ORs	Browning copper; Tiptaft	20.00
28B-61		Officers	Gilt on copper; Unknown	50.00

29TH INFANTRY BATTALION

"TOBIN'S TIGERS"/"VANCOUVER REGIMENT"

The Battalion was raised and mobilized in Vancouver, British Columbia under the authority of G.O. 36 March 15th, 1915. The Battalion sailed May 20th, 1915 with a strength of thirty-seven officers and one thousand and ninety other ranks under the command of Lieutenant-Colonel H. S. Tobin. The Battalion served in France and Belgium with the 6th Infantry Brigade, 2nd Division. It was disbanded September 15th, 1920.

BADGE NUMBER: 29

No. - 29A   **VANCOUVER/29/CANADA**

NOT AUTHORIZED

Makers: Ellis, Jacoby, Tiptaft
Fasteners: Lugs, Slides, Pin
Composition:
Other Ranks: Browning copper or brass
Officers: Unknown
Ref.: Babin, Meek, Stewart, Cox

Note: Two different makers exist;
1. Plain ribbons; Jacoby
2. Framed ribbons; Tiptaft *(Illustrated)*

Badge No.	Insignia	Rank	Description	Extremely Fine
29A-2	Cap	ORs	Browning copper; Jacoby	18.00
29A-4		ORs	Browning brass; Tiptaft	18.00
29A-21		Officers	Unknown	- -
29A-41	Collars	ORs	Browning copper; Jacoby	15.00
29A-43		ORs	Browning copper; Tiptaft	15.00
29A-61		Officers	Unknown	- -
	"C" Over Numbers			
29A-81	Collars	ORs	"C" over "29", Small "C"; Tiptaft	35.00
29A-91	Shoulders	ORs	Numeral: "29"; Ellis	14.00
29A-93		ORs	Title: "29TH (VANCOUVER) BAT'N/ CANADA"; Jacoby	25.00
29A-95		ORs	Title: "29TH (VANCOUVER) BAT'N/ CANADA; Tiptaft	25.00

No. -29B

OVERSEAS/CANADA/ VANCOUVER XXIX BATTALION

Makers: G & S Co.
Fasteners: Lugs
Composition:
Other Ranks: Unknown
Officers: Browning copper;
Superior construction
Ref.: Babin, Cox

Note: The Goldsmiths & Silversmiths Company Ltd. (G & S Co.), 112 Regent Street, London, England, was an established jeweller. The company produced finely designed badges and insignia mainly for officers.

Badge No.	Insignia	Rank	Description	Extremely Fine
29B-2	Cap	ORs	Unknown	- -
29B-21		Officers	Browning copper; G & S Co.	125.00
29B-41	Collars	ORs	Unknown	- -
29B-61		Officers	Browning copper; G & S Co.	25.00

No. - 29C   **29TH BATTALION PIPERS BADGE**

This cast clan badge was worn by the pipe band of the 29th Infantry Battalion.

AUDENTES FORTUNA JUVAT

Makers: Unknown
Fasteners: Lugs
Composition:
Pipers: Silver
Ref: Babin 40-8, Cox 495

Badge No.	Insignia	Rank	Description	Extremely Fine
29C-2	Cap	Pipers	White Metal	125.00

30TH INFANTRY BATTALION

"BRITISH COLUMBIA BATTALION"

The Battalion was raised in British Columbia with mobilization headquarters at Victoria under the authority of G.O. 36 March 15th, 1915. The Battalion sailed February 23rd, 1915 with a strength of thirty-five officers and nine hundred and eighty other ranks under the command of Lieutenant-Colonel J. A. Hall. In England the 30th Infantry Battalion became the 30th Reserve Battalion, which later was absorbed into the 1st Reserve Battalion. It was disbanded September 15th, 1920.

BADGE NUMBER: 30

No. - 30A   **30/BRITISH COLUMBIA/CANADA**

NOT AUTHORIZED

Makers: Caron, Ellis, Tiptaft, Unknown
Fasteners: Lugs
Composition:
Other Ranks: Browning copper or brass
Officers: Gilt on copper; or Browning copper Superior construction
Ref.: Babin, Stewart, Cox

Note: The maker of the caps and collars is not known.

Badge No.	Insignia	Rank	Description	Extremely Fine
30A-2	Cap	ORs	Browning copper; Unknown	30.00
30A-4		ORs	Browning brass; Unknown	20.00
30A-21		Officers	Browning copper; Unknown	40.00
30A-23		Officers	Gilt on copper; Unknown	50.00
30A-41	Collars	ORs	Browning copper; Unknown	12.00
30A-43		ORs	Browning brass; Unknown	60.00
30A-61		Officers	Browning copper; Unknown	12.00
30A-63		Officers	Gilt on copper; Unknown	22.00
	"C" Over Numbers			
30A-81	Collars	ORs	"C" bar "30", Small "C", Tiptaft	18.00
30A-91	Shoulders	ORs	Numeral: "30"; Ellis	12.00
30A-93		ORs	Numeral: "30"; Caron	12.00

No. - 30B   2/BRITISH COLUMBIA

Makers: Tiptaft, Unknown 1 & 2
Fasteners: Lugs, Slide
Composition:
Other Ranks: Browning brass; White metal
Officers: Blackened brass, with silver overlay on "2"
Ref.: Babin, Meek, Cox

Note: Three different die makers of this cap badge exist.
    1. Blunt leaf design with a pointed serif on the "2"; Tiptaft
    2. Pointed leaf design with a blunt serif on the "2"; Unknown-1. *(Illustrated)*
    3. Blunt leaf design with a blunt serif on the "2"; Unknown-2.

Badge No.	Insignia	Rank	Description	Extremely Fine
30B-2	Cap	ORs	Browning brass; Tiptaft	35.00
30B-4		ORs	Browning brass; Unknown-1	35.00
30B-6		ORs	White metal; Unknown-1	25.00
30B-8		ORs	White metal; Unknown-2	25.00
30B-21		Officers	Blackened brass with Silver overlay on "2" and "British Columbia"; Unknown	65.00
30B-41	Collars	ORs	Browning brass; Tiptaft	16.00
30B-43		ORs	Browning brass; Unknown-1	16.00
30B-45		ORs	White metal; Unknown-1	15.00
30B-47		ORs	White metal; Unknown-2	15.00
30B-61		Officers	Blackened brass with Wm. overlay on "2" and "British Columbia"; Unknown	20.00
30B-63		Officers	Gilt on copper	30.00

31ST INFANTRY BATTALION

"ALBERTA REGIMENT"

The Battalion was raised in Alberta with mobilization headquarters at Calgary, Alberta under the authority of G.O. 36 March 15th, 1915. The Battalion sailed May 17th, 1915 with a strength of thirty-six officers and one thousand and thirty-three other ranks under the command of Lieutenant-Colonel A. H. Bell. The Battalion served in France and Belgium with the 6th Infantry Brigade, 2nd Canadian Division. It was disbanded September 15th, 1920.

BADGE NUMBER: 31

No. - 31A   **ALBERTA OVERSEAS BATTN/XXXI**

TIPTAFT VARIETY HAS "N" IN THE ABBREVIATION OF BATTALLION "BATTN"

NOT AUTHORIZED

Makers: Caron, Ellis, Gaunt, Tiptaft, Unknown
Fasteners: Lugs, Tangs
Composition:
Other Ranks: Pickle brass; Browning copper
Officers: Browning copper; Superior construction
Ref.: Babin, Meek, Stewart, Cox

Note: Two different die makers of this cap badge exist.
1. Pointed leaf design with plain ribbons; Unknown
2. Blunt leaf design with framed ribbons; Tiptaft *(Illustrated)*

Badge No.	Insignia	Rank	Description	Extremely Fine
31A-2	Cap	ORs	Pickled brass; Unknown	20.00
31A-4		ORs	Browning copper; Unknown	18.00
31A-6		ORs	Browning copper; Tiptaft	18.00
31A-21		Officers	Browning copper; Unknown	40.00
31A-41	Collars	ORs	Pickled brass; Unknown	15.00
31A-43		ORs	Browning copper; Unknown	20.00
31A-45		ORs	Browning copper; Tiptaft	20.00
31A-61		Officers	Unknown	- -
		"C" Over Numbers		
31A-81	Collars	ORs	"C" over "31"; Gaunt	18.00
31A-83		ORs	"C" bar " 31", small "C"; Tiptaft	18.00
31A-91	Shoulders	ORs	Numeral: "31"; Caron	14.00
31A-93		ORs	Numeral: "31"; Ellis	15.00

No.- 31B   **"BATT" VARIETY**

SCULLY VARIETY HAS NO "N" IN
THE ABBREVIATION OF BATTALION
"BATT"

Photograph	**Makers:** Scully
Not Available	**Fasteners:** Lugs
At Press Time	**Composition:**
	Other Ranks: Pickle brass
	Officers: As above
	Ref.: Not previousley listed

Badge No.	Insignia	Rank	Description	Extremely Fine
31B-2	Cap	ORs	Pickled brass; Scully	20.00
31B-21		Officers	Unknown	- -
31B-41	Collars	ORs	Pickled brass; Scully	20.00
31B-61		Officers	Unknown	- -

32ND INFANTRY BATTALION

"MANITOBA AND SASKATCHEWAN REGIMENT"

The Battalion was raised in Manitoba and Saskatchewan with mobilization headquarters at Winnipeg, Manitoba under the authority of G.O. 36 March 15th, 1915. The Battalion sailed February 23rd, 1915 with a strength of thirty-five officers and nine hundred and sixty-two other ranks under the command of Lieutenant-Colonel H. J. Cowan. In England the Battalion became the 32nd Reserve Battalion and subsequently was absorbed into the 15th Reserve Battalion. It was disbanded September 15th, 1920.

BADGE NUMBER: 32

MANITOBA/SASKATCHEWAN/32/CANADA

NOT AUTHORIZED

Makers: Birks, Ellis, Gaunt, Tiptaft
Fasteners: Lugs, Slide
Composition:
Other Ranks: Browning copper or brass; Bronze
Officers: Browning copper; Sterling silver
Ref.: Babin, Meek, Stewart, Cox

Note: Two die makers of this cap badge exist.
1. The "2" of 32 is closed with the motto running under the leaf; Ellis
2. The "2" of 32 is open and the motto is clear of the leaf; Tiptaft *(Illustrated)*

Badge No.	Insignia	Rank	Description	Extremely Fine
32-2	Cap	ORs	Browning copper; Ellis	18.00
32-4		ORs	Browning brass; Tiptaft	20.00
32-21		Officers	Browning copper; Unknown	40.00
32-23		Officers	Sterling silver; Unknown	40.00
32-25		Officers	Gilt on copper; Ellis	40.00
32-41	Collars	ORs	Browning copper; Ellis	12.00
32-43		ORs	Browning copper; Tiptaft	10.00
32-61		Officers	Browning copper; Unknown	20.00
32-63		Officers	Sterling silver; Unknown	20.00
			"C" Over Numbers	
32-81	Collars	ORs	"C" over "32"; Gaunt	16.00
32-83		ORs	"C" bar "32", Small C; Tiptaft	16.00
32-91	Shoulders	ORs	Numeral: "32"; Birks	14.00
32-93		ORs	Numeral: "32"; Ellis	14.00

33RD INFANTRY BATTALION

The Battalion was raised and mobilized in London, Ontario under the authority of G.O. 86 July 1st, 1915. The Battalion sailed March 17th, 1916 under the command of Lieutenant-Colonel A. Wilson with a strength of forty officers and nine hundred and forty-six other ranks. The Battalion was absorbed into the 36th Infantry Battalion in England. It was disbanded September 15th, 1920.

BADGE NUMBER: 33

No. - 33A   **(CROWN) 33**

NOT AUTHORIZED

Makers: Caron, Tiptaft;
Unknown
Fasteners: Lugs
Composition:
Other Ranks: Browning copper
Officers: Sterling silver
Ref.: Babin

Note: The maker of the caps and collars is not known.

Badge No.	Insignia	Rank	Description	Extremely Fine
33A-2	Cap	ORs	Browning copper; Unknown	220.00
33A-21		Officers	Sterling silver; Unknown	300.00
33A-41	Collars	ORs	Browning copper; Unknown	20.00
33A-61		Officers	Sterling silver; Unknown	50.00
			"C" Over Numbers	
33A-81	Collars	ORs	"C" bar "33" Small "C"; Tiptaft	16.00
33A-91	Shoulders	ORs	Numeral: "33"; Caron	14.00

No. - 33B   33/CANADA

Makers: Tiptaft
Fasteners: Lugs
Composition:
 Other Ranks: Browning copper
Officers: Silver
Ref.: Babin, Meek, Stewart, Cox

Badge No.	Insignia	Rank	Description	Extremely Fine
33B-2	Cap	ORs	Browning copper; Tiptaft	50.00
33B-21		Officers	Silver; Tiptaft	50.00
33B-41	Collars	ORs	Browning copper; Tiptaft	18.00
33B-61		Officers	Silver; Tiptaft	20.00

34TH INFANTRY BATTALION

The Battalion was raised and mobilized in Guelph, Ontario under the authority of G.O. 86 July 1st, 1915. The Battalion sailed October 23rd, 1915 with a strength of forty-one officers and one thousand one hundred and two other ranks under the command of Lieutenant-Colonel A. J. Oliver. In England the Battalion was reorganized as the "Boys Battalion" and ultimately disbanded.

BADGE NUMBER: 34

No. - 34A   **OVERSEAS BATTN/34/CANADA**

NOT AUTHORIZED

Makers: Ellis, Tiptaft, Unknown
Fasteners: Lugs
Composition:
Other Ranks: Browning copper or brass
Officers: Silver overlay on numbers
Ref.: Babin, Meek, Stewart, Cox

Note: Two different die makers of this cap badge exist.
1. Pointed leaf design; Unknown *(Illustrated)*
2. Blunt leaf design; Tiptaft

Badge No.	Insignia	Rank	Description	Extremely Fine
34A-2	Cap	ORs	Browning copper; Unknown	25.00
34A-4		ORs	Browning brass; Tiptaft	25.00
34A-21		Officers	Browning copper, Silver overlay on on "34"; Tiptaft	40.00
34A-41	Collars	ORs	Browning copper; Unknown	20.00
34A-43		ORs	Browning brass; Tiptaft	20.00
34A-61		Officers	Browning copper, Silver overlay on "34"; Tiptaft	20.00
34A-91	Shoulders	ORs	Numeral: "34"; Ellis	12.00
34A-93		ORs	Title "34/CANADA"	15.00

No. - 34B   **OVERSEAS 34 BATTALION/CANADA**

Makers: Tiptaft
Fasteners: Lugs
Composition:
　Other Ranks: Browning copper
　　Officers: Unknown
Ref.: Not previously listed

Badge No.	Insignia	Rank	Description	Extremely Fine
34B-2	Cap	ORs	Browning copper; Tiptaft	25.00
34B-21		Officers	Unknown	- -
34B-41	Collars	ORs	Browning copper; Tiptaft	20.00
34B-61		Officers	Unknown	- -

35TH INFANTRY BATTALION

The Battalion was raised and mobilized in Toronto, Ontario under the authority of G.O. 86 July 1st, 1915. The Battalion sailed October 16th, 1915 under the command of Lieutenant-Colonel F. C. McCordick with a strength of forty-one officers and one thousand one hundred and five other ranks. In England the Battalion became the 35th Reserve Battalion and was subsequently absorbed into the 4th Reserve Battalion. It was disbanded September 15th, 1920.

BADGE NUMBER: 35

No. - 35A　　　　　　　　　　**35/CANADA**

NOT AUTHORIZED

Makers: Caron, Ellis, Tiptaft
Fasteners: Lugs
Composition:
Other Ranks: Browning copper
Officers: As above; Superior construction
Ref.: Babin, Meek, Stewart, Cox

Note: Two different die makers of this cap badge exist.
　　1. Pointed leaf design with small stem; Ellis *(Illustrated)*
　　2. Blunt leaf design with large stem; Tiptaft

Badge No.	Insignia	Rank	Description	Extremely Fine
35A-2	Cap	ORs	Browning copper; Ellis	22.00
35A-4		ORs	Browning copper; Tiptaft	22.00
35A-21		Officers	Browning copper; Unknown	25.00
35A-41	Collars	ORs	Browning copper; Ellis	10.00
35A-43		ORs	Browning copper; Tiptaft	10.00
35A-61		Officers	Browning copper; Unknown	20.00
35A-91	Shoulders	ORs	Numeral: "35"; Caron	12.00
35A-93		ORs	Numeral: "35"; Ellis	12.00

No. - 35B   **OVERSEAS 35 BATTALION/CANADA**

**Photograph
Not Available
At Press Time**

Makers: Unknown
Fasteners: Lugs
Composition:
 Other Ranks: Browning copper
 Officers: Unknown
Ref.: Not previously listed

Badge No.	Insignia	Rank	Description	Extremely Fine
35B-2	Cap	ORs	Browning copper; Unknown	100.00
35B-21		Officers	Unknown	- -
35B-41	Collars	ORs	Browning copper; Unknown	20.00
35B-61		Officers	Unknown	- -

36TH INFANTRY BATTALION

The Battalion was raised and mobilized in Hamilton, Ontario under the authority of G.O. 86 July 1st, 1915. The Battalion sailed June 19th, 1915 under the command of Lieutenant-Colonel E. C. Ashton with a strength of thirty-nine officers and one thousand and four other ranks. In England the Battalion was absorbed into the 3rd Reserve Battalion and was disbanded September 15th, 1920.

BADGE NUMBER: 36

No. - 36A   **36/CANADA**

NOT AUTHORIZED

Makers: Birks, Ellis, Lees
Tiptaft, Unknown
Fasteners: Lugs, Slide
Composition:
Other Ranks: Browning copper
Officers: Gilt on brass
Ref.: Babin, Meek, Stewart, Cox

Note: Two different die makers of this cap badge exist.
1. Large numerals for "36" with an open "C" in Canada; Lees *(Illustrated)*
2. Small numerals for "36" with a closed "C" in Canada; Tiptaft

Badge No.	Insignia	Rank	Description	Extremely Fine
36A-2	Cap	ORs	Browning copper; Lees	20.00
36A-4		ORs	Browning copper; Tiptaft	20.00
36A-21		Officers	Browning copper; Unknown	25.00
36A-23		Officers	Gilt on brass; Unknown	110.00
36A-41	Collars	ORs	Browning copper; Lees	10.00
36A-43		ORs	Browning copper; Tiptaft	10.00
36A-61		Officers	Browning copper; Unknown	18.00
36A-91	Shoulders	ORs	Numeral: "36"; Ellis	12.00
36A-93		ORs	Numeral: "36"; Birks	13.00

No. - 36B   **OVERSEAS BATTALION/36/CANADA**

**Photograph
Not Available
At Press Time**

Makers: Unknown
Fasteners: Lugs
Composition:
Other Ranks: Browning copper
Offiers: Unknown
Ref.: Not previously listed

Note: Only the collars are reported

Badge No.	Insignia	Rank	Description	Extremely Fine
36B-2	Cap	ORs	Unknown	- -
36B-21		Officers	Unknown	- -
36B-41	Collars	ORs	Browning copper	Rare
36B-61		Officers	Unknown	- -

37TH INFANTRY BATTALION

The Battalion was raised in Sault Ste. Marie in Northern Ontario with mobilization headquarters at Niagara Falls, Ontario under the authority of G.O. 86 July 1st, 1915. The Battalion sailed November 27th, 1915 under the command of Lieutenant-Colonel C. F. Bick with a strength of forty officers and one thousand one hundred and four other ranks. In England the Battalion was abosrbed by the 39th Infantry Battalion and was disbanded September 15th, 1920.

BADGE NUMBER: 37

No. - 37A   **CANADIAN OVERSEAS BATTALION/37**

Makers: Caron, Ellis, Tiptaft
Unknown 1 & 2
Fasteners: Slide, Lugs
Composition:
Other Ranks: Browning copper
Officers: Sterling silver
Ref.: Babin, Meek, Stewart, Cox

Note: Three makers produced caps and collars for the 37th Infantry Battalion, Tiptaft being one of them. A detailed description is not available for the other two.

Badge No.	Insignia	Rank	Description	Extremely Fine
37A-2	Cap	ORs	Browning copper; Unknown-1	27.50
37A-4		ORs	Browning copper; Unknown-2	27.50
37A-6		ORs	Browning copper; Tiptaft	30.00
37A-21		Officers	Sterling silver; Unknown	150.00
37A-41	Collars	ORs	Browning copper; Unknown-1	18.00
37A-43		ORs	Browning copper; Unknown-2	18.00
37A-45		ORs	Browning copper; Tiptaft	18.00
37A-61		Officers	Sterling silver; Unknown	30.00
37A-91	Shoulders	ORs	Numeral: "37"; Caron	12.00

No. - 37B OVERSEAS 37 BATTALION/CANADA

Makers: Tiptaft
Fasteners: Lugs
Composition:
 Other Ranks: Browning copper
 Officers: Unknown
Ref.: Not previously listed

Badge No.	Insignia	Description		Extremely Fine
37B-2	Cap	ORs	Browning copper; Tiptaft	50.00
37B-21		Officers	Unknown	
37B-41	Collars	ORs	Browning copper; Tiptaft	35.00
37B-61		Officers	Unknown	

38TH INFANTRY BATTALION

"ROYAL OTTAWA BATTALION"

The Battalion was raised and mobilized in Ottawa, Ontario under the authority of G.O. 86 July 1st, 1915. The Battalion sailed with a strength of thirty-seven officers and one thousand and thirty-eight other ranks for Bermuda on August 8th, 1915 as a Protective Garrison. On May 30th, 1916 the Battalion sailed for England under the command of Lieutenant-Colonel C. M. Edwards. The Battalion served in France and Belgium with the 12th Brigade, 4th Canadian Division. It was disbanded September 15th, 1920.

BADGE NUMBER: 38

OTTAWA OVERSEAS BATTALION/ADVANCE/38/CANADA

Makers: Gaunt, Hemsley, Inglis, Tiptaft; Unknown
Fasteners: Lugs
Composition:
Other Ranks: Pickled copper; Browning copper
Officers: White metal overlay on crown and crest; Gilt
Ref.: Babin, Meek, Stewart, Cox

Note: Three makers of this cap badge exist.
1. Small pointed leaf (39 mm), domed "38", with a small beaver; Hemsley, Inglis (Illustrated)
2. Small blunt leaf (40 mm), flat "38", with a large snarling beaver; Gaunt
3. Large blunt leaf (43 mm), flat "38", with a small beaver; Tiptaft

Badge No.	Insignia	Rank	Description	Extremely Fine
38-2	Cap	ORs	Pickled copper; Hemsley	18.00
38-4		ORs	Pickled brass; Gaunt	25.00
38-6		ORs	Browning copper; Hemsley	18.00
38-8		ORs	Browning copper; Tiptaft	25.00
38-21		Officers	Pickled copper, Wm. overlay on design; Hemsley	50.00
38-23		Officers	Gilt on copper; Unknown	30.00
38-41	Collars	ORs	Pickled copper; Hemsley	7.50
38-43		ORs	Browning copper; Hemsley	20.00
38-45		ORs	Browning copper; Tiptaft	15.00
38-61		Officers	Pickled copper, Wm. overlay on design	25.00
38-63		Officers	Gilt on copper; Unknown	20.00

Badge No.	Insignia	Rank	Description	Extremely Fine
		"C" Over Numbers		
38-81	Collars	ORs	"C" over "38"; Gaunt	16.00
38-83		ORs	"C bar 38"; Linked 3 and 8; Tiptaft	14.00
38-85		ORs	"C bar 38"; Open 3 and 8; Unknown	18.00
38-91	Shoulders	ORs	Numeral: "38"; Caron	20.00

39TH INFANTRY BATTALION

The Battalion was raised in Southeastern Ontario with mobilization headquarters at Belleville, Ontario under the authority of G.O. 86 July 1st, 1915. The Battalion sailed June 24th, 1915 under the command of Lieutenant-Colonel J. A. V. Preston with forty officers and one thousand and three other ranks. It was absorbed into the 6th Reserve Battalion in England and disbanded September 15th, 1920.

BADGE NUMBER: 39

No. - 39A   **39/CANADA**

Makers: Ellis, Jacoby, Tiptaft, Unknown 1 & 2
Fasteners: Tangs, Lugs
Composition:
Other Ranks: Pickled brass; Browning copper
Officers: As above
Ref.: Babin, Meek, Stewart, Cox

Note: Four makers of the cap badge exist.
1. Open 3 in "39" with four jewels in the crown arch; Jacoby
2. Closed 3 in "39" with five jewels in the crown arch; Tiptaft *(Illustrated)*
3. Open 3 in "39" with five jewels in the crown arch; Unknown-1
4. Closed 3 in "39" with three jewels in the crown arch; Unknown-2

Badge No.	Insignia	Rank	Description	Extremely Fine
39A-2	Cap	ORs	Pickled brass; Jacoby	20.00
39A-4		ORs	Browning copper; Jacoby	45.00
39A-6		ORs	Browning copper; Tiptaft	45.00
39A-8		ORs	Browning copper; Unknown-1	45.00
39A-10		ORs	Browning copper; Unknown-2	45.00
39A-21		Officers	Pickled brass; Unknown	450.00
39A-23		Officers	Browning copper; Unknown	25.00
39A-41	Collars	ORs	Pickled brass; Jacoby	15.00
39A-43		ORs	Browning copper; Jacoby	20.00
39A-45		ORs	Browning copper; Tiptaft	20.00
39A-47		ORs	Browning copper; Unknown-1	20.00
39A-49		ORs	Browning copper; Unknown-2	20.00
39A-61		Officers	Unknown	- -
39A-91	Shoulders	ORs	Numeral: "39"; Ellis	12.00

The following two badges are possibly a militia issue (1920 to 1936). More research is required to confirm this. They are similar to No. 47 which is a confirmed militia badge.

No. - 39B   **39/CANADA/PRAESTO UT PRAESTUM**

DESIGN WITHOUT BEAVER

Makers: Jacoby, Tiptaft
Fasteners: Lugs
Composition:
Other Ranks: Pickled copper or brass
Officers: Silver overlay on "39"
Ref.: Not previously listed

Note: Two makers of this cap badge exist
1. Open "3" in "39"; Jacoby *(Illustrated)*
2. Closed "3" in "39"; Tiptaft

Badge No.	Insignia	Rank	Description	Extremely Fine
39B-2	Cap	ORs	Pickled copper; Jacoby	150.00
39B-4		ORs	Pickled brass; Tiptaft	150.00
39B-21		Officers	Pickled copper, Silver overlay on "39" and "Canada"; Jacoby	200.00
39B-41	Collars	ORs	Pickled copper; Jacoby	50.00
39B-43		ORs	Pickled brass; Tiptaft	50.00
39B-61		Officers	Pickled copper, Silver overlay on "39" and "Canada"; Jacoby	75.00

No. - 39C   **39/CANADA/PRAESTO UT PRAESTUM**

DESIGN WITH BEAVER

Makers: Unknown
Fasteners: Lugs, Tangs
Composition:
Other Ranks: Browning copper
Officers: Silverplate
overlay on
"39" and "Canada"
Ref.: Not previously listed

Note: This badge is also known in white metal. This variety is rare.

Badge No.	Insignia	Rank	Description	Extremely Fine
39C-2	Cap	ORs	Browning copper; Unknown	100.00
39C-21		Officers	Browning copper, Silverplate overlay on "39" and "CANADA"; Unknown	750.00
39C-41	Collars	ORs	Browning copper; Unknown	20.00
39C-61		Officers	Browning copper, Silverplate overlay on "39" and "CANADA"; Unknown	50.00

40TH INFANTRY BATTALION

"NOVA SCOTIA BATTALION"

The Battalion was raised in Nova Scotia, under the authority of G.O. 86 July 1st, 1915. mobilization headquarters was at Halifax (Aldershot). The Battalion left Canada October 8th, 1915 under the command of Lieutenant-Colonel A. Vincent with a strength of forty officers and one thousand and ninety other ranks. In England the Battalion was absorded into the 17th and 26th Reserve Battalion and disbanded September 15th, 1920.

BADGE NUMBER: 40

N.S./OVERSEAS BATTALION/40/CANADA

Makers: Birks, Caron, Ellis, Hemsley, Inglis, Tiptaft, Unknown
Fasteners: Lugs
Composition:
Other Ranks: Pickled copper or brass; Browning brass
Officers: Silver
Ref.: Babin, Meek, Stewart, Cox

Note: Three makers of this cap badge exist.
1. Plain ribbons, plain numbers; Hemsley, Inglis *(Illustrated)*
2. Framed ribbons, plain numbers; Unknown
3. Framed ribbons, framed numbers; Tiptaft

Badge No.	Insignia	Rank	Description	Extremely Fine
40-2	Cap	ORs	Pickled copper; Hemsley, Inglis	20.00
40-4		ORs	Pickled brass; Hemsley, Inglis	20.00
40-6		ORs	Browning copper; Tiptaft	20.00
40-21		Officers	Silver; Unknown	50.00
40-41	Collars	ORs	Pickled copper; Hemsley, Inglis	15.00
40-43		ORs	Pickled brass; Hemsley, Inglis	12.50
40-45		ORs	Browning copper; Tiptaft	12.00
40-61		Officers	Silver; Unknown	20.00
40-91	Shoulders	ORs	Numeral: "40"; Caron	12.00
40-93		ORs	Numeral: "40"; Ellis	12.00
40-95		ORs	Numeral: "40"; Birks	12.00

41ST INFANTRY BATTALION

"CANADIENS FRANCAIS"

The Battalion was raised in Quebec under the authority of G.O. 86 July 1st, 1915. The mobilization headquarters was at Quebec City. The Battalion sailed October 18th, 1915 under the command of Lieutenant-Colonel L. A. Archambeault with thirty-six officers and one thousand and eighty-two other ranks. The Battalion was absorbed into the 10th Reserve Battalion in England and disbanded September 15th, 1920.

BADGE NUMBER: 41

No. - 41A   **41/BATTALION CANADIENS FRANCAIS**

Makers: Caron, Hemsley, Inglis
Fasteners: Lugs
Composition:
Other Ranks: Pickled copper or brass
Officers: Sterling silver
Ref.: Babin, Meek, Stewart, Cox

Note: Two makers of this cap badge exist.
1. Small beaver, small numbers; Hemsley, Inglis *(Illustrated)*
2. Large beaver, large numbers; Caron

Badge No.	Insignia	Rank	Description	Extremely Fine
41A-2	Cap	ORs	Pickled copper; Hemsley, Inglis	20.00
41A-4		ORs	Pickled brass; Hemsley, Inglis	25.00
41A-6		ORs	Pickled brass; Caron	20.00
41A-21		Officers	Pickled copper; Hemsley, Inglis	30.00
41A-23		Officers	Sterling silver; Caron	100.00
41A-41	Collars	ORs	Pickled copper; Hemsley, Inglis	16.00
41A-43		ORs	Pickled brass; Hemsley, Inglis	12.00
41A-45		ORs	Pickled brass; Caron	12.00
41A-61		Officers	Pickled copper; Caron	12.00
41A-63		Officers	Sterling silver; Caron	35.00
41A-91	Shoulders	ORs	Numeral: "41"; Caron	14.00
41A-93		ORs	Numeral: "41"; Ellis	14.00
41A-95		ORs	Title: "41" OVER CANADA; Unknown	25.00

No. - 41B   41/CANADA

INTERIM BADGE

Makers: As General List, Ellis
Fasteners: Lugs
Composition:
Other Ranks: "41" overlaid on General List
Ref.: Not previously listed

Note: Shoulder numeral overlay on General List. The badges are Ellis'.

Badge No.	Insignia	Rank	Description	Extremely Fine
41B-2	Cap	ORs	General List, Overlay on "41"; Ellis	100.00
41B-4		ORs	General List, Overlay on embossed brass "41"	100.00
41B-21		Officers	Unknown	- -
41B-41	Collars	ORs	Unknown	- -
41B-61		Officers	Unknown	- -

42ND INFANTRY BATTALION

"ROYAL HIGHLANDERS OF CANADA"

The Battalion was raised in Montreal, Quebec under the authority of G.O. 86 July 1st, 1915. The headquarters on mobilization was also Montreal. The Battalion sailed June 10th, 1915 with a strength of forty officers and nine hundred and seventy-eight other ranks under the command of Lieutenant-Colonel G. S. Cantlie. The Battalion served in France and Belgium with the 7th Infantry Brigade, 3rd Canadian Division. It was disbanded September 15th, 1920.

BADGE NUMBER: 42

No. - 42A

THE ROYAL HIGHLANDERS
/NEMO ME IMPUNE LACESSET
/BLACK WATCH

Makers: Caron, Ellis, McDougall's, Tiptaft, Unknown
Fasteners: Lugs
Composition:
Other Ranks: Browning copper or brass
Officers: Sterling silver; Silver gilt of three piece construction
Ref.: Babin, Meek, Stewart

Badge No.	Insignia	Rank	Description	Extremely Fine
42A-2	Glengarry	ORs	Browning copper; Unknown	65.00
42A-4		ORs	Browning brass; Unknown	85.00
42A-21		Officers	Silver gilt, Three piece construction, MacDougall's, London	350.00
42A-41	Collars	ORs	Browning brass; Unknown	100.00
42A-61		Officers	Sterling silver; Unknown	175.00
		"C" over Numbers		
42A-81	Collars	ORs	"C" Bar "42", Small "C"; Tiptaft	16.00
42A-83		ORs	"C" Bar "42", Large "C"; Tiptaft	16.00
42A-85		NCO	"C" Bar "42", Wm.; Unknown	16.00
42A-91	Shoulders	ORs	Numeral: "42"; Caron	14.00
42A-93		ORs	Numeral: "42"; Ellis	14.00
42A-95		ORs	Title: RHC (Royal Highlanders Canada); Unknown	12.00

**No. - 42B   FORTY SECOND/ NEMO ME IMPUNE LACESSET
/THE ROYAL HIGHLANDERS OF CANADA**

Makers: MacDougall, Unknown
Fasteners: Lugs
Composition:
Other Ranks: Browning copper or
brass
Officers: Silver gilt, two
piece construction
Ref.: Babin, Cox

Badge No.	Insignia	Rank	Description	Extremely Fine
42B-2	Glengarry	ORs	Browning copper; Unknown	100.00
42B-4		ORs	Browning brass; Unknown	100.00
42B-21		Officers	Silver gilt; Unknown	200.00
42B-23		Officers	Silver gilt, (2 pc const); MacDougall	1,250.00
42B-41	Collars	ORs	Browning copper; Unknown	25.00
42B-43		ORs	Browning brass; Unknown	25.00
42B-61		Officers	Thistle Type: Silver; Unknown	400.00

43RD INFANTRY BATTALION

"CAMERON HIGHLANDERS"

The Battalion was raised in Winnipeg, Manitoba which was also the mobilization headquarters under the authority of G.O. 86 July 1st, 1915. The Battalion left Canada June 1st, 1915 under the command of Lieutenant-Colonel R. M. Thomson with a strength of forty officers and nine hundred and ninety-eight other ranks. The Battalion served in France and Belgium with the 9th Infantry Brigade, 3rd Canadian Division. It was disbanded September 15th, 1920.

BADGE NUMBER: 43

No. - 43A   **CAMERON HIGHLANDERS OF CANADA**
/43/ULLAMH

SMALL "43" INSIDE CIRCLE - "ULLAMH"

Makers: Unknown
Fasteners: Lugs, Pins
Composition:
Other Ranks: Browning copper; White metal
Officers: Sterling silver
Ref.: Babin E-43, Cox

Badge No.	Insignia	Rank	Description	Extremely Fine
43A-2	Glengarry	ORs	Browning copper; Unknown	60.00
43A-21		Officers	Sterling silver; Unknown	110.00
43A-4		ORs	White metal; Unknown	425.00
43A-41	Collars	ORs	Browning copper; Unknown	20.00
43A-61		Officers	Sterling silver; Unknown	75.00
43A-63		Officers	Gilt on brass; Unknown	30.00
	"C" Over Numbers			
43A-81	Collars	ORs	"C" bar "43", Large "C"; Tiptaft	18.00
43A-91	Shoulders	ORs	Numeral: "43"; Unknown	14.00

No. - 43B　　　**CAMERON HIGHLANDERS OF CANADA**
/43/BATTN C.E.F. WINNIPEG

SMALL "43" INSIDE CIRCLE - "BATTN CEF WINNPEG"

Makers: Tiptaft, Unknown
Fasteners: Lugs
Composition:
　Other Ranks: Browning Copper
　　Officers: Unknown
Ref.: Meek

Note: Two makers of this cap badge exist
　　1. Void crown with small type for "Batt'n C.E.F."; Unknown
　　2. Solid crown with large type for "Batt'n C.E.F."; Tiptaft.

Badge No.	Insignia	Rank	Description	Extremely Fine
43B-2	Glengarry	ORs	Browning copper; Unknown	265.00
43B-4		ORs	Browning copper; Tiptaft	265.00
43B-21		Officers	Unknown	- -
43B-41	Collars	ORs	Browning copper; Unknown	20.00
43B-43		ORs	Browning copper; Tiptaft	20.00
43B-61		Officers	Unknown	- -

No. - 43C   **CAMERON HIGHLANDERS OF CANADA**
/OVERSEAS/43/BATTN CEF WINNIPEG

LARGE "43" ON CIRCLE - "BATTN C.E.F. WINNIPEG"

Makers: Unknown 1 & 2
Fasteners: Lugs
Composition:
Other Ranks: Browning copper or
brass; White metal
on copper
Officers: Sterling silver
Ref.: Babin E-43A, Stewart, Cox

Note: Two makers of this cap badge exist
1. A struck badge with a void crown; Unknown-1 *(Illustrated)*
2. A cast badge with a void crown; Unknown-2

Badge No.	Insignia	Rank	Description	Extremely Fine
43C-2	Glengarry	ORs	Browning copper; Unknown-1	25.00
43C-4		ORs	Browning brass; Unknown-1	25.00
43C-6		ORs	Wm. on copper; Unknown-1	45.00
43C-8		ORs	White metal, Cast; Unknown-2	175.00
43C-21		Officers	Sterling silver; Unknown	150.00
43C-41	Collars	ORs	Browning copper; Unknown-1	25.00
43C-61		Officers	Unknown	- -

No. - 43D   **CAMERON HIGHLANDERS OF CANADA**
/OVERSEAS/ULLAMH

Photograph
Not Available
At Press Time

Makers: Unknown
Fasteners: Lugs
Composition:
Other Ranks: White metal
Officers: Unknown
Ref.: Babin E-43B

Badge No.	Insignia	Rank	Description	Extremely Fine
43D-2	Glengarry	ORs	White metal	100.00
43D-21		Officers	Unknown	- -

44TH INFANTRY BATTLION

The Battalion was raised in Winnipeg, Manitoba under the authority of G.O. 86 July 1st, 1915. Mobilization headquarters was also in Winnipeg. The Battalion left Canada October 23rd, 1915 with a strength of thirty-six officers and one thousand and seventy-six other ranks under the command of Lieutenant-Colonel E. R. Wayland. The Battalion served in France and Belgium with the 10th Infantry Brigade, 4th Canadian Division. It was redesignated the "44th New Brunswick Battalion" and was disbanded September 15th, 1920.

BADGE NUMBER: 44

No. - 44A   **OVERSEAS/44/BATTALION/CANADA**

Makers: Ellis, Hemsley, Inglis, Tiptaft, Unknown
Fasteners: Lugs, Slide
Composition:
Other Ranks: Pickled copper or brass; Browning copper
Officers: Copper gilt; Unknown
Ref.: Babin, Meek, Stewart, Cox

Note: Two makers of this cap badge exist.
    1. Small crown; Detailed design for the sheaf of wheat; Hemsley, Inglis *(Illustrated)*
    2. Large crown; Course design for the sheaf of wheat; Tiptaft

Badge No.	Insignia	Rank	Description	Extremely Fine
44A-2	Cap	ORs	Pickled copper; Hemsley, Inglis	18.00
44A-4		ORs	Pickled brass; Hemsley, Inglis	18.00
44A-6		ORs	Pickled brass; Tiptaft	18.00
44A-8		ORs	Browning copper; Tiptaft	18.00
44A-21		Officers	Gilt on copper; Unknown	- -
44A-41	Collars	ORs	Pickled copper; Hemsley, Inglis	25.00
44A-43		ORs	Pickled brass; Hemsley, Inglis	25.00
44A-45		ORs	Pickled brass; Tiptaft	25.00
44A-47		ORs	Browning copper; Tiptaft	25.00
44A-61		Officers	Gilt on copper; Unknown	- -
	"C" Over Numbers			
44A-81	Collars	ORs	"C" bar "44", Large "C"; Tiptaft	20.00
44A-91	Shoulders	ORs	Numeral: "44"; Ellis	16.00

No. - 44B   **44/CANADA**

Makers: Tiptaft
Fasteners: Lugs
Composition:
Other Ranks: Pickled Silver Gilt
Officers: Green enamelled numbers on gilt copper
Ref.: Babin, Cox

Badge No.	Insignia	Rank	Description	Extremely Fine
44B-2	Cap	ORs	Pickled silver, gilt	150.00
44B-21		Officers	Copper gilt with green enamel	100.00
44B-41	Collars	ORs	Unknown	- -
44B-61		Officers	Copper gilt with green enamel	75.00

45TH INFANTRY BATTALION

"MANITOBA REGIMENT"

The Battalion was raised in Manitoba with mobilization headquarters at Brandon under the authority of G.O. 86 July 1st, 1915. The Battalion sailed March 13th, 1916 under the command of Lieutenant-Colonel F. J. Clarke with a strength of thirty-eight officers and seven hundred and twenty other ranks. In England the Battalion was absorbed into the 11th Reserve Battalion. It was disbanded September 15th, 1920.

BADGE NUMBER: 45

MANITOBA/OVERSEAS
/45/BATTALION/CANADA

Makers: Ellis, Hemsley, Inglis, Tiptaft
Fasteners: Lugs
Composition:
Other Ranks: Pickled copper or brass; Browning copper; Blackened brass
Officers: Unknown
Ref.: Babin E-45, Meek, Stewart, Cox

Note: Two makers of this cap badge exist.
1. A stemless leaf design; Standing buffalo; Hemsley, Inglis *(Illustrated)*
2. A stem leaf design; Pawing buffalo; Tiptaft

Badge No.	Insignia	Rank	Description	Extremely Fine
45-2	Cap	ORs	Pickled copper; Hemsley, Inglis	35.00
45-4		ORs	Pickled brass; Hemsley, Inglis	35.00
45-6		ORs	Browning copper; Tiptaft	35.00
45-8		ORs	Blackened brass; Tiptaft	35.00
45-21		Officers	Unknown	- -
45-41	Collars	ORs	Pickled copper; Hemsley, Inglis	20.00
45-43		ORs	Pickled brass; Hemsley, Inglis	20.00
45-45		ORs	Browning copper; Tiptaft	20.00
45-47		ORs	Blackened brass; Tiptaft	20.00
45-61		Officers	Unknown	- -
45-91	Shoulders	ORs	Numeral: "45"; Ellis	16.00

46TH INFANTRY BATTALION

"SOUTH SASKATCHEWAN BATTALION"

The Battalion was raised in Saskatchewan with mobilization headquarters at Moose Jaw under the authority of G.O. 86 July 1st, 1915. The Battalion sailed October 23rd, 1915 under the command of Lieutenant-Colonel H. Snell with a strength of thirty-six officers and one thousand one hundred and fifteen other ranks. The Battalion served in France and Belgium with the 10th Infantry Brigade, 4th Canadian Division. It was disbanded September 15th, 1920.

BADGE NUMBER: 46

SOUTH SASKATCHEWAN
/XLVI/OVERSEAS/CANADA

There are a large number of makers for the 46th Infantry Battalion Cap and Collar badges. In order to identify the badges easily we have divided the badges first by the position of the Wheat Sheaves.

No. - 46A **ARMS OF SASKATCHEWAN -**
SHEAVES OF WHEAT STAGGERED

Makers: Dingwall, Ellis, Tiptaft
Fasteners: Lugs, Slide, Tangs
Composition:
Other Ranks: Pickled brass;
Browning copper
or brass;
Blackened brass
Officers: Gilt
Ref.: Babin, Meek, Stewart, Cox

Note: Two makers of this cap badge exist
1. A buffalo with a single curved tail; Dingwall *(Illustrated)*
2. A buffalo with a double curved tail, solid or void; Tiptaft

Badge No.	Insignia	Rank	Description	Extremely Fine
46A-2	Cap	ORs	Pickled brass; Dingwall	20.00
46A-4		ORs	Browning copper; Dingwall	16.00
46A-6		ORs	Browning copper, Solid; Tiptaft	16.00
46A-8		ORs	Browning copper, Void; Tiptaft	16.00
46A-10		ORs	Blackened copper; Dingwall	30.00
46A-12		ORs	Blackened brass, Void; Tiptaft	30.00
46A-21		Officers	Gilt on copper; Dingwall	30.00

Badge No.	Insignia	Rank	Description	Ectremely Fine
46A-41	Collars	ORs	Pickled brass; Dingwall	15.00
46A-43		ORs	Browning copper; Dingwall	15.00
46A-45		ORs	Browning copper, Solid; Tiptaft	15.00
46A-47		ORs	Browning copper, Void; Tiptaft	15.00
46A-49		ORs	Blackened copper; Dingwall	15.00
46A-51		ORs	Blackened brass, Void; Tiptaft	15.00
46A-61		Officers	Gilt on copper; Dingwall	16.00
		"C" Over Numbers		
46B-81	Collars	ORs	"C" over "46", Large C; Tiptaft	25.00
46B-91	Shoulders	ORs	Numeral: "46"; Ellis	18.00

No. - 46B

**ARMS OF SASKATCHEWAN -
SHEAVES OF WHEAT IN LINE**

**Photograph
Not Available
At Press Time**

Makers: Service Supply,
Fasteners: Lugs, Slide, Tangs
Composition:
Other Ranks: Brass;
Browning copper or brass;
Officers: Unknown
Ref.: Babin, Meek, Stewart, Cox

Note: These badges were issued with and without a void between the leaf and the "Canada" ribbon.

Badge No.	Insignia	Rank	Description	Extremely Fine
46B-2	Cap	ORs	Browning brass, Solid; Service Supply	30.00
46B-4		ORs	Browning brass, Void; Service Supply	30.00
46B-21		Officers	Unknown	- -
46B-41	Collars	ORs	Browning brass, Solid; Service Supply	25.00
46B-43		ORs	Browning brass, Void; Service Supply	25.00
46B-61		Officers	Unknown	- -

47TH INFANTRY BATTALION

The Battalion was raised in British Columbia under the authority of G.O. 86 July 1st, 1915. The mobilization headquarters was at New Westminster. The Battalion sailed November 13th, 1915, under the command of Lieutenant-Colonel W. N. Winsby with a strength of thirty-six officers and one thousand one hundred and fourteen other ranks. The Battalion served in France and Belgium with the 10th Infantry Brigade, 4th Canadian Division. The Battalion was redesignated the "47th Western Ontario Battalion" in February of 1918. It was disbanded September 15th, 1920.

BADGE NUMBER: 47

47/B./CANADA/C.

Jacoby # 1

Makers: Caron, Ellis, Gaunt Jacoby, Tiptaft
Fasteners: Lugs, Pin
Composition:
Other Ranks: Browning copper; Blackened copper
Officers: Gilt on copper; Blackened copper with silver overlay on design
Ref.: Babin, Meek, Stewart, Cox

Jacoby # 2

Note: Three makers of this cap badge exist.
1. Stylized leaf; Jacoby *(Illustrated)*
2. Regular leaf with plain ribbons (40 mm); Jacoby *(Illustrated)*
3. Regular leaf with framed ribbons (43 mm); Tiptaft

Badge No.	Insignia	Rank	Description	Extremely Fine
			Stylized Maple Leaf - Jacoby	
47-2	Cap	ORs	Blackened copper; Jacoby	50.00

Badge No.	Insignia	Rank	Description	Extremely Fine
			Regular Maple Leaf - Jacoby, Tiptaft	
47-4	Cap	ORs	Browning copper; Jacoby	20.00
47-6		ORs	Blackened copper; Tiptaft	18.00
47-21		Officers	Copper gilt; Jacoby	25.00
47-23		Officers	Blackened copper, Silver overlay; Tiptaft	50.00
47-41	Collars	ORs	Browning copper; Jacoby	10.00
47-43		ORs	Blackened copper; Tiptaft	15.00
47-61		Officers	Copper gilt; Jacoby	18.00
47-63		Officers	Blackened copper, Silver overlay; Tiptaft	23.00
			"C" Over Numbers	
47-81	Collars	ORs	"C" over "47"; Gaunt	18.00
47-83		ORs	"C" bar "47", Large "C"; Tiptaft	18.00
47-85		NCO	"C" bar "47", Small thin "C"	20.00
47-91	Shoulders	ORs	Numeral: "47"; Caron	14.00
47-93		ORs	Numeral: "47"; Ellis	12.00
47-95		ORs	Title: "47TH CANADA"; Jacoby	25.00
47-97		ORs	Title: "47TH CANADA"; Tiptaft	25.00

48TH INFANTRY BATTALION

The Battalion was raised in British Columbia under the authority of G.O. 86 July 1st, 1915. The mobilization headquarters was at Victoria. The Battalion sailed July 1st, 1915 with a strength of thirty-eight officers and one thousand and twenty other ranks, under the command of Lieutenant-Colonel W. J. H. Holmes. In England the Battalion was redesignated the "3rd Pioneer Battalion (48th Canadians)" and served in France and Belgium with the 3rd Canadian Division. On May 31st, 1917 the Battalion was broken up to provide reinforcements for the Canadian Corps in the field.

BADGE NUMBER: 48

B. 48 C./CANADA

Makers: Caron, Tiptaft,
Unknown 1 & 2
Fasteners: Lugs
Composition:
Other Ranks: Pickled copper
or brass;
Browning brass
Officers: Pickled copper;
Superior
construction;
Ref.: Babin, Meek, Stewart, Cox

Note: Three makers of this cap badge exist but it is difficult to distinguish one from the other.

Badge No.	Insignia	Rank	Description	Extremely Fine
48-2	Cap	ORs	Pickled copper; Unknown-1	100.00
48-4		ORs	Pickled brass; Unknown-2	50.00
48-6		ORs	Browning brass'; Tiptaft	20.00
48-21		Officers	Pickled copper; Unknown-2	65.00
48-41	Collars	ORs	Pickled brass; Unknown-1	25.00
48-43		ORs	Browning brass; Tiptaft	25.00
48-61		Officers	Unknown	- -
48-91	Shoulders	ORs	Numeral: "48" ; Caron	14.00

49TH INFANTRY BATTALION

The Battalion was raised in Edmonton, Alberta under the authority of G.O. 86 July 1st, 1915. The mobilization headquarters was also at Edmonton. The Battalion sailed June 4th, 1915 with a strength of thirty-six officers and nine hundred and ninety-six other ranks under the command of Lieutenant-Colonel W. A. Griesbach. The Battalion served in France and Belgium with the 7th Infantry Brigade, 3rd Canadian Division. It was disbanded September 15th, 1920.

BADGE NUMBER: 49

EDMONTON/49/OVERSEAS/BATTALION/CANADA

Makers: Caron, Ellis, Hemsley, Inglis, Tiptaft
Fasteners: Lugs, Slide
Composition:
Other Ranks: Pickled copper or brass; Browning copper
Officers: Unknown
Ref.: Babin, Cox

Note: Two makers of this cap badge exist.
1. Wide numbers; Short ribbons; Hemsley, Inglis *(Illustrated)*
2. Narrow numbers; Long ribbons; Tiptaft

Badge No.	Insignia	Rank	Description	Extremely Fine
49A-2	Cap	ORs	Pickled copper; Hemsley, Inglis	25.00
49A-4		ORs	Pickled brass; Hemsley, Inglis	25.00
49A-6		ORs	Browning copper; Tiptaft	25.00
49A-21		Officers	Unknown	- -
49A-41	Collars	ORs	Pickled copper; Hemsley, Inglis	16.00
49A-43		ORs	Pickled brass; Hemsley, Inglis	18.00
49A-45		ORs	Browning copper; Tiptaft	18.00
49A-61		Officers	Unknown	- -
		"C" Over Numbers		
49A-81	Collars	ORs	"C" over "49"; Unknown	25.00
49A-91	Shoulders	ORs	Numeral: "49"; Caron	12.00
49A-93		ORs	Numeral: "49"; Ellis	14.00

No. - 49B   **CANADA/49/EDMONTON REGIMENT**

Makers: Gaunt, Scully, Tiptaft
Fasteners: Lugs
Composition:
   Other Ranks: Brass;
               Browning brass;
               Blackened brass
      Officers: Unknown; Brass
Ref.: Babin, Meek, Stewart, Cox

Note: It is questionable as to whether this badge belongs to the C.E.F. or militia period.
Three makers of this cap badge exist
1. A brass badge; Scully
2. Browning brass badge with a large eared cat; Gaunt
3. Blackened brass badge with a small eared cat; Tiptaft *(Illustrated)*

Badge No.	Insignia	Rank	Description	Extremely Fine
49B-2	Cap	ORs	Brass; Scully	25.00
49B-4		ORs	Browning brass; Gaunt	25.00
49B-6		ORs	Blackened brass; Tiptaft	25.00
49B-21		Officers	Unknown	- -
49B-41	Collars	ORs	Brass; Scully	14.00
49B-43		ORs	Browning brass; Gaunt	14.00
49B-45		ORs	Blackened brass; Tiptaft	14.00
49B-61		Officers	Unknown	16.00

No. - 49C   **PIPER'S BADGE**
          CANADA/49/EDMONTON REGIMENT

Makers: Unknown
Fasteners: Lugs
Composition:
   Other Ranks: Brass
      Officers:
Ref.: Babin 40-3, Cox 530

Badge No.	Insignia	Rank	Description	Extremely Fine
49C-2	Cap	ORs	Brass	Rare

50TH INFANTRY BATTALION

"CALGARY REGIMENT"

The Battalion was raised and mobilized in Calgary, Alberta under the authority of G.O. 86 July 1st, 1915. The Battalion left Canada on October 27th, 1915 under the command of Lieutenant-Colonel E. G. Mason with a strength of forty-one officers and one thousand and thirty-six other ranks. The Battalion served in France and Belgium with the 10th Infantry Brigade, 4th Canadian Division. It was disbanded September 15th, 1920.

BADGE NUMBER: 50

No. - 50A   **OVERSEAS/BN/CALGARY/50/CANADA**

Makers: Caron, Ellis, Tiptaft, Unknown
Fasteners: Lugs
Composition:
Other Ranks: Pickled copper; Browning copper or brass
Officers: Gilt on copper
Ref.: Babin, Meek, Stewart, Cox

Note: Three makers of this cap badge exist.
  1. Pointed "5"; Large letters. The leaf is 38 mm wide; Caron *(Illustrated)*
  2. Blunt "5"; Small letters. The leaf is 36 mm wide; Tiptaft
  3. Blunt "5"; Small letters. The leaf is 35 mm wide; Unknown

Badge No.	Insignia	Rank	Description	Extremely Fine
50A-2	Cap	ORs	Pickled copper; Caron	18.00
50A-4		ORs	Browning copper; Caron	18.00
50A-6		ORs	Browning copper; Tiptaft	18.00
50A-8		ORs	Browning brass; Unknown	24.00
50A-21		Officers	Gilt on copper; Unknown	18.00
50A-41	Collars	ORs	Pickled copper; Caron	12.00
50A-43		ORs	Browning copper; Caron	12.00
50A-45		ORs	Browning copper; Tiptaft	15.00
50A-61		Officers	Unknown	- -
			"C" Over Numbers	
50A-81	Collars	ORs	"C" bar "50", Small "C"; Tiptaft	18.00
50A-91	Shoulders	ORs	Numeral: "50"; Ellis	14.00

No. - 50B   **50/CANADIAN INFANTRY**

Makers: G & S Co., Tiptaft,
Unknown
Fasteners: Lugs
Composition:
Other Ranks: Browning copper
Officers: Browning copper
with silver overlay
on design
Ref.: Babin, Meek, Stewart, Cox

Note: Three makers of this cap badge exist.
1. Large lettering; Five centre stripes; Tiptaft *(Illustrated)*
2. Small lettering; Four centre stripes; Unknown
3. Goldsmiths & Silvesmiths Co. badges are always stamped "G & S CO".

Badge No.	Insignia	Rank	Description	Extremely Fine
50B-2	Cap	ORs	Browning copper; Tiptaft	20.00
50B-4		ORs	Browning copper; Unknown	20.00
50B-6		ORs	Browning copper; G & S Co.	20.00
50B-21		Officers	Browning copper, Silver overlay on design; G & S Co.	175.00
50B-41	Collars	ORs	Browning copper; Tiptaft	12.00
50B-43		ORs	Browning copper; Unknown	12.00
50B-45		ORs	Browning copper; C & S Co.	12.00
50B-61		Officers	Browning copper, Silver overlay on design	14.00

51ST INFANTRY BATTALION

"EDMONTON REGIMENT"

The Battalion was raised and mobilized in Edmonton, Alberta under the authority of G.O. 86 July 1st, 1915. The Battalion sailed March 4th, 1916 with a strength of thirty-seven officers and one thousand and fifty-five other ranks under the command of Lieutenant-Colonel R. De L. Harwood. In England the Battalion was used for Garrison Duty. It was disbanded September 15th, 1920.

BADGE NUMBER: 51

No. - 51A   **EDMONTON/OVER 51 SEAS/CANADA**

WITH "OVERSEAS" VARIETY

Makers: Ellis, Hemsley, Inglis, Tiptaft
Fasteners: Lugs, Pin
Composition:
Other Ranks: Pickled copper or brass; Browning copper
Officers: Pickled copper; Superior construction
Ref.: Babin, Meek, Stewart, Cox

Note: Two makers of this cap badge exist.
1. Small "5"; Pointed leaf design; Hemsley. Inglis *(Illustrated)*
2. Large "5"; Blunt leaf design; Tiptaft

Badge No.	Insignia	Rank	Description	Extremely Fine
51A-2	Cap	ORs	Pickled copper; Hemsley, Inglis	30.00
51A-4		ORs	Pickled brass; Hemsley, Inglis	32.00
51A-6		ORs	Browning copper; Hemsley, Inglis	30.00
51A-8		ORs	Browning copper; Tiptaft	30.00
51A-21		Officers	Pickled copper; Pin; Hemsley, Inglis	60.00
51A-41	Collars	ORs	Pickled copper; Hemsley, Inglis	14.00
51A-43		ORs	Pickled brass; Hemsley, Inglis	14.00
51A-45		ORs	Browning copper; Hemsley, Inglis	14.00
51A-61		Officers	Pickled copper; Pin; Hemsley, Inglis	16.00
51A-91	Shoulders	ORs	Numeral: "51"; Ellis	12.00

No. - 51B   EDMONTON/51/CANADA

WITHOUT "OVERSEAS" VARIETY

NOT AUTHORIZED

Makers: Service Supply
Fasteners: Lugs
Composition:
 Other Ranks: Browning copper
        Officers: Unknown
Ref.: Cox

Badge No.	Insignia	Rank	Description	Extremely Fine
51B-2	Cap	ORs	Browning copper	100.00
51B-21		Officers	Unknown	- -
51B-41	Collars	ORs	Browning copper	25.00
51B-61		Officers	Unknown	- -

52ND INFANTRY BATTALION

"NEW ONTARIO REGIMENT"

The Battalion was raised in Western Ontario under the authority of G.O. 86 July 1st, 1915. The mobilization headquarters was at Port Arthur. The Battalion sailed November 23rd, 1916 under the command of Lieutenant-Colonel J. A. D. Hulme with a strength of forty officers and one thousand and thirty-two other ranks. The Battalion served in France and Belgium with the 9th Infantry Brigade, 3rd Canadian Division. It was disbanded September 15th, 1920.

BADGE NUMBER: 52

NEW ONTARIO/52/CANADA

Makers: Caron, Ellis, Service
Supply, Tiptaft;
Unknown
Fasteners: Lugs
Composition:
Other Ranks: Pickled copper;
Blackened brass
Officers: Unknown
Ref.: Babin, Meek, Stewart, Cox

Note: Four makers of this cap badge exist. They are very difficult to distinguish.

Badge No.	Insignia	Rank	Description	Extremely Fine
52-2	Cap	ORs	Pickled copper; Unknown	20.00
52-4		ORs	Blackened brass; Tiptaft	22.00
52-21		Officers	Pickled copper, Wm. overlay on design	50.00
52-41	Collars	ORs	Pickled copper; Unknown	7.50
52-43		ORs	Blackened brass; Tiptaft	7.50
52-61		Officers	Pickled copper, Wm. overlay on design	25.00
52-91	Shoulders	ORs	Numeral: "52"; Caron	10.00
52-93		ORs	Numeral: "52"; Ellis	12.00
52-95		ORs	Title: "52" bar "CANADA"; Tiptaft	15.00

53RD INFANTRY BATTALION

The Battalion was raised in Saskatchewan and Manitoba under the authority of G.O. 86 July 1st, 1915. The mobilization headquarters was at Winnipeg, Manitoba. The Battalion left Canada March 29th, 1916 under the command of Lieutenant-Colonel R. M. Dennistoun with a strength of thirty-five officers and one thousand and sixty-three other ranks. In England the Battalion was absorbed into the 15th Reserve Battalion. It was disbanded September 15th, 1920.

BADGE NUMBER: 53

CANADA/53/OVERSEAS BATTALION

Makers: Caron, Dingwall, Tiptaft
Fasteners: Lugs, Tangs, Pin
Composition:
Other Ranks: Pickled copper; Browning copper
Officers: As above; Superior construction
Ref.: Babin, Meek, Stewart, Cox

Note: Two makers of this cap badge exist. This Dingwall badge was issued with a void or solid field.
1. Open "5"; Large crown; Dingwall
2. Closed "5"; Small crown; Tiptaft

Badge No.	Insignia	Rank	Description	Extremely Fine
53-2	Cap	ORs	Pickled copper, Solid; Dingwall	18.00
53-4		ORs	Pickled copper, Void; Dingwall	18.00
53-6		ORs	Browning copper, Solid; Dingwall	18.00
53-8		ORs	Browning copper, Solid; Tiptaft	18.00
53-21		Officers	Browning copper; Pin; Dingwall	35.00
53-41	Collars	ORs	Pickled copper, Solid; Dingwall	18.00
53-43		ORs	Pickled copper, Void; Dingwall	18.00
53-45		ORs	Browning copper, Solid; Dingwall	18.00
53-47		ORs	Browning copper, Solid; Tiptaft	18.00
53-61		Officers	Browning copper; Pin; Dingwall	25.00
53-91	Shoulders	ORs	Numeral: "53"; Caron	12.00

54TH INFANTRY BATTALION

"KOOTENAY BATTALION"

The Battalion was raised in Southern British Columbia under the authority of G.O. 86 July 1st, 1915. The mobilization headquarters was at Nelson, British Columbia. The Battalion sailed November 22nd, 1915 under the command of Lieutenant-Colonel W. M. Davis with a strength of thirty-six officers and one thousand one hundred and eleven other ranks. The Battalion served with the 11th Infantry Brigade, 4th Canadian Division. The Battalion was redesignated the 54th "Central Ontario" Battalion August 1917. It was disbanded September 15th, 1920.

BADGE NUMBER: 54

KOOTENAY/OVERSEAS BATTALION 54
/B. C. CANADA

Makers: Caron, Ellis, Gaunt, Jacoby, Tiptaft
Fasteners: Lugs, Tangs
Composition:
Other Ranks: Pickled brass; Browning copper; Blackened copper
Officers:
  A: Browning copper with silver overlay on crown
  B: Browning copper with white metal overlay on crown
  C: Browning copper with silver overlay on "Crown" and "54"
Ref.: Babin, Meek, Stewart, Cox

Note: Three makers of this cap badge exist.
1. Overseas and Battalion ribbons rest on "54"; Large "54"; Jacoby
2. Overseas and Battalion ribbons do not rest on "54"; Large "54"; Tiptaft (*Illustrated*)
3. Overseas and Battalion ribbons do not rest on "54"; Small "54"; Unknown

Badge No.	Insignia	Rank	Description	Extremely Fine
54-02	Cap	ORs	Pickled brass; Unknown	22.00
54-04		ORs	Browning copper; Jacoby	20.00
54-06		ORs	Blackened copper; Tiptaft	20.00

Badge No.	Insignia	Rank	Description	Extremely Fine
54-21	Cap	Officers	Browning copper, Silver overlay on crown	50.00
54-23		Officers	Browning copper, Wm. overlay on crown	50.00
54-25		Officers	Browning copper, Silver overlay on crown and "54"; Tiptaft	50.00
54-27		Officers	Browning copper, Silver overlay on "54"; Jacoby	50.00
54-41	Collars	ORs	Pickled brass; Jacoby	14.00
54-43		ORs	Browning copper; Jacoby	14.00
54-45		ORs	Blackened copper; Tiptaft	14.00
54-61		Officers	Browning copper, Silver overlay on crown and "54"; Tiptaft	25.00
54-63		Officers	Browning copper, Silver overlay on "54"; Jacoby	25.00

"C" Over Numbers

Badge No.	Insignia	Rank	Description	Extremely Fine
54-81	Collars	ORs	"C" over "54"; Gaunt	15.00
54-83		ORs	"C" bar "54", Small "C"; Tiptaft	20.00
54-85		ORs	"C" bar "54", Large "C"; Tiptaft	20.00
54-91	Shoulders	ORs	Numeral: "54"; Caron	12.00
54-93		ORs	Numeral: "54"; Ellis	14.00
54-95		ORs	Title: 54th (Kootenay) Batn Canada; Jacoby	25.00
54-97		ORs	Title: 54th (Kootenay) Batn Canada; Tiptaft	25.00

55TH INFANTRY BATTALION

"NEW BRUNSWICK/P.E.I. BATTALION"

The Battalion was raised in New Brunswick and Prince Edward Island under the authority of G.O. 86 July 1st, 1915. The mobilization headquarters was at Sussex, New Brunswick. The Battalion sailed October 30th, 1915 under the command of Lieutenant-Colonel J. R. Kirkpatrick with a strength of forty-two officers and one thousand and ninety-seven other ranks. The Battalion was absorbed into the 17th and 26th Reserve Battalions. It was disbanded September 15th, 1920.

BADGE NUMBER: 55

No. - 55A   NEW BRUNSWICK P.E.I./55/
OVERSEAS BATTALION/CANADA

WITHOUT "AMPERSAND" VARIETY

Makers: Caron, Hemsley, Inglis,
Service Supply, Tiptaft
Unknown
Fasteners: Lugs
Composition:
Other Ranks: Pickled copper or
brass; Browning
copper or brass;
Officers: Pickled copper;
Silver
Ref.: Babin, Meek, Stewart, Cox

Note: Three makers of this cap badge exist.
1. Plain ribbons; Small laurel leaves on each side of "55"; Hemsley, Inglis *(Illustrated)*
2. Framed ribbons; Large laurel leaves on each side of "55"; Tiptaft
3. Service Supply cap badge in brass recorded but not described.

Badge No.	Insignia	Rank	Description	Extremely Fine
55A-2	Cap	ORs	Pickled copper; Hemsley, Inglis	20.00
55A-4		ORs	Pickled brass; Hemsley, Inglis	40.00
55A-6		ORs	Browning copper; Hemsley, Inglis	20.00
55A-8		ORs	Browning copper; Tiptaft	20.00
55A-10		ORs	Browning brass; Service Supply	25.00
55A-21		Officers	Pickled copper; Pin; Hemsley, Inglis	40.00
55A-41	Collars	ORs	Pickled copper; Hemsley; Inglis	20.00
55A-43		ORs	Browning copper; Hemsley; Inglis	20.00
55A-45		ORs	Browning copper; Tiptaft	20.00
55A-47		ORs	Browning brass; Service Supply	16.00
55A-61		Officers	Pickled copper; Pin; Hemsley, Inglis	20.00
55A-63		Officers	Silver; Unknown	50.00
55A-91	Shoulders	ORs	Numeral: "55"; Caron	14.00

No. - 55B

**NEW BRUNSWICK & P.E.I./55/
OVERSEAS BATTALION/CANADA**

WITH "AMPERSAND" VARIETY

Makers: Tiptaft
Fasteners: Lugs
Composition:
  Other Ranks: Browning copper
    Officers: Unknown
Ref.: Babin 55-A

Badge No.	Insignia	Rank	Description	Extremely Fine
55B-2	Cap	ORs	Browning copper; Tiptaft	45.00
55B-21		Officers	Unknown	- -
55B-41	Collars	ORs	Browning copper; Tiptaft	15.00
55B-61		Officers	Unknown	- -

56TH INFANTRY BATTALION

"CALGARY BATTALION"

The Battalion was raised and mobilized in Calgary, Alberta, under the authority of G.O. 86 July 1st, 1915. The Battalion left Canada March 23rd, 1916 under the command of Lieutenant-Colonel W. C. G. Armstrong with a strength of forty officers and one thousand and seventy other ranks. In England the Battalion was absorbed into the 9th Reserve Battalion. It was disbanded September 15th, 1920.

BADGE NUMBER: 56

OVERSEAS BATTALION/56/CALGARY/CANADA

Makers: Birks, Caron, Ellis, Hemsley, Inglis, Tiptaft Unknown
Fasteners: Lugs, Pin
Composition:
Other Ranks: Pickled copper or brass; Browning copper
Officers: Unknown
Ref.: Babin, Meek, Stewart, Cox

Note: Three makers of this cap badge exist.
1. Small lettering in legend; Wide "5"; Hemsley, Inglis *(Illustrated)*
2. Large lettering in legend; Narrow "5"; Tiptaft
3. Unknown - insufficient data available.

Badge No.	Insignia	Rank	Description	Extremely Fine
56-2	Cap	ORs	Pickled copper; Hemsley, Inglis	18.00
56-4		ORs	Pickled brass; Hemsley, Inglis	18.00
56-6		ORs	Browning copper; Tiptaft	18.00
56-21		Officers	Unknown	- -
56-41	Collars	ORs	Pickled copper; Hemsley, Inglis	7.50
56-43		ORs	Pickled brass; Hemsley, Inglis	7.50
56-45		ORs	Browning copper; Tiptaft	20.00
56-61		Officers	Unknown	- -
56-91	Shoulders	ORs	Numeral: "56"; Caron	14.00
56-93		ORs	Numeral: "56"; Ellis	12.00
56-95		ORs	Numeral: "56"; Birks	12.00

57TH INFANTRY BATTALION

"CANADIENS FRANCAIS"

The Battalion was raised and mobilized in Quebec City, Quebec under the authority of G.O. 103A August 15th, 1915. The Battalion sailed June 2nd, 1916 under the command of Lieutenant-Colonel E. T. Paquette with a strength of eighteen officers and four hundred and nineteen other ranks. In England, the Battalion was absorbed into the 69th Battalion. It was disbanded September 19th, 1920.

BADGE NUMBER: 57

FAIS CE QUE DOIS/57/
BATTALION CANADIENS FRANCAIS

Makers: Caron, Ellis,
General List, Tiptaft
Fasteners: Lugs
Composition:
Other Ranks: Pickled brass;
Browning brass;
Blackened brass
Officers: Heavy, superior two
piece construction
Ref.: Babin, Meek, Stewart, Cox

Note: Two makers of this cap badge exist.
    1. The centre circle is flat across the diameter; Caron *(Illustrated)*
    2. The centre circle is convex across the diameter; Tiptaft

Badge No.	Insignia	Rank	Description	Extremely Fine
57-2	Cap	ORs	Pickled brass; Caron	25.00
57-4		ORs	Browning brass; Caron	25.00
57-6		ORs	Blackened brass; Tiptaft	25.00
57-21		Officers	Pickled brass, Two piece construction; Caron	55.00
57-41	Collars	ORs	Pickled brass; General List	5.00
57-43		ORs	Browning brass; General List	5.00
57-61		Officers	Pickled brass; General List	10.00
57-91	Shoulders	ORs	Numeral: "57"; Caron	12.00
57-93		ORs	Numeral: "57"; Ellis	12.00

58TH INFANTRY BATTALION

The Battalion was raised in Central Ontario under the authority of G.O. 103A August 15th, 1915. The mobilization headquarters was at Niagara-on-the-Lake, Ontario. The Battalion sailed November 22nd, 1915 with a strength of forty officers and one thousand and ninety-one other ranks under the command of Lieutenant-Colonel H. A. Genet. The Battalion served in France and Belgium with the 9th Infantry Brigade, 3rd Canadian Division. It was disbanded September 15th, 1920.

BADGE NUMBER: 58

No. - 58A   **58/CANADA**

Makers: Birks, Ellis, Lees
Service Supply, Tiptaft
Fasteners: Lugs, Slide
Composition:
Other Ranks: Browning copper
Officers: Browning copper;
Unknown
Ref.: Babin, Meek, Stewart, Cox

Note: Three types of this cap badge exist.
1. Large leaf (50 mm); Small "58"; Pointed "5"; Tiptaft *(Illustrated)*
2. Large leaf (52 mm); Large "58"; Blunt "5"; Lees
3. Small leaf (46 mm); Small "58"; Framed numbers; Service Supply

Badge No.	Insignia	Rank	Description	Extremely Fine
58A-2	Cap	ORs	Browning copper; Lees	18.00
58A-4		ORs	Browning copper; Tiptaft	18.00
58A-6		ORs	Browning copper; Service Supply	18.00
58A-21		Officers	Browning copper; Unknown	- -
58A-41	Collars	ORs	Browning copper; Lees	40.00
58A-43		ORs	Browning copper: Tiptaft	40.00
58A-45		ORs	Browning copper; Service Supply	40.00
58A-61		Officers	Unknown	- -
			"C" Over Numbers	
58A-81	Collars	ORs	"C" over "58"; Gaunt	15.00
58A-83		ORs	"C" bar "58", Small "C"; Tiptaft	15.00
58A-91	Shoulders	ORs	Numeral "58"; Caron	12.00
58A-93		ORs	Numeral "58"; Ellis	12.00
58A-95		ORs	Numeral "58"; Birks	12.00

No. - 58B   **OVERSEAS BATTALION/58/CANADA**

Makers: Tiptaft
Fasteners: Lugs
Composition:
 Other Ranks: Browning copper
                or brass
        Officers: Gilt on copper
Ref.: Babin, Cox

Badge No.	Insignia	Rank	Description	Extremely Fine
58B-2	Cap	ORs	Browning copper; Tiptaft	45.00
58B-4		ORs	Browning brass; Tiptaft	45.00
58B-21		Officers	Gilt on copper; Tiptaft	75.00
58B-41	Collars	ORs	Browning copper; Tiptaft	20.00
58B-43		ORs	Browning brass; Tiptaft	20.00
58B-61		Officers	Gilt on copper; Tiptaft	30.00

59TH INFANTRY BATTALION

The Battalion was raised in Eastern Ontario and Western Quebec under the authority of G.O. 103A August 15th, 1915. The mobilization headquarters was near Kingston at Barriefield, Ontario. The Battalion left Canada April 5th, 1916 with a strength of thirty-six officers and one thousand and seventy-three other ranks under the command of Lieutenant-Colonel H. J. Dawson. In England the Battalion was absorbed into the 39th Infantry Battalion. It was disbanded September 15th, 1920.

BADGE NUMBER: 59

No. - 59A   **OVERSEAS/BATTALION/59/ FOY POUR DEVOIR/CANADA**

Makers: Ellis, Hemsley
Fasteners: Lugs
Composition:
Other Ranks: Pickled copper or brass
Officers: Pickled copper with silver overlay on design
Ref.: Babin, Meek, Stewart, Cox

Badge No.	Insignia	Rank	Description	Extremely Fine
59A-2	Cap	ORs	Pickled copper, Void; Hemsley	27.50
59A-4		ORs	Pickled copper, Solid; Hemsley	27.50
59A-6		ORs	Pickled brass, Void; Hemsley	35.00
59A-21		Officers	Pickled copper, Silver overlay on design, Void; Hemsley	50.00
59A-41	Collars	ORs	Pickled copper, Void; Hemsley	7.50
59A-43		ORs	Pickled brass, Void; Hemsley	15.00
59A-61		Officers	Pickled copper, Silver overlay on design, Void; Hemsley	30.00
59A-91	Shoulders	ORs	Numeral: "59"; Ellis	14.00

No. - 59B   59/OVERSEAS/ROY POUR DEVOIR/CANADA

TIPTAFT ERROR MOTTO "ROY POUR DEVOIR"

Makers: Tiptaft
Fasteners: Lugs
Compositon:
Other Ranks: Browning copper;
    Blackened copper
    Officers: Unknown
Ref.: Cox

Badge No.	Insignia	Rank	Description	Extremely Fine
59B-2	Cap	ORs	Browning copper; Tiptaft	30.00
59B-4		ORs	Blackened copper; Tiptaft	30.00
59B-21		Officers	Unknown	- -
59B-41	Collars	ORs	Browning copper; Tiptaft	15.00
59B-43		ORs	Blackened copper; Tiptaft	15.00
59B-61		Officers	Unknown	- -

No. - 59C   59/OVERSEAS/FOY POUR DEVOIR/CANADA

CORRECT MOTTO "FOY POUR DEVOIR"

A corrected badge was issued by Tiptaft, probably after realizing their error in spelling "Foy" with an "R". This badge is similar to badge No. 59B

Makers: Kinnear, Tiptaft, Unknown
Fasteners: Lugs, Pin
Composition:
Other Ranks: Browning copper; Blackened copper
Officers: Browning copper with silver overlay on "59"
Ref.: Babin, Meek

Note: Two makers of this cap badge exist.
1. Large leaf (39 x 41 mm) with small "59"; Kinnear *(Illustrated)*
2. Small leaf (38 x 36 mm) with large "59"; Tiptaft

Badge No.	Insignia	Rank	Description	Extremely Fine
59C-2	Cap	ORs	Browning copper; Kinnear	18.00
59C-4		ORs	Browning copper; Tiptaft	30.00
59C-6		ORs	Blackened copper; Tiptaft	30.00
59C-21		Officers	Browning copper with silver overlay on "59"; Unknown	125.00
59C-41	Collars	ORs	Browning copper; Kinnear	15.00
59C-43		ORs	Browning copper; Tiptaft	10.00
59C-45		ORs	Blackened copper; Tiptaft	15.00
59C-61		Officers	Browning copper with silver overlay on "59"; Unknown	30.00

60TH INFANTRY BATTALION

"VICTORIA RIFLES OF CANADA"

The Battalion was raised and mobilized in Montreal, Quebec under the authority of G.O. 103A August 15th, 1915. The Battalion sailed November 6th, 1915 under the command of Lieutenant-Colonel F. A. Gascoigne, with a strength of forty officers and one thousand and twenty-four other ranks. The Battalion served in France and Belgium with the 9th Infantry Brigade, 3rd Canadian Division. It was disbanded September 15th, 1920.

BADGE NUMBER: 60

OVERSEAS/60/BATTALION/CANADA

Makers: Caron, Ellis, Hemsley, Inglis, Tiptaft
Fasteners: Lugs, Pins
Compositon:
Other Ranks: Pickled copper or brass; Browning copper
Officers: Pickled copper
Ref.: Babin, Meek, Stewart, Cox

Note: Two makers of this cap badge exist.
    1. Four jewels in the upper band of the crown; Hemsley, Inglis *(Illustrated)*
    2. Five jewels in the upper band of the crown; Tiptaft

Badge No.	Insignia	Rank	Description	Extremely Fine
60-2	Cap	ORs	Pickled copper; Hemsley, Inglis	18.00
60-4		ORs	Pickled brass; Tiptaft	18.00
60-6		ORs	Browning copper; Hemsley, Inglis	18.00
60-8		ORs	Browning copper; Tiptaft	18.00
60-21		Officers	Pickled copper; Hemsley, Inglis	25.00
60-41	Collars	ORs	Pickled brass; Hemsley, Inglis	15.00
60-43		ORs	Browning copper; Hemsley, Inglis	10.00
60-45		ORs	Browning copper; Tiptaft	12.00
60-61		Officers	Pickled brass, Pin; Hemsley, Inglis	15.00
60-91	Shoulders	ORs	Numeral: "60"; Caron	12.00
60-93		ORs	Numeral: "60"; Ellis	12.00

61ST INFANTRY BATTALION

"WINNIPEG BATTALION"

The Battalion was raised and mobilized in Winnipeg, Manitoba under the authority of G.O. 103A August 15th, 1915. The Battalion sailed from Canada on April 5th, 1916 under the command of Lieutenant-Colonel F. J. Murray with a strength of thirty-seven officers and one thousand and ninety-one other ranks. In England the Battalion was absorbed into the 11th Reserve Battalion. It was disbanded September 15th, 1920.

BADGE NUMBER: 61

WINNIPEG/61/OVERSEAS BATTALION/CANADA

Makers: Dingwall, Ellis, Hemsley, Inglis, Tiptaft
Fasteners: Lugs, Tangs
Composition:
Other Ranks: Pickled copper or brass
Officers: As above; Superior construction
Ref.: Babin, Meek, Stewart, Cox

Note: Three makers of this cap badge exist
1. Pointed leaf design with large lettering in legend; Hemsley, Inglis *(Illustrated)*
2. Pointed leaf design with small lettering in legend; Dingwall
3. Blunt leaf design with large lettering in legend; Tiptaft

Badge No.	Insignia	Rank	Description	Extremely Fine
61-2	Cap	ORs	Pickled copper; Hemsley, Inglis	22.00
61-4		ORs	Pickled brass; Hemsley, Inglis	22.00
61-6		ORs	Pickled copper; Dingwall	22.00
61-8		ORs	Pickled copper; Tiptaft	22.00
61-21		Officers	Pickled copper; Unknown	35.00
61-41	Collars	ORs	Pickled copper; Hemsley, Inglis	14.00
61-43		ORs	Pickled copper; Dingwall	14.00
61-45		ORs	Pickled copper; Tiptaft	14.00
61-61		Officers	Pickled copper; Unknown	22.00
61-91	Shoulders	ORs	Numeral: "61"; Ellis	12.00

62ND INFANTRY BATTALION

"BRITISH COLUMBIA BATTALION"

The Battalion was raised in Southern British Columbia under the authority of G.O. 103A August 15th, 1915. The mobilization headquarters was at Vancouver, British Columbia. The Battalion sailed March 23rd, 1916 under the command of Lieutenant-Colonel J. Hulme with a strength of thirty-six officers and one thousand and thirty-seven other ranks. The Battalion was absorbed into the 30th Reserve Battalion in England. It was disbanded September 15th, 1920.

BADGE NUMBER: 62

BRITISH COLUMBIA/62/CANADA

Makers: Allan, Birks, Ellis, Tiptaft
Fasteners: Lugs, Pins
Composition:
Other Ranks: Browning copper; Blackened brass
Officers: Gilt on brass
Ref.: Babin, Meek, Stewart, Cox

Note: Three makers of this cap badge exist.
1. Large leaf, Open "6" with large lettering in legend; Allan
2. Large leaf, Closed "6" with small lettering in legend; Tiptaft *(Illustrated)*
3. Small leaf, Closed "6" with small lettering in legend; Birks

Badge No.	Insignia	Rank	Description	Extremely Fine
62-2	Cap	ORs	Browning copper; Allan	18.00
62-4		ORs	Blackened brass; Allan	20.00
62-6		ORs	Browning copper; Tiptaft	18.00
62-21		Officers	Gilt on brass; Birks	65.00
62-41	Collars	ORs	Browning copper; Allan	14.00
62-43		ORs	Blackened brass; Allan	14.00
62-45		ORs	Browning copper; Tiptaft	14.00
62-61		Officers	Browning copper; pin; Allan	25.00
62-63		Officers	Gilt on brass; Birks	30.00
62-91	Shoulders	ORs	Numeral: "62"; Ellis	12.00
62-93		ORs	Title: "62" bar "CANADA"	20.00
62-95		ORs	Title: "BRITISH COLUMBIA / CANADA"; Allan	25.00

63RD INFANTRY BATTALION

The Battalion was raised in Alberta under the authority of G.O. 103A August 15th, 1915. Mobilization headquarters was at Edmonton, Alberta. The Battalion sailed April 22nd, 1916 with a strength of thirty-six officers and one thousand and eighteen other ranks under the command of Lieutenant-Colonel G. B. McLeod. The Battalion was absorbed by the 9th Reserve Battalion in England. It was disbanded September 15th, 1920.

BADGE NUMBER: 63

No. - 63A   **CANADA/OVERSEAS/63/EDMONTON**

Makers: Caron, Jacoby, Tiptaft
Fasteners: Lugs
Composition:
Other Ranks: Pickled copper;
Blackened brass
Officers:
    A: Silverplate
    B: Gilt on copper
Ref.: Babin, Meek, Stewart, Cox

Note: Two makers exist of this cap badge exist.
    1. Large rifles; "63" on Edmonton ribbon; Jacoby *(Illustrated)*
    2. Small rifles; "63" above Edmonton ribbon; Tiptaft

Badge No.	Insignia	Rank	Description	Extremely Fine
63A-2	Cap	ORs	Pickled copper; Jacoby	35.00
63A-4		ORs	Blackened brass; Tiptaft	120.00
63A-21		Officers	Silverplate; Unknown	450.00
63A-23		Officers	Gilt on copper; Jacoby	50.00
63A-41	Collars	ORs	Pickled copper; Jacoby	10.00
63A-43		ORs	Blackened brass; Tiptaft	15.00
63A-61		Officers	Gilt on copper; Jacoby	20.00
63A-91	Shoulders	ORs	Numeral: "63"; Caron	14.00

No. - 63B   63/EDMONTON

Makers: Unknown
Fasteners: Lugs
Composition:
Other Ranks: Browning copper
Officers: Unknown
Ref.: Not previously listed

Badge No.	Insignia	Rank	Description	Extremely Fine
63B-2	Cap	ORs	Browning copper; Unknown	100.00
63B-21		Officers	Unknown	- -
63B-41	Collars	ORs	Browning copper; Unknown	25.00
63B-61		Officers	Unknown	- -

No. - 63C   OVERSEAS BATTALION CANADA/63

Makers: Caron for Eaton's
Fasteners: Lugs, Pin
Compositon:
Other Ranks: Pickled copper with white metal centre
Officers: As above; With pin fasteners
Ref.: Not previously listed

Badge No.	Insignia	Rank	Description	Extremely Fine
63C-2	Cap	ORs	Pickled copper, Wm. centre, Lugs; Caron	350.00
63C-21		Officers	Pickled copper, Wm. centre, Pin; Caron	350.00

64TH INFANTRY BATTALION

The Battalion was raised in the Provinces of New Brunswick, Nova Scotia and Prince Edward Island with mobilization headquarters at Halifax, Nova Scotia, under the authority of G.O. 103A August 15th, 1915. The Battalion sailed March 31st, 1916 under the command of Lieutenant-Colonel H. M. Campbell with a strength of thirty-eight officers and one thousand and eighty-nine other ranks. The 64th was broken up in England and provided drafts for the 40th Battalion and several reserve battalions. The Battalion was disbanded September 15th, 1920.

BADGE NUMBER: 64

OVERSEAS BATTALION/64/CANADA

Makers: Caron, Hemsley, Inglis, Tiptaft
Fasteners: Lugs
Composition:
Other Ranks: Pickled copper or brass; Blackened brass
Officers: Unknown
Ref.: Babin, Meek, Stewart, Cox

Note: Two makers of this cap badge exist.
    1. Laurel leaves surrounding the centre circle are overlapping; Hemsley, Inglis
    2. Laurel leaves surrounding the centre circle are separate; Tiptaft

Badge No.	Insignia	Rank	Description	Extremely Fine
64-2	Cap	ORs	Pickled copper; Hemsley, Inglis	30.00
64-4		ORs	Pickled brass; Hemsley, Inglis	30.00
64-6		ORs	Blackened brass; Tiptaft	30.00
64-21		Officers	Unknown	- -
64-41	Collars	ORs	Pickled copper; Hemsley, Inglis	14.00
64-43		ORs	Pickled brass; Hemsley, Inglis	14.00
64-45		ORs	Blackened brass; Tiptaft	14.00
64-61		Officers	Unknown	- -
64-91	Shoulders	ORs	Numeral: "64"; Caron	15.00

65TH INFANTRY BATTALION

"SASKATCHEWAN BATTALION"

The Battalion was raised in Saskatchewan and Manitoba under the authority of GO 103A August 15th, 1915. The mobilization headquarters was at Saskatoon, Saskatchewan. The Battalion sailed June 18th, 1916 with a strength of thirty-three officers and one thousand and forty other ranks under the command of Lieutenant-Colonel N. Lang. In England the Battalion was absorbed into the 44th, 46th, 54th and the 72nd Battalions. It was disbanded September 15th, 1920.

BADGE NUMBER: 65

65/OVERSEAS BATTALION/
SASKATCHEWAN/CANADA

Makers: Ellis, Hemsley, Inglis, Tiptaft
Fasteners: Lugs, Pin
Composition:
Other Ranks: Pickled copper or brass, Browning copper; Blackened brass
Officers: Unknown
Ref.: Babin, Meek, Stewart, Cox

Note: Three makers of this cap badge exist.
1. Wide numeral "65"; Large lettering for "Canada"; Hemsley, Inglis *(Illustrated)*
2. Narrow numeral "65"; Small lettering for "Canada"; Tiptaft
3. A third variety exists but there is insufficient data available at present.

Badge No.	Insignia	Rank	Description	Extremely Fine
65-2	Cap	ORs	Pickled copper; Hemsley, Inglis	16.00
65-4		ORs	Pickled brass; Hemsley, Inglis	16.00
65-6		ORs	Browning copper; Hemsley, Inglis	16.00
65-8		ORs	Blackened brass; Tiptaft	70.00
65-21		Officers	Unknown	- -
65-41	Collars	ORs	Pickled copper; Hemsley, Inglis	20.00
65-43		ORs	Pickled brass; Hemsley, Inglis	20.00
65-45		ORs	Browning copper; Hemsley, Inglis	20.00
65-47		ORs	Blackened brass; Hemsley, Inglis	20.00
65-61		Officers	Unknown	- -
65-91	Shoulders	ORs	Numeral: "65"; Ellis	12.00

66TH INFANTRY BATTALION

The Battalion was raised and mobilized in Edmonton, Alberta under the authority of G.O. 103A August 15th, 1915. The Battalion sailed April 28th, 1916 under the command of Lieutenant-Colonel J. W. McKinery with a strength of thirty-six officers and one thousand and seventy-one other ranks. The Battalion was absorbed into the 9th Reserve Battalion in England and was disbanded September 15th, 1920.

BADGE NUMBER: 66

No. - 66A   **66/CANADA**

Makers: Jackson, Unknown
Fasteners: Lugs, Pin
Composition:
Other Ranks: Browning copper
or brass
Officers:
    A: Browning copper
    B: Sterling silver
Ref.: Babin, Meek, Stewart, Cox

Note: Two makers of this cap badge exist.
    1. Narrow "66"; Without rings inside the band of the crown; Jackson *(Illustrated)*
    2. Wide "66"; Rings inside the band of the crown; Unknown

Badge No.	Insignia	Rank	Description	Extremely Fine
66A-2	Cap	ORs	Browning copper; Jackson	25.00
66A-4		ORs	Browning copper; Unknown	25.00
66A-6		ORs	Browning brass; Jackson	25.00
66A-21		Officers	Browning copper; Unknown	35.00
66A-23		Officers	Sterling silver; Unknown	50.00
66A-41	Collars	ORs	Browning copper; Jackson	15.00
66A-43		ORs	Browning brass; Jackson	10.00
66A-45		ORs	Browning copper; Unknown	22.00
66A-61		Officers	Browning copper; Unknown	25.00
66A-63		Officers	Sterling silver; Unknown	50.00
66A-91	Shoulders	ORs	Numeral: "66"; Unknown	- -
66A-93		ORs	Title: "66 CANADA Scroll"; Jackson	20.00
66A-95		ORs	Title: "66 CANADA Scroll"; Unknown	20.00

No. - 66B   **66/EDMONTON**

Makers: Unknown
Fasteners: Lugs
Composition:
  Other Ranks: Browning Copper
        Officers: Unknown
Ref.: Not previously listed

Badge No.	Insignia	Rank	Extremely Description	Fine
66B-2	Cap	ORs	Browning copper; Unknown	125.00
66B-21		Officers	Unknown	- -
66B-41	Collars	ORs	Browning copper; Unknown	30.00
66B-61		Officers	Unknown	- -

67TH INFANTRY BATTALION

"WESTERN SCOTS"

The Battalion was raised and mobilized at Victoria, British Columbia under the authority of GO 103A August 15th, 1915. The Battalion sailed April 21st, 1916 with a strength of thirty-four officers and one thousand and forty-five other ranks under the command of Lieutenant-Colonel L. Ross. The Battalion was redesignated the 67th Pioneer Battalion and then the 4th Pioneer Battalion. It was disbanded September 15th, 1920.

BADGE NUMBER: 67

No. - 67A   **WESTERN SCOTS BRITISH COLUMBIA**
/OVERSEAS/67/SABAID

Makers: Caron, Ellis, Tiptaft, Unknown
Fasteners: Lugs
Composition:
Other Ranks: Browning copper; Blackened brass
Officers:
    A: Blackened brass with silver or white metal overlay on design
    B: Gilt on brass
Ref.: Babin, Meek, Stewart, Cox

Note: Two makers of this cap badge exist.
  1. Large lettering; Pointed top "7"; Unknown *(Illustrated)*
  2. Small lettering; Flat top "7"; Tiptaft

Badge No.	Insignia	Rank	Description	Extremely Fine
67A-2	Glengarry	ORs	Browning copper; Unknown	75.00
67A-4		ORs	Blackened brass; Unknown	125.00
67A-6		ORs	Blackened brass; Tiptaft	50.00
67A-21		Officers	Blackened brass, Wm. overlay on design; Unknown	120.00
67A-23		Officers	Blackened brass, Silver overlay on design; Tiptaft	225.00
67A-25		Officers	Gilt on brass; Unknown	50.00
67A-27		Officers	Silver	75.00

Badge No.	Insignia	Rank	Description	Extremely Fine
67A-41	Collars	ORs	Browning copper; Unknown	20.00
67A-43		ORs	Blackened brass; Unknown	18.00
67A-45		ORs	Blackened brass; Tiptaft	18.00
67A-61		Officers	Blackened brass, Wm. overlay on design Unknown	60.00
67A-63		Officers	Blackened brass, Silver overlay on design; Unknown	75.00
67A-65		Officers	Gilt on brass; Unknown	60.00
67A-91	Shoulders	ORs	Numeral: "67"; Caron	14.00
67A-93		ORs	Numeral: "67"; Ellis	15.00

No. - 67B   **OVERSEAS BATTALION CANADA/67**

Photograph
Not Available
At Press Time

Makers: Caron for Eaton's
Fasteners: Lugs
Composition:
Other Ranks: Pickled copper with white metal centre
Officers: Pickled copper with silver centre
Ref.: Not previously listed

Badge No.	Insignia	Rank	Description	Extremely Fine
67B-2	Cap	ORs	Pickled copper, Wm. centre; Caron	275.00
67B-21		Officers	Pickled copper, Silver centre; Caron	250.00

68TH INFANTRY BATTALION

"REGINA BATTALION"

The Battalion was raised in Saskatchewan with mobilization headquarters at Regina under the authority of G.O. 103A August 15th, 1915. The Battalion sailed April 28th, 1916 with a strength of thirty-four officers and one thousand and sixty-seven other ranks under the command of Lieutenant-Colonel P. E. Perrett. The Battalion was absorbed into the 32nd Battalion in England and disbanded September 20th, 1920.

BADGE NUMBER: 68

OVERSEAS BATTALION/68/REGINA/CANADA

Makers: Caron, Ellis, Hemsley, Inglis, Scully, Tiptaft
Fasteners: Lugs
Composition:
Other Ranks: Pickled copper; Browning copper or brass
Officers: As above; superior construction
Ref.: Babin, Meek, Stewart, Cox

Note: Two makers of this cap badge exist.
1. Small lettering in the legend with detailed design for the sheaves of wheat; Hemsley, Inglis *(Illustrated)*
2. Large lettering in the legend with course design for the sheaves of wheat; Tiptaft

Badge No.	Insignia	Rank	Description	Extremely Fine
68-2	Cap	ORs	Pickled copper; Hemsley, Inglis	18.00
68-4		ORs	Browning copper; Hemsley, Inglis	18.00
68-6		ORs	Browning brass; Tiptaft	120.00
68-21		Officers	Unknown	- -
68-41	Collars	ORs	Pickled copper; Hemsley, Inglis	15.00
68-43		ORs	Browning copper; Hemsley, Inglis	15.00
68-45		ORs	Browning brass; Tiptaft	25.00
68-61		Officers	Unknown	- -
68-91	Shoulders	ORs	Numeral: "68"; Caron	12.00
68-93		ORs	Numeral: "68"; Ellis	12.00
68-95		ORs	Title: "CANADA /68 INF/ REGINA BATTALION"; Scully	25.00

69TH INFANTRY BATTALION

The Battalion was raised in Quebec with mobilization headquarters at Montreal under authority of G.O. 103A August 15th, 1915. The Battalion sailed April 17th, 1916 under the command of Lieutenant-Colonel J. A. Dansereau with a strength of thirty-four officers and one thousand and twenty-three other ranks. The Battalion was absorbed into the 10th Reserve Battalion in England. It was disbanded September 15th, 1920.

BADGE NUMBER: 69

SERVICE/69/OUTRE MER
/JE ME SOUVIENS/CANADA

Makers: Hemsley, Inglis, Tiptaft
Fasteners: Lugs
Composition:
Other Ranks: Pickled copper or brass; Browning copper
Officers: Browning copper; Silverplate
Ref.: Babin, Meek, Stewart, Cox

Note: Two makers of this cap badge exist.
    1. Small lettering; Three large maple leaves on crest; Hemsley, Inglis *(Illustrated)*
    2. Large lettering; Three small maple leaves on crest; Tiptaft

Badge No.	Insignia	Rank	Description	Extremely Fine
69-2	Cap	ORs	Pickled copper; Hemsley, Inglis	20.00
69-4		ORs	Pickled brass; Hemsley, Inglis	20.00
69-6		ORs	Browning copper: Hemsley, Inglis	20.00
69-8		ORs	Browning copper:Tiptaft	20.00
69-21		Officers	Browning copper, silver overlay of design; Hemsley, Inglis	75.00
69-23		Officers	Silverplate; Hemsley, Inglis	110.00
69-41	Collars	ORs	Pickled copper; Hemsley, Inglis	10.00
69-43		ORs	Pickled brass: Hemsley, Inglis	10.00
69-45		ORs	Browning copper; Tiptaft	10.00
69-61		Officers	Browning copper, Silver overlay of design; Hemsley, Inglis	30.00
69-91	Shoulders	ORs	Numeral: "69"; Ellis	14.00

70TH INFANTRY BATTALION

The Battalion was raised in Southwestern Ontario with mobilization headquarters at London, Ontario under the authority of G.O. 103A August 15th, 1915. The Battalion sailed April 24th, 1916 with a strength of thirty-five officers and nine hundred and thirty-six other ranks under the command of Lieutenant-Colonel R. I. Towers. The Battalion was absorbed into the 39th Infantry Battalion. It was disbanded September 15th, 1920.

BADGE NUMBER: 70

OVERSEAS BATTALION/70/CANADA

Makers: Caron, Hemsley, Inglis, Tiptaft
Fasteners: Lugs
Composition:
Other Ranks: Pickled copper or brass
Officers: Pickled copper with silver overlay on "70"
Ref.: Babin, Meek, Stewart, Cox

Badge No.	Insignia	Rank	Description	Extremely Fine
70-2	Cap	ORs	Pickled copper; Hemsley, Inglis	35.00
70-4		ORs	Pickled brass; Hemsley, Inglis	35.00
70-21		Officers	Pickled copper, Silver overlay on "70" Hemsley, Inglis	60.00
70-41	Collars	ORs	Pickled copper; Hemsley, Inglis	16.00
70-43		ORs	Pickled brass; Hemsley, Inglis	12.00
70-61		Officers	Pickled copper, Silver overlay on "70" Hemsley, Inglis	30.00
		"C" Over Numbers		
70-81	Collars	ORs	"C" Bar "70", Small "C"; Tiptaft	20.00
70-91	Shoulders	ORs	Numeral: "70"; Caron	14.00

71ST INFANTRY BATTALION

The Battalion was raised and mobilized in Woodstock, Ontario under the authority of G.O. 103A August 15th, 1915. The Battalion sailed April 21st, 1916 with a strength of thirty-five officers and nine hundred and sixty-three other ranks under the command of Lieutenant-Colonel D. M. Sutherland. The Battalion was absorbed into the 44th, 51st, 54th and 74th Battalions. It was disbanded September 15th, 1920.

BADGE NUMBER: 71

OVERSEAS BATTALION/71/CANADA

Makers: Caron, Unknown
Fasteners: Lugs
Composition:
Other Ranks: Pickled copper; Browning copper
Officers:
  A. Browning copper with silver overlay on "71"
  B. Browning copper with white metal overlay on "71"
Ref.: Babin, Meek, Stewart, Cox

Badge No.	Insignia	Rank	Description	Extremely Fine
71-2	Cap	ORs	Pickled copper; Caron	60.00
71-4		ORs	Browning copper; Caron	60.00
71-21		Officers	Browning copper, Wm. overlay on "71"; Caron	100.00
71-23		Officers	Browing copper, silver overlay on "71"; Caron	65.00
71-41	Collars	ORs	Pickled copper; Caron	15.00
71-43		ORs	Browning copper; Caron	15.00
71-61		Officers	Browning copper, Wm. overlay on "71"; Caron	35.00
71-63		Officers	Browning copper, silver overlay on "71"; Caron	45.00
71-91	Shoulders	ORs	Numeral: "71"; Caron	12.00
71-93		ORs	Title: "71" over "CANADA"; Caron	20.00

72ND INFANTRY BATTALION

"SEAFORTH HIGHLANDERS"

The Battalion was raised in British Columbia with mobilization headquarters at Vancouver under the authority of G.O. 103A August 15th, 1915. The Battalion sailed April 23rd, 1916 under the command of Lieutenant-Colonel J. A. Clark with a strength of thirty-four officers and one thousand and ninety-four other ranks. The Battalion served in France and Belgium with the 12th Infantry Brigade, 4th Canadian Division. It was disbanded September 15th, 1920.

BADGE NUMBER: 72

72/CUIDICH'N RICH

Makers: Allan, Ellis, Hemsley, Tiptaft, Unknown
Fasteners: Lugs, Tangs, Pin
Composition:
Other Ranks: White metal; Blackened brass
Officers: Sterling silver; Silverplated brass
Ref.: Babin, Meek, Stewart, Cox

Note: Three different makers of this cap badge exist.
1. The eyebrows and nose are one continuous line; Allan *(Illustrated)*
2. The eyebrows and nose are on two separate lines; Hemsley
3. The wreath surrounding the deer's head is wide with large leaves; Tiptaft

Badge No.	Insignia	Rank	Description	Extremely Fine
72-2	Glengarry	ORs	White metal; Allan	35.00
72-4		ORs	White metal; Hemsley	35.00
72-6		ORs	White metal; Tiptaft	35.00
72-21		Officers	Silver-plated brass; Unknown	75.00
72-23		Officers	Sterling silver (HM); Unknown	300.00
72-41	Collars	ORs	White metal	30.00
72-43		ORs	Blackened brass, Lugs; Allan	15.00
72-45		ORs	Blackened brass, Lugs; Tiptaft	15.00
72-61		Officers	Blackened brass, Pin; Allan	15.00
72-63		Officers	Sterling silver (HM); Unknown	275.00
	"C" Over Numbers			
72-81	Collars	ORs	"C" Bar "72", Small "C"; Tiptaft	18.00

Badge No.	Insignia	Rank	Description	Extremely Fine
72-91	Shoulders	ORs	Numeral: "72"; Ellis	12.00
72-93		ORs	Title: "72" over "HIGHLANDERS"	18.00
72-95		ORs	Title: "SEAFORTH HIGHLANDERS / CANADA"; Allan	25.00
72-97		ORs	Title: "SEAFORTH HIGHLANDERS / CANADA"; Tiptaft	25.00

73RD INFANTRY BATTALION

"ROYAL HIGHLANDERS OF CANADA"

The Battalion was raised in Western Quebec and Eastern Ontario with mobilization headquarters at Montreal, Quebec under the authority of G.O. 103A August 15th, 1915. The Battalion sailed March 31st, 1916, under the command of Lieutenant-Colonel P. Davidson with a strength of thirty-six officers and one thousand and thirty-three other ranks. The Battalion served in France and Belgium with the 12th Infantry Brigade, 4th Canadian Division. The Battalion was withdrawn April 14th, 1917 after suffering heavy casualties at Vimy Ridge. It was replaced by the 85th Battalion and the men of the 73rd were absorbed by the 13th, 42nd and 85th Battalions. It was disbanded September 15th, 1920.

BADGE NUMBER: 73

ROYAL HIGHLANDERS/73/C.E.F./CANADA

Makers: Hemsley, Scully, Tiptaft
Fasteners: Lugs
Composition:
Other Ranks: Pickled copper; Browning copper or brass
Officers: Gilt on Copper
Ref.: Babin, Meek, Stewart, Cox

Note: Two makers of this cap badge exist, Hemsley and Tiptaft, they are very difficult to distinguish from each other.

Badge No.	Insignia	Rank	Description	Extremely Fine
73-2	Glengarry	ORs	Pickled copper; Hemsley	235.00
73-4		ORs	Browning copper; Tiptaft	120.00
73-6		ORs	Browning brass; Tiptaft	120.00
73-21		Officers	Gilt on copper; Hemsley	200.00
Maple Leaf Design				
73-41	Collars	ORs	Pickled copper; Hemsley	25.00
73-43		ORs	Browning copper; Tiptaft	60.00
73-45		ORs	Browning brass; Tiptaft	60.00
73-61		Officers	Gilt on copper; Hemsley	100.00
Saint Andrew Design				
73-47	Collars	ORs	Unknown	--
73-63		Officers	Browning copper	50.00
73-91	Shoulders	ORs	Numeral: "73"; Unknown	14.00
73-93		ORs	Title: "73 RH" over "CANADA"; Scully	16.00
73-95		ORs	Title: "73 RH"; Unknown	16.00

74TH INFANTRY BATTALION

The Battalion was raised in the counties of Peel and York, Ontario under the authority of GO 103A August 15th, 1915. The mobilization headquarters was at Camp Niagara, Ontario. The Battalion sailed March 29th, 1916 with a strength of thirty-four officers and one thousand and forty-six other ranks under the command of Lieutenant-Colonel J. M. McCausland. In England the Battalion was absorbed into the 50th, 51st, 52nd Infantry Battalions and the 2nd Mounted Rifles Battalion. It was disbanded September 15th, 1920.

BADGE NUMBER: 74

No. - 74A   **74/OVERSEAS/CANADA**

Makers: Caron, Ellis, Tiptaft
Unknown
Fasteners: Lugs, Slide
Composition:
Other Ranks: Browning copper
Officers: As above; Superior construction
Ref.: Babin, Meek, Stewart, Cox

Note: Two makers of this cap badge exist.
1. Pointed leaf design with a large "7"; Ellis *(Illustrated)*
2. Blunt leaf design with a small "7"; Tiptaft

Badge No.	Insignia	Rank	Description	Extremely Fine
74A-2	Cap	ORs	Browning copper; Ellis	22.00
74A-4		ORs	Browning copper; Tiptaft	20.00
74A-21		Officers	Browning copper; Unknown	30.00
74A-41	Collars	ORs	Browning copper; Ellis	15.00
74A-43		ORs	Browning copper; Tiptaft	15.00
74A-61		Officers	Browning copper; Unknonw	20.00
74A-91	Shoulders	ORs	Numeral: "74"; Caron	12.00
74A-93		ORs	Numeral: "74"; Ellis	12.00

No. - 74B   **OVERSEAS BATTALION CANADA/74**

Makers: Caron for Eaton's
Fasteners: Lugs, Pin
Composition:
Other Ranks: Pickled copper with white metal overlay
Officers: As above but gilt
Ref.: Not previously listed

Note: Collars are not known.

Badge No.	Insignia	Rank	Description	Extremely Fine
74B-2	Cap	ORs	Pickled copper, Wm. overlay on centre; Caron	300.00
74B-21		Officers	Gilt, Wm. overlay on centre; Caron	395.00

75TH INFANTRY BATTALION

The Battalion was raised in Southern Ontario with mobilization headquarters at Toronto, Ontario under the authority of G.O. 103A August 15th, 1915. The Battalion sailed March 29th, 1916 under the command of Lieutenant-Colonel S. G. Beckett, with a strength of thirty-six officers and one thousand one hundred and fourteen other ranks. The Battalion served in France and Belgium with the 11th Infantry Brigade, 4th Canadian Division. It was disbanded September 15th, 1920.

BADGE NUMBER: 75

No. - 75A   **OVERSEAS BATTALION/75**

Makers: Caron, Ellis, Tiptaft
Unknown
Fasteners: Lugs
Composition:
Other Ranks: Browning copper
Officers: As above; Superior
construction
Ref.: Babin, Meek, Stewart, Cox

Note: Two makers of this cap badge exist.
1. A garter belt design with six eyelets; Ellis
2. A garter belt design with eight eyelets; Tiptaft *(Illustrated)*

Badge No.	Insignia	Rank	Description	Extremely Fine
75A-2	Cap	ORs	Browning copper; Ellis	20.00
75A-4		ORs	Browning copper; Tiptaft	20.00
75A-21		Officers	Browning copper; Unknown	30.00
75A-41	Collars	ORs	Browning copper; Ellis	50.00
75A-43		ORs	Browning copper; Tiptaft	50.00
75A-61		Officers	Browning copper; Unknown	75.00
	"C" Over Numbers			
75A-81	Collars	ORs	"C" over "75", Small "C"; Tiptaft	16.00
75A-91	Shoulders	ORs	Numeral: "75"; Caron	12.00
75A-93		ORs	Numeral: "75"; Ellis	12.00
75A-95		ORs	Title: "75" over "CANADA", Large; Ellis	20.00
75A-97		ORs	Title: "75" over "CANADA", Large; Tiptaft	20.00
75A-99		ORs	Title: "75" over "CANADA", Small; Unknown	20.00

No. - 75B   **OVERSEAS BATTALION CANADA/75**

Makers: Caron for Eaton's
Fasteners: Lugs, Pin
Composition:
Other Ranks: Pickled copper with
white metal overlay
Officers: As above but gilt
Ref.: Not previously listed

Note: Collars are not known.

Badge No.	Insignia	Rank	Description	Extremely Fine
75B-2	Cap	ORs	Pickled copper, Wm. overlay on centre; Caron	150.00
75B-21		Officers	Gilt, Wm. overlay on centre; Caron	395.00

76TH INFANTRY BATTALION

The Battalion was raised in Barrie, Ontario with mobilization headquarters at Niagara, Ontario under the authority of G.O. 103A August 15th, 1915. The Battalion sailed April 23rd, 1916 under the command of Lieutenant-Colonel J. Ballantine with a strength of thirty-six officers and one thousand and six other ranks. In England the Battalion was absorbed into the 36th Infantry Battalion (3rd Reserve Battalion). It was disbanded September 15th, 1920.

BADGE NUMBER: 76

76/OVERSEAS/CANADA
AUTHORIZED SEPTEMBER 27, 1915

Makers: Caron, Ellis, Tiptaft
Fasteners: Lugs
Composition:
Other Ranks: Browning copper
Officers: Browning copper
with silver overlay
on "76" and "Canada"
Ref.: Babin, Meek, Stewart, Cox

Note: Three makers of this cap badge exist.
1. Pointed leaf design with "Overseas" in large lettering; Small leaf 39 mm high; Ellis *(Illustrated)*
2. Blunt leaf design with "Overseas" in small lettering; Small leaf 42 mm high; Tiptaft
3. Blunt leaf design with "Overseas" in large lettering; Large leaf 49 mm high; Tiptaft

Badge No.	Insignia	Rank	Description	Extremely Fine
76-2	Cap	ORs	Browning copper, Small lettering; Ellis;	20.00
76-4		ORs	Browning copper, Small lettering; Tiptaft	25.00
76-6		ORs	Browning copper, Large lettering; Tiptaft	25.00
76-21		Officers	Browning copper, Silver overlay on "76" and "Canada"; Ellis	90.00
76-41	Collars	ORs	Browning copper, (32 mm); Ellis	18.00
76-43		ORs	Browning copper, (33 mm); Tiptaft	20.00
76-45		ORs	Browning copper, (34 mm); Tiptaft	20.00
76-61		Officers	Browning copper, Silver overlay on "76" and "Canada"; Ellis	25.00
76-91	Shoulders	ORs	Numeral: "76"; Caron	12.00

77TH INFANTRY BATTALION

"OTTAWA BATTALION"

The Battalion was raised and mobilized in Ottawa, Ontario under the authority of G.O. 103A August 15th, 1915. The Battalion left Canada June 19th, 1916 with a strength of thirty-eight officers and one thousand and seven other ranks under the command of Lieutenant-Colonel D. R. Street. In England the Battalion was broken up to provide replacements for the 46th and 73rd Infantry Battalions. It was disbanded September 15th, 1920.

BADGE NUMBER: 77

77/OTTAWA/OVERSEAS BATTALION/C.E.F.

Makers: Caron, Hemsley, Tiptaft, Unknown
Fasteners: Lugs, Pin
Composition:
Other Ranks: Pickled copper or brass; Blackened brass
Officers:
  A: Pickled copper, "Ottawa" void
  B: Gilt on copper
Ref.: Babin, Meek, Stewart, Cox

Note: The Hemsley cap badge was issued with both a void and a solid "Ottawa".

Note: Two makers of this cap badge exist.
  1. Fine leaf design; Pointed "7's"; Hemsley *(Illustrated)*
  2. Course leaf design; Blunt "7's"; Tiptaft

Badge No.	Insignia	Rank	Description	Extremely Fine
77-2	Cap	ORs	Pickled copper, Solid; Hemsley	20.00
77-4		ORs	Pickled copper, Void; Hemsley	50.00
77-6		ORs	Pickled brass; Tiptaft	20.00
77-8		ORs	Blackened brass; Tiptaft	20.00
77-21		Officers	Pickled copper, Void; Hemsley	55.00
77-23		Officers	Gilt on copper; Unknown	50.00
77-41	Collars	ORs	Pickled copper; Hemsley	20.00
77-43		ORs	Pickled brass; Tiptaft	20.00
77-45		ORs	Blackened brass; Tiptaft	20.00
77-61		Officers	Pickled copper; Hemsley	30.00
77-91	Shoulders	ORs	Numeral: "77"; Caron	12.00

78TH INFANTRY BATTALION

"WINNIPEG GRENADIERS"

The Battalion was raised and mobilized in Winnipeg, Manitoba under the authority of G.O. 103A August 15th, 1915. The Battalion sailed May 20th, 1916 under the command of Lieutenant-Colonel J. Kirkcaldy with a strength of thirty-seven officers and one thousand and ninety-seven other ranks. The Battalion served in France and Belgium with the 12th Infantry Brigade, 4th Canadian Division. The Battalion was disbanded September 15th, 1920.

BADGE NUMBER: 78

78/WINNIPEG GRENADIERS

Makers: Caron, Dingwall, Tiptaft
Fasteners: Lugs, Tangs
Composition:
Other Ranks: Blackened copper
or brass
Officers: Pickled copper
Ref.: Babin, Meek, Stewart, Cox

Note: Two makers of this cap badge exist.
1. Wide "8"; Dingwall *(Illustrated)*
2. Narrow "8"; Tiptaft

Badge No.	Insignia	Rank	Description	Extremely Fine
78-2	Cap	ORs	Blackened copper; Dingwall	20.00
78-4		ORs	Blackened copper, Tiptaft	20.00
78-6		ORs	Blackened brass, Dingwall	25.00
78-8		ORs	Blackened brass; Tiptaft	25.00
78-21		Officers	Pickled copper; Unknown	30.00
78-41	Collars	ORs	Blackened copper; Dingwall	10.00
78-43		ORs	Blackened brass; Tiptaft	10.00
78-61		Officers	Pickled copper; Unknown	20.00
			"C" Over Numbers	
78-81	Collars	ORs	"C" over "78", Small C; Tiptaft	16.00
78-91	Shoulders	ORs	Numeral: "78"; Caron	12.00

79TH INFANTRY BATTALION

"MANITOBA BATTALION"

The Battalion was raised in Manitoba and mobilized at Brandon Manitoba under the authority of G.O. 103A August 15th, 1915. The Battalion sailed April 24th, 1916 with a strength of thirty-seven officers and one thousand and ninety-five other ranks under the command of Lieutenant-Colonel G. Clinglan. The Battalion was absorbed into the 17th Reserve Battalion. It was disbanded September 15th, 1920.

BADGE NUMBER: 79

79/OVERSEAS BATTALION/MANITOBA/CANADA

Makers: Caron, Hemsley, Inglis, Tiptaft
Fasteners: Lugs, Pins
Composition:
Other Ranks: Pickled copper or brass
Officers: Unknown
Ref.: Babin, Meek, Stewart, Cox

Note: Two makers of this cap badge exist.
1. Small wide "79"; Plain ribbons; Hemsley, Inglis *(Illustrated)*
2. Tall narrow "79"; Framed ribbons; Tiptaft

Badge No.	Insignia	Rank	Description	Extremely Fine
79-2	Cap	ORs	Pickled copper; Hemsley, Inglis	85.00
79-4		ORs	Pickled brass; Tiptaft	20.00
79-21		Officers	Unknown	- -
79-41	Collars	ORs	Pickled copper; Hemsley, Inglis	20.00
79-43		ORs	Pickled brass; Tiptaft	15.00
79-61		Officers	Unknown	- -
79-91	Shoulders	ORs	Numeral: "79"; Caron	12.00

80TH INFANTRY BATTALION

The Battalion was raised in Eastern Ontario under the authority of G.O. 103A, August 15th, 1915. The mobilization headquarters was at Barriefield, Ontario. The Battalion left Canada on May 16th, 1916 under the command of Lieutenant-Colonel W. G. Ketcheson with a strength of thirty-five officers and one thousand and forty-one other ranks. The Battalion was absorbed into the 51st Infantry Battalion in England. It was disbanded September 15th, 1920.

BADGE NUMBER: 80

OVERSEAS BATTALION PARATUS/80/CANADA

Makers: Caron, Hemsley, Inglis
Fasteners: Lugs
Composition:
Other Ranks: Pickled copper
Officers: Silver overlay on design
Ref.: Babin, Meek, Stewart, Cox

Note: Both the badge and collars were issued with either a void or solid field.

Badge No.	Insignia	Rank	Description	Extremely Fine
80-2	Cap	ORs	Pickled copper, Solid; Hemsley, Inglis	50.00
80-4		ORs	Pickled copper, Void; Hemsley, Inglis	20.00
80-21		Officers	Pickled copper, Silver overlay on design, Void; Hemsley, Inglis	175.00
80-41	Collars	ORs	Pickled copper, Solid; Hemsley, Inglis	20.00
80-43		ORs	Pickled copper, Void; Hemsley, Inglis	10.00
80-61		Officers	Pickled copper, Silver overlay on design, Void; Hemsley, Inglis	50.00
80-91	Shoulders	ORs	Numeral: "8"; Caron	14.00

81ST INFANTRY BATTALION

The Battalion was raised and mobilized in Toronto, Ontario under the authority of G.O. 103A August 15th, 1915. The Battalion sailed April 28th, 1916 with a strength of thirty-six officers and one thousand and sixty-seven other ranks, under the command of Lieutenant-Colonel B. H. Belson. In England the Battalion was absorbed into the 35th Reserve Battalion. It was disbanded September 15th, 1920.

BADGE NUMBER: 81

No. - 81A　　　　　　　**81/OVERSEAS/CANADA**

Makers: Caron, Hemsley, Inglis, Ryrie Bros., Tiptaft, Unknown
Fasteners: Lugs
Composition:
Other Ranks: Pickled copper; Browning copper
Officers: Pickled copper with silver overlay on "81"
Ref.: Babin, Meek, Stewart, Cox

Note: Three makers of this cap badge exist.
　　1. Wide lettering of "Canada"; Plain ribbons; Hemsley, Inglis *(Illustrated)*
　　2. Narrow lettering of "Canada"; Plain ribbons; Tiptaft
　　3. Wide lettering of "Canada"; Framed numbers and ribbons; Ryrie

Badge No.	Insignia	Rank	Description	Extremely Fine
81A-2	Cap	ORs	Pickled copper; Hemsley, Inglis	22.00
81A-4		ORs	Browning copper; Tiptaft	25.00
81A-6		ORs	Browning copper; Ryrie Bros.	25.00
81A-21		Officers	Pickled copper/Silver overlay on "81"; Unknown	65.00
81A-41	Collars	ORs	Pickled copper; Hemsley, Inglis	15.00
81A-43		ORs	Browning copper; Tiptaft	15.00
81A-45		ORs	Browning copper; Ryrie Bros.	30.00
81A-61		Officers	Pickled copper/Silver overlay on "81"; Unknown	35.00
81A-91	Shoulders	ORs	Numeral: "81"; Caron	12.00

No. - 81B   **OVERSEAS BATTALION CANADA/81**

Makers: Caron for Eaton's
Fasteners: Lugs, Pin
Composition:
Other Ranks: Pickled copper with white metal overlay centre
Officers: Gilt on copper with silver overlay on centre
Ref.: Babin, Cox

Note: No collars issued.

Badge No.	Insignia	Rank	Description	Extremely Fine
81B-2	Cap	ORs	Pickled copper, Wm. overlay on centre	225.00
81B-21		Officers	Gilt on copper, Silver overlay on centre	300.00

82ND INFANTRY BATTALION

"CALGARY BATTALION"

The Battalion was raised and mobilized in Calgary, Alberta under the authority of G.O. 103A August 15th, 1915. The Battalion left Canada on May 20th, 1916 under the command of Lieutenant-Colonel W. A. Lowry with a strength of thirty-four officers and one thousand and six other ranks. The Battalion was absorbed into the 9th Reserve Battalion in England. It was disbanded September 15th, 1920.

BADGE NUMBER: 82

OVERSEAS BATTALION/82/CALGARY/CANADA

Makers: Black, Caron, Chauncey, Hemsley, Inglis
Fasteners: Lugs
Composition:
Other Ranks: Pickled copper; Browning copper
Officers: Unknown
Ref.: Babin, Meek, Stewart, Cox

Note: Two makers of this cap badge exist.
    1. Three jewels in the arch of the crown with a plain crest; Hemsley, Inglis, Black. *(Illustrated)*
    This is one of those badges where the dies must have been shared between manufacturers or one manufacturer produced to order with different maker's marks.
    2. Four jewels in the arch of the crown with a framed crest; Chauncey

Badge No.	Insignia	Rank	Description	Extremely Fine
82-2	Cap	ORs	Pickled copper; Hemsley, Inglis, Black	20.00
82-4		ORs	Browning copper; Hemsley, Inglis, Black	20.00
82-6		ORs	Browning copper; Chauncey	20.00
82-21		Officers	Unknown	- -
82-41	Collars	ORs	Pickled copper; Hemsley, Inglis, Black	15.00
82-43		ORs	Browning copper; Hemsley, Inglis, Black	15.00
82-45		ORs	Browning copper; Chauncey	15.00
82-61		Officers	Unknown	- -
82-91	Shoulders	ORs	Numeral: "82"; Caron	14.00

83RD INFANTRY BATTALION

"QUEEN'S OWN RIFLES"

The Battalion was raised and mobilized in Toronto, Ontario under the authority of G.O. 103A August 15th, 1915. The Battalion sailed April 28th, 1916 with a strength of thirty-five officers and one thousand and eighty-one other ranks under the command of Lieutenant-Colonel R. Pellatt. In England the Battalion was absorbed into the 12th Reserve Battalion. It was disbanded September 15th, 1920.

BADGE NUMBER: 83

No. - 83A   **QUEEN'S OWN RIFLES OF CANADA
/83/OVERSEAS BATTALION**

AUTHORIZED FEBRUARY 16, 1916

Makers: Caron, Ellis, Reich
Fasteners: Lugs
Composition:
Other Ranks: Browning copper
or brass
Officers: Pickled brass
Ref.: Babin, Stewart, Cox

Note: Three different makers of this cap badge exist. However the differences are slight and the badge variations are difficult to distinguish. Little is known about the Folkstone badge.
  1. The Ellis badge has a blunt top "3" *(Illustrated)*
  2. The Reich badge has a pointed top "3"
  3. Only a collar of the Folkstone badge is known at this time. The collar carries the
     maker's mark: F. J. _____ Son
                          74 Tontine St.,
                          Folkstone, England.

Badge No.	Insignia	Rank	Description	Extremely Fine
83A-2	Cap	ORs	Browning copper; Ellis	45.00
83A-4		ORs	Browning brass; Reich	45.00
83A-21		Officers	Pickled brass; Ellis	50.00
83A-41	Collars	ORs	Browning copper; Ellis	20.00
83A-43		ORs	Browning brass; Reich	20.00
83A-45		ORs	Browning copper; F.J. _____ Son	30.00
83A-61		Officers	Pickled brass; Ellis	40.00
83A-91	Shoulders	ORs	Numeral: "83"; Caron	14.00

No. - 83B   **CANADIAN EXPEDITIONARY FORCE/83**

Makers: Ellis
Fasteners: Lugs
Composition:
  Other Ranks: Pickled brass
    Officers: Unknown
Ref.: Babin, Meek, Cox

Badge No.	Insignia	Rank	Description	Extremely Fine
83B-2	Cap	ORs	Pickled brass; Ellis	45.00
83B-21		Officers	Unknown	- -
83B-41	Collars	ORs	Pickled brass; Ellis	50.00
83B-61		Officers	Unknown	- -

No. - 83C   **OVERSEAS BATTALION CANADA/83**

Makers: Caron for Eaton's
Fasteners: Lugs, Pin
Composition:
  Other Ranks: Pickled copper with white metal overlay
    Officers: Gilt on copper with silver overlay
Ref.: Not previously listed

Note: Collars not issued

Badge No.	Insignia	Rank	Description	Extremely Fine
83C-2	Cap	ORs	Pickled copper, Wm. overlay on centre	225.00
83C-21		Officers	Gilt on copper, Silver overlay on centre	250.00

84TH INFANTRY BATTALION

The Battalion was raised and mobilized in Toronto, Ontario under the authority of G.O. 103A August 15th, 1915. The Battalion left Canada June 18th, 1916 with a strength of thirty-six officers and nine hundred and thirteen other ranks under the command of Lieutenant-Colonel W. D. Stewart. The Battalion was broken up and absorbed into the 73rd and 75th Infantry Battalions in England. It was disbanded September 15th, 1920.

BADGE NUMBER: 84

No. - 84A   **OVERSEAS BATTALION**
                          /84/CANADA/REX VOCAT

Makers: Caron, Unknown
Fasteners: Lugs, Pin
Composition:
  Other Ranks: Browning copper
      Officers: Browning copper
Ref.: Babin, Meek, Stewart, Cox

Badge No.	Insignia	Rank	Description	Extremely Fine
84A-2	Cap	ORs	Pickled copper, Solid; Unknown	75.00
84A-4		ORs	Browning copper, Solid; Unknown	60.00
84A-6		ORs	Browning copper, Void; Unknown	75.00
84A-21		Officers	Browning copper; Unknown	65.00
84A-41	Collars	ORs	PIckled copper, Solid; Unknown	60.00
84A-43		ORs	Browning copper, Void; Unknown	60.00
84A-61		Officers	Browning copper; Unknown	60.00
84A-91	Shoulders	ORs	Numeral: "84"; Caron	14.00

No. - 84B   OVERSEAS BATTALION CANADA/84

Makers: Caron for Eaton's
Fasteners: Lugs, Pin
Composition:
Other Ranks: Pickled copper with white metal overlay
Officers: Gilt on copper with silver overlay
Ref.: Not previously listed

Note: No collars issued

Badge No.	Insignia	Rank	Description	Extremely Fine
84B-2	Cap	ORs	Pickled copper, Wm. overlay on centre	200.00
84B-21		Officers	Gilt on copper, Silver overlay on centre	300.00

85TH INFANTRY BATTALION

"NOVA SCOTIA HIGHLANDERS"

The Battalion was raised in Nova Scotia with mobilization headquarters at Halifax under the authority of G.O. 103A August 15th, 1915. The Battalion sailed October 12th, 1916 with a strength of thirty-four officers and one thousand and one other ranks under the command of Lieutenant-Colonel E. C. Phinney. The Battalion served in France and Belgium when it replaced the 73rd in the 12th Infantry Brigade, 4th Canadian Division. It was disbanded September 15th, 1920.

BADGE NUMBER: 85

No. - 85A **CANADA/NOVA SCOTIA HIGHLANDERS OVERSEAS/85/SOIL NA FEAR FEARAIL**

Makers: Caron, Hemsley, Inglis, Tiptaft
Fasteners: Lugs
Composition:
Other Ranks: Pickled copper or brass; Browning brass
Officers:
  A: Pickled brass with white metal overlay on design
  B: Gilt on copper with silver overlay on design
Ref.: Babin, Meek, Stewart, Cox

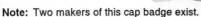

Note: Two makers of this cap badge exist.
1. The maple leaf design is void on either side of the tongue, above the final scroll and all ribbons are plain; Hemsley, Inglis *(Illustrated)*
2. The maple leaf design is solid with all ribbons framed; Tiptaft

Badge No.	Insignia	Rank	Description	Extremely Fine
85A-2	Cap	ORs	Pickled copper; Hemsley, Inglis	50.00
85A-4		ORs	Pickled brass; Hemsley, Inglis	55.00
85A-6		ORs	Browning brass; Tiptaft	50.00
85A-21		Officers	Pickled brass, Wm. overlay on design; Hemsley, Inglis	250.00
85A-23		Officers	Gilt on copper, Silver overlay on design; Tiptaft	400.00

Badge No.	Insignia	Rank	Description	Extremely Fine
		Maple Leaf Design		
85A-41	Collars	ORs	Pickled copper; Hemsley, Inglis	100.00
85A-43		ORs	Pickled brass. Hemsley, Inglis	100.00
85A-45		ORs	Browning brass; Tiptaft	100.00
85A-61		Officers	Pickled copper, Silver overlay on design; Hemsley, Inglis	150.00
		Scroll Design		
85A-47	Collars	ORs	Pickled brass; Hemsley, Inglis	25.00
85A-49		ORs	Browning brass; Tiptaft	25.00
85A-63		Officers	Pickled brass, Silver overlay on circle; Hemsley, Inglis	75.00
85A-91	Shoulders	ORs	Numeral: "85"; Caron	14.00

No. - 85B   OVERSEAS BATTALIONS CANADA/85

Makers: Caron for Eaton's
Fasteners: Lugs, Pin
Composition:
Other Ranks: Pickled copper with white metal overlay on centre
Officers: Gilt with silver overlay on centre
Ref.: Not previously listed

Note: No collars issued

Badge No.	Insignia	Rank	Description	Extremely Fine
85B-2	Cap	ORs	Pickled copper, Wm. overlay on centre	225.00
85B-21		Officers	Gilt on copper, Silver overlay on centre	225.00

No. - 85C   **85/CANADA**

INTERIM BADGE

Makers: As General List
Fasteners: Lugs
Composition:
Other Ranks: "85" overlay on
General List
Officers: Unknown
Ref.: Not previously listed

Note: The ease of manufacturing has lead to many counterfeits.

Badge No.	Insignia	Rank	Description	Extremely Fine
85C-2	Cap	ORs	General List, "85" overlay	50.00
85C-21		Officers	Unknown	- -
85C-41	Collars	ORs	Unknown	- -
85C-61		Officers	Unknown	- -

86TH INFANTRY BATTALION

"86TH MACHINE GUN BATTALION"

The Battalion was raised in Southern Ontario with mobilization headquarters at Hamilton under the authority of G.O. 151 December 22nd, 1915. The battalion sailed May 22nd, 1916 under the command of Lieutenant-Colonel W. W. Stewart with a strength of thirty-six officers and one thousand and seventy-two other ranks. In England the Battalion was reorganized as the Canadian Machine Gun Depot. It was disbanded September 15th, 1920.

BADGE NUMBER: 86

86/CANADA/OVERSEAS/MACHINE GUN BATTALION

Makers: Caron, Lees
Fasteners: Lugs
Composition:
Other Ranks: Browning copper or brass
Officers: Browning copper
Ref.: Babin, Meek, Stewart, Cox

Badge No.	Insignia	Rank	Description	Extremely Fine
86-2	Cap	ORs	Browning copper; Lees	45.00
86-21		Officers	Browning copper; Lees	45.00
86-41	Collars	ORs	Browning copper; Lees	20.00
86-43		ORs	Browning brass; Lees	50.00
86-61		Officers	Browning copper; Lees	25.00
86-91	Shoulders	ORs	Numeral: "86"; Caron	14.00
86-93		ORs	Title: "86 MG"; Lees	20.00

87TH INFANTRY BATTALION

"CANADIAN GRENADIER GUARDS"

The Battalion was raised in Quebec with mobilization headquarters at Montreal under the authority of G.O. 151 December 22nd, 1915. The Battalion sailed April 26th, 1916 under the command of Lieutenant-Colonel J. P. Rexford with a strength of thirty-six officers and one thousand and twenty-six other ranks. The Battalion served in France and Belgium with the 11th Infantry Brigade, 4th Canadian Division. It was disbanded September 15th, 1920.

BADGE NUMBER: 87

G R R G/CANADA

Makers: Caron, Gaunt, Hemsley, Tiptaft
Fasteners: Lugs
Composition:
Other Ranks: Pickled copper or brass
Officers:
    A. Pickled copper with silver overlay on cypher;
    B. Pickled brass with brass overlay on cypher
Ref.: Babin, Meek, Stewart, Cox

Note: Two makers of this cap badge exist.
1. The flame has fourteen points with a narrow ring joining the flame to the grenade; Hemsley *(Illustrated)*
2. The flame has seventeen points with a wide ring joining the flame to the grenade; Tiptaft

Gaunt and Goldsmiths & Silversmith & Co. in England possibly made badges for this battalion. If they did, naturally the number of makers will increase.

Badge No.	Insignia	Rank	Description	Extremely Fine
87-2	Cap	ORs	Pickled copper; Hemsley	150.00
87-4		ORs	Pickled brass; Hemsley	25.00
87-6		ORs	Pickled brass; Tiptaft	25.00
87-21		Officers	Pickled copper, Silver overlay on Cypher; Hemsley	200.00
87-23		Officers	Pickled brass, Brass overlay on Cypher; Tiptaft	40.00

Badge No.	Insignia	Rank	Description	Extremely Fine
			Maple Leaf and Cypher Design	
87-41	Collars	ORs	Pickled copper; Hemsley	50.00
87-43		ORs	Pickled brass; Tiptaft	50.00
87-61		Officers	Silverplate; Unknown	30.00
			"87/CGG" Design	
87-45	Collars	ORs	Browning copper; Unknown	75.00
87-63		Officers	Unknown	- -
			"C" Over Numbers	
87-81	Collars		"C" over "87"; Unknown	25.00
87-91	Shoulders	ORs	Numeral: "87"; Caron	14.00
87-93		ORs	Numeral: "87"; Gaunt	14.00

88TH INFANTRY BATTALION

"VICTORIA FUSILIERS"

The Battalion was raised and mobilized in Victoria, British Columbia under the authority of G.O. 151 December 22nd, 1915. The Battalion sailed June 2nd, 1916 under the command of Lieutenant-Colonel H. J. R. Cullin with a strength of thirty-four officers and one thousand and twenty-nine other ranks. In England the Battalion was absorbed into the 30th Reserve Battalion. It was disbanded September 15th, 1920.

BADGE NUMBER 88

No. - 88A   **B.C./BATT 88 C.E.F./VICTORIA FUSILIERS**

Makers: Caron, Ellis, Tiptaft
Unknown
Fasteners: Lugs
Composition:
Other Ranks: Browning brass
Officers: Gilt on brass;
Superior
construction
Ref.: Babin, Meek, Cox

Note: Two makers of this cap badge exist.
1. The central "8's" are flat and small with no period after "Batt"; Ellis *(Illustrated)*
2. The central "8's" are raised and large with a period after "Batt"; Tiptaft

Badge No.	Insignia	Rank	Description	Extremely Fine
88A-2	Cap	ORs	Browning brass; Ellis	45.00
88A-4		ORs	Browning brass; Tiptaft	45.00
88A-21		NCO	Gilt on brass; Ellis	60.00
Maple Leaf Design:				
88A-41	Collars	ORs	Browning brass; Unknown	30.00
88A-61		NCO	Unknown	- -
Grenade Design:				
88A-43	Collars	ORs	Browning brass; Ellis	18.00
88A-45		ORs	Browning brass; Tiptaft	18.00
88A-63		NCO	Gilt on brass; Ellis	25.00
88A-91	Shoulders	ORs	Numeral: "88"; Caron	14.00

No. - 88B   88/IN VIRTUTE VICTORIA/VICTORIA FUSILIERS

Makers: Gaunt
Fasteners: Tangs
Composition:
Other Ranks: Unknown
Officers:
  A: Browning copper
  B: Silver gilt
Ref.: Babin, Stewart

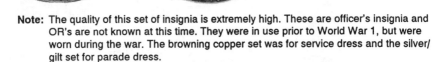

Note: The quality of this set of insignia is extremely high. These are officer's insignia and OR's are not known at this time. They were in use prior to World War 1, but were worn during the war. The browning copper set was for service dress and the silver/ gilt set for parade dress.

Badge No.	Insignia	Rank	Description	Extremely Fine
88B-2	Cap	ORs	Unknown	- -
88B-21		Officers	Browning copper; Gaunt	220.00
88B-23		Officers	Silver gilt; Gaunt	250.00
88B-41	Collars	ORs	Unknown	- -
88B-61		Officers	Browning copper; Gaunt	40.00
88B-63		Officers	Silver gilt; Gaunt	50.00

89TH INFANTRY BATTALION

"ALBERTA BATTALION"

The Battalion was raised in Alberta with mobilization headquarters at Calgary under the authority of G.O. 151 December 15th, 1915. The Battalion sailed June 2nd, 1916 under the command of Lieutenant-Colonel W. W. Nasmyth with a strength of thirty-three officers and nine hundred and sixty-nine other ranks. In England the Battalion was absorbed into the 9th Reserve Battalion. It was disbanded September 15th, 1920.

BADGE NUMBER: 89

ALBERTA/89/OVERSEAS BATTALION/CANADA

Makers: Black, Caron, Hemsley, Inglis, Tiptaft, Unknown
Fasteners: Lugs
Composition:
Other Ranks: Pickled copper or brass; Browning copper
Officers: Pickled copper
Ref.: Babin, Meek, Stewart, Cox

Note: Three makers of this cap badge exist.
1. The "8" design is broken with a closed "S" configuration; Wide "89"; Small crown; Hemsley, Inglis, Black. *(Illustrated)*
2. The "8" design is broken with a closed "S" configuration; Wide "89"; Large crown; Unknown
3. The "8's" are solid and all the ribbons are framed; Tiptaft

Badge No.	Insignia	Rank	Description	Extremely Fine
89-2	Cap	ORs	Pickled copper; Hemsley, Inglis, Black	50.00
89-4		ORs	Pickled brass, Hemsley, Inglis, Black	50.00
89-6		ORs	Pickled brass, Unknown	50.00
89-8		ORs	Browning copper; Tiptaft	55.00
89-21		Officers	Pickled copper; Hemsley, Inglis, Black	65.00
89-41	Collars	ORs	Pickled copper; Hemsley, Inglis, Black	18.00
89-43		ORs	Pickled brass; Unknown	18.00
89-45		ORs	Browning copper; Tiptaft	15.00
89-61		Officers	Pickled copper; Hemsley, Inglis, Black	20.00
89-91	Shoulders	ORs	Numeral: "89"; Caron	14.00
89-93		ORs	Title: "89 CANADA" Ribbon; Black	22.00

90TH INFANTRY BATTALION

"WINNIPEG RIFLES"

The Battalion was raised and mobilized in Winnipeg, Manitoba under the authority of G.O. 151 December 22nd, 1915. The Battalion sailed June 2nd, 1916 under the command of Lieutenant-Colonel W. A. Monroe, with a strength of thirty-six officers and one thousand and eighty-seven other ranks. In England the Battallion was absorbed into the 11th Infantry Battalion. It was disbanded September 15th, 1920.

BADGE NUMBER 90:

No. - 90A   **2/HOSTI ACIE NOMINATI**

Makers: Dingwall, Hicks, Unknown
Fasteners: Lugs
Composition:
Other Ranks: Pickled copper;
Browning copper
Officers: Pickled copper
Ref.: Babin, Meek, Stewart, Cox

Note: Three makers of this cap badge exist.
1. Plain centre tine on trident; Five folds on the ribbon ends; Dingwall
2. Barbed centre tine on trident; Four folds on the ribbon ends; Hicks *(Illustrated)*
3. The third cap variety is not recorded only the collars, which have a wide "0" in "90" while the other two have narrow or oval "0's"

Badge No.	Insignia	Rank	Description	Extremely Fine
90A-2	Cap	ORs	Pickled copper; Dingwall	28.00
90A-4		ORs	Browning copper; Hicks	28.00
90A-21		Officers	Pickled copper; Unknown	40.00
90A-23		Officers	Silver plate; Hicks	50.00
90A-41	Collars	ORs	Pickled copper; Dingwall	18.00
90A-43		ORs	Browning copper; Hicks	18.00
90A-45		ORs	Browning copper; Unknown	20.00
90A-61		Officers	Pickled copper; Unknown	22.00
90A-91	Shoulders	ORs	Numeral: "90"; Caron	14.00

No. - 90B   **90/CANADA**

Makers: As General List
Fasteners: Lugs
Composition:
Other Ranks: General List
                      With "90" overlay
Ref.: Not previously listed

Badge No.	Insignia	Rank	Description	Extremely Fine
90B-2	Cap	ORs	General List, "90" overlay	200.00
90B-21		Officers	Unknown	- -
90B-41	Collars	ORs	Unknown	- -
90B-61		Officers	Unknown	- -

91ST INFANTRY BATTALION

"ELGIN BATTALION"

The Battalion was raised in Elgin County, Ontario with mobilization headquarters at St. Thomas under the authority of G.O. 151 December 22nd, 1915. The Battalion sailed June 29th, 1916 under the command of Lieutenant-Colonel W. J Green with a strength of thirty-two officers and nine hundred and five other ranks. In England the Battalion was absorbed into the 12th Reserve Battalion. It was disbanded September 15th, 1920.

BADGE NUMBER: 91

OVERSEAS ELGIN CANADA/91/DUTY FIRST

Makers: Caron, Unknown
Fasteners: Lugs
Composition:
Other Ranks: Pickled copper or brass;
Browning copper
Officers: Pickled copper with silver overlay on "91"
Ref.: Babin, Meek, Stewart, Cox

Badge No.	Insignia	Rank	Description	Extremely Fine
91-2	Cap	ORs	Pickled copper; Unknown	35.00
91-4		ORs	Pickled brass; Unknown	35.00
91-6		ORs	Browning copper; Unknown	40.00
91-21		Officers	Pickled copper, Silver overlay on "91" Unknown	75.00
91-41	Collars	ORs	Pickled copper; Unknown	18.00
91-43		ORs	Browning copper; Unknown	18.00
91-61		Officers	Pickled copper, Silver overlay on "91" Unknown	30.00
91-91	Shoulders	ORs	Numeral: "91"; Caron	12.00

92ND INFANTRY BATTALION

"48TH HIGHLANDERS"

The Battalion was raised and mobilized in Toronto, Ontario under the authority of G.O. 103A August 15th, 1915. The Battalion sailed May 22nd, 1916 under the command of Lieutenant-Colonel G. G. Chisholm with a strength of thirty-six officers and one thousand and ninety-six other ranks. In England the Battalion was absorbed into the 5th Reserve Battalion. It was disbanded September 15th, 1920.

BADGE NUMBER: 92

No. - 92A   DILEAS CU BRATH/92/CANADA OVERSEAS

FULL BUCKLE VARIETY

NOT AUTHORIZED

Makers: Caron, Ellis
Fasteners: Lugs
Composition:
Other Ranks: Browning copper;
                Blackened copper;
                White metal
Officers: Sterling silver
Ref.: Babin, Meek, Stewart

Note: It is interesting to note that the Canadian made full buckle variety was not the authorized design. Prints made December 23rd, 1915 show the half buckle variety as the badge authorized.

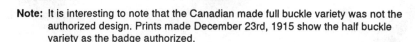

Badge No.	Insignia	Rank	Description	Extremely Fine
92A-2	Glengarry	ORs	White metal; Ellis	85.00
92A-21		Officers	Sterling silver; Ellis	125.00
92A-41	Collars	ORs	Browning copper; Ellis	30.00
92A-43		ORs	Blackened copper; Ellis	30.00
92A-61		Officers	Sterling silver; Ellis	40.00
92A-91	Shoulders	ORs	Numeral: "92"; Caron	14.00

No. - 92B　　　　**DILEAS GU BRATH/92/OVERSEAS**

HALF BUCKLE VARIETY

AUTHORIZED DECEMBER 21, 1915

Makers: Tiptaft
Fasteners: Lugs
Composition:
Other Ranks: Browning copper;
Glengarry: White metal
Officers: Sterling silver
Ref.: Cox

Badge No.	Insignia	Rank	Description	Extremely Fine
92B-2	Glengarry	ORs	Browning copper; Tiptaft	60.00
92B-21		Officers	Sterling silver; Tiptaft	125.00
92B-23		ORs	White metal; Tiptaft	35.00
92B-41	Collars	ORs	Browning copper; Tiptaft	30.00
92B-61		Officers	Sterling silver; Tiptaft	40.00

No. - 92C　　　　**OVERSEAS BATTALION CANADA/ 92**

Makers: Caron for Eaton's
Fasteners: Lugs, Pin
Composition:
Other Ranks: Pickled copper with white metal overlay
Officers: Gilt on copper with silver overlay
Ref.: Not previously listed

Note: No collars issued.

Badge No.	Insignia	Rank	Description	Extremely Fine
92C-2	Cap	ORs	Pickled copper, Wm. overlay on centre	300.00
92C-21		Officers	Gilt on copper, Silver overlay on centre	300.00

No. - 92D   **1ST 92ND DRAFT**

Makers: Unknown
Fasteners: Pin
Compositon:
 Other Ranks: White metal;
                            Browning copper
               Officers: Unknown
Ref.: Babin, Cox

Note: Collars are not known. The original issue of this badge carried a pin (brooch) back. Lugs were not original issue and therefore were added at a later date.

Badge No.	Insignia	Rank	Description	Extremely Fine
92D-2	Glengarry	ORs	White metal; Unknown	2,400.00
92D-4		ORs	Browning copper; Unknown	Extremely Rare
92D-21		Officers	Unknown	- -

93RD INFANTRY BATTALION

"PETERBOROUGH BATTALION"

The Battalion was raised in Peterborough County, Ontario with mobilization headquarters at Peterborough under the authority of G.O. 151 December 22nd, 1915. The Battalion sailed July 15th, 1916 under the command of Lieutenant-Colonel T. J. Johnston with a strength of thirty-six officers and eight hundred and sixty-eight other ranks. In England the Battalion was absorbed into the 39th Infantry Battalion. It was disbanded September 15th, 1920.

BADGE NUMBER: 93

PETERBORO/93/OVERSEAS BATTALION/CANADA

Makers: Caron, Hemsley,
    Inglis, Tiptaft
Fasteners: Lugs
Composition:
Other Ranks: Pickled copper or
    brass;
    Browning copper
Officers: Browning copper
Ref.: Babin, Meek, Stewart, Cox

Note: Two makers of this cap badge exist.
1. The Ontario crest is narrow with all ribbons being plain; Hemsley, Inglis *(Illustrated)*
2. The Ontario crest is wide and all ribbons have framed edges; Tiptaft

Badge No.	Insignia	Rank	Description	Extremely Fine
93-2	Cap	ORs	PIckled copper; Hemsley, Inglis	22.00
93-4		ORs	Pickled brass; Hemsley, Inglis	22.00
93-6		ORs	Browning copper; Tiptaft	25.00
93-21		Officers	Browning copper; Hemsley, Inglis	30.00
93-41	Collars	ORs	PIckled copper; Hemsley, Inglis	12.00
93-43		ORs	Browning copper; Tiptaft	7.50
93-61		Officers	Browning copper; Hemsley, Inglis	15.00
93-91	Shoulders	ORs	Numeral: "93"; Caron	12.00

94TH INFANTRY BATTALION

"NEW ONTARIO BATTALION"

The Battalion was raised in Northern Ontario with mobilization headquarters at Port Arthur under the authority of G.O. 151 December 22nd, 1915. The Battalion sailed June 29th, 1916 under the command of Lieutenant-Colonel H. A. C. Machin with a strength of thirty-six officers and one thousand and nine other ranks. In England the Battalion was broken up and absorbed by the 17th and 32nd Reserve Battalions. It was disbanded September 15th, 1920.

BADGE NUMBER: 94

NEW ONTARIO/94/OVERSEAS BATTALION/CANADA

Makers: Caron, Maybee's
Fasteners: Lugs
Composition:
Other Ranks: Browning copper
Officers: Browning copper
Ref.: Babin, Meek, Stewart, Cox

Badge No.	Insignia	Rank	Description	Extremely Fine
94-2	Cap	ORs	Browning copper; Maybee's	34.00
94-21		Officers	Browning copper; Maybee's	36.00
94-41	Collars	ORs	Browning copper; Maybee's	25.00
94-61		Officers	Browning copper; Maybee's	25.00
94-91	Shoulders	ORs	Numeral: "94"; Caron	12.00
94-93		ORs	Title: "BEAVER OVER CAN 93 ADA"; Maybee's	25.00

95TH INFANTRY BATTALION

The Battalion was raised and mobilized in Toronto, Ontario under the authority of G.O. 151 December 22nd, 1915. The Battalion sailed June 2nd, 1916 under the command of Lieutenant-Colonel R. K. Barker with a strength of thirty-six officers and one thousand and sixty-one other ranks. In England the Battalion was absorbed into the 5th Reserve Battalion. It was disbanded September 15th, 1920.

BADGE NUMBER: 95

No. - 95A   NUMQUAM DORMIMUS/95/CANADA OVERSEAS

Makers: Caron, Ellis, Tiptaft
Fasteners: Lugs
Composition:
Other Ranks: Pickled brass;
Browning copper;
Antiqued copper
Officers: Pickled copper
Ref.: Babin, Meek, Stewart, Cox

Note: Two makers of this cap badge exist
1. Pointed leaf design with a broken "9" in "95", Plain ribbon; Ellis *(Illustrated)*
2. Blunt leaf design with a solid "9" in "95", Framed ribbon; Tiptaft.

Badge No.	Insignia	Rank	Description	Extremely Fine
95A-2	Cap	ORs	Pickled brass; Ellis	25.00
95A-4		ORs	Antiqued copper; Ellis	25.00
95A-6		ORs	Browning copper; Tiptaft	25.00
95A-21		Officers	Pickled copper; Ellis	25.00
95A-41	Collars	ORs	Pickled brass; Ellis	12.00
95A-43		ORs	Antiqued copper; Ellis	12.00
95A-45		ORs	Browning copper; Tiptaft	12.00
95A-61		Officers	Pickled copper; Ellis	14.00
95A-91	Shoulders	ORs	Numeral: "95"; Caron	12.00

No. - 95B   **OVERSEAS BATTALION CANADA/95**

Makers: Caron for Eaton's
Fasteners: Lugs, Pin
Composition:
Other Ranks: White metal overlay
on pickled copper
Officers: Gilt on copper with
silver overlay
Ref.: Not previously listed

Note: No collars were issued.

Badge No.	Insignia	Rank	Description	Extremely Fine
95B-2	Cap	ORs	Pickled copper, Wm. overlay on centre	240.00
95B-21		Officers	Gilt on copper, Silver overlay on centre	250.00

96TH INFANTRY BATTALION

"CANADIAN HIGHLANDERS"

The Battalion was raised in Saskatoon and district with mobilization headquarters at Saskatoon, Saskatchewan under the authority of G.O. 151 December 22nd, 1915. The Battalion sailed September 27th, 1916 under the command of Lieutenant-Colonel J. Glenn with a strength of twenty-nine officers and seven hundred and sixty-eight other ranks. In England the Battalion was absorbed into the 92nd Infantry Battalion. It was disbanded September 15th, 1920.

BADGE NUMBER: 96

CANADIAN HIGHLANDERS BATTALION/96

Makers: Caron, Dingwall, Tiptaft
Fasteners: Lugs, Tangs
Composition:
Other Ranks: Pickled copper or brass; Browning brass
Pipers: Sterling silver
Officers: Sterling silver
Ref.: Babin, Meek, Stewart, Cox

Note: Two makers of this cap badge exist, Dingwall and Tiptaft, they are very difficult to distinguish from each other. The collars can be identified by the plain ribbons used by Dingwall and framed ribbons by Tiptaft.

Badge No.	Insignia	Rank	Description	Extremely Fine
96A-2	Glengarry	ORs	Pickled copper, Lugs; Dingwall	50.00
96A-4		ORs	Pickled brass, Tangs; Dingwall	40.00
96A-6		ORs	Browning brass; Tiptaft	45.00
96A-8		Pipers	Sterling silver; Dingwall	110.00
96A-21		Officers	Sterling silver; Dingwall	110.00
Maple Leaf Type:				
96A-41	Collars	ORs	Pickled copper; Dingwall	75.00
96A-43		ORs	Pickled brass; Dingwall	20.00
96A-45		ORs	Browning brass; Tiptaft	15.00
96A-61		Officers	Unknown	- -
Saint Andrew's Cross Type:				
96A-47	Collars	ORs	Pickled copper	100.00
96A-91	Shoulders	ORs	Numeral: "96"; Caron	12.00

97TH INFANTRY BATTALION

"TORONTO AMERICANS"

The Battalion was raised and mobilized in Toronto, Ontario under the authority of G.O. 151 December 22nd, 1915. The Battalion sailed September 19th, 1916 under the command of Lieutenant-Colonel A. B. Clark with a strength of thirty-one officers and seven hundred and ninety-eight other ranks. This Battalion was one of four raised from American volunteers. In England the Battalion was absorbed into the R.C.R. and P.P.C.L.I. Depot Units. It was disbanded September 15th, 1920.

BADGE NUMBER: 97

No.- 97A   CANADA 97 OVERSEAS/ACTA NON VERBA

AUTHORIZED MAY 27TH, 1916

Makers: Ellis, Lees
Fasteners: Lugs
Composition:
 Other Ranks: Browning copper
  Officers: Unknown
Ref.: Babin, Stewart, Cox

Note: Lees and Ellis both used the same dies to produce this badge. It is interesting to note that the main crest of this badge and that of 212, 213 and 237 is the Arms of the Family of Washington.

Badge No.	Insignia	Rank	Description	Extremely Fine
97A-2	Cap	ORs	Browning copper, Lees	20.00
97A-4		ORs	Browning copper; Ellis	20.00
97A-21		Officers	Unknown	- -
97A-41	Collars	ORs	Browning copper; Lees	7.50
97A-43		ORs	Browning copper; Ellis	7.50
97A-61		Officers	Unknown	- -
97A-91	Shoulders	ORs	Numeral: "97"; Caron	12.00

No. - 97B   CANADA 97 OVERSEAS/AMERICAN LEGION

NOT AUTHORIZED

Makers: Caron, Lees, Tiptaft
Fasteners: Lugs, Pin
Composition:
Other Ranks: Browning copper
Officers: Browning copper
with white metal
overlay on design
Ref.: Babin, Meek, Cox

Note: Two makers of this cap badge exist.
1. The "9" is closed with the legend having large letters; Lees
2. The "9" is open with the legend having small letters; Tiptaft.

Badge No.	Insignia	Rank	Description	Extremely Fine
97B-2	Cap	ORs	Browning copper, Lugs; Lees	35.00
97B-4		ORs	Browning copper; Tiptaft	35.00
97B-21		Officers	Browning copper, Wm. overlay on design; Lees	65.00
97B-41	Collars	ORs	Browning copper; Lees	10.00
97B-43		ORs	Browning copper; Tiptaft	16.00
97B-61		Officers	Browning copper, Pin; Lees	30.00

No. - 97C   OVERSEAS BATTALION CANADA/97

Makers: Caron for Eaton's
Fasteners: Lugs, Pin
Composition:
Other Ranks: Pickled copper with
white metal overlay
Officers: Gilt on copper with
silver overlay
Ref.: Not previously listed

Note: No collars issued

Badge No.	Insignia	Rank	Description	Extremely Fine
97C-2	Cap	ORs	Pickled copper, Wm. overlay on centre; Caron	275.00
97C-21		Officers	Gilt on copper, Silver overlay on centre on centre; Caron	275.00

98TH INFANTRY BATTALION

"LINCOLN AND WELLAND BATTALION"

The Battalion was raised in the Lincoln and Welland Counties of Ontario with mobilization headquarters at Welland under the authority of G.O. 151 December 22nd, 1915. The Battalion sailed July 16th, 1916 under the command of Lieutenant-Colonel H. A. Rose with a strength of thirty-six officers and one thousand and fifty other ranks. In England the Battalion was absorbed into the 12th Reserve Battalion. It was disbanded September 15th, 1920.

BADGE NUMBER: 98

LINCOLN & WELLAND OVERSEAS/98/CANADA

AUTHORIZED FEBRUARY 1, 1916

Makers: Caron, Ellis, Tiptaft
Fasteners: Lugs
Composition:
Other Ranks: Browning copper
Officers:
    A: Browning copper
        with silver overlay
        on "98" and
        "Canada";
    B: Browning copper
        with gilt overlay
        on design
Ref.: Bain, Meek, Stewart, Cox

Note: Two makers of this cap badge exist.
    1. Pointed leaf design with a narrow crown; Ellis *(Illustrated)*
    2. Blunt leaf design with a wide crown; Tiptaft

Badge No.	Insignia	Rank	Description	Extremely Fine
98-2	Cap	ORs	Browning copper; Ellis	120.00
98-4		ORs	Browning copper; Tiptaft	120.00
98-21		Officers	Browning copper, Silver overlay on "98" and "Canada"; Ellis	125.00
98-23		Officers	Browning copper, Gilt overlay	145.00
98-41	Collars	ORs	Browning copper; Ellis	40.00
98-43		ORs	Browning copper; Tiptaft	40.00
98-61		Officers	Browning copper, Silver overlay on "98" and "Canada"; Ellis	45.00
98-91	Shoulders	ORs	Numeral: "98"; Caron	12.00

99TH INFANTRY BATTALION

"ESSEX BATTALION"

The Battalion was raised in Essex County, Ontario with mobilization headquarters at Windsor under the authority of G.O. 151 December 22nd, 1915. The Battalion sailed June 2nd, 1916 under the command of Lieutenant-Colonel T. B. Welch with a strength of thirty-six officers and eight hundred and twenty-five other ranks. In England the Battalion was absorbed into the 35th Reserve Battalion which in turn was absorbed into the 4th Reserve Battalion. It was disbanded September 15th, 1920.

BADGE NUMBER: 99

No. - 99A

ACTA NON VERBA/99/
CANADA ESSEX OVERSEAS

Makers: Caron, Unknown
Fasteners: Lugs
Composition:
Other Ranks: Pickled copper;
Browning copper
or brass
Officers:
    A: Pickled copper
    B: Sterling silver, void
Ref.: Babin, Meek, Stewart, Cox

Badge No.	Insignia	Rank	Description	Extremely Fine
99A-2	Cap	ORs	Pickled copper; Unknown	50.00
99A-4		ORs	Browning brass; Unknown	50.00
99A-21		Officers	Pickled copper; Unknown	325.00
99A-23		Officers	Sterling silver, void; Unknown	75.00
99A-41	Collars	ORs	Pickled copper; Unknown	20.00
99A-43		ORs	Browning copper; Unknown	40.00
99A-61		Officers	Unknown	- -
99A-91	Shoulders	ORs	Numeral: "99"; Caron	12.00

No. - 99B   99/CANADA

INTERIM BADGE

Makers: As General List
Fasteners: Lugs
Composition:
Other Ranks: Unofficial, "99" overlay on General List
Officers: Unknown
Ref.: Not previously listed

Badge No.	Insignia	Rank	Description	Extremely Fine
99B-2	Cap	ORs	General List, "99" overlay	110.00
99B-21		Officers	Unknown	- -
99B-41	Collars	ORs	General List, "99" overlay	65.00
99B-61		Officers	Unknown	- -

100TH INFANTRY BATTALION

"WINNIPEG GRENADIERS"

The Battalion was raised and mobilized in Winnipeg, Manitoba under the authority of G.O. 151 December 22nd, 1915. The Battalion sailed September 19th, 1916 under the command of Lieutenant-Colonel J. B. Mitchell with a strength of thirty-one officers and eight hundred and eighty other ranks. In England the Battalion was absorbed into the 11th Reserve Battalion. It was disbanded September 15th, 1920.

BADGE NUMBER: 100

100/WINNIPEG GRENADIERS

Makers: Caron, Dingwall, Tiptaft; Unknown
Fasteners: Lugs
Composition:
Other Ranks: Pickled copper or brass; Blackened copper or brass
Officers: Blackened copper
Ref.: Babin, Meek, Stewart, Cox

Note: Two makers of this cap badge exist.
1. The number "100" is high on the grenade ball with small flame points; Dingwall *(Illustrated)*
2. The number "100" is low on the grenade ball with large flame points; Tiptaft

Badge No.	Insignia	Rank	Description	Extremely Fine
100-2	Cap	ORs	Blackened copper; Dingwall	25.00
100-4		ORs	Blackened brass; Tiptaft	25.00
100-21		Officers	Blackened copper; Unknown	25.00
100-41	Collars	ORs	Pickled copper; Dingwall	12.00
100-43		ORs	Pickled brass; Tiptaft	12.00
100-61		Officers	Unknown	- -
100-91	Shoulders	ORs	Numeral: "100"; Caron	14.00
100-93		ORs	Title: "100" over "CANADA"Large; Caron	18.00
100-95		ORs	Title: "CANADA" curved; Tiptaft	18.00
100-97		ORs	Title: "100" over "CANADA" Small; Unknown	18.00

101ST INFANTRY BATTALION

"ROYAL WINNIPEG RIFLES/WINNIPEG LIGHT INFANTRY"

The Battalion was raised and mobilized in Winnipeg, Manitoba under the authority of G.O. 151 December 22nd, 1915. The Battalion sailed June 29th, 1916 under the command of Lieutenant-Colonel D. McLean with a strength of thirty-six officers and one thousand and twenty-five other ranks. In England the Battalion was absorbed into the 17th Reserve Battalion. It was disbanded September 15th, 1920.

BADGE NUMBER: 101

WINNIPEG LIGHT INFANTRY
/101/OVERSEAS BATTALION/CANADA

Makers: Caron, Hemsley, Inglis, Tiptaft
Fasteners: Lugs
Composition:
Other Ranks: Pickled copper or brass; Browning copper or brass
Officers: Pickled copper with silver overlay on design
Ref.: Babin, Meek, Stewart, Cox

Note: Two makers of this cap badge exist.
1. Pointed leaf design with legend having small lettering; Plain ribbons; Hemsley *(Illustrated)*
2. Blunt leaf design with legend having large lettering; Framed ribbons; Tiptaft

Badge No.	Insignia	Rank	Description	Extremely Fine
101-2	Cap	ORs	Pickled copper; Hemsley, Inglis	25.00
101-4		ORs	Pickled brass; Hemsley, Inglis	25.00
101-6		ORs	Browning copper; Tiptaft	25.00
101-21		Officers	Pickled copper, Silver overlay on design; Hemsley	110.00
101-41	Collars	ORs	Pickled copper; Hemsley, Inglis	18.00
101-43		ORs	Pickled brass; Hemsley, Inglis	12.00
101-45		ORs	Browning brass; Tiptaft	12.00
101-61		Officers	Pickled copper, Silver overlay on design; Hemsley	50.00
101-91	Shoulders	ORs	Numeral: "101"; Caron	12.00
101-93		ORs	Numeral: "101"; Tiptaft	14.00

102ND INFANTRY BATTALION

"NORTH BRITISH COLUMBIANS"

The Battalion was raised in Northern British Columbia with mobilization headquarters at Comox under the authority of G.O. 151, December 22nd, 1915. The Battalion sailed June 20th, 1916 under the command of Lieutenant-Colonel J. W. Warden with a strength of thirty-seven officers and nine hundred and sixty-eight other ranks. The Battalion served in France and Belgium with the 11th Infantry Brigade, 4th Canadian Division. It was disbanded September 15th, 1920.

BADGE NUMBER: 102

No. - 102A
**C.E.F./OVERSEAS/102
/NORTH BRITISH COLUMBIANS/CANADA**

"OVERSEAS" VARIETY

Makers: Allan, Caron, Tiptaft
Fasteners: Lugs
Composition:
Other Ranks: Browning copper
or brass
Officers: Unknown
Ref.: Not previously listed

Note: Two makers of this cap badge exist.
1. The head-dress feather design is weak; small lettering in the legend; Allan
2. The head-dress design is strong with good individual feather design; large lettering; Tiptaft *(Illustrated)*

Badge No.	Insignia	Rank	Description	Extremely Fine
102A-2	Cap	ORs	Browning copper; Allan	75.00
102A-4		ORs	Browning copper; Tiptaft	75.00
102A-6		ORs	Browning brass; Allan	75.00
102A-21		Officers	Unknown	- -
102A-41	Collars	ORs	Browning copper; Allan	10.00
102A-43		ORs	Browning copper; Tiptaft	10.00
102A-45		ORs	Browning brass; Allan	15.00
102A-61		Officers	Unknown	- -
			"C" Over Numbers	
102A-81	Collars	ORs	"C" bar "102", Large "C"; Tiptaft	25.00
102A-91	Shoulders	ORs	Numeral: "102"; Caron	14.00
102A-93		ORs	Title: "NORTH BRITISH/102/ COLUMBIANS"; Allan	20.00

No. - 102B

**C.E.F./102/NORTH
BRITISH COLUMBIANS/CANADA**

WITHOUT "OVERSEAS" VARIETY

NOT AUTHORIZED

Makers: Allan, Tiptaft
Fasteners: Lugs
Composition:
Other Ranks: Browning copper;
Blackened brass
Officers:
A: Browning copper;
B: Silverplate
Ref.: Babin, Meek, Stewart, Cox

Note: Two makers of this badge exist. Both are 50 x 42 mm.
1. The "102" has narrow numbers; One band on the headdress; Allan *(Illustrated)*
2. The "102" has wide numbers; Three bands on the headdress; Tiptaft

Badge No.	Insignia	Rank	Description	Extremely Fine
102B-2	Cap	ORs	Browning copper; Allan	35.00
102B-4		ORs	Blackened brass; Tiptaft	45.00
102B-21		Officers	Browning copper; Unknown	65.00
102B-23		Officers	Silverplate; Unknown	250.00
102B-41	Collars	ORs	Browning copper; Allan	10.00
102B-43		ORs	Blackened brass; Tiptaft	15.00
102B-61		Officers	Browning copper; Unknown	35.00

No. - 102C

**C.E.F./102/NORTH
BRITISH COLUMBIANS/CANADA**

Makers: Unknown
Fasteners: Lugs
Composition:
Pipers: White metal
Ref.: Babin 40-4, Cox 603

Note: This badge is cast.

Badge No.	Insignia	Rank	Description	Extremely Fine
102C-2	Cap	Pipers	White metal	900.00

103RD INFANTRY BATTALION

The Battalion was raised and mobilized in Victoria, British Columbia under the authority of G.O. 151 December 22nd, 1915. The Battalion sailed July 24th, 1916 under the command of Lieutenant-Colonel E. C. J. Henniker with a strength of thirty-seven officers and nine hundred and thirty-nine other ranks. In England the Battalion was absorbed into the 16th Reserve Battalion. It was disbanded September 15th, 1920.

BADGE NUMBER: 103

103RD C.E.F./RESNON VERBA/CANADA

Makers: Caron, Jacoby, Tiptaft
Fasteners: Lugs
Composition:
Other Ranks: Pickled brass;
Blackened brass
Officers: White metal
Ref.: Babin, Meek, Stewart, Cox

Note: Two makers of this cap badge exist.
1. Block style type with plain ribbon; Jacoby *(Illustrated)*
2. Round style type with framed ribbons; Tiptaft

Badge No.	Insignia	Rank	Description	Extremely Fine
103-2	Cap	ORs	Pickled brass; Jacoby	35.00
103-4		ORs	Blackened brass; Jacoby	35.00
103-6		ORs	Blackened brass; Tiptaft	35.00
103-21		Officers	White metal; Unknown	210.00
103-41	Collars	ORs	Pickled brass; Jacoby	12.00
103-43		ORs	Blackened brass; Jacoby	12.00
103-45		ORs	Blackened brass; Tiptaft	12.00
103-61		Officers	White metal; Unknown	50.00
103-91	Shoulders	ORs	Numeral: "103"; Caron	14.00
103-93			Title: "103RD BATT. C.E.F./CANADA"; Jacoby	25.00
103-94			Title: "103RD BATTN. C.E.F./CANADA"; Tiptaft	25.00

Note: Shoulder titles by Jacoby used the short form "Batt.", while Tiptaft used "Battn.".

104TH INFANTRY BATTALION

The Battalion was raised in New Brunswick with mobilization headquarters at Sussex under the authority of G.O. 151 December 22nd, 1915. The Battalion sailed June 29th, 1916 under the command of Lieutenant-Colonel G. W. Fowler with a strength of forty-two officers and one thousand and eighty-four other ranks. The Battalion was absorbed into the 13th Reserve Battalion. It was disbanded September 15th, 1920.

BADGE NUMBER: 104

No. - 104A   **PRO IMPERA/OVERSEAS BATTALION /104/CANADA**

Makers: Caron, G & S Co., Hemsley, Tiptaft, Unknown
Fasteners: Lugs
Composition:
Other Ranks: Pickled copper or brass; Browning copper or brass
Officers:
    A: Sterling silver;
    B: Sterling silver with gold overlay on design
Ref.: Babin, Meek, Stewart, Cox

Note: Three makers of this badge exist.
1. The ship has a half furled sail; The "O" in "104" is oval; Hemsley. *(Illustrated)* This badge was issued in either solid and void patterns.
2. The ship has a half furled sail; The "O" in "104" is round; Tiptaft. This badge is known only in solid pattern.
3. The ship has a furled sail; The "O" in "104" is oval; G. & S. Co.

Badge No.	Insignia	Rank	Description	Extremely Fine
104A-2	Cap	ORs	Pickled copper, Void; Hemsley	20.00
104A-4		ORs	Pickled brass, Solid; Hemsley	20.00
104A-6		ORs	Browning copper, Void; Hemsley	20.00
104A-8		ORs	Browning copper, Solid; Tiptaft	20.00
104A-10		ORs	Browning brass, Void; G & S Co.	20.00
104A-21		Officers	Sterling silver; Unknown	85.00
104A-23		Officers	Sterling silver, Gold overlay on design; G & S Co.	85.00
104A-41	Collars	ORs	Pickled copper, Void; Hemsley	12.00
104A-43		ORs	Pickled brass, Solid; Hemsley	12.00
104A-45		ORs	Browning copper, Void; Hemsley	12.00
104A-47		ORs	Browning copper, Solid; Tiptaft	12.00
104A-61		Officers	Unknown	- -
104A-91	Shoulders	ORs	Numeral: "104"; Caron	12.00
104A-93		ORs	Title: "104/CANADA"	20.00

No. - 104B   **OVERSEAS BATTALION/104/CANADA**

Makers: Caron
Fasteners: Lugs
Composition:
 Other Ranks: Browning copper
          Officers: Sterling silver
Ref.: Not previously listed

Badge No.	Insignia	Rank	Description	Extremely Fine
104B-2	Cap	ORs	Browning copper; Caron	35.00
104B-21		Officers	Sterling silver; Caron	100.00
104B-41	Collars	ORs	Unknown	- -
104B-61		Officers	Unknown	- -

105TH INFANTRY BATTALION

"P.E.I. HIGHLANDERS"

The Battalion was raised in Prince Edward Island with mobilization headquarters at Charlottetown, under the authority of G.O. 151 December 22nd, 1915. The Battalion sailed July 16th, 1916, under the command of Lieutenant-Colonel A. E. Ings with a strength of thirty-seven officers and one thousand and eighty-seven other ranks. In England the Battalion was absorbed into the 104th Infantry Battalion. It was disbanded September 15th, 1920.

BADGE NUMBER: 105

CANADA/PRINCE EDWARDS ISLAND HIGHLANDERS/105

Makers: Birks, Caron, Hemsley, Tiptaft
Fasteners: Lugs
Composition:
Other Ranks: Pickled copper or brass; Browning brass
Officers: Silverplate with copper centre
Ref.: Babin, Meek, Stewart, Cox

Note: Two makers of this cap badge exist.
1. Pointed leaf design with small letters in the legend; Plain ribbons; Hemsley
2. Blunt leaf design with large letters in the legend; Framed ribbons; Tiptaft

Badge No.	Insignia	Rank	Description	Extremely Fine
105-2	Cap	ORs	Pickled copper; Hemsley	35.00
105-4		ORs	Pickled brass; Hemsley	25.00
105-6		ORs	Browning copper; Tiptaft	30.00
105-21		Officers	Silverplate with copper centre	700.00
Six Maple Leaves Design				
105-41	Collars	ORs	Pickled copper; Hemsley	12.00
105-43		ORs	Pickled brass; Hemsley	12.00
105-61		Officers	Unknown	- -
Maple Leaf Design				
105-45	Collars	ORs	Browning copper; Tiptaft	12.00
105-63		Officers	Silverplate	50.00
105-91	Shoulders	ORs	Numeral: "105"; Caron	14.00
105-93		ORs	Numeral: "105"; Birks	14.00

106TH INFANTRY BATTALION

"NOVA SCOTIA RIFLES"

The Battalion was raised in Nova Scotia with mobilization headquarters at Truro under the authority of G.O. 151 December 22nd, 1915. The Battalion sailed July 16th, 1916, under the command of Lieutenant-Colonel R. Innes with a strength of thirty-six officers and one thousand and nine other ranks. In England the Battalion was absorbed into the 23rd Reserve Battalion. It was disbanded September 15th, 1920.

BADGE NUMBER: 106

NOVA SCOTIA RIFLES/106/
OVERSEAS BATTALION/CANADA

Makers: Birks, Caron, Hemsley, Tiptaft
Fasteners: Lugs
Composition:
Other Ranks: Pickled copper or brass; Browning copper
Officers: Pickled copper
Ref.: Babin, Meek, Stewart, Cox

Note: Two makers of this cap badge exist.
1. Pointed leaf design, wide lettering in legend; Hemsley *(Illustrated)*
2. Blunt leaf design; narrow lettering in legends; Tiptaft

Badge No.	Insignia	Rank	Description	Extremely Fine
106-2	Cap	ORs	Pickled copper; Hemsley	40.00
106-4		ORs	Pickled brass; Hemsley	25.00
106-6		ORs	Browning copper; Tiptaft	25.00
106-21		Officers	Pickled copper; Hemsley	40.00
106-41	Collars	ORs	Pickled copper; Hemsley	30.00
106-43		ORs	Pickled brass; Hemsley	16.00
106-45		ORs	Browning copper; Tiptaft	16.00
106-61		Officers	Pickled copper; Hemsley	16.00
106-91	Shoulders	ORs	Numeral: "106"; Caron	12.00
106-93		ORs	Numeral: "106"; Birks	12.00

107TH INFANTRY BATTALION

"WINNIPEG BATTALION"

The Battalion was raised and mobilized in Winnipeg, Manitoba under the authority of G.O. 151 December 22nd, 1915. The Battalion sailed September 19th, 1916 under the command of Lieutenant-Colonel G. Campbell with a strength of thirty-two officers and nine hundred and sixty-five other ranks. In England the Battalion was redesignated the 107th Pioneer Battalion and served in France in that capacity. It was disbanded September 15th, 1920.

BADGE NUMBER: 107

No. - 107A   OVERSEAS 107 BATTALION/WINNIPEG

Makers: Caron, Dingwall, Tiptaft
Fasteners: Lugs
Composition:
Other Ranks: Pickled brass;
Browning copper;
Blackened brass
Officers: Silverplate
Ref.: Babin, Meek, Stewart, Cox

Note: Two makers of this cap badge exist.
  1. Thick type for numbers; Large type for letters; Dingwall *(Illustrated)*
  2. Narrow type for numbers; Small type for letters; Tiptaft

Badge No.	Insignia	Rank	Description	Extremely Fine
107A-2	Cap	ORs	Pickled brass; Dingwall	25.00
107A-4		ORs	Browning copper; Dingwall	25.00
107A-6		ORs	Blackened brass; Tiptaft	25.00
107A-21		Officers	Silverplate; Dingwall	125.00
107A-41	Collars	ORs	Pickled brass; Dingwall	20.00
107A-43		ORs	Browning copper; Dingwall	10.00
107A-56		ORs	Blackened brass; Tiptaft	20.00
107A-61		Officers	Silverplate; Dingwall	50.00
107A-91	Shoulders	ORs	Numeral: "107"; Caron	14.00
107A-93		ORs	Title: "INF. 107 BATT/ CANADA"; Dingwall	25.00

No. - 107B   **107 CANADA**

INTERIM BADGE

Photograph
Not Available
At Press Time

Makers: As General List
Fasteners: Lugs
Composition:
Other Ranks: General List with
"107" overlay
Officers: Unknown
Ref.: Not previously listed

Badge No.	Insignia	Rank	Description	Extremely Fine
107B-2	Cap	ORs	General List, "107" overlay	65.00
107B-21		Officers	Unknown	- -
107B-41	Collars	ORs	Unknown	- -
107B-61		Officers	Unknown	- -

No. - 107C   **PIPER'S BADGE
FOLLOW ME/107/WINNIPEG/
OVERSEAS BATTALION/CANADA**

Makers: Unknown
Fasteners: Lugs
Composition:
Other Ranks:
Officers: Unknown
Ref.: Not previously listed

Badge No.	Insignia	Rank	Description	Extremely Fine
107C-2	Cap	ORs	Collar over Anulas	Rare
107C-21		Officers	Unknown	- -

108TH INFANTRY BATTALION

"SELKIRK AND MANITOBA BATTALION"

The Battalion was raised in Manitoba with mobilization headquarters at Selkirk under the authority of G.O. 151 December 22nd, 1915. The Battalion sailed September 19th, 1916 under the command of Lieutenant-Colonel G.. H. Bradbury, with a strength of thirty-two officers and eight hundred and forty-three other ranks. In England the Battalion was absorbed into the 14th Reserve Battalion. It was disbanded September 15th, 1920.

BADGE NUMBER: 108

No. - 108A   **OVERSEAS BATTALION/108/CANADA**

Makers: Birks, Caron
Fasteners: Lugs, Pin
Composition:
Other Ranks: Browning copper
or brass
Officers: Sterling silver
Ref.: Babin, Cox

Badge No.	Insignia	Rank	Description	Extremely Fine
108A-2	Cap	ORs	Browning copper; Birks	40.00
108A-4		ORs	Browning brass; Birks	35.00
108A-21		Officers	Sterling silver; Birks	65.00
108A-41	Collars	ORs	Browning copper; Birks	20.00
108A-43		ORs	Browning brass; Birks	20.00
108A-61		Officers	Sterling silver; Birks	35.00
108A-91	Shoulders	ORs	Numeral: "108"; Caron	15.00
108A-93		ORs	Title: "INF 108 BATT/CANADA"	25.00

No. - 108B

OVERSEAS BATTALION/
SELKIRK MANITOBA/CANADA/108

Makers: Dingwall, Tiptaft
Fasteners: Lugs
Composition:
Other Ranks: Pickled copper
or brass
Officers: Unknown
Ref.: Babin, Meek, Stewart, Cox

Note: Two makers of this cap badge exist.
1. Thick type for "Canada" and "108"; Vein leaf design; Dingwall *(Illustrated)*
2. Narrow type for "Canada" and "108"; Flat leaf design; Tiptaft

Badge No.	Insignia	Rank	Description	Extremely Fine
108B-2	Cap	ORs	Pickled copper; Dingwall	28.00
108B-4		ORs	Pickled brass; Tiptaft	28.00
108B-21		Officers	Unknown	- -
108B-41	Collars	ORs	Pickled copper; Dingwall	15.00
108B-43		ORs	Pickled brass; Tiptaft	15.00
108B-61		Officers	Unknown	- -

109TH INFANTRY BATTALION

"VICTORIA AND HALIBURTON BATTALION"

The Battalion was raised in the Victoria and Haliburton Counties of Ontario with mobilization headquarters at Lindsay under the authority of G.O. 151 December 22nd, 1915. The Battalion sailed July 24th, 1916 under the command of Lieutenant-Colonel J. J. H. Fee with a strength of thirty-five officers and seven hundred and sevety-five other ranks. In England the Battalion was broken up and absorbed into the 20th, 21st, 38th and 124th Battalions. It was disbanded September 15th, 1920.

BADGE NUMBER: 109

109 OVERSEAS CANADA/
VICTORIA & HALIBURTON/WHERE DUTY LEADS

Makers: Caron, Ellis, Kinnear,
      Tiptaft, Unknown
Fasteners: Lugs
Composition:
 Other Ranks: Browning copper
    Officers: As above
Ref.: Babin, Meek, Stewart, Cox

Note: Three makers of this cap badge exist.
    1. Thick type "109"; Wide wreath design; Ellis. This badge is only
       known in the void pattern.
    2. Thin type "109"; Medium wreath design; Kinnear and Desterre. *(Illustrated)*
       This badge is available in either a solid or void pattern.
    3. Thin, tall type; Thin wreath design; Tiptaft

Badge No.	Insignia	Rank	Description	Extremely Fine
109-2	Cap	ORs	Browning copper, Void; Ellis	20.00
109-4		ORs	Browning copper, Void; Kinnear	20.00
109-6		ORs	Browning copper, Solid; Kinnear	30.00
109-8		ORs	Browning copper, Void; Tiptaft	20.00
109-21		Officers	Browning copper, Solid; Unknown	30.00
109-41	Collars	ORs	Browning copper, Void; Ellis	20.00
109-43		ORs	Browning copper, Void; Kinnear	20.00
109-45		ORs	Browning copper, solid; Kinnear	20.00
109-47		ORs	Browning copper, Void; Tiptaft	20.00
109-61		Officers	Browning copper, Solid; Unknown	20.00
109-91	Shoulders	ORs	Numeral: "109"; Caron	12.00
109-93		ORs	Title: "V & H/109/CANADA"	25.00
109-95		Officers	Title: "VICTORIA/109/HALIBURTON CANADA"	25.00

110TH INFANTRY BATTALION

"PERTH BATTALION"

The Battalion was raised in Perth County Ontario with mobilization headquarters at Stratford under the authority of G.O. 151 December 22nd, 1915. The Battalion sailed November 1st, 1916 under the command of J. L. Youngs with a strength of twenty-six officers and six hundred and thirty-five other ranks. In England the Battalion was absorbed into the 8th Reserve Battalion. It was disbanded September 15th, 1920.

BADGE NUMBER: 110

No. - 110A   OVERSEAS 110 BATTALION/PERTH/CANADA

Makers: Caron, Hemsley, Inglis, Tiptaft
Fasteners: Lugs
Composition:
Other Ranks: Pickled copper or brass; Browning copper
Officers: Pickled copper with silver overlay on design
Ref.: Babin, Meek, Stewart, Cox

Note: Two makers of this cap badge exist.
  1. Thick, large type for "110" and Perth; Hemsley, Inglis *(Illustrated)*
  2. Narrow, small type for "110" and Perth; Tiptaft

Badge No.	Insignia	Rank	Description	Extremely Fine
110A-2	Cap	ORs	Pickled copper; Hemsley, Inglis	25.00
110A-4		ORs	Pickled copper; Tiptaft	25.00
110A-6		ORs	Pickled brass; Hemsley, Inglis	25.00
110A-8		ORs	Browning copper; Tiptaft	25.00
110A-21		Officers	Pickled copper, Silver overlay on design; Hemsley	85.00
110A-41	Collars	ORs	Pickled copper; Hemsley, Inglis	15.00
110A-43		ORs	Pickled copper; Tiptaft	15.00
110A-45		ORs	Browning copper; Tiptaft	15.00
110A-61		Officers	Pickled copper, Silver overlay on design; Hemsley	30.00
110A-91	Shoulders	ORs	Numeral: "110"; Caron	25.00
110A-93		ORs	Title: "110/CANADA"; Hemsley	25.00

No. - 110B   **OVERSEAS BATTALION/110/CANADA**

Makers: Caron
Fasteners: Pin
Composition:
Other Ranks: Browning copper
Officers: Silver overlay on "110"
Ref.: Not previously listed

Badge No.	Insignia	Rank	Description	Extremely Fine
110B-2	Cap	ORs	Browning copper; Caron	35.00
110B-21		Officers	Browning copper, Silver overlay on "110"; Caron	100.00
110B-41	Collars	ORs	Browning copper; Caron	20.00
110B-61		Officers	Browning copper, Silver overlay on "110"; Caron	30.00

No. - 110C   **OVERSEAS BATTALION CANADA/110**

Photograph
Not Available
At Press Time

Makers: Caron for Eaton's
Fasteners: Pin
Composition:
Other Ranks: Pickled copper with white metal overlay on centre
Officers: Pickled copper with silver overlay on centre
Ref.: Not previously listed

Note: Collars not issued.

Badge No.	Insignia	Rank	Description	Extremely Fine
110C-2	Cap	ORs	Pickled copper, Wm. overlay on centre; Caron	175.00
110C-21		Officers	Pickled copper, Silver overlay on centre; Caron	225.00

111TH INFANTRY BATTALION

"SOUTH WATERLOO BATTALION"

The Battalion was raised in Waterloo Country, Ontario with mobilization headquarters at Galt under the authority of G.O. 151 December 22nd, 1915. The Battalion sailed September 27th, 1916, under the command of Lieutenant-Colonel J. D. Clarke with a strength of twenty-five officers and six hundred and thirty-seven other ranks. In England the Battalion was absorbed into the 35th Reserve Battalion. It was disbanded September 15th, 1920.

BADGE NUMBER: 111

No. - 111A

SOUTH WATERLOO /OVERSEAS 111 BATTALION/CANADA

Makers: Caron, Hemsley, Inglis, Tiptaft
Fasteners: Lugs, Pin
Composition:
Other Ranks: Pickled copper or brass; Browning copper
Officers:
A: Silver overlay on design
B: Sterling silver
Ref.: Babin, Meek, Stewart, Cox

Note: Two makers of this cap badge exist.
1. Thick type for numbers "111"; Ribbon on Canada is not framed; Hemsley, Inglis *(Illustrated)*
2. Narrow type for numbers "111"; Ribbon on Canada is framed; Tiptaft

Badge No.	Insignia	Rank	Description	Extremely Fine
111A-2	Cap	ORs	Pickled copper; Hemsley, Inglis	35.00
111A-4		ORs	Pickled brass; Hemsley, Inglis	40.00
111A-6		ORs	Browning copper; Tiptaft	35.00
111A-21		Officers	PIckled copper, Silver overlay on design; Hemsley, Inglis	100.00
111A-41	Collars	ORs	Pickled copper; Hemsley, Inglis	10.00
111A-43		ORs	Pickled brass; Hemsley, Inglis	10.00
111A-45		ORs	Browning copper, Solid; Tiptaft	10.00
111A-47		ORs	Browning copper, Void; Tiptaft	10.00
111A-61		Officers	Pickled copper, Silver overlay on thistle; Hemsley, Inglis	20.00
111A-63		Officers	Sterling silver; Tiptaft	100.00
111A-91	Shoulders	ORs	Numeral: "111"; Caron	16.00

No. - 111B **111/CANADA**

Photograph
Not Available
At Press Time

Makers: Tiptaft
Fasteners: Lugs
Composition:
Other Ranks: Browning Copper
Officers: Unknown
Ref.: Cox

Badge No.	Insignia	Rank	Description	Extremely Fine
111B-2	Cap	ORs	Browning copper; Tiptaft	50.00
111B-21		Officers	Unknown	- -
111B-41	Collars	ORs	Browning copper; Tiptaft	35.00
111B-61		Officers	Unknown	- -

No. - 111C **OVERSEAS BATTALION CANADA/111**

Makers: Caron for Eaton's
Fasteners: Lugs
Composition:
Other Ranks: White metal overlay on pickled copper
Officers: Silver overlay on pickled copper
Ref.: Not previously listed

Note: Collars are not known.

Badge No.	Insignia	Rank	Description	Extremely Fine
111C-2	Cap	ORs	Pickled copper, Wm overlay on centre; Caron	250.00
111C-21		Officers	Pickled copper, Silver overlay on centre; Caron	275.00

112TH INFANTRY BATTALION

"NOVA SCOTIA OVERSEAS BATTALION"

The Battalion was raised in Nova Scotia with mobilzation headquarters at Windsor, Nova Scotia under the authority of G.O. 151 December 22nd, 1915. The Battalion sailed July 24th, 1916 under the command of Lieutenant-Colonel H. B. Tremaine with a strength of thirty-six officers and one thousand and ninety other ranks. In England the Battalion was absorbed into the 26th Reserve Battalion. It was disbanded September 15th, 1920.

BADGE NUMBER: 112

NOVA SCOTIA 112 OVERSEAS BATTALION/ CANADA/HONOR ET HONESTAS

Makers: Brown, Caron, Tiptaft, Unknown
Fasteners: Lugs
Composition:
Other Ranks: Pickled brass; Blackened brass
Officers: Pickled brass with silver overlay on "112"
Ref.: Babin, Meek, Stewart, Cox

Note: Three makers of this cap badge exist.
   1. Thick type "112". The fish has a large dorsel fin; Brown *(Illustrated)*
   2. Thin type "112". The fish has a small dorsel fin; Tiptaft
   3. Thick type "112". The fish has a small dorsel fin; Unknown

Badge No.	Insignia	Rank	Description	Extremely Fine
112-2	Cap	ORs	Pickled brass; Brown	24.00
112-4		ORs	Blackened brass; Tiptaft	24.00
112-6		ORs	Blackened brass; Unknown	24.00
112-21		Officers	Pickled brass, Silver overlay on "112"; Brown	150.00
112-41	Collars	ORs	Pickled brass; Brown	14.00
112-43		ORs	Blackened brass; Tiptaft	14.00
112-45		ORs	Blackened brass; Unknown	11.00
112-61		Officers	Pickled brass, Silver overlay on "112"; Brown	50.00
112-91	Shoulders	ORs	Numeral: "112"; Caron	12.00
112-93		ORs	Numeral: "112"; Tiptaft	12.00
112-95		ORs	Title: "112/"CANADA"; Tiptaft	18.00

113TH INFANTRY BATTALION

"LETHBRIDGE HIGHLANDERS"

The Battalion was raised and mobilized in Lethbridge Alberta, under the authority of G.O. 151 December 22nd, 1915. The Battalion sailed September 27th, 1916 under the command of Lieutenant-Colonel W. A. Pryce Jones with a strength of thirty officers and eight hundred and eighty-three other ranks. In England the Battalion was absorbed into the 17th Reserve Battalion. It was disbanded September 15th, 1920.

BADGE NUMBER: 113

OVERSEAS BATTALION/113/
CANADA/LETHBRIDGE HIGHLANDERS

Makers: Black, Caron, Hemsley, Tiptaft
Fasteners: Lugs
Composition:
Other Ranks: Pickled copper
Officers:
A: Gilt
B: Pickled copper with silver overlay on centre design
Ref.: Babin, Meek, Stewart, Cox

Note: Three makers of this cap badge exist.
1. Bonnet badge: The three of "113" has a pointed serif; Plain ribbons, 59 mm in height; Hemsley, Black *(Illustrated)*
2. Small cap badge: The three of "113" has a pointed serif; Plain ribbons, 45 mm in height; Hemsley, Black
3. Bonnet badge: The three of "113" has a blunt serif; Framed ribbons; 57 mm in height; Tiptaft

Badge No.	Insignia	Rank	Description	Extremely Fine
113-2	Cap	ORs	Pickled copper, Large; Hemsley, Black	75.00
113-4		ORs	Pickled copper, Small; Hemsley, Black	35.00
113-21		Officers	Gilt on copper, Large; Hemsley, Black	150.00
113-6	Bonnett	ORs	Pickled copper, Large; Tiptaft	75.00
113-23		Officers	Pickled copper, Silver overlay on centre design; Hemsley	150.00
113-41	Collars	ORs	Pickled copper; Hemsley, Black	20.00
113-43		ORs	Pickled copper; Tiptaft	85.00
113-61		Officers	Gilt on copper; Hemsley, Black	20.00
113-91	Shoulders	ORs	Numeral: "113"; Caron	14.00
113-93		ORs	Numeral: "113", Great coat size	25.00

114TH INFANTRY BATTALION

"BROCK'S RANGERS"

The Battalion was raised in Haldimand County and the Six Nations Indian Reserve, with mobilization headquarters at Cayuga under the authority of G.O. 151 December 22nd, 1915. The Battalion sailed November 1st, 1916 under the command of Lieutenant-Colonel A. T. Thompson with a strength of thirty officers and six hundred and seventy-nine other ranks. In England the Battalion was broken up and absorbed into the 35th and 36th Infantry Battalions. It was disbanded September 15th, 1920.

BADGE NUMBER: 114

FOR KING AND COUNTRY HALDIMAND/114/ BROCK'S RANGERS/CANADA/OVERSEAS

AUTHORIZED JANUARY 27, 1916

Makers: Caron, Ellis, Tiptaft
Fasteners: Lugs
Composition:
Other Ranks: Pickled brass;
Browning copper
Officers: Sterling silver
Ref.: Babin, Meek, Stewart, Cox

Note: Two makers of this cap badge exist.
1. Pointed leaf design; plain ribbons; Ellis *(Illustrated)*
2. Blunt leaf design; framed ribbons; Tiptaft

Badge No.	Insignia	Rank	Description	Extremely Fine
114-2	Cap	ORs	Pickled brass; Ellis	30.00
114-4		ORs	Browning copper; Ellis	30.00
114-6		ORs	Browning copper; Tiptaft	30.00
114-21		Officers	Sterling silver; Ellis	75.00
114-41	Collars	ORs	Pickled brass; Ellis	10.00
114-43		ORs	Browning copper; Ellis	20.00
114-45		ORs	Browning copper: Tiptaft	20.00
114-61		Officers	Sterling silver; Ellis	40.00
114-91	Shoulders	ORs	Numeral: "114"; Caron	14.00

Note: The Tiptaft collars have an error in the spelling of Haldimand, the "M" is replaced by a "W".

115TH INFANTRY BATTALION

"NEW BRUNSWICK BATTALION"

The Battalion was raised in New Brunswick with mobilization headquarters at Saint John under the authority of G.O. 151 December 22nd, 1915. The Battalion sailed July 24th, 1916 under the command of Lieutenant-Colonel F. V. Wedderburn with a strength of thirty-four officers and eight hundred and one other ranks. In England the Battalion was absorbed into the 112th Infantry Battalion. It was disbanded September 15th, 1920.

BADGE NUMBER: 115

NEW BRUNSWICK/115/
OVERSEAS BATTALION/CANADA

Makers: Caron, Ellis, Tiptaft
Fasteners: Lugs
Composition:
Other Ranks: Pickled copper or brass; Browning copper
Officers:
A: Pickled copper with white metal overlay on design
B: Pickled copper
Ref.: Babin, Meek, Stewart, Cox

Note: Two makers of this cap badge exist.
　　　1. Pointed leaf design; Plain ribbons; Ellis *(Illustrated)*
　　　2. Blunt leaf design; Framed ribbons; Tiptaft

Badge No.	Insignia	Rank	Description	Extremely Fine
115-2	Cap	ORs	Pickled copper; Ellis	24.00
115-4		ORs	Pickled brass; Ellis	22.00
115-6		ORs	Browning copper; Tiptaft	24.00
115-21		Officers	Pickled copper, Wm. overlay on design; Ellis	85.00
115-41	Collars	ORs	Pickled brass; Ellis	15.00
115-43		ORs	Browning copper; Tiptaft	10.00
115-61		Officers	Pickled copper, Wm. overlay on design; Ellis	30.00
115-91	Shoulders	ORs	Numeral: "115"; Caron	14.00

116TH INFANTRY BATTALION

"ONTARIO COUNTY INFANTRY BATTALION"

The 116th Infantry Battalion was raised in Ontario County, Ontario with mobilization headquarters at Uxbridge under the authority of G.O. 151 December 22nd, 1915. The Battalion sailed July 23rd, 1916 with a strength of thirty-six officers and nine hundred and forty-three other ranks under the command of Lieutenant-Colonel S. Sharpe. The Battalion served in France and Belgium replacing the 60th Battalion on February 11th, 1917 with the 9th Infantry Brigade, 3rd Canadian Division. It was disbanded September 15th, 1920.

BADGE NUMBER: 116

CANADA OVERSEAS BATTALION/116

AUTHORIZED JANUARY 18, 1916

Makers: Birks, Caron, Ellis/Ryrie, F. S. & Firmin, Tiptaft
Fasteners: Lugs
Composition:
Other Ranks: Pickled copper; Browning copper; Blackened copper
Officers:
   A: Pickled copper with white metal overlay on design
   B: Browning copper with white metal circle insert with "116"
   C: Browning copper with white metal overlay on design
Ref.: Babin, Meek, Stewart, Cox

Note: Three makers of this cap badge exist.
1. Three large jewels in crown band; Closed "6" in "116"; Ellis/Ryrie
2. Five large jewels in crown band; Open "6" in "116"; Fermin *(Illustrated)*
3. Five large jewels in crown band; Closed "6" in "116"; Tiptaft

Badge No.	Insignia	Rank	Description	Extremely Fine
116-2	Cap	ORs	Pickled copper; Ellis, Ryrie	20.00
116-4		ORs	Browning copper; Firmin	22.00
116-6		ORs	Browning copper, Tiptaft	22.00
116-8		ORs	Blackened copper; Tiptaft	22.00

Badge No.	Insignia	Rank	Description	Extremely Fine
116-21	Cap	Officers	Pickled copper, Wm. overlay on design; Ellis	65.00
116-23		Officers	Browning copper, Wm. circle insert with "116"; Firmin	75.00
116-25		Officers	Browning copper, Wm. overlay on design; Tiptaft	65.00
116-41	Collars	ORs	Pickled copper; Ellis, Ryrie	14.00
116-43		ORs	Browning copper; Firmin	14.00
116-45		ORs	Browning copper; Tiptaft	14.00
116-47		ORs	Blackened copper; Tiptaft	14.00
116-61		Officers	Pickled copper, Wm. overlay on design; Ellis	35.00
116-63		Officers	Browning copper, Wm. circle insert with "116"; Firmin	45.00
116-65		Officers	Browning copper, Wm. overlay on design; Tiptaft	35.00
		"C" Over Numbers		
116-81	Collars	ORs	"C" bar "116", Large C; Tiptaft	25.00
116-91	Shoulders	ORs	Numeral: "116"; Birks	18.00
116-93		ORs	Numeral: "116"; Caron	18.00

117TH INFANTRY BATTALION

"EASTERN TOWNSHIP BATTALION"

The Battalion was raised in Eastern Quebec, with mobilization headquarters at Sherbrooke under the authority of G.O. 151 December 22nd, 1915. The Battalion sailed August 14th, 1916 under the command of Lieutenant-Colonel L. J. Gilbert with a strength of thirty-six officers and nine hundred and forty-three other ranks. In England the Battalion was absorbed into the 23rd Reserve Battalion. It was disbanded September 15th, 1920.

BADGE NUMBER: 117

EASTERN TOWNSHIPS/117/CANADA/
OVERSEAS BATTALION/C.E.F.

Makers: Birks, Hemsley, Tiptaft
Fasteners: Lugs
Composition:
Other Ranks: Pickled copper or brass;
Officers: Pickled copper
    A: White metal overlay on "117"
    B: White metal overlay on design
Ref.: Babin, Meek, Stewart, Cox

Note: Two makers of this cap badge exist.
1. Pointed leaves; Wide numbers; Hemsley *(Illustrated)*
2. Blunt leaves; Narrow numbers; Tiptaft

Badge No.	Insignia	Rank	Description	Extremely Fine
117-2	Cap	ORs	Pickled copper; Hemsley	18.00
117-4		ORs	Pickled copper; Tiptaft	18.00
117-6		ORs	Pickled brass; Hemsley	20.00
117-8		ORs	Pickled brass; Tiptaft	20.00
117-21		Officers	Pickled copper, Wm. overlay on "117"; Tiptaft	90.00
117-23		Officers	Pickled copper, Wm. overlay on design; Hemsley	90.00
117-41	Collars	ORs	Pickled copper; Hemsley	14.00
117-43		ORs	Pickled copper; Tiptaft	14.00
117-45		ORs	Pickled brass; Hemsley	14.00
117-47		ORs	Pickled brass; Tiptaft	14.00
117-61		Officers	Pickled copper, Wm. overlay on "117"; Tiptaft	30.00
117-63		Officers	Pickled copper, Wm. overlay on design; Hemsley	30.00
117-91	Shoulders	ORs	Numeral: "117"; Birks	14.00
117-93		ORs	Title: "CAN 117 ADA"	25.00

118TH INFANTRY BATTALION

"NORTH WATERLOO OVERSEAS BATTALION"

The Battalion was raised in Northern Waterloo County, Ontario with mobilization headquarters at Kitchener under the authority of G.O. 151 December 22nd, 1915. The Battalion sailed January 26th, 1917 under the command of Lieutenant-Colonel W. M. O. Lochead with a strength of fifteen officers and two hundred and thirty-one other ranks. In England the Battalion was absorbed into the 25th Reserve Battalion. It was disbanded September 15th, 1920.

BADGE NUMBER: 118

No. - 118A   **NORTH WATERLOO/118/**
OVERSEAS BATTALION/CANADA

Makers: Caron, Hemsley, Tiptaft
Fasteners: Lugs, Pin
Composition:
Other Ranks: Pickled copper;
Browning copper
Officers: Pickled copper with
white metal overlay
on "118"
Ref.: Babin, Meek, Stewart, Cox

Note: Two makers of this cap badge exist.
1. Legend in small type; Plain ribbons; Hemsley *(Illustrated)*
2. Legend in large type; Framed ribbons; Tiptaft

Badge No.	Insignia	Rank	Description	Extremely Fine
118A-2	Cap	ORs	Pickled copper; Hemsley	30.00
118A-4		ORs	Browning copper; Tiptaft	30.00
118A-21		Officers	Pickled copper, Wm. overlay on "118"; Hemsley	100.00
118A-41	Collars	ORs	Pickled copper; Hemsley	10.00
118A-43		ORs	Browning copper; Tiptaft	10.00
118A-61		Officers	Pickled copper, Wm. overlay on "118"; Hemsley	45.00
118A-91	Shoulders	ORs	Numeral: "118"; Caron	15.00
118A-93		ORs	Title: "118" over "CANADA"	20.00

No. - 118B   OVERSEAS BATTALION/118/CANADA

Makers: Caron
Fasteners: Lugs
Composition:
Other Ranks: Browning copper;
Officers: Browning copper
with white metal
overlay on "118"

Ref.: Cox

Badge No.	Insignia	Rank	Description	Extremely Fine
118B-2	Cap	ORs	Browning copper; Caron	50.00
118B-21		Officers	Browning copper, Wm. overlay on "118"; Caron	100.00
118B-41	Collars	ORs	Browning copper; Caron	22.00
118B-61		Officers	Browning copper, Wm. overlay on "118"; Caron	30.00

No. - 118C   OVERSEAS BATTALION CANADA/118

Photograph
Not Available
At Press Time

Makers: Caron for Eaton's
Fasteners: Lugs
Composition:
Other Ranks: Pickled copper with
white metal overlay
Officers: Gilt on copper with
silver overlay on
centre
Ref.: Not previously listed

Note: Collars not issued

Badge No.	Insignia	Rank	Description	Extremely Fine
118C-2	Cap	ORs	Pickled copper, Wm. overlay on centre	150.00
118C-21		Officers	Gilt on copper, Silver overlay on centre	200.00

119TH INFANTRY BATTALION

"ALGOMA OVERSEAS BATTALION"

The Battalion was raised in the Algoma and Manitoulin areas of Ontario with mobilization headquarters at Sault Ste. Marie under the authority of G.O. 151 December 22nd, 1915. The Battalion sailed August 9th, 1916 under the command of Lieutenant-Colonel T. P. T. Rowland with a strength of thirty-two officers and nine hundred and thirty-five other ranks. In England the Battalion was absorbed into the 8th Reserve Battalion. It was disbanded September 15th, 1920.

BADGE NUMBER: 119

OVERSEAS ALGOMA BATTALION/119/CANADA

AUTHORIZED JUNE 16, 1916

Makers: Caron, Hemsley, Patterson, Tiptaft
Fasteners: Lugs
Composition:
Other Ranks: Pickled copper or brass
Officers: Pickled copper with white metal overlay on design
Ref.: Babin, Meek, Stewart, Cox

Note: Two makers of this cap badge exist.
  1. Small type for all letters with the legend on plain ribbons; Hemsley, Patterson (*Illustrated*)
  2. Large type for all letters with the legend on framed ribbons; Tiptaft

Badge No.	Insignia	Rank	Description	Extremely Fine
119-2	Cap	ORs	Pickled copper; Hemsley, Patterson	24.00
119-4		ORs	Pickled brass; Hemsley, Patterson	20.00
119-6		ORs	PIckled brass; Tiptaft	20.00
119-21		Officers	Pickled copper, Wm. overlay on design; Hemsley, Patterson	85.00
119-41	Collars	ORs	Pickled copper; Hemsley, Patterson	15.00
119-43		ORs	Pickled brass; Hemsley, Patterson	10.00
119-45		ORs	Pickled brass; Tiptaft	10.00
119-61		Officers	Pickled copper, Wm. overlay on design; Hemsley, Patterson	25.00
119-91	Shoulders	ORs	Numeral: "119"; Caron	14.00

120TH INFANTRY BATTALION

"13TH ROYAL REGIMENT/HAMILTON BATTALION"

The Battalion was raised and mobilized in Hamilton, Ontario under the authority of G.O. 151 December 22nd, 1915. The Battalion sailed August 14th, 1916 under the command of Lieutenant-Colonel D. G. Fearman with a strength of thirty-two officers and eight hundred and thirty-eight other ranks. In England the Battalion was absorbed into the 2nd Reserve Battalion. It was disbanded September 15th, 1920.

BADGE NUMBER: 120

No. - 120A   **120/CITY OF HAMILTON/CANADA OVERSEAS**

AUTHORIZED MARCH 4, 1916

Makers: Birks, Lees, Tiptaft, Unknown
Fasteners: Lugs
Composition:
Other Ranks: Pickled brass; Browning copper
Officers:
   A. Gilt on copper
   B. Browning copper with silver overlay on "120" and legend

Ref.: Babin

Note: Three makers of this cap badge exist.
   1. Narrow type for "Canada Overseas"; Pointed leaf design; Unknown *(Illustrated)*
   2. Narrow type for "Canada Overseas"; Blunt leaf design; Lees
   3. Wide type for "Canada Overseas"; Blunt leaf design; Tiptaft

Badge No.	Insignia	Rank	Description	Extremely Fine
120A-2	Cap	ORs	Pickled brass; Unknown	25.00
120A-4		ORs	Browning copper; Lees	20.00
120A-6		ORs	Browning copper; Tiptaft	20.00
120A-21		Officers	Gilt on copper; Lees	50.00
120A-23		Officers	Browning copper, Silver. overlay on "120" and legend; Unknown	45.00
120A-41	Collars	ORs	Pickled brass; Unknown	15.00
120A-43		ORs	Browning copper; Lees	15.00
120A-45		ORs	Browning copper; Tiptaft	15.00
120A-61		Officers	Gilt on copper; Lees	25.00
120A-63		Officers	Browning copper, Silver overlay on "120" and legend; Unknown	30.00
120A-91	Shoulders	ORs	Numeral: "120"; Birks	14.00

No. - 120B   120/CITY OF HAMILTON/OVERSEAS BATTALION

Makers: Unknown
Fasteners: Lugs
Composition:
Other Ranks: Browning copper
Officers: White metal overlay on "120" and legend
Ref.: Not previously listed

Badge No.	Insignia	Rank	Description	Extremely Fine
120B-2	Cap	ORs	Browning copper; Unknown	25.00
120B-21		Officers	Browning copper, Wm. overlay on "120" and legend; Unknown	160.00
120B-41	Collars	ORs	Browning copper; Unknown	10.00
120B-61		Officers	Browning copper, Wm. overlay on "120" and legend; Unknown	50.00

No. - 120C   OVERSEAS BATTALION CANADA/120

Photograph Not Available At Press Time

Makers: Caron for Eaton's
Fasteners: Lugs, Pin
Composition:
Other Ranks: Pickled copper with White metal centre
Officers: Pickled copper with silver centre
Ref.: Not previously listed

Badge No.	Insignia	Rank	Description	Extremely Fine
120C-2	Cap	ORs	Pickled copper, Wm. centre	300.00
120C-21		Officers	Pickled copper, Silver centre	300.00

121ST INFANTRY BATTALION

"WESTERN IRISH"

The Battalion was raised and mobilized in New Westminster under the authority of G.O. 151 December 22nd, 1915. The battalion sailed August 14th, 1916 under the command of Lieutenant-Colonel A. W. McLelan with a strength of thirty-two officers and one thousand and thirty-three other ranks. In England the Battalion was absorbed into the 16th Reserve Battalion. It was disbanded September 15th, 1920.

BADGE NUMBER: 121

121/WESTERN IRISH/CANADA

Makers: Allan, Birks, Unknown
Fasteners: Lugs, Tangs
Composition:
Other Ranks: Browning copper
Pipers: Silver
Officers:
  A: Gilt on copper
  B: Pickled copper/gilt
Ref.: Babin, Meek, Stewart, Cox

Note: Three makers of this cap badge exist but the differences are so minor that distinguishing them is difficult. It is possible that more than one manufacturer used the same dies.

Badge No.	Insignia	Rank	Description	Extremely Fine
121-2	Cap	ORs	Browning copper; Allan	25.00
121-4		Pipers	Silver; Unknown	125.00
121-21		Officers	Gilt on copper; Unknown	38.00
121-23		Officers	Pickled copper, Gilt; Unknown	85.00
121-41	Collars	ORs	Browning copper; Allan	12.00
121-61		Officers	Pickled copper, Gilt; Unknown	25.00
121-91	Shoulders	ORs	Numeral: "121"; Birks	14.00
121-93		ORs	Title: "121ST WESTERN/IRISH/CANADA", Allan	25.00

122ND INFANTRY BATTALION

The Battalion was raised in the Muskoka District of Ontario with mobilization headquarters at Huntsville under the authority of G.O. 151 December 22nd, 1915. The Battalion sailed June 2nd, 1917 under the command of Lieutenant-Colonel D. M. Grant with a strength of twenty-six officers and six hundred and eighty-six other ranks. In England the Battalion was absorbed into the Canadian Forestry Depot. It was disbanded September 15th, 1920.

BAGDE NUMBER: 122

No. - 122A

MUSKOKA/122/
OVERSEAS BATTALION/CANADA

Makers: Birks, Ellis
Fasteners: Lugs
Composition:
Other Ranks: Browning copper
or brass
Officers: Browning copper
Ref.: Babin, Cox

Badge No.	Insignia	Rank	Description	Extremely Fine
122A-2	Cap	ORs	Browning copper; Ellis	120.00
122A-4		ORs	Browning brass; Ellis	45.00
122A-21		Officers	Browning copper; Ellis	100.00
122A-41	Collars	ORs	Browning copper; Ellis	20.00
122A-43		ORs	Browning brass; Ellis	20.00
122A-61		Officers	Browning copper; Ellis	40.00
122A-91	Shoulders	ORs	Numeral: "122"; Birks	14.00

No. - 122B   122/OVERSEAS/CANADA

AUTHORIZED JANUARY 27, 1916

Makers: Unknown 1 & 2
Fasteners: Lugs
Composition:
Other Ranks: Browning copper
Officers: Unknown
Ref.: Babin, Meek, Stewart, Cox

Note: Two makers of this cap badge exist.
1. A stylized pointed leaf design; Plain ribbons; Unknown-1 *(Illustrated)*
2. A standard blunt leaf design; Framed ribbons; Unknown-2

Badge No.	Insignia	Rank	Description	Extremely Fine
122B-2	Cap	ORs	Browning copper, Pointed; Unknown	100.00
122B-4		ORs	Browning copper, Blunt; Unknown	80.00
122B-21		Officers	Unknown	- -
122B-41	Collars	ORs	Browning copper, Pointed; Unknown	20.00
122B-43		ORs	Browning copper, Blunt; Unknown	50.00
122B-61		Officers	Unknown	- -

No. - 122C   OVERSEAS BATTALION CANADA
/122 /DUTY FIRST

Makers: Unknown
Fasteners: Lugs
Composition:
Other Ranks: Browning brass
Officers: Gilt on brass
Ref.: Not previously listed

Note: Collars are not known.

Badge No.	Insignia	Rank	Description	Extremely Fine
122C-2	Cap	ORs	Browning brass; Unknown	185.00
122C-21		Officers	Gilt on brass; Unknown	200.00

No. - 122D

**122/CANADA
INTERIM BADGE**

Photograph
Not Available
At Press Time

Makers: As General List
Fasteners: Lugs
Composition:
 Other Ranks: As General List
 Officers: Unknown
Ref.: Not previously listed

Badge No.	Insignia	Rank	Description	Extremely Fine
122D-2	Cap	ORs	General list, "122" overlay	150.00
122D-21		Officers	Unknown	- -
122D-41	Collars	ORs	Unknown	- -
122D-61		Officers	Unknown	- -

123RD INFANTRY BATTALION

"ROYAL GRENADIER OVERSEAS BATTALION 10TH REGIMENT"

The Battalion was raised and mobilized in Toronto, Ontario under the authority of G.O. 151 December 22nd, 1915. The Battalion sailed August 9th, 1916 under the command of Lieutenant-Colonel W. B. Kingsmill, with a strength of twelve officers and three hundred and sixty-nine other ranks. In England the Battalion was redesignated the 123rd Pioneer Battalion. It was disbanded September 15th, 1920.

BADGE NUMBER: 123

No. - 123A

HONI SOIT QUI MAL Y PENSE
/READY AYE READY
/CANADA OVERSEAS/123
/ROYAL GRENADIERS

Officers

Other Ranks

Makers: Birks, Caron, Ellis
Tiptaft, Unknown
Fasteners: Lugs
Composition:
Other Ranks: Browning copper;
Blackened copper
or brass; Brass;
Gilt on brass
Officers:
A. Gilt on copper
B. Sterling silver
C: Gilt on brass
Ref.: Babin, Meek, Stewart, Cox

Note: Two makers of this cap badge exist
1. The "3" in "123" has blunt serifs, and the ribbons are plain; Ellis *(Illustrated)*
2. The "3" in "123" has pointed serifs and the ribbons are framed; Tiptaft

Badge No.	Insignia	Rank	Description	Extremely Fine
123A-2	Cap	ORs	Browning copper; Ellis	18.00
123A-4		ORs	Blackened copper; Tiptaft	24.00
123A-6		ORs	Blackened brass; Ellis	24.00
123A-21		Officers	Gilt on copper; Unknown	85.00
123A-23		Officers	Sterling Silver; Ellis	100.00

Badge No.	Insignia	Rank	Description	Extremely Fine
123A-41	Collars	ORs	Brass; Ellis, Horizontal	30.00
123A-43		ORs	Brass; Tiptaft, Horizontal	30.00
123A-51		NCO	Gilt on brass; Ellis, Horizontaal	35.00
123A-53		NCO	Gilt on brass; Tiptaft, Horizontal	35.00
123A-61		Officers	Gilt on brass; Ellis, Perpendicular	35.00
123A-63		Officers	Gilt on brass; Tiptaft, Perpendicular	35.00
123A-91	Shoulders	ORs	Numeral: "123"; Caron	14.00
123A-93		ORs	Numeral: "123"; Birks	14.00
123A-95		ORs	Numeral: "123"; Tiptaft	14.00

No. - 123B   0VERSEAS BATTALION CANADA/123

Makers: Caron for Eaton's
Fasteners: Lugs, Pin
Composition:
Other Ranks: Pickled copper
Officers: Pickled copper with white metal overlay on centre
Ref.: Not previously listed

Note: Collars not issued.

Badge No.	Insignia	Rank	Description	Extremely Fine
123B-2	Cap	ORs	Pickled copper	175.00
123B-21		Officers	Pickled copper, Wm. overlay on centre	250.00

124TH INFANTRY BATTALION

"GOVERNOR GENERAL'S BODY GUARD"

The Battalion was raised and mobilized in Toronto, Ontario under the authority of G.O. 151 December 22nd, 1915. The Battalion sailed August 9th, 1916 under the command of Lieutenant-Colonel W. C. V. Chadwick with a strength of thirty-two officers and one thousand and four other ranks. In England the Battalion was redesignated the 124th Pioneer Battalion. It was disbanded September 15th, 1920.

BADGE NUMBER: 124

No. - 124A

G.G.B.G. AND M.H.
CANADA OVERSEAS BN/124

Makers: Birks, Caron, Ellis, Tiptaft
Fasteners: Lugs
Composition:
Other Ranks: Pickled copper;
Blackened copper
or brass
Officers: Gilt on copper
Ref.: Babin, Meek, Stewart, Cox

Note: Two makers of this cap badge exist.
   1. Pointed leaf design with the unicorn having a split tail (two tails); Ellis *(Illustrated)*
   2. Blunt leaf design with the unicorn having a single tail; Tiptaft

Note: The central device of the cap was used to make the collars.

Badge No.	Insignia	Rank	Description	Extremely Fine
124A-2	Cap	ORs	Pickled copper; Ellis	25.00
124A-4		ORs	Blackened copper; Ellis	20.00
124A-6		ORs	Blackened copper; Tiptaft	20.00
124A-8		ORs	Blackened brass; Tiptaft	20.00
124A-21		Officers	Gilt on copper; Ellis	65.00
124A-41	Collars	ORs	Pickled copper; Ellis	16.00
124A-43		ORs	Blackened copper; Ellis	16.00
124A-45		ORs	Blackened brass; Tiptaft	12.00
124A-61		Officers	Gilt on copper; Ellis	35.00
124A-91	Shoulders	ORs	Numeral: "124"; Caron	14.00
124A-93		ORs	Numeral: "124"; Birks	14.00
124A-95		ORs	Numeral: "124"; Tiptaft	14.00

No. - 124B   **OVERSEAS BATTALION CANADA/124**

Makers: Caron for Eaton's
Fasteners: Lugs, Pin
Composition:
Other Ranks: Pickled Copper
Officers: White metal overlay
on pickled copper
Ref.: Not previously listed

Note: Collars are not known.

Badge No.	Insignia	Rank	Description	Extremely Fine
124B-2	Cap	ORs	Pickled copper; Caron	200.00
124B-21		Officers	Pickled copper, Wm. overlay on centre; Caron	250.00

125TH INFANTRY BATTALION

The Battalion was raised in Brant County, Ontario with mobilization headquarters at Brantford, Ontario under the authority of G.O. 151 December 22nd, 1915. The Battalion sailed August 9th, 1916 under the command of Lieutenant-Colonel M. E. B. Cutcliffe with a strength of thirty-two officers and nine hundred and seventy-four other ranks. In England the Battalion was absorbed into the 8th Reserve Battalion. It was disbanded September 15th, 1920.

BADGE NUMBER: 125

FOR KING AND COUNTRY/125/
CANADA OVERSEAS

AUTHORIZED FEBRUARY 29, 1916

Makers: Birks, Caron, Hemsley, Inglis, Tiptaft
Fasteners: Lugs
Composition:
Other Ranks: Pickled brass
 Browning copper
Officers: Unknown
Ref.: Babin, Meek, Stewart, Cox

Note: Three makers of this cap badge exist.
1. Pointed leaf design with plain ribbons and five jewels in the band of the crown; Hemsley
2. Pointed leaf design with framed ribbons and thirteen jewels in band of crown; Inglis *(Illustrated)*
3. Blunt leaf design with framed ribbons and thirteen jewels in crown; Tiptaft.

Badge No.	Insignia	Rank	Description	Extremely Fine
125-2	Cap	ORs	Pickled brass; Hemsley	22.00
125-4		ORs	Browning copper; Inglis	18.00
125-6		ORs	Browning copper; Tiptaft	18.00
125-21		Officers	Unknown	- -
125-41	Collars	ORs	Pickled brass; Hemsley	15.00
125-43		ORs	Browning copper; Inglis	10.00
125-45		ORs	Browning copper; Tiptaft	10.00
125-61		Officers	Unknown	- -
125-91	Shoulders	ORs	Numeral: "125"; Caron	14.00
125-93		ORs	Numeral: "125"; Birks	14.00
125-95		ORs	Title: "125"/ "CANADA"; Tiptaft	18.00

126TH INFANTRY BATTALION

"PEEL BATTALION"

The Battalion was raised in the County of Peel, Ontario with mobilization headquarters at Toronto, Ontario under the authority of G.O. 151 December 22nd, 1915. The Battalion sailed August 14th, 1916 under the command of Lieutenant-Colonel F. J. Hamilton with a strength of thirty-two officers and eight hundred and twenty-two other ranks. In England the Battalion was broken up and absorbed into the 109th and 116th Infantry Battalions and the 8th Reserve Battalion. It was disbanded September 15th, 1920.

BADGE NUMBER: 126

PEEL/CANADA OVERSEAS/126

AUTHORIZED JANUARY 5, 1916

Makers: Caron, Ellis
Fasteners: Lugs
Composition:
Other Ranks: Pickled copper or brass; Browning copper; Blackened copper
Officers: Gilt on copper
Ref.: Babin, Meek, Stewart, Cox

Badge No.	Insignia	Rank	Description	Extremely Fine
126A-2	Cap	ORs	Pickled copper; Ellis	25.00
126A-4		ORs	Pickled brass; Ellis	25.00
126A-6		ORs	Browning copper; Ellis	25.00
126A-8		ORs	Blackened copper; Ellis	25.00
126A-21		Officers	Gilt on copper; Ellis	75.00
126A-41	Collars	ORs	PIckled copper; Ellis	20.00
126A-43		ORs	Pickled brass; Ellis	20.00
126A-45		ORs	Browning copper; Ellis	20.00
126A-47		ORs	Blackened copper; Ellis	20.00
126A-61		Officers	Gilt on copper; Ellis	40.00
126A-91	Shoulders	ORs	Numeral: "126"; Caron	14.00

No. - 126B   **OVERSEAS BATTALION CANADA/126**

Makers: Caron for Eaton's
Fasteners: Lugs, Pin
Composition:
Other Ranks: Pickled brass
Officers: Pickled copper
with white metal
overlay on design
Ref.: Not previously listed

Note: Collars are not known.

Badge No.	Insignia	Rank	Description	Extremely Fine
126B-2	Cap	ORs	Pickled brass; Caron	360.00
126B-21		Officers	Pickled copper, Wm. overlay in centre design; Caron	275.00

127TH INFANTRY BATTALION

"12TH YORK RANGERS"

The Battalion was raised in the County of York, Ontario with mobilization headquarters at Toronto, under the authority of G.O. 151 December 22nd, 1915. The Battalion sailed August 24, 1916 under the command of Lieutenant-Colonel F. F. Clarke with a strength of thirty-two officers and nine hundred and seventy-two other ranks. On November 8th, 1916 the Battalion was redesignated the 2nd Battalion, Canadian Railway Troops and served in France in this capacity. It was disbanded September 15th, 1920.

BADGE NUMBER: 127

No. - 127A   12TH REGT YORK RANGERS CELER ET AUDAY/ CANADA 127 OVERSEAS

AUTHORIZED JANUARY 17, 1916

Makers: Birks, Caron, Ellis, Tiptaft
Fasteners: Lugs
Composition:
Other Ranks: Pickled copper; Browning copper
Officers: Pickled copper; Browning copper White metal overlay on "127"
Ref.: Babin, Meek, Stewart, Cox

Note: Three makers of this cap badge exist.
1. Pointed leaf design with plain ribbons and a lion with "ears"; Ellis *(Illustrated)*
2. Blunt leaf design with framed ribbons and a lion without "ears"; Tiptaft
3. Blunt leaf design with plain ribbons and a lion with "ears"; Birks

Badge No.	Insignia	Rank	Description	Extremely Fine
127A-2	Cap	ORs	PIckled copper; Ellis	35.00
127A-4		ORs	Browning copper; Ellis	25.00
127A-6		ORs	Browning copper; Tiptaft	25.00
127A-8		ORs	Browning copper; Birks	25.00
127A-21		Officers	Pickled copper, Silver overlay on "127"; Ellis	70.00
127A-23		Officers	Browning copper, Silver overlay on "127"; Tiptaft	70.00
127A-25		Officers	Browning copper, Silver overlay on "127"; Birks	240.00

Badge No.	Insignia	Rank	Description	Extremely Fine
127A-41	Collars	ORs	Pickled copper; Ellis	16.00
127A-43		ORs	Browning copper; Ellis	16.00
127A-45		ORs	Browning copper; Tiptaft	16.00
127A-47		ORs	Browning copper; Birks	16.00
127A-61		Officers	Pickled copper, Silver overlay on "127"; Ellis	20.00
127A-63		Officers	Browning copper, Silver overlay on "127"; Tiptaft	20.00
127A-65		Officers	Browning copper, Silver overlay on "127"; Birks	20.00
127A-91	Shoulders	ORs	Numeral: "127"; Caron	14.00
127A-93		ORs	Numeral: "127"; Birks	14.00

No. - 127B   **OVERSEAS BATTALION CANADA/127**

Makers: Caron for Eaton's
Fasteners: Lugs
Composition:
Other Ranks: Pickled copper
Officers: Pickled copper with white metal overlay on centre
Ref.: Not previously listed

Note: Collars are not known.

Badge No.	Insignia	Rank	Description	Extremely Fine
127B-2	Cap	ORs	Pickled copper; Caron	175.00
127B-21		Officers	Pickled copper, Wm. overlay on centre; Caron	275.00

128TH INFANTRY BATTALION

The Battalion was raised and mobilized in Moosejaw, Saskatchewan under the authority of G.O. 151 December 22nd, 1915. The Battalion sailed August 15th, 1916 under the command of Lieutenant-Colonel F. Pawlett with a strength of thirty-two officers and nine hundred and eighty-eight other ranks. In England the Battalion was broken up and absorbed into the 15th and 19th Reserve Battalions. It was disbanded September 15th, 1920.

BADGE NUMBER: 128

OVERSEAS 128 BATTALION/
MOOSE JAW/CANADA

Makers: Caron,Hemsley, Inglis, Tiptaft
Fasteners: Lugs
Composition:
Other Ranks: Pickled copper or brass; Browning copper
Officers:
    A: Pickled copper;
    B: Silverplate on copper
Ref.: Babin, Meek, Stewart, Cox

Note: Two makers of this cap badge exist
    1. The wreath of maple leaves is sharp with plain ribbons; Hemsley, Inglis
    (Illustrated)
    2. The wreath of maple leaves is fuzzy with framed ribbons; Tiptaft.

Badge No.	Insignia	Rank	Description	Extremely Fine
128-2	Cap	ORs	Pickled copper; Hemsley, Inglis	25.00
128-4		ORs	Pickled brass; Hemsley, Inglis	25.00
128-6		ORs	Browning copper; Hemsley, Inglis	25.00
128-8		ORs	Browning copper; Tiptaft	25.00
128-21		Officers	Pickled copper; Hemsley, Inglis	25.00
128-23		Officers	Silverplate on copper; Unknown	25.00
128-41	Collars	ORs	Pickled copper; Hemsley, Inglis	15.00
128-43		ORs	Pickled brass; Hemsley, Inglis	15.00
128-45		ORs	Browning copper, Hemsley, Inglis	15.00
128-47		ORs	Browning copper; Tiptaft	15.00
128-91	Shoulders	ORs	Numeral: "128"; Caron	16.00
128-93		ORs	Title: CANADA/128/MOOSE JAW'S; Unknown	25.00

129TH INFANTRY BATTALION

"WENTWORTH BATTALION"

The Battalion was raised in the County of Wentworth, Ontario with mobilization headquarters at Dundas, Ontario under the authority of G.O. 151 December 22nd, 1915. The Battalion sailed August 24th, 1916 under the command of Lieutenant-Colonel W. E. S. Knowles with a strength of thirty-two officers and eight hundred and seven other ranks. In England the Battalion was broken up and absorbed into the 123rd and 124th Infantry Battalions and the 12th Reserve Battalion.

BADGE NUMBER: 129

129/CANADA OVERSEAS/WENTWORTH

AUTHORIZED MAY 15, 1916

Makers: Caron, Hemsley, Tiptaft
Fasteners: Lugs
Composition:
Other Ranks: Pickled copper or brass; Browning copper
Officers: Pickled copper White metal overlay on design Silver plate on copper
Ref.: Babin, Meek, Stewart, Cox

Note: Two makers of this cap badge exist.
1. The "129" is voided both top and bottom with all ribbons plain; Hemsley *(Illustrated)*
2. The "129" is voided only on top with all ribbons framed; Tiptaft.

Badge No.	Insignia	Rank	Description	Extremely Fine
129-2	Cap	ORs	Pickled copper; Hemsley	28.00
129-4		ORs	Pickled brass; Hemsley	28.00
129-6		ORs	Browning copper; Hemsley	35.00
129-8		ORs	Browning copper; Tiptaft	35.00
129-21		Officers	Pickled copper, Silver overlay on design; Hemsley	100.00
129-23		Officers	Silverplate on copper; Unknown	90.00
129-41	Collars	ORs	Pickled copper; Hemsley	16.00
129-43		ORs	Browning copper; Hemsley	16.00
129-45		ORs	Browning copper; Tiptaft	16.00
129-61		Officers	Pickled copper, Silver overlay on design; Hemsley	30.00
129-91	Shoulders	ORs	Numeral: "129"; Caron	14.00

130TH INFANTRY BATTALION

"LANARK AND RENFREW BATTALION"

The Battalion was raised in the Counties of Lanark and Renfrew with mobilization headquarters at Perth, Ontario under the authority of G.O. 151 December 22nd, 1915. The Battalion sailed September 27th, 1916 under the command of Lieutenant-Colonel J. F. de Hertel with a strength of twenty-five officers and five hundred and seventy-three other ranks. In England the Battalion was absorbed into the 12th Reserve Battalion. It was disbanded September 15th, 1920.

BADGE NUMBER: 130

LANARK & RENFREW OVERSEAS BATTALION
/130/FAC ET SPERA/CANADA

Makers: Caron, Hemsley, Tiptaft
Fasteners: Lugs
Composition:
Other Ranks: Pickled copper or brass; Browning copper
Officers: Pickled copper with white metal overlay on design
Ref.: Babin, Meek, Stewart, Cox

Note: Two makers of this cap badge exist. This badge was issued with both a void or solid centre.
1. Detailed maple leaves on surrounding wreath with plain ribbons; Hemsley *(Illustrated)*
2. Fuzzy maple leaves on surrounding wreath with framed ribbons; Tiptaft

Badge No.	Insignia	Rank	Description	Extremely Fine
130-2	Cap	ORs	Pickled copper, Void; Hemsley	18.00
130-4		ORs	Pickled brass, Solid; Hemsley	30.00
130-6		ORs	Browning copper, Void; Tiptaft	20.00
130-21		Officers	Pickled copper, Wm. overlay on design, Void; Hemsley	85.00
130-23		Officers	Pickled copper, Wm. overlay on design, Solid; Hemsley	120.00
130-41	Collars	ORs	Pickled copper, Void; Hemsley	20.00
130-43		ORs	Pickled brass, Solid; Hemsley	20.00
130-45		ORs	Browning copper, Void; Tiptaft	20.00
130-61		Officers	Pickled copper, Wm. overlay on design, Void; Hemsley	25.00
130-63		Officers	Pickled copper, Wm. overlay on design, Solid; Hemsley	35.00
130-91	Shoulders	ORs	Numeral: "130"; Caron	15.00

131ST INFANTRY BATTALION

"WESTMINSTER BATTALION"

The Battalion was raised and mobilized in New Westminster, British Columbia under the authority of G.O. 151 December 22nd, 1915. The Battalion sailed November 1st, 1916 under the command of Lieutenant-Colonel J. D. Taylor with a strength of thirty-two officers and nine hundred and fifty-four other ranks. In England the Battalion was absorbed into the 30th Infantry Battalion. It was disbanded September 15th, 1920.

BADGE NUMBER: 131

WESTMINSTER/131/CANADA

Makers: Allan, Birks
Fasteners: Tangs, Pin
Composition:
Other Ranks: Browning copper
Officers:
     A: Browning copper
     B: Gilt on copper
     C: Sterling silver
Ref.: Babin, Meek, Stewart, Cox

Note: At least three makers of this cap badge exist but they are difficult to identify.

Badge No.	Insignia	Rank	Description	Extremely Fine
131-2	Cap	ORs	Browning copper, Tangs; Allan	22.00
131-21		Officers	Browning copper, Pin; Allan	25.00
131-23		Officers	Gilt on copper, Pin; Allan	60.00
131-25		Officers	Sterling silver, Pin; Allan	75.00
131-41	Collars	ORs	Browning copper, Tangs; Allan	15.00
131-61		Officers	Browning copper, Pin; Allan	15.00
131-63		Officers	Gilt on copper, Pin; Allan	30.00
131-91	Shoulders	ORs	Numeral: "131"; Birks	15.00
131-93		ORs	Title: "131ST WESTMINSTER/CANADA"; Allan	25.00

132ND INFANTRY BATTALION

"NORTH SHORE BATTALION"

The Battalion was raised in Northern New Brunswick with mobilization headquarters at Chatham under the authority of G.O. 151 December 22nd, 1915. The Battalion sailed October 26th, 1916 under the command of Lieutenant-Colonel G. W. Mersereau with a strength of thirty-two officers and eight hundred and nine other ranks. In England the Battalion was absorbed into the 13th Reserve Battalion. It was disbanded September 15th, 1920.

BADGE NUMBER: 132

OVERSEAS/NORTH SHORE BATTALION
NEW BRUNSWICK/132/CANADA

Makers: Birks, Hemsley, Inglis, Tiptaft
Fasteners: Lugs
Composition:
Other Ranks: Pickled copper or brass; Browning copper
Officers: Pickled copper with white metal overlay on design
Ref.: Babin, Meek, Stewart, Cox

Note: Two makers of this cap badge exist. The badge was issued with both a void and a solid field.
1. Pointed leaf design with plain ribbons; Hemsley, Inglis *(Illustrated)*
2. Blunt leaf design with framed ribbon; Tiptaft

Badge No.	Insignia	Rank	Description	Extremely Fine
132-2	Cap	ORs	Pickled copper, Void; Hemsley, Inglis	22.00
132-4		ORs	Pickled copper, Solid; Hemsley, Inglis	18.00
132-6		ORs	Pickled brass, Solid; Hemsley, Inglis	35.00
132-8		ORs	Browning copper, Solid; Tiptaft	20.00
132-21		Officers	Pickled copper, Wm. overlay on design, Void; Hemsley, Inglis	60.00
132-23		Officers	Pickled copper, Wm. overlay on design, Solid; Hemsley, Inglis	60.00
132-41	Collars	ORs	Pickled copper, Void; Hemsley, Inglis	15.00
132-43		ORs	Pickled copper, Solid; Hemsley, Inglis	10.00
132-45		ORs	Browning copper; Tiptaft	10.00
132-61		Officers	Pickled copper, Wm. overlay on design, Void; Hemsley, Inglis	30.00
132-63		Officers	Pickled copper, Wm. overlay on design, Solid; Hemsley, Inglis	30.00
132-91	Shoulders	ORs	Numeral: "132"; Birks	15.00
132-93		ORs	Title: "CAN 132 ADA"	25.00

133RD INFANTRY BATTALION

"NORFOLK'S OWN"

The Battalion was raised in Norfolk County, Ontario with mobilization headquarters at Simcoe under the authority of G.O. 151 December 22nd, 1915. The Battalion sailed November 1st, 1916 under the command of Lieutenant-Colonel A. C. Pratt with a strength of twenty-one officers and six hundred and sixty-five other ranks. In England the Battalion was absorbed into the 23rd Reserve Battalion. It was disbanded September 15th, 1920.

BADGE NUMBER: 133

NORFOLK'S OWN/133/
OVERSEAS BATTALION/CANADA

AUTHORIZED MARCH 1, 1916

Makers: Birks, Caron, Hemsley, Tiptaft, Unknown
Fasteners: Lugs
Composition:
Other Ranks: Pickled copper or brass; Browning copper
Officers: Pickled copper with white metal overlay on design
Ref.: Babin, Meek, Stewart, Cox

Note: Three makers of this cap badge exist.
1. Pointed leaf design with small type and plain ribbons; Hemsley *(Illustrated)*
2. Blunt leaf design with large type and framed ribbons; Tiptaft.
3. Blunt leaf with framed ribbon and small type in lettering.

Badge No.	Insignia	Rank	Description	Extremely Fine
133-2	Cap	ORs	Pickled copper; Hemsley	25.00
133-4		ORs	Pickled copper; Unknown	25.00
133-6		ORs	Pickled brass; Hemsley	20.00
133-8		ORs	Browning copper; Tiptaft	25.00
133-21		Officers	Pickled copper, Wm. overlay on design; Hemsley	75.00
133-41	Collars	ORs	Pickled copper; Hemsley	15.00
133-43		ORs	Browning copper; Tiptaft	15.00
133-61		Officers	Pickled copper, Wm. overlay on design; Hemsley	25.00
133-91	Shoulders	ORs	Numeral: "133"; Caron	14.00
133-93		ORs	Numeral: "133"; Birks	14.00
133-95		ORs	Numeral: "133"; Unknown	14.00

134TH INFANTRY BATTALION

"48TH HIGHLANDERS"

The Battalion was raised and mobilized in Toronto, Ontario under the authority of G.O. 151 December 22nd, 1915. The battalion sailed August 9th, 1916 under the command of Lieutenant-Colonel A. A. Miller with a strength of thirty-two officers and one thousand and seventy-eight other ranks. In England the Battalion was absorbed into the 12th Reserve Battalion. It was disbanded September 15th, 1920.

BADGE NUMBER: 134

No. - 134A   48TH HIGHLANDERS/DILEAS CU BRATH /134/OVERSEAS/CANADA

AUTHORIZED JANUARY 17, 1916

Makers: Caron, Ellis, Tiptaft, Unknown
Fasteners: Lugs
Composition:
Other Ranks: Browning copper
Pipers: Silverplate on copper
Officers: Silverplate on copper
Ref.: Babin, Meek, Stewart, Cox

Note: Three makers of this cap badge exist.
1. A large buckle with void numbers "134"; Ellis *(Illustrated)*
2. A small buckle with solid numbers "134"; Tiptaft
3. A third variety of badge exists but its details are presently unknown.

Badge No.	Insignia	Rank	Description	Extremely Fine
134A-2	Glengarry	ORs	Browning copper; Ellis	50.00
134A-4		ORs	Browning copper; Tiptaft	45.00
134A-6		Pipers	Silverplate on copper; Ellis	125.00
134A-21		Officers	Silverplate on copper; Ellis	120.00
134A-41	Collars	ORs	Browning copper; Ellis	40.00
134A-43		ORs	Browning copper; Tiptaft	50.00
134A-61		Officers	Silverplate on copper; Ellis	25.00
134A-91	Shoulders	ORs	Numeral: "134"; Caron	15.00
134A-93		ORs	Title: "134" over "CANADA"	20.00

No. - 134B   134/CANADA

INTERIM BADGE

Photograph
Not Available
At Press Time

Makers: Unofficial
Fasteners: Lugs
Composition:
Other Ranks: General list with
"134" overlay
Officers: Unknown
Ref.: Not previously listed

Badge No.	Insignia	Rank	Description	Extremely Fine
134B-2	Cap	ORs	General List, "134" overlay	100.00
134B-21		Officers	Unknown	- -
134B-41	Collars	ORs	Unknown	- -
134B-61		Officers	Unknown	- -

135TH INFANTRY BATTALION

"MIDDLESEX BATTALION"

The Battalion was raised in the County of Middlesex, Ontario with mobilization headquarters at London under the authority of G.O. 151 December 22nd, 1915. The Battalion sailed August 24th, 1916 under the command of Lieutenant-Colonel B. Robson with a strength of thirty-two officers and nine hundred and ten other ranks. In England the Battalion was broken up and absorbed into the 116th, 125th and 134th Infantry Battalions and the 8th Reserve Battalion. It was disbanded September 15th, 1920.

BADGE NUMBER: 135

No. - 135A   **OVERSEAS/MIDDLESEX BATTALION
/CXXXV/C.O.E.F./CANADA**

Makers: Birks, Caron, Ellis, Unknown
Fasteners: Lugs
Compositon:
Other Ranks: Browning copper; or brass
Officers: Browing copper with white metal overlay on "CXXXV" and "CANADA"
Ref.: Babin, Meek, Stewart, Cox

Note: Two makers of this cap badge exist. Only a collar of the second maker has been found.

Badge No.	Insignia	Rank	Description	Extremely Fine
135A-2	Cap	ORs	Browning copper; Ellis	100.00
135A-4		ORs	Browning brass, Unknown	- -
135A-21		Officers	Browning copper, Wm. overlay on "CXXXV" and " CANADA"; Ellis	150.00
135A-41	Collars	ORs	Browning copper; Ellis	60.00
135A-43		ORs	Browning brass; Unknown	40.00
135A-61		Officers	Browning copper, Wm. overlay on "CXXXV" and "CANADA"; Ellis	35.00
135A-91	Shoulders	ORs	Numeral: "135"; Caron	14.00
135A-93		ORs	Numeral: "135"; Birks	14.00

No. - 135B   135/CANADA

INTERIM BADGE

Makers: General List
Fasteners: Lugs
Composition:
 Other Ranks: Numeral "135"
                         overlay on General
                         List
Ref.: Not previously listed

Badge No.	Insignia	Rank	Description	Extremely Fine
135B-2	Cap	ORs	General List, "135" Wm. overlay	50.00
135B-21		Officers	Unknown	- -
135B-41	Collars	ORs	General List, "135" Wm. overlay	25.00
135B-61		Officers	Unknown	- -

136TH INFANTRY BATTALION

The Battalion was raised in the Counties of Durham, Ontario and Pontiac, Quebec with mobilization headquarters at Kingston, Ontario under the authority of G.O. 151, December 22nd, 1915. The Battalion sailed September 27th, 1916 under the command of Lieutenant-Colonel R. W. Smart with a strength of eighteen officers and four hundred and ninety-two other ranks. In England the Battalion was broken up and absorbed into the 39th Infantry Battalion and the 6th Reserve Battalion. It was disbanded September 15th, 1920.

BADGE NUMBER: 136

No. - 136A   **DURHAM OVERSEAS BATTN CANADA /136/SEMPER PARATUS**

Makers: Caron, Hemsley, Inglis, Reynolds, Tiptaft
Fasteners: Lugs, Pin
Composition:
Other Ranks: Pickled brass, Browning copper
Officers: Gilt on brass
Ref.: Babin, Meek, Stewart, Cox

Note: Three makers of this cap badge exist.
    1. Pointed leaf design; Closed "3"; Reynolds *(Illustrated)*
    2. Pointed leaf design; Open "3"; Tiptaft
    3. Pointed leaf design; Hemsley, Inglis. This badge is not recorded below due to details not being available.

Badge No.	Insignia	Rank	Description	Extremely Fine
136A-2	Cap	ORs	Pickled brass; Reynolds	40.00
136A-4		ORs	Pickled brass; Tiptaft	40.00
136A-6		ORs	Browning copper, Reynolds	27.50
136A-21		Officers	Gilt on brass, Pin; Reynolds	50.00
136A-41	Collars	ORs	Pickled brass; Reynolds	15.00
136A-43		ORs	Pickled brass; Tiptaft	15.00
136A-45		ORs	Browning copper; Reynolds	8.00
136A-61		Officers	Gilt on brass, Pin; Reynolds	30.00
136A-91	Shoulders	ORs	Numeral: "136"; Caron	14.00

No. - 136B   136/CANADA

INTERIM BADGE

Makers: As General List
Fasteners: Lugs
Composition:
Other Ranks: Unofficial; "136" overlay on General List
Ref.: Not previously listed

Badge No.	Insignia	Rank	Description	Extremely Fine
136B-2	Cap	ORs	General List, "136" Wm. overlay	240.00
136B-21		Officers	Unknown	- -
136B-41	Collars	ORs	Unknown	- -
136B-61		Officers	Unknown	- -

137TH INFANTRY BATTALION

"DURHAM BATTALION"

The Battalion was raised and mobilized in Calgary, Alberta under the authority of G.O. 151 December 22nd, 1915. The Battalion sailed August 24th, 1916 under the command of Lieutenant-Colonel G. W. Moffit with a strength of thirty-two officers and nine hundred and thirty-two other ranks. In England the Battalion was absorbed into the 21st Reserve Battalion. It was disbanded September 15th, 1920.

BADGE NUMBER: 137

OVERSEAS/137/CALGARY/CANADA

Makers: Birks, Black, Hemsley, Tiptaft
Fasteners: Lugs, Pin
Composition:
Other Ranks: Pickled copper or brass
Officers: Pickled copper with white metal overlay on design
Ref.: Babin, Meek, Stewart, Cox

Note: Two makers of this cap badge exist.
1. Pointed leaf design; Narrow "Canada" ribbon; Black, Hemsley *(Illustrated)*
2. Blunt leaf design; Wide "Canada" ribbon; Tiptaft

Badge No.	Insignia	Rank	Description	Extremely Fine
137-2	Cap	ORs	Pickled copper; Black, Hemsley	27.50
137-4		ORs	Pickled copper; Tiptaft	27.50
137-6		ORs	Pickled brass; Black, Hemsley	30.00
137-21		Officers	Pickled copper, Wm. overlay on Design; Tiptaft	125.00
137-41	Collars	ORs	Pickled brass; Black, Hemsley	15.00
137-43		ORs	Pickled brass; Tiptaft	15.00
137-61		Officers	Pickled copper, Wm. overlay on design; Tiptaft	25.00
137-91	Shoulders	ORs	Numeral: "137" Birks	15.00
137-93		ORs	Title: "CAN 137 ADA"; Black	25.00

138TH INFANTRY BATTALION

"EDMONTON BATTALION"

The Battalion was raised and mobilized in Edmonton, Alberta under the authority of G.O. 151 December 22nd, 1915. The Battalion sailed August 24th, 1916 under the command of Lieutenant-Colonel R. Belcher with a strength of thirty-two officers and eight hundred and seventy other ranks. The Battalion was broken up and absorbed into the 47th, 50th, 128th, 137th and 175th Infantry Battalions. It was disbanded September 15th, 1920.

BADGE NUMBER: 138

No. - 138A   **OVERSEAS BATTALION/138/CANADA /EDMONTON ALBERTA**

Makers: Caron, Jackson, Tiptaft, Unknown
Fasteners: Lugs
Composition:
Other Ranks: Pickled copper or brass; Browning copper; Blackened brass
Officers: Gilt on silver
Ref.: Babin, Meek, Stewart, Cox

Note: Four makers of this cap badge exist.
1. Heavy lines inside crown band; Five jewels on crown arch; Blunt "1"; Jackson (*Illustrated*)
2. No lines inside crown band; Nine jewels on crown arch; Blunt "1"; Unknown. This is a cast badge.
3. Light lines inside crown band; Five jewels on crown arch; Pointed "1"; Tiptaft
4. Light lines inside crown band; Five jewels on crown arch; Blunt "1"; Unknown

Badge No.	Insignia	Rank	Description	Extremely Fine
138A-2	Cap	ORs	Pickled copper; Unknown	20.00
138A-4		ORs	Pickled brass; Jackson	20.00
138A-6		ORs	Pickled brass; Unknown, Cast	20.00
138A-8		ORs	Browning copper; Unknown, Cast	20.00
138A-10		ORs	Blackened brass; Tiptaft	20.00
138A-21		Officers	Gilt on silver; Jackson	35.00
138A-41	Collars	ORs	Pickled copper; Unknown	11.00
138A-43		ORs	Pickled brass; Jackson	11.00
138A-45		ORs	Pickled brass; Unknown	11.00
138A-47		ORs	Browning copper; Unknown	8.00
138A-49		ORs	Blackened brass; Tiptaft	11.00
138A-61		Officers	Gilt on silver; Jackson	20.00
138A-91	Shoulders	ORs	Numeral: "138"; Caron	14.00

No. - 138B   **138/EDMONTON**

Makers: Unknown
Fasteners: Lugs, Pin
Composition:
  Other Ranks: Browning copper
         Officers: Unknown
Ref.: Not previously listed

Badge No.	Insignia	Rank	Description	Extremely Fine
138B-2	Cap	ORs	Browning copper; Unknown	100.00
138B-21		Officers	Unknown	- -
138B-41	Collars	ORs	Browning copper; Unknown	25.00
138B-61		Officers	Unknown	- -

139TH INFANTRY BATTALION

"NORTHUMBERLAND BATTALION"

The Battalion was raised in Northumberland County, Ontario with mobilization headquarters at Cobourg under the authority of G.O. 151 December 22nd, 1915. The Battalion sailed September 27th, 1916 under the command of Lieutenant-Colonel W. H. Floyd with a strength of twenty-one officers and four hundred and ninety-five other ranks. In England the Battalion was broken up and absorbed into the 3rd and 36th Reserve Battalions. It was disbanded September 15th, 1920.

BADGE NUMBER: 139

EXCELSIOR/NORTHUMBERLAND OVERSEAS
BATTALION/139/CANADA

Makers: Birks, Hemsley, Tiptaft
Fasteners: Lugs
Composition:
Other Ranks: Pickled brass; Browning copper
Officers: Browning copper; Superior construction
Ref.: Babin, Meek, Stewart, Cox

Note: Two makers of this cap badge exist.
    1. Pointed ray design; Plain ribbons; Hemsley *(Illustrated)*
    2. Blunt ray design; Framed ribbons; Tiptaft.

Badge No.	Insignia	Rank	Description	Extremely Fine
139-2	Cap	ORs	Pickled brass; Hemsley	25.00
139-4		ORs	Browning copper; Tiptaft	25.00
139-21		Officers	Browning copper; Tiptaft	35.00
139-41	Collars	ORs	Pickled brass; Hemsley	16.00
139-43		ORs	Browning copper; Tiptaft	16.00
139-61		Officers	Browning copper; Tiptaft	20.00
139-91	Shoulders	ORs	Numeral: "139"; Birks	15.00

140TH INFANTRY BATTALION

The Battalion was raised in New Brunswick with mobilization headquarters at Saint John, under the authority of G.O. 151 December 22nd, 1915. The Battalion sailed September 27th, 1916 under the command of Lieutenant-Colonel L. H. Bee with a strength of thirty-three officers and eight hundred and twenty other ranks. In England the Battalion was broken up and absorbed into the R.C.R. and P.O.C.L.I. Depots and the 13th Reserve Battalion. It was disbanded September 15th, 1920.

BADGE NUMBER: 140

PRO IMPERA/OVERSEAS BATTALION/140/CANADA

Makers: Caron, Hemlsey, Tiptaft
Fasteners: Lugs
Composition:
Other Ranks: Pickled brass;
Browning copper
Officers: Pickled copper with
white metal overlay
on design
Ref.: Babin, Meek, Stewart, Cox

Note: Two makers of this cap badge exist
1. A voided crown with tall legend lettering; Hemsley *(Illustrated)*
2. A solid crown with short legend lettering; Tiptaft.

Badge No.	Insignia	Rank	Description	Extremely Fine
140-2	Cap	ORs	Pickled copper; Hemsley	40.00
140-4		ORs	Pickled brass; Hemsley	40.00
140-6		ORs	Browning copper; Hemsley	40.00
140-8		ORs	Browning copper; Tiptaft	40.00
140-21		Officers	Pickled copper, Wm. overlay on design; Hemsley	75.00
140-41	Collars	ORs	Pickled copper; Hemsley	15.00
140-43		ORs	Pickled brass; Hemsley	15.00
140-45		ORs	Browning copper; Hemsley	15.00
140-47		ORs	Browning copper; Tiptaft	15.00
140-61		Officers	Pickled copper, Wm. overlay on design; Hemsley	25.00
140-91	Shoulders	ORs	Numeral: "140"; Caron	14.00
140-93			Title: "140" over "CANADA"	18.00

141ST INFANTRY BATTALION

"BORDER BATTALION"

The Battalion was raised in the Rainy River district of Ontario, with mobilization headquarters at Fort Frances under the authority of G.O. 151 December 22nd 1915. The Battalion sailed April 29th, 1917 under the command of Lieutenant-Colonel D. C. McKenzie with a strength of seventeen officers and four hundred and sixty-six other ranks. In England the Battalion was absorbed into the 18th Reserve Battalion. It was disbanded September 15th, 1920.

BADGE NUMBER: 141

RAINY RIVER DISTRICT/
BORDER BULL MOOSE/CANADA 141 OVERSEAS

Makers: Unknown
Fasteners: Lugs, Pin
Composition:
Other Ranks: Pickled brass;
Browning copper
Officers:
A: Pickled brass;
B: Copper gilt;
C: Sterling silver
Ref.: Babin, Meek, Stewart, Cox

Note: Two makers of this cap badge exist, both are unknown.
1. Wide numbers "141", there is a hyphen between bull and moose. The badge is void. *(Illustrated)*
2. Narrow numbers "141", the badge is void.
The collars are all solid.

Badge No.	Insignia	Rank	Description	Extremely Fine
141-2	Cap	ORs	Pickled brass, Void; Unknown	30.00
141-4		ORs	Browning copper, Void; Unknown	25.00
141-6		ORs	Browning copper, Void; Unknown	25.00
141-21		Officers	Pickled brass, Void; Unknown	30.00
141-23		Officers	Copper gilt, Void; Unknown	40.00
141-25		Officers	Sterling silver; Void; Unknown	150.00
141-41	Collars	ORs	Pickled brass, Solid; Unknown	28.00
141-43		ORs	Browning copper, Solid; Unknown	20.00
141-61		Officers	Pickled brass, Solid; Unknown	30.00
141-63		Officers	Sterling silver, Solid; Unknown	50.00
141-91	Shoulders	ORs	Numeral: "141"; Unknown	14.00

142ND INFANTRY BATTALION

"LONDON'S OWN"

The Battalion was raised and mobilized in London, Ontario under the authority of G.O. 151 December 22nd, 1915. The Battalion sailed November 1st, 1916 under the command of Lieutenant-Colonel C. M. R. Graham with a strength of twenty-six officers and five hundred and seventy-four other ranks. In England the Battalion was absorbed into the 23rd Reserve Battalion. It was disbanded September 15th, 1920.

BADGE NUMBER: 142

No. - 142A

CANADA/OVERSEAS BATTALION /142/LONDON'S OWN

Makers: Birks, Caron, Hemsley
Fasteners: Lugs
Composition:
Other Ranks: Pickled brass
Officers: Pickled brass with white metal overlay on "142"
Ref.: Babin, Meek, Stewart, Cox

Note: Two makers of this cap badge exist.
1. Numeral "142" in thick type; Framed ribbons; Caron *(Illustrated)*
2. Numeral "142" in thin type; Plain ribbons; Hemsley.

Badge No.	Insignia	Rank	Description	Extremely Fine
142A-2	Cap	ORs	Pickled brass; Caron	30.00
142A-4		ORs	Pickled brass; Hemsley	30.00
142A-21		Officers	Pickled brass, Wm. overlay on "142"; Caron	60.00
142A-41	Collars	ORs	Pickled brass; Caron	15.00
142A-43		ORs	Pickled brass; Hemsley	15.00
142A-61		Officers	Pickled brass, Wm. overlay on "142"; Caron	40.00
142A-91	Shoulders	ORs	Numeral: "142"; Caron	14.00
142A-93		ORs	Numeral: "142"; Birks	14.00
142A-95		ORs	Title: "142" over "CANADA"	20.00

No. - 142B   142/CANADA

INTERIM BADGE

Makers: As General List
Fasteners: Lugs
Composition:
Other Ranks: Numeral "142"
overlay on
General list
Officers: Unknown
Ref.: Babin

Badge No.	Insignia	Rank	Description	Extremely Fine
142B-2	Cap	ORs	General List, "142" coppper overlay	290.00
142B-4		ORs	General List, "142", Wm. overlay	200.00
142B-21		Officers	Unknown	- -
142B-41	Collars	ORs	General list, "142", Wm. overlay	20.00
142B-61		Officers	Unknown	- -

143RD INFANTRY BATTALION

"B.C. BANTAMS"

The Battalion was raised in British Columbia, with mobilization headquarters at Victoria, under the authority of G.O. 151 December 22nd, 1915. The Battalion sailed February 17th, 1917 under the command of Lieutenant-Colonel A. B. Powley with a strength of thirty-two officers and eight hundred and eighty-two other ranks. In England the Battalion was broken up and absorbed into the 1st and 4th Reserve Battalions and the Canadian Railway Troops. It was disbanded September 15th, 1920.

BADGE NUMBER: 143

OVERSEAS /MULTUM IN PARVO/
B.C. BANTAMS/143/CANADA

Makers: Birks, Caron, Unknown
Fasteners: Lugs, Tangs, Pin
Composition:
Other Ranks: Pickled copper;
    Blackened copper
NCO: Sterling silver
Officers: Sterling silver
Ref.: Babin, Meek, Stewart, Cox

Badge No.	Insignia	Rank	Description	Extremely Fine
143-2	Cap	ORs	Pickled copper; Unknown	75.00
143-4		ORs	Blackened copper; Unknown	75.00
143-21		Officers	Sterling silver; Unknown	120.00
	Maple Leaf Design			
143-41	Collars	ORs	Pickled copper; Unknown	30.00
143-43		ORs	Blackened copper; Unknown	30.00
	Rooster Design			
143-45	Collars	NCO	Sterling silver, Large; Unknown	25.00
143-61		Officers	Sterling silver, Small; Unknown	20.00
143-91	Shoulders	ORs	Numeral: "143"; Caron	14.00
		ORs	Numeral: "143"; Birks	14.00

144TH INFANTRY BATTALION

"WINNIPEG RIFLES"

The Battalion was raised and mobilized in Winnpeg, Manitoba under the authority of G.O. 151 December 22nd, 1915. The Battalion sailed September 19th, 1916 under the command of Lieutenant-Colonel A. W. Morley with a strength of twenty-nine officers and nine hundred and sixty-two other ranks. In England the Battalion was absorbed into the 18th Reserve Battalion. It was disbanded September 15th, 1920.

BADGE NUMBER: 144

No. - 144A   3/HOSTI ACIE NOMINATI

(CORRECT LEGEND)

Makers: Birks, Dingwall, Ryrie, Tiptaft
Fasteners: Lugs, Tangs
Composition:
Other Ranks: Pickled copper;
Browning copper;
Blackened brass
Officers:
A: Sterling silver
B: Pickled copper with white metal overlay on "3" and legend
Ref.: Babin, Meek, Stewart, Cox

Note: Three makers of this cap badge exist. Another large size badge made in silver or white metal was auctioned by Denby. This is reputed to be a Pipe Major or R.S.M. Badge.
1. Void spear with a flat top cup leaning to the left; Dingwall *(Illustrated)*
2. Solid spear with a flat top cup leaning to the right; Tiptaft
3. Void spear with a round top cup leaning to the left; Birks.

Badge No.	Insignia	Rank	Description	Extremely Fine
144A-2	Cap	ORs	Pickled copper; Birks	40.00
144A-4		ORs	Browning copper; Dingwall	40.00
144A-6		ORs	Blackened brass; Tiptaft	35.00
144A-21		Officers	Sterling silver; Ryrie	150.00
144A-23		Officers	Pickled copper, Wm. overlay on "3" and legend; Birks	65.00
144A-41	Collars	ORs	Picled copper; Birks	10.00
144A-43		ORs	Browning copper; Dingwall	10.00
144A-45		ORs	Blackened brass; Tiptaft	10.00
144A-61		Officers	Pickled copper, Wm. overlay on "3" and legend; Birks	30.00
144A-91	Shoulders	ORs	Numeral: "144"; Birks	16.00

No. - 144B   **3/NOMINATI ACIE HOSTI**

(ERROR LEGEND)

Makers: Tiptaft
Fasteners: Lugs
Composition:
Other Ranks: Blackened brass
Officers: Unknown
Ref.: Babin, Cox

Note: This badge was made by Tiptaft. They also produced a corrected badge which is
listed under 144A. The "Error Legend" has "NOMINATI" as the first word instead
of "HOSTI".

Badge No.	Insignia	Rank	Description	Extremely Fine
144B-2	Cap	ORs	Blackened brass; Tiptaft	100.00
144B-21		Officers	Unknown	- -
144B-41	Collars	ORs	Blackened brass; Tiptaft	10.00
144B-61		Officers	Unknown	- -

145TH INFANTRY BATTALION

The Battalion was raised in the Kent and Westmoreland Counties of New Brunswick with mobilization headquarters at Moncton under the authority of G.O. 151 December 22nd, 1915. The Battalion sailed September 27th, 1916 under the command of Lieutenant-Colonel W. E. Forbes with a strength of nineteen officers and five hundred and twenty-four other ranks. In England the Battalion was absorbed into the 9th Reserve Battalion. It was disbanded September 15th, 1920.

BADGE NUMBER: 145

OVERSEAS BATTALION/145/N.B./CANADA

Makers: Birks, Hemsley, Tiptaft
Fasteners: Lugs
Composition:
Other Ranks: Pickled copper or brass
Officers:
  A: Pickled copper with white metal overlay on design
  B: Browning copper with silver overlay on design
Ref.: Babin, Meek, Stewart, Cox

Note: Two makers of this cap badge exist.
1. Pointed leaf design; Wide, thick numbers; Plain ribbons; Hemsley *(Illustrated)*
2. Blunt leaf design; Narrow, thin numbers; Framed ribbons; Tiptaft.

Badge No.	Insignia	Rank	Description	Extremely Fine
145-2	Cap	ORs	Pickled copper; Hemsley	20.00
145-4		ORs	Pickled brass; Hemsley	22.00
145-6		ORs	Pickled brass; Tiptaft	22.00
145-21		Officers	Pickled copper, Wm. overlay on design; Hemsley	65.00
145-23		Officers	Browning copper, Silver overlay on design; Tiptaft	70.00
145-41	Collars	ORs	Pickled copper; Hemsley	15.00
145-43		ORs	Pickled brass; Hemsley	16.00
145-45		ORs	Pickled brass; Tiptaft	16.00
145-61		Officers	Pickled copper, Wm. overlay on design; Hemsley	25.00
145-63		Officers	Browning copper, Silver overlay on design; Tiptaft	25.00
145-91	Shoulders	ORs	Numeral: "145"; Birks	14.00

146TH INFANTRY BATTALION

The Battalion was raised in South Eastern Ontario with mobilization headquarters at Kingston under the authority of G.O. 151, December 22nd, 1915. The Battalion sailed September 9th, 1916 under the command of Major C. A. Lorne with twenty-six officers and five hundred and eighty-one other ranks. In England the Battalion was absorbed into the 12th Reserve Battalion. It was disbanded September 15th, 1920.

BADGE NUMBER: 146

AUDAX IN AROUIS/OVERSEAS BATTALION /146/CANADA

Makers: Birks, Coates, Hemsley, Kinnear, Tiptaft
Fasteners: Lugs
Composition:
Other Ranks: Pickled copper or brass; Browning copper
Officers:
    A: Sterling silver
    B: Browning copper with white metal overlay on design
Ref.: Babin, Meek, Stewart, Cox

Note: The caps and collars were issued with either a void or solid field. The badge produced by F. W. Coates of Kingston is cast.

Badge No.	Insignia	Rank	Description	Extremely Fine
146-2	Cap	ORs	Pickled copper, Solid; Hemsley, Kinnear	18.00
146-4		ORs	Pickled copper, Void; Hemsley, Kinnear	18.00
146-6		ORs	Pickled brass, Solid; Hemsley, Kinnear	18.00
146-8		ORs	Browning copper, Solid; Tiptaft	20.00
146-10		ORs	Browning copper, Void; Coates	20.00
146-21		Officers	Sterling silver, Void; Hemsley, Kinnear	75.00
146-23		Officers	Browning copper, Wm. overlay on design; Tiptaft	75.00
Maple Leaf Design				
146-41	Collars	ORs	Pickled copper, Solid; Hemsley	25.00
146-43		ORs	Pickled copper, Void; Hemsley	25.00
146-61		Officers	Sterling silver, Void; Hemsley	40.00
146-63		Officers	Browning copper, Solid, Wm. overlay on design; Tiptaft	40.00
Central Overlay Design				
146-65	Collars	Officers	Silver, "146" in gilt	50.00
146-91	Shoulders	ORs	Numeral: "146"; Birks	14.00
146-93		ORs	Numeral: "146"; Tiptaft	14.00

147TH INFANTRY BATTALION

"GREY BATTALION"

The Battalion was raised in Grey County, Ontario with mobilization headquarters at Owen Sound under the authority of G.O. 151 December 22nd, 1915. The Battalion sailed November 14th, 1916 under the command of Lieutenant-Colonel G. F. McFarland with a strength of thirty-two officers and nine hundred and ten other ranks. In England the Battalion was absorbed into the 8th Reserve Battalion. It was disbanded September 15th, 1920.

BADGE NUMBER: 147

No. - 147A   **GREY/OVER 147 SEAS/CANADA**

Makers: Ellis, Hemsley, Tiptaft
Fasteners: Lugs
Composition:
Other Ranks: Pickled copper;
Browning copper
or brass
Officers: Gilt on copper
Ref.: Babin, Cox

Note: Three makers of this cap badge exist.
    1. Small, Pointed leaf design (42 mm); Hemsley
    2. Large, Pointed leaf design (48 mm); Ellis *(Illustrated)*
    3. Large, Blunt leaf design (48 mm); Tiptaft

Badge No.	Insignia	Rank	Description	Extremely Fine
147A-2	Cap	ORs	Pickled copper, Small; Hemsley,	55.00
147A-4		ORs	Browning copper, Large; Ellis	35.00
147A-6		ORs	Browning brass, Large; Tiptaft	35.00
147A-21		Officers	Gilt on copper; Unknown	100.00
147A-41	Collars	ORs	Pickled copper; Hemsley	20.00
147A-43		ORs	Browning brass; Ellis	10.00
147A-45		ORs	Browning brass; Tiptaft	10.00
147A-61		Officers	Unknown	- -
147A-91	Shoulders	ORs	Numeral: "147"; Unknown	14.00
147A-93		ORs	Title: "147/CANADA"; Tiptaft	25.00

No. - 147B   **OVERSEAS BATTALION CANADA/147**

Makers: Caron for Eaton's
Fasteners: Lugs, Pin
Composition:
Other Ranks: Pickled copper with
white metal overlay
on design
Officers: Pickled copper
with silver overlay
on design
Ref.: Not previously listed

Note: Collars not issued

Badge No.	Insignia	Rank	Description	Extremely Fine
147B-2	Cap	ORs	Pickled copper, Wm. overlay on design	250.00
147B-21		Officers	Pickled copper, Silver overlay on design	250.00

148TH INFANTRY BATTALION

The Battalion was raised in the Montreal area of Quebec with mobilization headquarters at Montreal under the authority of G.O. 151 December 22nd, 1915. The Battalion sailed September 27th, 1916 under the command of Lieutenant-Colonel A. A. McGee with a strength of thirty-two officers and nine hundred and fifty-three other ranks. In England the Battalion was absorbed into the 20th Reserve Battalion. It was disbanded September 15th, 1920.

BADGE NUMBER: 148

OVERSEAS CANADA BATTALION/148/
GRAND ESCVNT AVCTA LABORE

Makers: Birks, Hemsley, Tiptaft
Fasteners: Lugs
Composition:
Other Ranks: Pickled brass;
Browning copper;
Brass
Officers:
A: Pickled brass with silver overlay on design
B: Sterling silver
Ref.: Babin, Meek, Stewart, Cox

Note: Three makers of this cap badge exist.
1. No periods in legend; Large pointed "1"; Hemsley (Illustrated)
2. Two periods in legend, Large plain "1"; Birks
3. No periods in legend, Small pointed "1"; Tiptaft.

Badge No.	Insignia	Rank	Description	Extremely Fine
148-2	Cap	ORs	Pickled brass, Solid; Hemsley	27.50
148-4		ORs	Pickled brass, Void; Hemsley	27.50
148-6		ORs	Browning copper, Void; Birks	27.50
148-8		ORs	Brass, Void; Tiptaft	27.50
148-21		Officers	Pickled brass, Silver overlay, Void; Hemsley	350.00
148-23		Officers	Sterling silver, Void; Birks	250.00
148-41	Collars	ORs	Pickled brass, Solid; Hemsley	20.00
148-43		ORs	Pickled brass, Void; Hemsley	20.00
148-45		ORs	Browning copper,Void; Birks	20.00
148-61		Officers	Pickled brass, Silver overlay, Void Hemsley	35.00
148-63		Officers	Sterling silver, Void; Birks	50.00
148-91	Shoulders	ORs	Numeral: "148"; Unknown	15.00
148-93		ORs	Title: "148" over "CANADA" curved up	20.00
148-95		ORs	Title: "148" over "CANADA" curved down	20.00

149TH INFANTRY BATTALION

"LAMBTON BATTALION"

The Battalion was raised in Lambton County, Ontario with mobilization headquarters at Watford, under the authority of G.O. 151 December 22nd, 1915. The Battalion sailed March 28th, 1917 under the command of Lieutenant-Colonel G. G. C. Kelly with a strength of eighteen officers and four hundred and thirty-nine other ranks. In England the Battalion was broken up and absorbed into the 4th and 25th Reserve Battalions. It was disbanded September 15th, 1920.

BADGE NUMBER: 149

No. - 149A OVERSEAS BATTALION/
149/LAMBTONS/CANADA

Makers: Inglis
Fasteners: Lugs
Composition:
Other Ranks: Pickled copper or brass
Officers: Pickled copper with white metal overlay on design
Ref.: Babin, Meek, Stewart, Cox

Badge No.	Insignia	Rank	Description	Extremely Fine
149A-2	Cap	ORs	Pickled copper; Inglis	27.50
149A-4		ORs	PIckled brass; Inglis	50.00
149A-21		Officers	Pickled copper, Wm. overlay on design; Inglis	95.00
149A-41	Collars	ORs	Pickled copper; Inglis	18.00
149A-61		Officers	Pickled copper, Wm. overlay on design; Inglis	40.00
149A-91	Shoulders	ORs	Numeral: "149"; Unknown	14.00

No. - 149B   **OVERSEAS BATTALION CANADA/149**

Makers: Caron for Eaton's
Fasteners: Lugs, Pin
Composition:
Other Ranks: Pickled copper with white metal overlay
Officers: Pickled copper with silver overlay
Ref.: Not previously listed

Note: Collars not issued

Badge No.	Insignia	Rank	Description	Extremely Fine
149B-2	Cap	ORs	Pickled copper, Wm. overlay, Lugs	225.00
149B-21		Officers	Pickled copper, Silver overlay, Pin	225.00

No. - 149C   **149/CANADA**

INTERIM BADGE

Makers: As General List
Fasteners: Lugs
Composition:
Other Ranks: Unofficial, "149" overlay on General List
Ref.: Not previously listed

Badge No.	Insignia	Rank	Description	Extremely Fine
149C-2	Cap	ORs	General List, 149 overlay	125.00
149C-21		Officers	Unknown	- -
149C-41	Collars	ORs	General List, 149 overlay	30.00
149C-61		Officers	Unknown	- -

150TH INFANTRY BATTALION

"150TH CARABINIERS MONT ROYAL"

The Battalion was raised in the Montreal area with mobilization headquarters at Montreal, Quebec under the authority of G.O. 151 December 22nd, 1915. The Battalion sailed September 27th, 1916 under the command of Lieutenant-Colonel H. Barre with a strength of twenty-four officers and five hundred and fifteen other ranks. In England the Battalion was broken up and absorbed into the 13th, 22nd, 24th and 87th Infantry Battalions and the 5th Canadian Mounted Rifles.

BADGE NUMBER: 150

CANADA/150/D'OUTRE-MER/ CARABINIERS MONT-ROYAL

Makers: Hemsley, Tiptaft
Fasteners: Lugs
Composition:
Other Ranks: Pickled copper or brass, Browning copper
Officers: Pickled copper with white metal overlay on design
Ref.: Babin, Meek, Stewart, Cox

Note: Two makers of this cap badge exist.
1. Narrow rifle straps; Plain ribbons; Hemsley *(Illustrated)*
2. Wide rifle straps; Framed ribbons; Tiptaft.

Badge No.	Insignia	Rank	Description	Extremely Fine
150-2	Cap	ORs	Pickled copper, Solid; Hemsley	25.00
150-4		ORs	Pickled copper, Void; Hemsley	100.00
150-6		ORs	Pickled brass, Solid; Hemsley	85.00
150-8		ORs	Browning copper; Tiptaft	30.00
150-21		Officers	Pickled copper, Wm. overlay on design; Hemsley	75.00
150-23		Officers	Pickled copper, Wm. overlay on "150" and "D'outre-mer"; Tiptaft	75.00
150-41	Collars	ORs	Pickled copper; Hemsley	10.00
150-43		ORs	Pickled brass; Hemsley	10.00
150-43		ORs	Browning copper; Tiptaft	10.00
150-61		Officers	Pickled copper, Wm. overlay on design; Hemsley	35.00
150-63		Officers	Pickled copper, Wm. overlay on "150" and "D'outre0mer"; Tiptaft	35.00
150-91	Shoulders	ORs	Numeral: "150"	12.00
150-93		ORs	"150" over "CANADA"	25.00

151ST INFANTRY BATTALION

"151ST CENTRAL ALBERTA BATTALION"

The Battalion was raised in Central Alberta with mobilization headquarters at Camp Sarcee under the authority of G.O. 151 December 22nd, 1915. The Battalion sailed October 4th, 1916 under the command of Lieutenant-Colonel J. W. Arnott with a strength of twenty-nine officers and nine hundred and twenty-five other ranks. In England the Battalion was broken up and absorbed into the 9th, 11th and 21st Reserve Battalions. It was disbanded September 15th, 1920.

BADGE NUMBER: 151

No. - 151A   CENTRAL ALBERTA CANADA/151/OVERSEAS

Makers: Birks, Jackson
Fasteners: Lugs
Composition:
Other Ranks: Pickled copper; Browning copper
Officers: Gilt on copper
Ref: Babin, Cox

Badge No.	Insignia	Rank	Description	Extremely Fine
151A-2	Cap	ORs	Pickled copper; Jackson	40.00
151A-4		ORs	Browning copper; Jackson	40.00
151A-21		Officers	Gilt on copper; Jackson	60.00
151A-41	Collars	ORs	Pickled copper; Jackson	10.00
151A-43		ORs	Browning copper; Jackson	10.00
151A-61		Officers	Gilt on copper; Jackson	25.00
151A-91	Shoulders	ORs	Numeral "151"; Birks	14.00

No. - 151B

CENTRAL ALBERTA BATTALION
/151/OVERSEAS

LEGEND WITHOUT "CANADA"

Makers: Jackson
Fasteners: Lugs, Pin
Composition:
Other Ranks: Browning copper
Officers:
A: Copper gilt
B: Sterling silver
Ref.: Babin, Meek, Stewart, Cox

Badge No.	Insignia	Rank	Description	Extremely Fine
151B-2	Cap	ORs	Browning copper; Jackson	37.50
151B-21		Officers	Gilt on copper; Jackson	60.00
151B-23		Officers	Sterling silver; Jackson	125.00
151B-41	Collars	ORs	Browning copper; Jackson	30.00
151B-61		Officers	Gilt on copper; Jackson	25.00
151B-63		Officers	Sterling silver; Jackson	50.00

No. - 151C　　　　**CENTRAL ALBERTA BATTALION**
/151/OVERSEAS/CANADA

LEGEND WITH "CANADA" BELOW BEAVER

Makers: Hemsley, Tiptaft
Fasteners: Lugs
Composition:
Other Ranks: White metal with browning copper; Pickled copper or brass
　　　　Officers: Unknown
Ref.: Not previously listed

Note: Two makers exist. Collars of both makers and the Tiptaft cap have been identified. The Hemsley cap has not been seen.
1. Plain Canada ribbon with thick type numbers; Hemsley
2. Framed Canada ribbon with thin type numbers; Tiptaft. *(Illustrated)*

Badge No.	Insignia	Rank	Description	Extremely Fine
151C-2	Cap	ORs	Unknown; Hemsley	- -
151C-4		ORs	Wm. 8-pointed star overlaid with collar badge; Tiptaft	Rare
151C-21		Officers	Unknown	- -
151C-41	Collars	ORs	Pickled copper; Hemsley	75.00
151C-43		ORs	Pickled brass; Hemsley	75.00
151C-45		ORs	Browning copper; Tiptaft	75.00
151C-61		Officers	Unknown	- -

No. - 151D　　　　**151/EDMONTON**

Makers: Unknown
Fasteners: Lugs
Composition:
Other Ranks: Browning copper
　　　　Officers: Unknown
Ref.: Not previously listed

Badge No.	Insignia	Rank	Description	Extremely Fine
151D-2	Cap	ORs	Browning copper	500.00
151D-41	Collars	ORs	Browning copper	30.00

152ND INFANTRY BATTALION

"WEYBURN EAST BATTALION"

The Battalion was raised in the Weyburn area with mobilization headquarters at Weyburn, Saskatchewan under the authority of G.O. 151 December 22nd, 1915. The Battalion sailed October 4th, 1916 under the command of Lieutenant-Colonel S. B. Nells with a strength of twenty-nine officers and seven hundred and forty-three other ranks. In England the Battalion was broken up and absorbed into the 15th and 32nd Reserve Battalions. It was disbanded September 15th, 1920.

BADGE NUMBER: 152

WEYBURN 152 ESTEVAN/
OVERSEAS BATTALION/CANADA

Makers: Birks, Roden, Tiptaft
Fasteners: Lugs
Composition:
Other Ranks: Pickled copper;
Browning copper;
Brass
Officers: Sterling silver
Ref.: Babin, Meek, Stewart, Cox

Note: Two makers of this cap badge exist.
1. Plain ribbons with thin type for numbers; Roden *(Illustrated)*
2. Framed ribbons with thick type for numbers; Tiptaft

Badge No.	Insignia	Rank	Description	Extremely Fine
152-2	Cap	ORs	Pickled copper; Roden	125.00
152-4		ORs	Browning copper; Roden	175.00
152-6		ORs	Browning brass; Tiptaft	150.00
152-21		Officers	Sterling silver; Roden	525.00
152-41	Collars	ORs	Pickled copper; Roden	30.00
152-43		ORs	Browning copper; Roden	25.00
152-45		ORs	Browning brass; Tiptaft	25.00
152-61		Officers	Sterling silver; Roden	100.00
152-91	Shoulders	ORs	Numeral: "152"; Birks	14.00

153RD INFANTRY BATTALION

"WELLINGTON BATTALION"

The Battalion was raised in Wellington County with mobilization headquarters at Guelph, Ontario under the authority of G.O. 151 December 22nd, 1915. The Battalion sailed April 29th, 1917 under the command of Lieutenant-Colonel R. T. Pritchard with a strength of seventeen officers and five hundred and eleven other ranks. In England the Battalion was broken up and absorbed into the 4th and 25th Reserve Battalions. It was disbanded September 15th, 1920.

BADGE NUMBER: 153

WELLINGTON/153/VIRTUTIS FORTUKNA COMES/ OVERSEAS/CANADA

Makers: Caron, Ellis
Fasteners: Lugs
Composition:
Other Ranks: Browning copper; Brass
Officers: Browning copper with silver overlay on "153" and "Canada"
Ref.: Babin, Meek, Stewart, Cox

Badge No.	Insignia	Rank	Description	Extremely Fine
153-2	Cap	ORs	Browning copper; Ellis	110.00
153-4		ORs	Browning brass; Ellis	150.00
153-21		Officers	Browning copper, Silver overlay on "153" and "Canada"; Ellis	190.00
153-41	Collars	ORs	Browning brass; Ellis	60.00
153-61		Officers	Browning copper, Silver overlay on "153" and "Canada"; Ellis	60.00
153-91	Shoulders	ORs	Numeral: "153"; Caron	12.00
153-93		ORs	Title: "153" over "CANADA"; Caron	16.00

154TH INFANTRY BATTALION

"STORMONT, DUNDAS AND GLENGARRY HIGHLANDERS"

The Battalion was raised in the Counties of Stormont, Dundas and Glengarry, Ontario with mobilization headquarters at Cornwall, under the authority of G.O. 151 December 22nd, 1915. The Battalion sailed October 25th, 1916 under the command of Lieutenant-Colonel A. G. F. McDonald with a strength of twenty-nine officers and eight hundred and seventy-two other ranks. In England the Battalion was absorbed into the 6th Reserve Battalion. It was disbanded September 15th, 1920.

BADGE NUMBER: 154

OVERSEAS BATTALION/154/
STORMONT DUNDAS/GLENGARRY/CANADA

Makers: Hemsley, Tiptaft
Fasteners: Lugs
Composition:
Other Ranks: Pickled copper or brass
Officers:
    A: Pickled copper with silver overlay on design
    B: Sterling silver
Ref.: Babin, Meek, Stewart, Cox

Note: Two makers of this cap badge exist
  1. Plain ribbons; Hemsley *(Illustrated)*
  2. Framed ribbons; Tiptaft.

Badge No.	Insignia	Rank	Description	Extremely Fine
154-2	Cap	ORs	Pickled copper; Hemsley	45.00
154-4		ORs	Pickled brass; Hemsley	45.00
154-6		ORs	Browning copper; Tiptaft	45.00
154-21		Officers	Pickled copper, Silver overlay on design; Hemsley	45.00
154-23		Officers	Sterling silver; Tiptaft	100.00
154-41	Collars	ORs	Pickled copper; Hemsley	18.00
154-43		ORs	Pickled brass; Hemsley	25.00
154-45		ORs	Browning copper; Tiptaft	25.00
154-61		Officers	Pickled copper, Silver overlay on design; Hemsley	35.00
154-63		Officers	Sterling silver; Tiptaft	35.00
154-91	Shoulders	ORs	Numeral: "154"	14.00

155TH INFANTRY BATTALION

"QUINTE BATTALION"

The Battalion was raised in the Counties of Hastings and Prince Edward, Ontario with mobilization headquarters at Barriefield under the authority of G.O. 151 December 22nd, 1915. The Battalion sailed October 18th, 1916 under the command of Lieutenant-Colonel M. K. Adams with a strength of twenty-nine officers and eight hundred and twenty-six other ranks. In England the Battalion was broken up and absorbed into the 154th Infantry Battalion and the 6th Reserve Battalion. It was disbanded September 15th, 1920.

BADGE NUMBER: 155

No. - 155A **QUINTE/OVERSEAS BATTALION /155/CANADA**

Makers: Birks, Caron, Hemsley, Tiptaft, Unknown
Fasteners: Lugs
Composition:
Other Ranks: Pickled copper or brass; Browning copper
Officers: Pickled copper or brass; Superior construction
Ref.: Babin, Meek, Stewart, Cox

Note: Three makers of this cap badge exist.
1. Three periods in the legend; Plain ribbons; Hemsley *(Illustrated)*
2. Two periods in the legend; Framed ribbons; Tiptaft
3. For the third variety only an ORs collar is known, thus details are not listed.

Badge No.	Insignia	Rank	Description	Extremely Fine
155A-2	Cap	ORs	Pickled copper, Solid; Hemsley	35.00
155A-4		ORs	Pickled brass, Solid; Hemsley	35.00
155A-6		ORs	Pickled copper, Void; Hemsley	25.00
155A-8		ORs	Pickled brass, Void; Hemsley	25.00
155A-10		ORs	Browning copper, Solid; Tiptaft	25.00
155A-21		Officers	Pickled copper, Void; Unknown	40.00
155A-23		Officers	Pickled brass, Void; Unknown	25.00
155A-41	Collars	ORs	Pickled copper, Solid; Hemsley	15.00
155A-43		ORs	Pickled copper, Void; Hemsley	30.00
155A-45		ORs	Browning copper; Tiptaft	30.00
155A-61		Officers	Pickled copper, Void; Unknown	30.00
155A-91	Shoulders	ORs	Numeral: "155"; Caron	16.00
155A-93		ORs	Numeral: "155"; Birks	16.00

No. - 155B   **OVERSEAS BATTALION CANADA/155**

Makers: Caron for Eaton's
Fasteners: Lugs, Pin
Composition:
Other Ranks: Pickled copper
with white metal
overlay
Officers: Pickled copper
with gilt overlay
Ref.: Not previously listed

Note: Collars not issued

Badge No.	Insignia	Rank	Description	Extremely Fine
155B-2	Cap	ORs	Pickled copper, Wm. overlay on centre	150.00
155B-21		Officers	Pickled copper, Gilt overlay on centre	325.00

156TH INFANTRY BATTALION

"156TH LEEDS AND GRENVILLE BATTALION"

The Battalion was raised in Leeds and Grenville Counties of Ontario, with mobilization headquarters at Brockville under the authority of G.O. 151 December 22nd, 1915. The Battalion sailed October 18th, 1916 under the command of Lieutenant-Colonel T. C. D. Bedeil with a strength of twenty-eight officers and seven hundred and seventy-eight other ranks. In England the Battalion was broken up and absorbed into the 2nd, 21st and 38th Infantry Battalions, the P.O.C.O.I., and the 6th Reserve Battalion. It was disbanded September 15th, 1920.

BADGE NUMBER: 156

No. - 156A   **LEEDS & GRENVILLE
OVERSEAS BATTALION/156/CANADA**

Makers: Hemsley, Tiptaft, Unknown
Fasteners: Lugs
Composition:
Other Ranks: Pickled copper or brass; Browning copper; Blackened brass
Officers: Pickled copper with white metal overlay on design
Ref.: Babin, Meek, Stewart, Cox

Note: There are three makers with five different die variations of this badge, the void and solid field dividing the makers.
1. Thick neck beaver; Plain ribbons; Hemsley *(Illustrated)*
2. Thin neck, well designed beaver; Plain ribbons; Void; Unknown
3. Poorly designed rat-like beaver; Framed ribbons; Solid; Tiptaft.

Badge No.	Insignia	Rank	Description	Extremely Fine
156A-2	Cap	ORs	Pickled copper, Void; Hemsley	25.00
156A-4		ORs	Pickled copper, Solid; Hemsley	45.00
156A-6		ORs	Pickled brass, Void; Hemsley	40.00
156A-8		ORs	Pickled brass, Void; Hemsley	40.00
156A-10		ORs	Pickled brass, Void; Unknown	40.00
156A-12		ORs	Browning copper, Void; Unknown	25.00
156A-14		ORs	Blackened brass, Solid; Tiptaft	30.00
156A-21		Officers	Pickled copper, Wm. overlay on design; Hemsley	100.00

Badge No.	Insignia	Rank	Description	Extremely Fine
156A-41	Collars	ORs	Pickled copper, Solid; Hemsley	15.00
156A-43		ORs	Pickled brass, Solid; Hemsley	15.00
156A-45		ORs	Pickled brass, Void; Hemsley	15.00
156A-47		ORs	Browning copper, Void; Unknown	15.00
156A-49		ORs	Blackened brass, Solid; Tiptaft	15.00
156A-61		Officers	Pickled brass, Silver overlay on design; Hemsley	50.00
156A-91	Shoulders	ORs	Numeral: "156"; Unknown	15.00
156A-93		ORs	Title: "156 CANADA"	25.00

No. - 156B   OVERSEAS BATTALION CANADA/156

**Photograph
Not Available
At Press Time**

Makers: Caron for Eaton's
Fasteners: Lugs, Pin
Composition:
Other Ranks: Pickled copper with white metal overlay
Officers:
  A: Pickled copper with gilt overlay
  B: Pickled copper with silver overlay
Ref.: Not previously listed

Badge No.	Insignia	Rank	Description	Extremely Fine
156B-2	Cap	ORs	Pickled copper, Wm. overlay	150.00
156B-21		Officers	Pickled copper, Gilt overlay	200.00
156B-23		Officers	Pickled copper, Silver overlay	200.00

157TH INFANTRY BATTALION

"SIMCOE FORESTERS"

.The Battalion was raised in Simcoe County, Ontario with mobilization headquarters at Barrie, under the authority of G.O. 151 December 22nd, 1915. The Battalion sailed October 18th, 1916 under the command of Lieutenant-Colonel D. H. MacLaren with a strength of thirty-two officers and nine hundred and sixty-six other ranks. In England the Battalion was broken up and absorbed into the 19th, 116th and 125th Infantry Battalions and the 8th Reserve Battalion. It was disbanded September 15th, 1920.

BADGE NUMBER: 157

No. - 157A   OVERSEAS/SIMCOE/FORESTERS/157/CANADA

AUTHORIZED JUNE 7, 1916

Makers: Ellis, Hemsley
Fasteners: Lugs, Pin
Composition:
Other Ranks: Pickled copper or brass; Browning copper
Officers:
    A: Silver overlay on leaf and "157"
    B: As above, but silver overlay now also on "Canada"
Ref.: Babin, Meek, Stewart, Cox

Note: Two makers of this badge exist.
1. Three periods; the maple leaf overlaps the crown; a flat badge; Ellis
2. Four periods; the maple leaf barely touches the crown; a domed badge; Hemsley

Badge No.	Insignia	Rank	Description	Extremely Fine
157A-2	Cap	ORs	Pickled brass, Solid; Hemsley	25.00
157A-4		ORs	Browning copper, Solid; Hemsley	35.00
157A-6		ORs	Browning copper, Void; Ellis	50.00
157A-21		Officers	Pickled copper, Silver overlay on leaf and "157"; Ellis	290.00
157A-23		Officers	Pickled copper, Silver overlay on leaf and "157" and "Canada"; Hemsley	300.00
157A-41	Collars	ORs	Pickled brass, Solid; Hemsley	20.00
157A-43		ORs	Browning copper,Solid; Hemsley	18.00
157A-61		Officers	Pickled copper, Silver overlay on leaf, "157"; Ellis	35.00
157A-63		Officers	Pickled copper, Silver overlay on leaf, "157" and "Canada"; Hemsley	35.00

No. - 157B   **OVERSEAS BATTALION CANADA**
/157/DUTY FIRST

Makers: Birks, Caron, Unknown
Fasteners: Lugs
Composition:
Other Ranks: Browning copper
with white metal
overlay
Officers: Browning brass
with silver overlay
Ref.: Babin, Cox

Note: This badge is of cast construction.

Badge No.	Insignia	Rank	Description	Extremely Fine
157B-2	Cap	ORs	Browning copper, Wm. overlay	385.00
157B-21		Officers	Browning brass, Silver overlay	400.00
157B-91	Shoulders	ORs	Numeral: "157"; Caron	14.00
157B-93		ORs	Numeral: "157"; Birks	14.00
157B-95		Officers	Numeral: "157"; Sterling silver	180.00??

No. - 157C   **157/CANADA**

INTERIM BADGE

Makers: As General List
Fasteners: Lugs
Composition:
Other Ranks: Unofficial, "157"
overlay on General
List
Officers: Unknown
Ref.: Not previously listed

Note: The shoulder numeral and the numeral overlay on the General List are identical.

Badge No.	Insignia	Rank	Description	Extremely Fine
157C-2	Cap	ORs	General List, "157" overlay	100.00
157C-21		Officers	Unknown	- -
157C-41	Collars	ORs	Unknown	- -
157C-61		Officers	Unknown	- -
157C-91	Shoulders	ORs	Numeral: "157"; Unknown	15.00

158TH INFANTRY BATTALION

"DUKE OF CONNAUGHT'S OWN"

The Battalion was raised and mobilized in Vancouver, British Columbia under the authority of G.O. 151 December 22nd, 1915. The Battalion sailed November 14th, 1916 under the command of Lieutenant-Colonel C. Milne with a strength of thirty-one officers and nine hundred and sixty-six other ranks. In England the Battalion was absorbed into the 1st Reserve Battalion. It was disbanded September 15th, 1920.

BADGE NUMBER: 158

THE DUKE OF CONNAUGHT'S OWN/(OVERSEAS) BATTALION/BRITISH COLUMBIA/158/CANADA

Makers: Allan, Birks
Fasteners: Tangs, Pin
Composition:
Other Ranks: Browning copper
Officers: Browning copper; Superior construction
Ref.: Babin, Meek, Stewart, Cox

Badge No.	Insignia	Rank	Description	Extremely Fine
158-2	Cap	ORs	Browning copper; Allan	25.00
158-21		Officers	Browning copper, Pin; Allan	35.00
158-41	Collars	ORs	Browning copper; Allan	12.00
158-61		Officers	Browning copper, Pin; Allan	15.00
158-91	Shoulders	ORs	Numeral: "158"; Birks	14.00
158-93		ORs	Title: "THE DUKE OF CONNAUGHT'S OWN" "CANADA"; Allan	25.00

159TH INFANTRY BATTALION

"1ST ALGONQUIN"

The Battalion was raised in the Nipissing and Sudbury areas of Ontario with mobilization headquarters at Haileybury under the authority of G.O. 151 December 22nd, 1915. The Battalion sailed November 1, 1916 under the command of Lieutenant-Colonel E. F. Armstrong with a strength of thirty-two officers and nine hundred and seventy-two other ranks. In England the Battalion was absorbed into the 8th Reserve Battalion. It was disbanded September 15th, 1920.

BADGE NUMBER: 159

1ST ALGONQUINS 159 OVERSEAS/CANADA

Makers: Birks, Caron, Ellis; Tiptaft
Fasteners: Lugs
Composition:
Other Ranks: Browning copper; Blackened copper
Officers:
  A. Browning copper with silver overlay on "159"
  B. Sterling silver
Ref.: Babin, Meek, Stewart, Cox

Note: Two makers of this cap badge exist.
1. Maple leaves have fine veins and in the number "159" the nine is a closed variety; Ellis *(Illustrated)*
2. Maple leaves have course veins and in the number "159" the nine is an open variety; Tiptaft.

Badge No.	Insignia	Rank	Description	Extremely Fine
159-2	Cap	ORs	Browning copper; Ellis	25.00
159-4		ORs	Blackened copper; Tiptaft	25.00
159-21		Officers	Browning copper, Silver overlay on "159"; Ellis	100.00
159-23		Officers	Sterling silver; Ellis	110.00
159-41	Collars	ORs	Browning copper; Ellis	10.00
159-43		ORs	Blackened copper; Tiptaft	35.00
159-61		Officers	Browning copper, Silver overlay on "159"; Ellis	25.00
159-91	Shoulders	ORs	Numeral: "159"; Caron	14.00
159-93		ORs	Numeral: "159"; Birks	14.00

160TH INFANTRY BATTALION

"BRUCE BATTALION"

The Battalion was raised in Northern Ontario with mobilization headquarters at Walkerton under the authority of G.O. 151 December 22nd, 1915. The Battalion sailed October 17th, 1916 under the command of Lieutenant-Colonel A. Weir with a strength of thirty-one officers and nine hundred and sevety eight other ranks. In England the Battalion was absorbed into the 4th Reserve Battalion. It was disbanded September 15th, 1920.

BADGE NUMBER: 160

BRUCE/CANADA OVERSEAS/160

Makers: Hemsley, Tiptaft, Unknown
Fasteners: Lugs
Composition:
Other Ranks: Pickled brass; Browning copper
Officers:
  A: Pickled brass with silver overlay
  B: Browning copper with silver overlay
  C: Gilt brass with silver overlay
Ref.: Babin, Meek, Stewart, Cox

Note: Two makers of this cap badge exist.
  1. Pointed maple leaf design; Thick numerals; Hemsley *(Illustrated)*
  2. Blunt maple leaf design; Thin numerals; Tiptaft.

Badge No.	Insignia	Rank	Description	Extremely Fine
160-2	Cap	ORs	Pickled brass; Hemsley	100.00
160-4		ORs	Pickled brass; Tiptaft	25.00
160-6		ORs	Browning copper; Hemsley	100.00
160-21		Officers	Pickled brass, Silver overlay; Hemsley	70.00
160-23		Officers	Browning copper, Silver overlay; Hemsley	50.00
160-25		Officers	Gilt brass, Silver overlay; Hemsley	185.00
160-27		Officers	Pickled brass, Silver overlay; Tiptaft	85.00
160-41	Collars	ORs	Pickled brass; Hemsley	8.00
160-43		ORs	Pickled brass; Tiptaft	8.00
160-45		ORs	Browning copper; Hemsley	8.00
160-61		Officers	Pickled brass, Silver overlay; Tiptaft	20.00
160-91	Shoulders	ORs	Numeral: "160"; Unknown	14.00
160-93		ORs	Title: "Bruce"; Unknown	8.00
160-95		ORs	Title: "160 over CANADA"; Unknown	20.00

161ST INFANTRY BATTALION

The Battalion was raised in Huron County, Ontario with mobilization headquarters at London, under the authority of G.O. 151 December 22nd, 1915. The Battalion sailed November 1st, 1916 under the command of Lieutenant-Colonel H. B. Combe with a strength of twenty-eight officers and seven hundred and forty-nine other ranks. In England the Battalion was absorbed into the 4th Reserve Battalion. It was disbanded September 15th, 1920.

BADGE NUMBER: 161

HURON/OVERSEAS 161 BATTALION/CANADA

Makers: Birks, Ellis,
Hemsley, Tiptaft
Fasteners: Lugs
Composition:
Other Ranks: Pickled brass;
Browning copper
Officers: Pickled brass with
white metal overlay
on design
Ref.: Babin, Meek, Stewart, Cox

Note: Two makers of this cap badge exist.
1. Wide type for "CANADA" with plain ribbons; Hemsley *(Illustrated)*
2. Thin type for "CANADA" with framed ribbons; Tiptaft

Badge No.	Insignia	Rank	Description	Extremely Fine
161-2	Cap	ORs	Pickled brass; Hemsley	25.00
161-4		ORs	Browning copper; Tiptaft	20.00
161-21		Officers	PIckled brass, Wm. overlay on design; Hemsley	50.00
161-41	Collars	ORs	Pickled brass; Hemsley	15.00
161-43		ORs	Browning copper; Tiptaft	15.00
161-61		Officers	Pickled brass, Wm. overlay on design; Hemsley	20.00
161-91	Shoulders	ORs	Numeral: "161"; Birks	12.00
161-93		ORs	Numeral: "161"; Ellis	12.00

162ND INFANTRY BATTALION

"PARRY SOUND BATTALION"

The Battalion was raised and mobilized in Parry Sound, Ontario under the authority of G.O. 151 December 22nd, 1915. The Battalion sailed November 1st, 1916 under the command of Lieutenant-Colonel J. Arthurs with a strength of thirty officers and seven hundred and sixty-six other ranks. In England the Battalion was broken up and absorbed into the 3rd and 4th Reserve Battalions. It was disbanded September 15th, 1920.

BADGE NUMBER: 162

PARRY 162 SOUND/CANADA OVERSEAS

AUTHORIZED MARCH 11, 1916

Makers: Birks, Caron, Roden
Fasteners: Lugs
Composition:
  Other Ranks: Browning copper
                or brass
    Officers: Sterling silver
Ref.: Babin, Meek, Stewart, Cox

Badge No.	Insignia	Rank	Description	Extremely Fine
162-2	Cap	ORs	Browning copper; Roden	80.00
162-4		ORs	Browning brass; Roden	150.00
162-21		Officers	Sterling silver; Roden	150.00
162-41	Collars	ORs	Browning copper; Roden	35.00
162-61		Officers	Sterling silver; Roden	45.00
162-91	Shoulders	ORs	Numeral: "162"; Caron	12.00
162-93		ORs	Numeral: "162"; Birks	12.00

163RD INFANTRY BATTALION

"CANADIENS FRANCAIS"

The Battalion was raised in Quebec, with mobilization headquarters at Montreal under the authority of G.O. 151 December 22nd, 1915. On May 24th, 1916 the Battalion was moved to Bermuda for garrison duty. On November 27th, 1916 the Battalion sailed for England under the command of Lieutenant-Colonel H. DesRosiers with a strength of thirty-eight officers and eight hundred and twenty-two other ranks. In England the Battalion was absorbed into the 10th Reserve Battalion. It was disbanded September 15th, 1920.

BADGE NUMBER: 163

CANADIENS-FRANCAIS/QUI S'Y FROTTE S'Y PIQVE /163/D'OUTRE-MER

Makers: Caron, Hemsley; Lamontagne
Fasteners: Lugs, Pin
Composition:
Other Ranks: Pickled copper or brass
Officers: Pickled copper, Gilt copper Silver overlay on design
Ref.: Babin, Meek

Note: There are two makers of this cap badge.
1. Solid crown; Hemsley *(Illustrated)*
2. Void crown; Lamontagne.

Badge No.	Insignia	Rank	Description	Extremely Fine
163-2	Cap	ORs	Pickled copper, Void; Lamontagne	25.00
163-4		ORs	Pickled brass, Solid; Hemsley	27.00
163-21		Officers	Pickled copper, Silver overlay on design; Hemsley	55.00
163-23		Officers	Gilt copper, Pin; Hemsley	100.00
163-41	Collars	ORs	Pickled copper; Lamontagne	12.00
163-43		ORs	Pickled brass; Hemsley	18.00
163-61		Officers	Pickled copper, Silver overlay on design; Hemsley	30.00
163-91	Shoulders	ORs	Numeral: "163"; Caron	14.00
163-93		ORs	Title: "163" over "CANADA" curving upwards	18.00

164TH INFANTRY BATTALION

"HALTON AND DUFFERIN BATTALION"

The Battalion was raised in the Counties of Halton and Dufferin, Ontario with mobilization headquarters at Orangeville under the authority of G.O. 151 December 22nd, 1915. The Battalion sailed April 11th, 1917 under the command of Lieutenant-Colonel P. Domvillle with a strength of twenty-six officers and seven hundred and ten other ranks. In England the Battalion was absorbed into the 8th Reserve Battalion. It was disbanded September 15th, 1920.

BADGE NUMBER: 164

OVERSEAS BATTALION/164/ CANADA/HALTON & DUFFERIN

AUTHORIZED MARCH 29, 1916

Makers: Birks, Caron, Lees, Tiptaft
Fasteners: Lugs, Pin
Composition:
Other Ranks: Browning copper
Officers: Sterling silver
Ref.: Babin, Meek, Stewart, Cox

Note: Two makers of this cap badge exist.
  1. Large beaver; Wide numbers; Lees
  2. Small beaver; Narrow numbers; Tiptaft. *(Illustrated)*

Badge No.	Insignia	Rank	Description	Extremely Fine
164-2	Cap	ORs	Browning copper, Large Beaver; Lees	30.00
164-4		ORs	Browning copper, Small Beaver; Tiptaft	28.00
164-21		Officers	Sterling silver; Lees	60.00
Matching Cap Design				
164-41	Collars	ORs	Browning copper; Lees	15.00
164-43		ORs	Browning copper; Tiptaft	14.00
164-61		Officers	Sterling silver; Lees	30.00
Maple Leaf Design				
164-45	Collars	ORs	Browning copper; Unknown	50.00
164-91	Shoulders	ORs	Numeral: "164"; Caron	12.00
164-93		ORs	Numeral: "164"; Birks	12.00

165TH INFANTRY BATTALION

"165TH FRENCH ACADIAN BATTALION"

The Battalion was raised in the Maritime Provinces with mobilization headquarters at Moncton, New Brunswick under the authority of G.O. 151 December 22nd, 1915. The Battalion sailed March 28th, 1917 under the command of Lieutenant-Colonel L. C. D'Aigle with a strength of twenty-four officers and five hundred and twenty-six other ranks. In England the Battalion was absorbed into the 13th Reserve Battalion. It was disbanded September 15th, 1920.

BADGE NUMBER: 165

AVE MARIS STELLA/ACADIENS D'OUTRE MER /165/CANADA

Makers: Birks, Hemsley, Unknown
Fasteners: Lugs
Composition:
Other Ranks: Pickled brass
Officers:
    A. Gilt on brass
    B. Sterling silver
Ref.: Babin, Meek, Stewart, Cox

Note: This badge was issued with and without a red colour patch behind central star. The badges with the colour patch have a small strip of metal in the form of a bracket to hold in the piece of red cloth.

Badge No.	Insignia	Rank	Description	Extremely Fine
165-2	Cap	ORs	Pickled brass with red colour patch; Hemsley	30.00
165-4		ORs	Pickled brass without red colour patch; Hemsley	30.00
165-21		Officers	Gilt on brass; Unknown	37.50
165-23		Officers	Pickled brass, Silver overlay on design; Hemsley	180.00
165-41	Collars	ORs	Pickled brass with red colour patch; Hemsley	11.00
165-43		ORs	Pickled brass without red colour patch; Hemsley	11.00
165-61		Officers	Gilt on brass; Unknown	18.00
165-63		Officers	Pickled brass, Silver overlay on design; Hemsley	18.00
165-91	Shoulders	ORs	Numeral: "165"; Birks	12.00
165-93		ORs	Title: "165 CANADA"	22.00

166TH INFANTRY BATTALION

"QUEEN'S OWN RIFLES OF CANADA"

The Battalion was raised and mobilized in Toronto, Ontario under the authority of G.O. 151 December 22nd, 1915. The Battalion sailed October 13th, 1916 under the command of Lieutenant-Colonel W. G. Mitchell with a strength of thirty-two officers and eight hundred and fifty-nine other ranks. In England the Battalion was absorbed into the 12th Reserve Battalion. It was disbanded September 15th, 1920.

BADGE NUMBER: 166

QUEEN'S OWN RIFLES OF CANADA /166/OVERSEAS BATTALION

AUTHORIZED FEBRUARY 17, 1916

Makers: Birks, Caron, Hemsley, Tiptaft, Unknown
Fasteners: Lugs
Composition:
Other Ranks: Pickled copper; Browning copper; Silverplated copper; White metal
Officers:
A: Sterling silver
B: White metal
C: Pickled copper with siver overlay
Ref.: Babin, Meek, Stewart, Cox

Note: Two makers of this cap badge exist.
1. Tall numbers with small type; Hemsley *(Illustrated)*
2. Short numbers with large type; Tiptaft

Badge No.	Insignia	Rank	Description	Extremely Fine
166-2	Cap	ORs	Pickled copper; Hemsley	30.00
166-4		ORs	Pickled brass; Hemsley	30.00
166-6		ORs	Browning copper; Unknown	30.00
166-8		ORs	Silverplated copper; Unknown	40.00
166-21		Officers	White metal; Tiptaft	45.00
166-23		Officers	Sterling silver; Tiptaft	85.00
166-25		Officers	Pickled copper, Silver overlay; Hemsley	100.00
166-41	Collars	ORs	Pickled copper; Hemsley	10.00
166-43		ORs	Pickled brass; Hemsley	15.00
166-61		Officers	White metal; Tiptaft	20.00
166-91	Shoulders	ORs	Numeral: "166"; Caron	12.00
166-93		ORs	Numeral: "166"; Birks	12.00
166-95		ORs	Title: "CROWN/QOR"/"CANADA"; Unknown	20.00

167TH INFANTRY BATTALION

"CANADIENS FRANCAIS"

The Battalion was raised in Quebec,with mobilization headquarters at Quebec City under the authority of G.O. 151 December 22nd, 1915. The Battalion was formed under the command of Lieutenant-Colonel O. Readman and redesignated the Quebec Recruiting Depot. It was disbanded September 15th, 1920.

BADGE NUMBER: 167

167/167 E BATTALION CANADIENS FRANCAIS F.E.C.
/TOUJOURS DROIGT

Makers: Birks, Caron, Hemsley
Fasteners: Lugs
Composition:
Other Ranks: Pickled brass; Browning copper
Officers: Pickled brass with silver overlay on design
Ref.: Babin, Meek, Stewart

Note: Two makers of this cap badge exist.
1. Small shield; Narrow numbers; Hemsley *(Illustrated)*
2. Large shield; Wide numbers; Caron

Badge No.	Insignia	Rank	Description	Extremely Fine
167-2	Cap	ORs	Pickled brass; Hemsley	30.00
167-4		ORs	Browning copper; Caron	30.00
167-21		Officers	Pickled brass, Silver overlay on design; Hemsley	135.00
167-41	Collars	ORs	PIckled brass; Hemsley	12.00
167-43		ORs	Browning copper; Caron	75.00
167-61		Officers	Pickled brass, Silver overlay on design; Hemsley	35.00
167-91	Shoulders	ORs	Numeral: "167"; Birks	12.00
167-93		ORs	Title: "167/CANADA"; Hemsley	18.00

168TH INFANTRY BATTALION

The Battalion was raised in Oxford County, Ontario with mobilization headquarters at Woodstock under the authority of G.O. 151 December 22nd, 1915. The Battalion sailed November 1st, 1916 under the command of Lieutenant-Colonel W. K. McMullen with a strength of twenty-six officers and six hundred and eighty-eight other ranks. In England the Battalion was broken up and absorbed into the 4th and 6th Reserve Battalions.

BADGE NUMBER: 168

No. - 168A   **OVERSEAS BATTALION CANADA/168**

Makers: Caron, Ellis, Unknown
Fasteners: Lugs, Pin
Composition:
Other Ranks: Pickled brass;
Browning copper;
Blackened copper
Officers:
  A. Pickled brass with silver overlay on design
  B. Browning copper with silver overlay on numbers
Ref.: Babin, Meek, Stewart, Cox

Note: Three makers of this cap badge exist.
1. Blunt maple leaf design, small "168"; Heavy veins; Ellis *(Illustrated)*
2. Blunt maple leaf design, small "168", Fine veins; Caron
3. Pointed maple leaf design, large "168", domed centre; Hemsley

Badge No.	Insignia	Rank	Description	Extremely Fine
168A-2	Cap	ORs	Pickled brass; Caron	50.00
168A-4		ORs	Browning copper; Ellis	40.00
168A-6		ORs	Browning copper; Hemsley	40.00
168A-8		ORs	Blackened copper; Ellis	40.00
168A-21		Officers	Pickled brass, Silver overlay on "168" Caron	100.00
168A-23		Officers	Browning copper, Silver overlay on "168";Ellis	100.00
168A-41	Collars	ORs	Pickled brass; Caron	20.00
168A-43		ORs	Browning copper; Ellis	20.00
168A-44		ORs	Browning copper; Hemsley	- -
168A-61		Officers	Pickled brass, Silver overlay on "168"; Caron	30.00
168A-63		Officers	Browning copper, Silver overlay on "168"; Ellis	30.00
168A-65		Officers	Sterling silver; Unknown	30.00
168A-91	Shoulders	ORs	Numeral: "168"; Caron	12.00
168A-93		ORs	Title: "168/CANADA"; Caron	14.00

No. - 168B   **OVERSEAS BATTALION CANADA/168**

Makers: Caron for Eaton's
Fasteners: Lugs, Pin
Composition:
Other Ranks: Pickled copper with white metal overlay on centre
Officers: Gilt on copper with silver overlay on centre
Ref.: Not previously listed

Note: Collars not issued

Badge No.	Insignia	Rank	Description	Extremely Fine
168B-2	Cap	ORs	Pickled copper, Wm. overlay on centre	110.00
168B-21		Officers	Gilt on copper, Silver overlay on centre	225.00

No. - 168C   **168/CANADA**

INTERIM BADGE

Makers: As General List
Fasteners: Lugs
Composition:
Other Ranks: Unofficial, "168" overlay on General List
Officers: Unknown
Ref.: Not previously listed

Badge No.	Insignia	Rank	Description	Extremely Fine
168C-2	Cap	ORs	General List, "168" overlay	275.00
168C-21		Officers	Unknown	- -
168C-41	Collars	ORs	General List, "168" overlay	35.00
168C-61		Officers	Unknown	- -

169TH INFANTRY BATTALION

"109TH REGIMENT"

The Battalion was raised and mobilized in Toronto, Ontario under the authority of G.O. 69 July 15th, 1916. The Battalion sailed October 26th, 1916 under the command of Lieutenant-Colonel J. G. Wright with a strength of thirty-two officers and eight hundred and eight-seven other ranks. In England the Battalion was absorbed into the 5th Reserve Battalion.

BADGE NUMBER: 169

**No. - 169A   169TH REGT OVERSEAS BATTALION
C.E.F. REX VOCAT/169/CANADA**

AUTHORIZED FEBRUARY 11, 1916

Makers: Caron, Unknown
Fasteners: Lugs, Pin
Composition:
Other Ranks: Browning copper or brass
Officers: Browning copper
Ref.: Babin, Meek, Stewart, Cox

Note: Two makers of this cap badge exist. The makers have not been identified.
1. Plain "169" - Solid and void *(Illustrated)*
2. Framed "169" - Void.
In Lieutenant-Colonel J. G. Wright's request for authorization of the proposed badge design, he also proposed that no special badge be made for the officers and that both officers and other ranks wear the same badge.

Badge No.	Insignia	Rank	Description	Extremely Fine
169A-2	Cap	ORs	Browning copper, Solid, Plain; Caron	30.00
169A-4		ORs	Browning copper, Void, Plain; Caron	30.00
169A-6		ORs	Browning copper, Void, Framed; Unknown	30.00
169A-8		ORs	Browning brass, Void, Plain; Caron	35.00
169A-21		Officers	Unknown	- -
169A-41	Collars	ORs	Browning copper, Solid, Plain; Caron	18.00
169A-43		ORs	Browning copper, Void, Plain; Caron	18.00
169A-45		ORs	Browning copper, Void, Plain; Caron	18.00
169A-61		Officers	Unknown	- -
169A-91	Shoulders	ORs	Numeral: "169"; Caron	12.00
169A-93		ORs	Numeral: "169"; Unknown	12.00
169A-95		ORs	Title: "169" / "CANADA"; Caron	18.00

No. - 169B   **OVERSEAS BATTALION CANADA/169**

Makers: Caron for Eaton's
Fasteners: Lugs, Pin
Composition:
Other Ranks: Pickled copper with
white metal overlay
on design
Officers: Gilt on copper
Ref.: Not previously listed

Note: Collars are not known.

Badge No.	Insignia	Rank	Description	Extremely Fine
169B-2	Cap	ORs	Pickled copper, Wm. overlay on centre	250.00
169B-21		Officers	Gilt on copper, Silver overlay on centre	300.00

No. - 170B   **OVERSEAS BATTALION CANADA/170**

Makers: Caron for Eaton's
Fasteners: Lugs, Pin
Composition:
Other Ranks: Pickled copper with white metal overlay on design
Officers:
A: Pickled copper with gilt overlay
B: Gilt on copper
Ref.: Not previously listed

Note: Collars are not known.

Badge No.	Insignia	Rank	Description	Extremely Fine
170B-2	Cap	ORs	Pickled copper, Wm. overlay on centre, Lugs; Caron	320.00
170B-21		Officers	Pickled copper, Gilt overlay on centre, Pin; Caron	340.00
170B-23		Officers	Gilt on copper, Pin; Caron	325.00

171ST INFANTRY BATTALION

"THE QUEBEC RIFLES"

The Battalion was raised in Quebec with mobilization headquarters at Quebec City under the authority of G.O. 69 July 15th, 1916. The Battalion sailed November 24th, 1916 under the command of Lieutenant-Colonel Sir W. Price with a strength of twenty-seven officers and five hundred and seventy-four other ranks. In England the Battalion was broken up and absorbed into the 148th Infantry Battalion, the 5th Pioneers and the 20th Reserve Battalion. It was disbanded September 15th, 1920.

BADGE NUMBER: 171

QUEBEC RIFLES/171/OVERSEAS BATTALION/CANADA

Makers: Hemsley
Fasteners: Lugs
Composition:
Other Ranks: Pickled copper or brass
Officers: Pickled copper with white metal overlay on design
Ref.: Babin, Meek , Stewart, Cox

Badge No.	Insignia	Rank	Description	Extremely Fine
171-2	Cap	ORs	Pickled copper; Hemsley	30.00
171-4		ORs	Pickled brass; Hemsley	30.00
171-21		Officers	Pickled copper, Wm. overlay on design; Hemsley	90.00
171-41	Collars	ORs	Pickled copper; Hemsley	15.00
171-43		ORs	Pickled brass; Hemsley	18.00
171-61		Officers	Pickled copper, Wm. overlay on design; Hemsley	20.00
171-91	Shoulders	ORs	Numeral: "171"; Unknown	14.00
171-93		ORs	Title: "171" over "CANADA"; Hemsley	20.00

172ND INFANTRY BATTALION

"ROCKY MOUNTAIN RANGERS"

The Battalion was raised in the Kamloops area of British Columbia, with mobilization headquarters at Kamloops under the authority of G.O. 69, July 15th, 1916. The Battalion sailed October 25th, 1916 under the command of Lieutenant-Colonel J. R. Vicars with a strength of thirty-two officers and nine hundred and seventy-two other ranks. In England the Battalion was absorbed into the 24th Reserve Battalion. It was disbanded September 15th, 1920.

BADGE NUMBER: 172

B.C./ROCKY MOUNTAIN RANGERS /C.E.F./172/CANADA

Makers: Allan, Caron, Unknown
Fasteners: Lugs, Pin
Composition:
Other Ranks: Browning copper or brass
Officers: Browning copper; Superior construction
Ref.: Babin, Meek, Stewart, Cox

Note: Three makers of this cap badge exist.
1. Plain ribbons; Pointed leaf; Allan (*Illustrated*)
2. Framed ribbons; Blunt leaf; Unknown
3. Another variety of which few details are known, has framed ribbons and numbers. This variety is not listed.

Badge No.	Insignia	Rank	Description	Extremely Fine
172-2	Cap	ORs	Browning copper; Allan	32.50
172-4		ORs	Browning brass;; Unknown	32.50
172-21		Officers	Browning copper, Pin; Allan	35.00
172-41	Collars	ORs	Browning copper; Allan	15.00
172-43		ORs	Browning brass; Unknown	15.00
172-61		Officers	Browning copper, Pin; Allan	20.00
172-91	Shoulders	ORs	Numeral: "172"; Caron	14.00
172-93		ORs	Title: "172 BATTALION/CANADA"; Allan	25.00

173RD INFANTRY BATTALION

"CANADIAN HIGHLANDERS"

The Battalion was raised and mobilized in Hamilton, Ontario, under the authority of G.O. 69 July 15th, 1916. The Battalion sailed November 14th, 1916 under the authority of Lieutenant-Colonel W. H. Bruce with a strength of thirty-two officers and nine hundred and thirty other ranks. In England the Battalion was absorbed into the 2nd Reserve Battalion. It was disbanded September 15th, 1920.

BADGE NUMBER: 173

No. 173A   **173/ALBAINN CU BRATH/OVERSEAS /CANADIAN HIGHLANDERS**

AUTHORIZED FEBRUARY 29, 1916

Makers: Caron, Lees
Fasteners: Lugs
Composition:
Other Ranks: Browning copper or brass; White metal
Officers:
A: Silverplated
B: Browning copper with white metal overlay on design
Ref.: Babin, Meek, Stewart, Cox

Note: A minor variety exists with the badge not voided between the leaf and the ribbon. Both are struck by Lees.

Badge No.	Insignia	Rank	Description	Extremely Fine
173A-2	Glengarry	ORs	Browning copper; Lees	35.00
173A-4		ORs	Browning brass; Lees	24.00
173A-6		ORs	Browning brass, Solid; Lees	40.00
173A-21		Officers	White metal; Lees	60.00
173A-23		Officers	Silverplated; Lees	110.00
173A-25		Officers	Browning copper, Wm. overlay on design; Lees	120.00
173A-41	Collars	ORs	Browning copper; Lees	22.00
173A-43		ORs	Browning brass; Lees	10.00
173A-61		Officers	Browning copper, Wm. overlay on design; Lees	50.00
173A-91	Shoulders	ORs	Numeral: "173"; Caron	14.00

No. - 173B

ALBAINN 91 CU BRATH/
173RD OVERSEAS BATTALION

Photograph
Not Available
At Press Time

Makers: Unknown
Fasteners: Lugs
Composition:
 Other Ranks: White metal
 Officers: Unknown
Ref.: Not previously listed

Note: Possibly an interim badge made by adding a ribbon to the badge of the 91st Highlanders.

Badge No.	Insignia	Rank	Description	Extremely Fine
173B-2	Glengarry	ORs	White metal; Unknown	Rare
173B-21		Officers	Unknown	- -
173B-41	Collars	ORs	Unknown	- -
173B-61		Officers	Unknown	- -

174TH INFANTRY BATTALION

"CAMERON HIGHLANDERS OF CANADA"

The Battalion was raised in the Provinces of Manitoba, Saskatchewan and Alberta with mobilization headquarters at Winnipeg, Manitoba under the authority of G.O. 69 July 15th, 1916. The Battalion sailed April 29th, 1917 under the command of Lieutenant-Colonel H. F. Osler with a strength of fourteen officers and two hundred and seventy-five other ranks. In England the Battalion was broken up and absorbed into the 11th and 14th Reserve Battalions. It was disbanded September 15th, 1920.

BADGE NUMBER: 174

CAMERON HIGHLANDERS OF CANADA
/174/OVERSEAS/ULLAMH

Makers: McDougall
Fasteners: Lugs
Composition:
Other Ranks: Pickled copper; White metal; Brass
Officers:
A: Silverplate on white metal
B: Silverplate on copper
Ref.: Babin, Meek, Stewart, Cox

Note: A minor variety exists with a solid crown and numbers.

Badge No.	Insignia	Rank	Description	Extremely Fine
174-2	Glengarry	ORs	Pickled copper, Solid; McDougall	165.00
174-4		ORs	Pickled copper, Void; McDougall	165.00
174-21		Officers	White metal; McDougall	275.00
174-23		Officers	Silverplate on Wm.; McDougall	225.00
174-25		Officers	Silverplate on Copper; McDougall	200.00
174-41	Collars	ORs	Pickled copper; McDougall	85.00
174-61		Officers	Silverplate on Wm.; McDougall	85.00
174-91	Shoulders	ORs	Numeral "174", Unknown	15.00

175TH INFANTRY BATTALION

"MEDICINE HAT BATTALION"

The Battalion was raised in the Medicine Hat district of Alberta with mobilization headquarters at Medicine Hat under the authority of G.O. 69 July 15th, 1916. The Battalion sailed October 4th, 1916 under the command of Lieutenant-Colonel N. Spencer with a strength of thirty officers and eight hundred and forty-seven other ranks. It was disbanded September 15th, 1920.

BADGE NUMBER: 175

No. - 175A

**OVER 175 SEAS
/MEDICINE HAT/CANADA**

Makers: Caron, Ellis
Fasteners: Lugs
Compositon:
Other Ranks: Browning copper
Officers: Browning copper with white metal overlay on "175"
Ref.: Babin, Cox

Badge No.	Insignia	Rank	Description	Extremely Fine
175A-2	Cap	ORs	Browning copper; Ellis	300.00
175A-21		Officers	Browning copper, Wm. overlay on "175"; Ellis	400.00
175A-41	Collars	ORs	Browning copper; Ellis	25.00
175A-61		Officers	Browning copper, Wm. overlay on "175"; Ellis	50.00
175A-91	Shoulders	ORs	Numeral: "175"; Caron	15.00
175A-93		ORs	Title: "175" / "CANADA"; Tiptaft	22.00

No. - 175B

MEDICINE HAT/
OVERSEAS 175 BATTALION/CANADA

Makers: Cook, Tiptaft
Fasteners: Lugs
Composition:
Other Ranks: Pickled copper or brass
Officers: Pickled brass with white metal overlay on design
Ref.: Babin, Meek, Stewart, Cox

Note: Two makers of this cap badge exist.
  1. Small hat with small numbers; Cook *(Illustrated)*
  2. Large hat with large numbers; Tiptaft

Badge No.	Insignia	Rank	Description	Extremely Fine
175B-2	Cap	ORs	Pickled copper; Cook	25.00
175B-4		ORs	Pickled brass; Tiptaft	25.00
175B-21		Officers	Pickled brass, Wm. overlay on design; Tiptaft	50.00
175B-41	Collars	ORs	Pickled copper; Cook	18.00
175B-43		ORs	Pickled brass; Tiptaft	15.00
175B-91		Officers	Pickled brass, Wm. overlay on design; Tiptaft	30.00

176TH INFANTRY BATTALION

"NIAGARA RANGERS"

The Battalion was raised in the Counties of Lincoln and Welland, Ontario with mobilization headquarters at St. Catharines under the authority of G.O. 69 July 15th, 1916. The Battalion sailed April 29th, 1917 under the command of Lieutenant-Colonel D. Sharpe with a strength of eighteen officers and four hunded and forty-six other ranks. In England the Battalion was absorbed into the 12th Reserve Battalion. It was disbanded September 15th, 1920.

BADGE NUMBER: 176

OVERSEAS BATTALION/NIAGARA RANGERS
/176/CANADA

AUTHORIZED JUNE 5, 1916

Makers: Caron, Hemsley
Fasteners: Lugs, Pin
Composition:
Other Ranks: Pickled copper or brass
Officers: Pickled copper with white metal overlay on design
Ref.: Babin, Meek, Stewart, Cox

Badge No.	Insignia	Rank	Description	Extremely Fine
176-2	Cap	ORs	Pickled copper; Hemsley	30.00
176-4		ORs	Pickled brass; Hemsley	40.00
176-21		Officers	Pickled copper, Wm. overlay on design; Hemsley	110.00
176-41	Collars	ORs	Pickled copper; Hemsley	18.00
176-43		ORs	Pickled brass; Hemsley	24.00
176-61		Officers	Pickled copper, Wm. overlay on design; Hemsley	30.00
176-91	Shoulders	ORs	Numeral: "176"; Caron	14.00
176-93		ORs	Title: "CAN 176 ADA"; Hemsley	25.00

177TH INFANTRY BATTALION

"SIMCOE FORESTERS"

The Battalion was raised in Simcoe County, Ontario with mobilization headquarters at Barrie under the authority of G.O. 69 July 15th, 1916. The Battalion sailed May 3rd, 1917 under the command of Lieutenant-Colonel J. B. McPhee with a strength of nineteen officers and five hundred and forty-nine other ranks. In England the Battalion was absorbed into the 3rd Reserve Battalion. It was disbanded September 15th, 1920.

BADGE NUMBER: 177

No. - 177A **OVERSEAS/SIMCOE FORESTERS /177/CANADA**

Makers: Caron, Ellis, Hemsley
Fasteners: Lugs
Composition:
Other Ranks: Pickled copper; Browning copper
Officers:
A: Pickled copper with white metal overlay on design
B: Browning copper with white metal overlay on design
Ref.: Babin, Meek, Stewart, Cox

Note: This cap badge has two makers.
1. The Hemsley badge, which is domed, has four periods in the outer circle. The "77's" are curved right, and it is found with a solid or void field. *(Illustrated)*
2. The Ellis badge, which is flat, has three periods in the outer circle. The "77's" are straight and it is also found with a solid or void field.

Badge No.	Insignia	Rank	Description	Extremely Fine
177A-2	Cap	ORs	Pickled copper, Solid; Hemsley	50.00
177A-4		ORs	Pickled copper, Void; Hemsley	50.00
177A-6		ORs	Browning copper, Solid; Ellis	25.00
177A-8		ORs	Browning copper, Void; Ellis	25.00
177A-21		Officers	Pickled copper, Wm. overlay on design; Hemsley	45.00
177A-23		Officers	Browning copper, Wm. Overlay on design; Ellis	45.00

Badge No.	Insignia	Rank	Description	Extremely Fine
177A-41	Collars	ORs	Pickled copper; Hemsley	8.00
177A-43		ORs	Browning copper; Ellis	8.00
177A-61		Officers	Pickled copper, Wm. overlay on design; Hemsley	40.00
177A-63		Officers	Browning copper, Wm. overlay on design; Ellis	40.00
177A-91	Shoulders	ORs	Numeral: "177"; Caron	14.00
177A-93		ORs	Numeral: "177"; Unknown	14.00

No . - 177B   **OVERSEAS BATTALION CANADA /177/DUTY FIRST**

Makers: Unknown
Fasteners: Lugs
Compositon:
  Other Ranks: Browning copper
  Officers: Gilt on copper
Ref.: Not previously listed

Note: The maker of this badge has not been identified. The badge appears to be cast. The shoulder numerals are listed with the badge due to the similar design of the numbers. There are no recorded collars.

Badge No.	Insignia	Rank	Description	Extremely Fine
177B-2	Cap	ORs	Browning copper	350.00
177B-21		Officers	Gilt on copper	450.00
177B-91	Shoulders	ORs	Numeral: "177"	20.00

No. - 177C   OVERSEAS BATTALION CANADA/177

Photograph
Not Available
At Press Time

Makers: Caron for Eaton's
Fasteners: Lugs, Pin
Composition:
Other Ranks: Pickled copper with white metal overlay in centre
Officers: Gilt on copper with silver overlay on centre
Ref.: Babin, Cox

Note: Collars not issued.

Badge No.	Insignia	Rank	Description	Extremely Fine
177C-2	Cap	ORs	Pickled copper, Wm. overlay in centre	300.00
177C-21		Officers	Gilt on copper, silver overlay on centre	350.00

No. - 177D   177/CANADA

INTERIM BADGE

Photograph
Not Available
At Press Time

Makers: As General List
Fasteners: Lugs
Composition:
Other Ranks: Unofficial, "177" overlay on General List
Ref.: Babin, Cox

Badge No.	Insignia	Rank	Description	Extremely Fine
177D-2	Cap	ORs	General List, "177" overlay	200.00
177D-21		Officers	Unknown	- -
177D-41	Collars	ORs	Unknown	- -
177D-61		Officers	Unknown	- -

178TH INFANTRY BATTALION

"CANADIENS FRANCAIS"

The Battalion was raised in Quebec and Eastern Ontario with mobilization headquarters at Victoriaville, Quebec under the authority of G.O. 69 July 15th, 1916. The Battalion sailed March 4th, 1917 under the command of Lieutenant-Colonel L. de la B. Girouard with a strength of twenty officers and four hundred and fifteen other ranks. In England the Battalion was absorbed into the 10th Reserve Battalion. It was disbanded September 15th, 1920.

BADGE NUMBER: 178

No. - 178A   CANADIENS-FRANCAIS/D'OUTRE-MER/
ATHABASKA DRUMMOND/
178/VOULOIR C'EST POUVOIR/NICOLET

Makers: Caron, Hemsley
Fasteners: Lugs
Composition:
Other Ranks: Pickled copper
Officers: Pickled copper with white metal overlay on design
Ref.: Babin, Meek, Stewart, Cox

Badge No.	Insignia	Rank	Description	Extremely Fine
178A-2	Cap	ORs	Pickled copper; Hemsley	25.00
178A-21		Officers	Pickled copper, Wm. overlay on design; Hemsley	125.00
178A-41	Collars	ORs	Pickled copper; Hemsley	18.00
178A-61		Officers	Pickled copper, Wm. overlay on design; Hemsley	25.00
178A-91	Shoulders	ORs	Numeral: "178"; Caron	16.00

No. - 178B   CANADIEN-FRANCAIS/
D'OUTRE MER PROVINCE QUEBEC
/178/VOULOIR C'EST DE POUVOIR

(NOTE LEGEND CHANGE)

Makers: Hemsley
Fasteners: Lugs
Composition:
Other Ranks: Pickled brass
Officers: Pickled brass with
white metal overlay
on design
Ref.: Babin, Cox

Note: This badge was issued with either a void or solid field.

Badge No.	Insignia	Rank	Description	Extremely Fine
178B-2	Cap	ORs	Pickled brass, Solid; Hemsley	25.00
178B-4		ORs	Pickled brass, Void; Hemsley	25.00
178B-21		Officers	Pickled brass, Wm. overlay on design; Hemsley	125.00
178B-41	Collars	ORs	Pickled brass, Solid; Hemsley	18.00
178B-43		ORs	Pickled brass, Void; Hemsley	18.00
178B-61		Officers	Pickled brass, Wm. overlay on design; Hemsley	20.00

No. - 178C   CANADIEN FRANCAIS/178/
BATTALIONS OVERSEAS/
VOULOIR C'EST DE POUVOIR/
D'OUTRE MER

Makers: Unknown
Fasteners: Lugs
Composition:
Other Ranks: Copper
Officers: Unknown
Ref.: Not previously listed

Note: Collars are not known.

Badge No.	Insignia	Rank	Description	Extremely Fine
178C-2	Cap	ORs	Copper; Unknown	150.00
178C-21		Officers	Unknown	- -

179TH INFANTRY BATTALION

"CAMERON HIGHLANDERS OF CANADA"

The Battalion was raised and mobilized in Winnipeg, Manitoba under the authority of G.O. 69 July 15th, 1916. The Battalion sailed October 4th, 1916 under the command of Lieutenant-Colonel J. Y. Reid with a strength of thirty-two officers and eight hundred and ninety-other ranks. In England the Battalion was absorbed into the 17th Reserve Battalion. It was disbanded September 15th, 1920.

BADGE NUMBER: 179

CAMERON HIGHLANDERS OF CANADA /179/OVERSEAS

Makers: Caron, Dingwall
Fasteners: Lugs, Tangs
Composition:
Other Ranks: Silverplate on copper; Pickled copper; Browning copper
Officers: Sterling silver
Ref.: Babin, Meek, Stewart, Cox

Note: One maker is known but there are two varieties of this cap badge.
1. A wreath of thistles and maple leaves with crossed boughs.
2. A wreath of thistles and maple leaves without crossed boughs.

Badge No.	Insignia	Rank	Description	Extremely Fine
		Cap without "Crossed boughs"		
179-2	Glengarry	ORs	Silverplate on copper; Dingwall	150.00
179-21		Officers	Sterling silver; Dingwall	225.00
		Cap with "Crossed boughs"		
179-4	Glengarry	ORs	Silverplate on copper; Dingwall	55.00
179-23		Officers	Browning copper; Dingwall	100.00
		Matching Cap Collar Design		
179-41	Collars	ORs	Browning copper; Dingwall	30.00
		Maple Leaf and Thistle Design		
179-43	Collars	ORs	Pickled copper; Dingwall	30.00
179-45		ORs	Browning copper; Dingwall	30.00
179-61		Officers	Gilt and silver, Pin; Dingwall	40.00
179-91	Shoulders	ORs	Numeral: "179"; Caron	14.00

180TH INFANTRY BATTALION

"SPORTSMEN BATTALION"

The Battalion was raised and mobilized in Toronto, Ontario under the authority of G.O. 69 July 15th, 1916. The Battalion sailed November 15th, 1916 under the command of Lieutenant-Colonel R. H. Greer with a strength of thirty-one officers and eight hundred and thirty-three other ranks. In England the Battalion was absorbed into the 3rd Reserve Battalion. It was disbanded September 15th, 1920.

BADGE NUMBER: 180

No. - 180A   **SPORTSMAN/180/CANADA/OVERSEAS**

AUTHORIZED FEBRUARY 19, 1916

Makers: Caron, Unknown
Fasteners: Lugs
Composition:
Other Ranks: Blackened copper or brass
Officers: Sterling silver or
Ref.: Babin, Meek, Stewart, Cox

Badge No.	Insignia	Rank	Description	Extremely Fine
180A-2	Cap	ORs	Blackened copper; Unknown	27.50
180A-4		ORs	Blackened brass; Unknown	27.50
180A-21		Officers	Sterling silver; Unknown	80.00
180A-41	Collars	ORs	Blackened copper; Unknown	10.00
180A-43		ORs	Blackened brass; Unknown	15.00
180A-61		Officers	Sterling silver; Unknown	25.00
180A-91	Shoulders	ORs	Numeral: "180"; Caron	14.00

No. - 180B   **OVERSEAS BATTALION CANADA/180**

Photograph
Not Available
At Press Time

Makers: Caron for Eaton's
Fasteners: Lugs, Pin
Composition:
Other Ranks: Pickled copper with
white metal overlay
on centre
Officers: Gilt on copper with
silver overlay on
centre
Ref.: Babin, Meek, Stewart, Coxs

Note: Collars not issued

Badge No.	Insignia	Rank	Description	Extremely Fine
180B-2	Cap	ORs	Pickled copper, Wm. overlay on centre; Caron	300.00
180B-21		Officers	Gilt on copper, Silver overlay on centre; Caron	350.00

181ST INFANTRY BATTALION

"BRANDON BATTALION"

The Battalion was raised in the Brandon district of Manitoba with mobilization headquarters at Brandon, under the authority of G.O. 69 July 15th, 1916. The Battalion sailed April 18th, 1917 under the command of Lieutenant-Colonel D. W. Beaubier with a strength of twenty officers and five hundred and ninety-seven other ranks. In England the Battalion was absorbed into the 18th Reserve Battalion. It was disbanded September 15th, 1920.

BADGE NUMBER: 181

OVERSEAS 181 BATTALION/BRANDON CANADA

AUTHORIZED MAY 17, 1916

Makers: Caron, Reesor, Unknown
Fasteners: Lugs, Pin
Composition:
Other Ranks: Pickled copper or brass
Officers:
    A: Pickled copper with silver overlay on "181"
    B: Gilt on copper
Ref.: Babin, Meek, Stewart, Cox

Note: Two makers of this cap badge exist.
1. Narrow or oval "8"; Reesor *(Illustrated)*
2. Wide or round "8"; Unknown.

Badge No.	Insignia	Rank	Description	Extremely Fine
181-2	Cap	ORs	Pickled copper; Ressor	40.00
181-4		ORs	Pickled brass; Unknown	35.00
181-21		Officers	Pickled copper, Silver overlay on "181"; Reesor	125.00
181-23		Officers	Gilt on copper, Pin; Reesor	125.00
181-41	Collars	ORs	Pickled copper; Ressor	15.00
181-43		ORs	Pickled brass; Unknown	15.00
181-61		Officers	Pickled copper, Silver overlay on "181"; Reesor	20.00
181-91	Shoulders	ORs	Numeral: "181"; Caron	14.00
181-93		ORs	Title: "CAN 181 ADA OVERSEAS"; Reesor	25.00

182ND INFANTRY BATTALION

"ONTARIO COUNTY BATTALION"

The Battalion was raised in the County of Ontario, Ontario with mobilization headquarters at Whitby under the authority of G.O. 69 July 15th, 1916. The Battalion sailed May 3rd, 1917 under the command of Lieutenant-Colonel A. A. Cockburn with a strength of nine officers and two hundred and eight other ranks. In England the Battalion was absorbed into the 18th Reserve Battalion. It was disbanded September 15th, 1920.

BADGE NUMBER: 182

CANADA OVERSEAS ONTARIO BATTALION/182

AUTHORIZED MARCH 25, 1916

Makers: Ellis, Hemsley, Unknown
Fasteners: Lugs
Composition:
 Other Ranks: Pickled brass
 Officers: Sterling silver
Ref.: Babin, Meek, Stewart, Cox

Note: Two makers of this cap badge exist.
1. Blunt leaf design; Wide crown; Ellis *(Illustrated)*
2. Pointed leaf design; Narrow crown; Hemsley.

Badge No.	Insignia	Rank	Description	Extremely Fine
182-2	Cap	ORs	Pickled brass; Ellis	60.00
182-4		ORs	Pickled brass; Hemsley	55.00
182-21		Officers	Sterling silver; Ellis	115.00
182-41	Collars	ORs	Pickled brass; Ellis	35.00
182-43		ORs	Pickled brass; Hemsley	35.00
182-61		Officers	Sterling silver; Ellis	50.00
182-91	Shoulders	ORs	Numeral: "182"	Unknown

183RD INFANTRY BATTALION

"MANITOBA BEAVERS"

The Battalion was raised in Manitoba with mobilization headquarters at Winnipeg under the authority of G.O. 69 July 15th, 1916. The Battalion sailed October 4th, 1916 under the command of Lieutenant-Colonel W. T. Edgecombe with a strength of thirteen officers and four hundred and thirty-one other ranks. In England the Battalion was broken up to supply reinforcements for the 100th, 107th, 108th and 144th Infantry Battalions. It was disbanded September 15th, 1920.

BADGE NUMBER: 183

No. - 183A

183/MANITOBA BEAVERS/ OVERSEAS BATTALION/CANADA

AUTHORIZED MARCH 23, 1916

Makers: Caron, Dingwall
Fasteners: Lugs, Tangs, Pin
Compositon:
Other Ranks: Pickled copper or brass
Officers: Pickled brass, Superior construction
Ref.: Babin, Meek, Stewart, Cox

Note: This cap badge was issued with either a void or solid field.

Badge No.	Insignia	Rank	Description	Extremely Fine
183A-2	Cap	ORs	Pickled copper, Solid; Dingwall	45.00
183A-4		ORs	Pickled brass, Void; Dingwall	35.00
183A-21		Officers	Pickled brass, Void, Pin; Dingwall	45.00
183A-41	Collars	ORs	Pickled copper; Dingwall	25.00
183A-61		Officers	Pickled copper, Pin; Dingwall	30.00
183A-91	Shoulders	ORs	Numeral: "183"; Caron	14.00
183A-93		ORs	Title: "183/CANADA/OVERSEAS	50.00
183A-95		ORs	BATTALION"; Dingwall	

No. - 183B   183/CANADA

INTERIM BADGE

Makers: Caron, As General List
Fastener: As General List
Composition:
Other Ranks: As General List with "183" overlaid
Ref.: Not previously listed

Photograph
Not Available
At Press Time

Badge No.	Insignia	Rank	Description	Extremely Fine
183B-2	Cap	ORs	General List, "183" overlay; Caron	50.00

184TH INFANTRY BATTALION

The Battalion was raised in Southern Manitoba with mobilization headquarters at Winnipeg under the authority of G.O. 69 July 15th, 1916. The Battalion sailed November 1st, 1916 under the command of Lieutenant-Colonel W. H. Sharpe with a strength of thirty-two officers and one thousand and forty-two other ranks. In England the Battalion was absorbed into the 11th Reserve Battlion. It was disbanded September 15th, 1920.

BADGE NUMBER: 184

184/OVERSEAS CANADA BATTALION

NOT AUTHORIZED

Makers: Caron, Dingwall,
Unknown
Fasteners: Lugs, Tangs
Composition:
Other Ranks: Pickled copper;
Blackened brass,
Officers: Unknown
Ref.: Babin, Meek, Stewart, Cox

Note: Two makers of this cap badge exist.
1. Dingwall *(Illustrated)*
2. Unknown; Little is known about the style of this badge.

Badge No.	Insignia	Rank	Description	Extremely Fine
184-2	Cap	ORs	Pickled copper; Dingwall	40.00
184-4		ORs	Blackened brass; Unknown	40.00
184-21		Officers	Unknown	- -
			Leaf Type - Sideview of Buffalo	
184-41	Collars	ORs	Pickled copper; Dingwall	20.00
184-43		ORs	Blackened brass; Unknown	20.00
184-61		Officers	Unknown	- -
			Leaf Type - Head of Buffalo	
184-45	Collars	ORs	Pickled copper; Dingwall	40.00
184-63		Officers	Unknown	- -
			Matching Cap Type	
184-47	Collars	ORs	Pickled copper; Unknown	80.00
185-65		Officers	Unknown	- -
184-91	Shoulders	ORs	Numeral: "184"; Caron	14.00
184-93		ORs	Title: "OVERSEAS CANADA BATTALION/184"; Unknown	25.00

185TH INFANTRY BATTALION

"CAPE BRETON HIGHLANDERS"

The battalion was raised in Cape Breton, Nova Scotia under the authority of G.O. 69 July 15, 1916 and had its mobilization headquarters at Broughton, Cape Breton. Lieutenant-Colonel F. P. Day was commanding.

BADGE NUMBER: 185

No. - 185A **CANADA/CAPE BRETON HIGHLANDERS /185/OVERSEAS/SIOL NA FEAR FEARAIL**

NOT AUTHORIZED

Makers: Caron, Hemsley, Tiptaft
Fasteners: Lugs
Composition:
Other Ranks: Pickled copper or brass
Officers:
   A. Pickled copper with white metal overlay on design
   B. Silverplate on copper
   C: Gilt on copper
Ref.: Babin, Meek, Stewart, Cox

Note: Two makers of this cap badge exist.
   1. Void between the crest and the maple leaf; Hemsley *(Illustrated)*
   2. Solid between the crest and the maple leaf; Tiptaft

Badge No.	Insignia	Rank	Description	Extremely Fine
185A-2	Glengarry	ORs	Pickled copper; Hemsley	35.00
185A-4		ORs	Pickled copper; Tiptaft	35.00
185A-6		ORs	Pickled brass; Hemsley	90.00
185A-8		ORs	Pickled brass; Tiptaft	90.00
185A-21		Officers	Pickled copper, Wm. overlay on design	275.00
185A-23		Officers	Gilt on copper; Tiptaft	300.00
185A-25		Officers	Silverplate on copper; Tiptaft	250.00
Maple Leaf Design				
185A-41	Collars	ORs	Pickled copper; Hemsley	70.00
185A-43		ORs	Pickled brass; Hemsley	70.00
185A-45		ORs	Pickled brass; Tiptaft	70.00
185A-61		Officers	Pickled copper, Wm. overlay on design; Hemsley	150.00

Badge No.	Insignia	Rank	Description	Extremely Fine
		Scroll Design		
185A-47	Collars	ORs	Pickled copper; Hemsley	40.00
185A-49		ORs	Pickled copper; Tiptaft	40.00
185A-63		Officers	Pickled copper, Wm. overlay on design; Hemsley	120.00
185A-65		Officers	Pickled copper, Wm. overlay on design; Tiptaft	100.00
185A-91	Shoulders	ORs	Numeral: "185"; Caron	20.00

No. - 185B   OVERSEAS BATTALION CANADA/185

**Photograph
Not Available
At Press Time**

Makers: Caron for Eaton's
Fasteners: Lugs, Pin
Composition:
Other Ranks: Pickled copper with white metal overlay on design
Officers: Gilt on copper with silver overlay on centre
Ref.: Not previously listed

Note: Collars are not known for this cap.

Badge No.	Insignia	Rank	Description	Extremely Fine
185B-2	Cap	ORs	Pickled copper, Wm. overlay on design	300.00
185B-21		Officers	Gilt on copper, Silver overlay on centre	350.00

186TH INFANTRY BATTALION

"KENT BATTALION"

The Battalion was raised in Kent County, Ontario with mobilization headquarters at Chatham under the authority of G.O. 69 July 15th, 1916. The Battalion sailed March 28th, 1917 under the command of Major N. Smith with a strength of eighteen officers and four hundred and sixty-nine other ranks. In England the Battalion was absorbed into the 4th Reserve Battalion. It was disbanded September 15th, 1920.

BADGE NUMBER: 186

No. - 186A   **KENT OVERSEAS BATTN CANADA /186/USQUE AD ARAS**

Makers: Caron, Wellings
Fasteners: Lugs
Composition:
Other Ranks: Browning copper; Blackened copper or brass
Officers: Browning copper with white metal overlay on "186"
Ref.: Babin, Meek

Note: Shoulder numerals are not known.

Badge No.	Insignia	Rank	Description	Extremely Fine
186A-2	Cap	ORs	Browning copper; Wellings	45.00
186A-4		ORs	Blackened copper; Wellings	50.00
186A-6		ORs	Blackened brass; Wellings	45.00
186A-21		Officers	Browning copper. Wm. overlay on "186"; Wellings	300.00
186A-41	Collars	ORs	Blackened copper; Wellings	30.00
186A-61		Officers	Browning copper, Wm. overlay on "186"; Wellings	75.00
186A-91	Shoulders	ORs	Numeral: "186";	Unknown

No. - 186B   OVERSEAS BATTALION CANADA/186

Makers: Caron for Eaton's
Fasteners: Lugs, Pin
Composition:
Other Ranks: Pickled copper with white metal overlay on centre
Officers: Gilt on copper with silver overlay on centre
Ref.: Not previously listed

Note: Collars are not known for this cap.

Badge No.	Insignia	Rank	Description	Extremely Fine
186B-2	Cap	ORs	Pickled copper, Wm. overlay on centre	300.00
186B-21		Officers	Gilt on copper, Silver overlay on centre	350.00

187TH INFANTRY BATTALION

"CENTRAL ALBERTA BATTALION"

The Battalion was raised in the District of Red Deer, Alberta with mobilization headquarters at Red Deer under the authority of G.O. 69 July 15th, 1916. The Battalion sailed December 20th, 1916 under the command of Lieutenant-Colonel C. W. Robinson with a strength of twenty-four officers and seven hundred and forty-four other ranks. In England the Battalion was absorbed into the 21st Reserve Battalion. It was disbanded September 15th, 1920.

BADGE NUMBER: 187

CENTRAL ALBERTA/187/
OVERSEAS BATTALION CANADA

AUTHORIZED MAY 23, 1916

Makers: Black, Caron, Unknown
Fasteners: Lugs
Composition:
Other Ranks: Pickled copper or brass
Officers:
   A. Pickled brass with white metal overlay on design
   B. Browning copper with silver overlay on "187"
   C: Browning copper with silver overlay on "187" and "Canada"
Ref.: Babin, Meek, Stewart, Cox

Note: Two makers of this cap badge exist.
  1. The "8" of 187 has a cross over centre; Black *(Illustrated)*
  2. The "8" of 187 is flat and has no cross over line, a smooth centre; Unknown.

Badge No.	Insignia	Rank	Description	Extremely Fine
187-2	Cap	ORs	Pickled copper; Black	25.00
187-4		ORs	Pickled brass; Black	75.00
187-21		Officers	Pickled brass, Wm. overlay on design; Unknown	225.00
187-23		Officers	Browning copper, Silver overlay on "187"; Black	85.00
187-25		Officers	Browning copper, Silver overlay on "187" and Canada; Black	165.00

Badge No.	Insignia	Rank	Description	Extremely Fine
187-41	Collars	ORs	Pickled copper; Black	12.00
187-61		Officers	Pickled brass, Wm. overlay on design; Unknown	85.00
187-63		Officers	Browning copper, Silver overlay on "187"; Black	25.00
187-65		Officers	Browning copper, Silver overlay on "187" and Canada; Black	25.00
187-91	Shoulders	ORs	Numeral: "187"; Caron	14.00
187-93		Officers	Title: "187" / "CANADA"; Unknown	25.00

188TH INFANTRY BATTALION

"SASKATCHEWAN BATTALION"

The Battalion was raised in Northern Saskatchewan with mobilization headquarters at Prince Albert under the authority of G.O. 69 July 15th, 1916. The Battalion sailed October 13th, 1916 under the command of Lieutenant-Colonel C. J. Donaldson with a strength of thirty-two officers and one thousand and four other ranks. In England the Battalion was absorbed into the 15th Reserve Battalion. It was disbanded September 15th, 1920.

BADGE NUMBER: 188

SASKATCHEWAN OVERSEAS BATTALION
/188/CANADA

NOT AUTHORIZED

Makers: Dingwall, Tiptaft, Hemsley
Fasteners: Lugs, Tangs
Composition:
Other Ranks: Pickled copper;
Browning copper
Officers: Browning copper
with silver overlay
on "188"
Ref.: Babin, Meek, Stewart, Cox

Note: Three makers of this cap badge exist.
1. Flat axes with wide type "188" and plain ribbons; Dingwall *(Illustrated)*
2. Flat axes with narrow type "188" and framed ribbons; Tiptaft
3. Broad axes with wide type "188" and plain ribbons; Hemsley.

Badge No.	Insignia	Rank	Description	Extremely Fine
		Flat Axe Variety		
188-2	Cap	ORs	Pickled copper;Dingwall	25.00
188-4		ORs	Browning copper; Tiptaft	25.00
188-21		Officers	Browning copper, Silver overlay on "188", Lugs, Canada; Tiptaft	100.00
188-41	Collars	ORs	Pickled copper; Dingwall	12.00
188-43		ORs	Browning copper; Tiptaft	12.00
188-61		Officers	Browning copper, Silver overlay on "188", Lugs, Canada	25.00
188-91	Shoulders	ORs	Numeral: "188"; Caron	15.00
188-93		ORs	Title: "CANADA" over "188"	
			Wide "88's"; Dingwall	25.00
			Narrow "88's"; Tiptaft	25.00

Badge No.	Insignia	Rank	Description	Extremely Fine
		Broad Axe Variety		
188-6	Cap	ORs	Pickled brass; Hemsley	95.00
188-23		Officers	Unknown	---
188-45	Collars	ORs	Pickled brass; Hemsley	12.00
188-63		Officers	Unknown	---

189TH INFANTRY BATTALION

"CANADIENS FRANCAIS"

The Battalion was raised in Eastern Quebec with mobilization headquarters at Fraserville under the authority of G.O. 69 July 15th, 1916. The Battalion sailed September 27th, 1916 under the command of Lieutenant-Colonel P. A. Piuze with a strength of twenty-six officers and five hundred and ninety-five other ranks. In England the Battalion was absorbed into the 69th Infantry Battalion. It was disbanded September 15th, 1920.

BADGE NUMBER: 189

189/BATTALION/CANADIENS FRANCAIS/ D'OUTRE MER/J'Y SVIS EN GARDE

NOT AUTHORIZED

Makers: Caron, Tiptaft
Fasteners: Lugs
Composition:
Other Ranks: Pickled brass;
Browning copper
Officers: Sterling silver
Ref.: Babin, Meek, Stewart, Cox

Note: Two makers of this cap badge exist.
1. The field carrying the inscription "Battalion Canadien Francais D'Outre Mer" is convex; Tiptaft
2. The field carrying the inscription "Battalion Canadien Francais D'Outre Mer" is concave; Caron

Badge No.	Insignia	Rank	Description	Extremely Fine
189-2	Cap	ORs	Pickled brass; Tiptaft	25.00
189-4		ORs	Pickled brass; Caron	25.00
189-6		ORs	Browning copper; Caron	25.00
189-21		Officers	Sterling silver; Caron	100.00
189-41	Collars	ORs	Pickled brass; Tiptaft	15.00
189-43		ORs	Pickled brass; Caron	15.00
189-61		Officers	Sterling silver; Caron	60.00
189-91	Shoulders	ORs	Numeral: "189"; Caron	15.00
189-93		ORs	Title: "189" over "CANADA"; Caron	20.00
189-95		ORs	Title: "189" over "Rifle", Pin; Unknown	25.00

190TH INFANTRY BATTALION

"WINNIPEG RIFLES"

The Battalion was raised in Winnipeg and District with mobilization headquarters at Winnipeg, Manitoba under the authority of G.O. 69 July 15th, 1916. The Battalion sailed May 3rd, 1917 under the command of Lieutenant-Colonel G. K. Watson with a strength of fifteen officers and three hundred and seventy-two other ranks. In England the Battalion was absorbed into the 18th Reserve Battalion. It was disbanded September 15th, 1920.

BADGE NUMBER: 190

4/HOSTI ACIE NOMINATI

AUTHORIZED MAY 12, 1916

Makers: Birks, Caron, Dingwall
Fasteners: Lugs, Pin
Composition:
Other Ranks: Pickled brass
Officers: Pickled brass with white metal overlay on "4" and motto
Ref.: Babin, Meek, Stewart, Cox

Note: Two makers of this cap badge exist.
    1. The cup leans forward to the left and has a rounded top; Birks (Illustrated)
    2. The cup is straight and the top is slanted down to the right; Dingwall

Badge No.	Insignia	Rank	Description	Extremely Fine
190-2	Cap	ORs	Pickled brass; Birks	55.00
190-4		ORs	Pickled brass; Dingwall	55.00
190-21		Officers	Pickled brass, Wm. overlay on "4" and motto; Dingwall	100.00
190-41	Collars	ORs	Pickled brass, Small "9"; Birks	12.00
190-43		ORs	Pickled brass, Large "9"; Dingwall	15.00
190-61		Officers	Pickled brass, Pin; Dingwall	25.00
190-91	Shoulders	ORs	Numeral: "190"; Caron	14.00

191ST INFANTRY BATTALION

"SOUTH ALBERTA REGIMENT"

The Battalion was raised in McLeod and the surrounding area with mobilization headquarters at McLeod, Alberta under the authority of G.O. 69 July 15th, 1916. The Battalion sailed March 28th, 1917 under the command of Lieutenant-Colonel W. C. Bryan with a strength of six officers and two hundred and forty-six other ranks. In England the Battalion was absorbed into the 21st Reserve Battalion. It was disbanded September 15th, 1920.

BADGE NUMBER: 191

191/OVERSEAS BATTALION/
SOUTHERN ALBERTA/CANADA

AUTHORIZED JULY 12, 1916

Makers: Black, Caron
Fasteners: Lugs
Composition:
Other Ranks: Pickled brass
Officers:
    A: Pickled brass with white metal overlay on "191"
    B: Pickled brass with white metal overlay on design
Ref.: Babin, Meek, Stewart, Cox

Badge No.	Insignia	Rank	Description	Extremely Fine
191-2	Cap	ORs	Pickled brass; Black	100.00
191-21		Officers	Pickled brass, Wm. overlay on design; Black	135.00
191-23		Officers	Pickled brass, Wm. overlay on "191"; Black	135.00
191-41	Collars	ORs	Pickled brass; Black	20.00
191-61		Officers	Pickled brass, Wm. overlay on design; Black	40.00
191-63		Officers	Pickled brass, Wm. overlay on "191"; Black	40.00
191-91	Shoulders	ORs	Numeral: "191"; Caron	14.00
191-93		ORs	Title: "191" / "CANADA"; Black	40.00
191-95		Officers	Title: "191/CANADA", Wm. overlay; Black	50.00

192ND INFANTRY BATTALION

"CROW'S NEST PASS BATTALION"

The Battalion was raised in Blairmore and District with mobilization headquarters at Blairmore, Alberta under the authority of G.O. 69 July 15th, 1916. The Battalion sailed November 1st, 1916 under the command of Captain H. E. Lyon with a strength of twenty-three officers and four hundred and twenty-four other ranks. In England the Battalion was absorbed into the 9th Reserve Battalion. It was disbanded September 15th, 1920.

BADGE NUMBER: 192

CROW'S NEST PASS/192/OVERSEAS BATTALION /ALBERTA/CANADA

AUTHORIZED JULY 3, 1916

Makers: Black, Caron, Tiptaft, Unknown
Fasteners: Lugs
Compositon:
Other Ranks: Pickled copper or brass; Browning copper
Officers:
    A: White metal
    B: Pickled copper with white metal overlay on design
Ref.: Babin, Meek, Stewart, Cox

Note: Two makers of this cap badge exist. They are very difficult to distinguish from one another.

Badge No.	Insignia	Rank	Description	Extremely Fine
192-2	Cap	ORs	Pickled copper; Black	75.00
192-4		ORs	Pickled brass; Black	75.00
192-6		ORs	Browning copper; Tiptaft	75.00
192-21		Officers	White metal; Unknown	165.00
192-23		Officers	Pickled copper, Wm. overlay on design; Black	100.00
192-41	Collars	ORs	Pickled copper; Black	35.00
192-43		ORs	Pickled brass; Black	12.00
192-45		ORs	Browning copper; Tiptaft	12.00
192-61		Officers	White metal; Unknown	85.00
192-63		Officers	Sterling silver, Pin; Unknown	35.00
192-65		Officers	Pickled copper, Wm. overlay on design; Black	50.00
192-91	Shoulders	ORs	Numeral: "192"; Caron	14.00

193RD INFANTRY BATTALION

"NOVA SCOTIA HIGHLANDERS"

The Battalion was raised in Nova Scotia, with mobilization headquarters at Truro under the authority of G.O. 69 July 15th, 1916. The Battalion sailed October 13th, 1916 under the command of Lieutenant-Colonel J. Stanfield with a strength of thirty-two officers and one thousand and twenty other ranks. In England the Battalion was absorbed into the 17th Reserve Battalion. It was disbanded September 15th, 1920.

BADGE NUMBER: 193

NOVA SCOTIA HIGHLANDERS OVERSEAS
/193/SIOL NA FEAR FEARAIL

NOT AUTHORIZED

Makers: Caron, Hemsley, Tiptaft, Unknown
Fasteners: Lugs
Composition:
Other Ranks: Pickled copper or brass
Officers:
　　　　A. Silverplate on copper
　　　　B. Pickled copper with white metal overlay on design
Ref.: Babin, Meek, Stewart, Cox

Note: Two makers of this cap badge exist.
1. Plain ribbons with a void either side of the shield below the Annulas; Hemsley *(Illustrated)*
2. Framed ribbons with a solid badge either side of the shield; Tiptaft

Badge No.	Insignia	Rank	Description	Extremely Fine
193-2	Glengarry	ORs	Pickled copper; Hemsley	65.00
193-4		ORs	Pickled brass; Hemsley	65.00
193-6		ORs	Pickled brass; Tiptaft	60.00
193-21		Officers	Pickled copper, Wm. overlay on design; Hemsley	200.00
193-23		Officers	Silverplate on copper; Unknown	200.00

Badge No.	Insignia	Rank	Description	Extremely Fine
			Maple Leaf Design	
193-41	Collars	ORs	Pickled copper; Hemsley	70.00
193-43		ORs	Pickled brass; Hemsley	70.00
193-45		ORs	Pickled brass; Tiptaft	100.00
193-61		Officers	Pickled copper, Wm. overlay on design; Hemsley	150.00
193-63		Officers	Silverplate on copper; Unknown	100.00
			Scroll Design	
193-47	Collars	ORs	Pickled copper; Hemsley	50.00
193-49		ORs	Pickled copper; Tiptaft	50.00
193-65		Officers	Pickled copper, Wm. overlay on design; Hemsley	100.00
193-67		Officers	Pickled copper, Wm. overlay on design; Tiptaft	100.00
193-91	Shoulders	ORs	Numeral: "193"; Caron	14.00

194TH INFANTRY BATTALION

"EDMONTON HIGHLANDERS"

The Battalion was raised in Edmonton and District with mobilization headquarters at Edmonton, Alberta under the authority of G.O. 69 July 15th, 1916. The Battalion sailed November 14th, 1916 under the command of Lieutenant-Colonel W. C. Craig with a strength of thirty-one officers and nine hundred and six other ranks. In England the Battalion was absorbed into the 9th Reserve Battalion. It was disbanded September 15th, 1920.

BADGE NUMBER: 194

EDMONTON HIGHLANDERS/194/
OVERSEAS BATTALION/CANADA

AUTHORIZED JULY 18, 1916

Makers: Caron, Hemsley, Jackson, Tiptaft
Fasteners: Lugs
Composition:
Other Ranks: Pickled brass; Blackened brass
Officers: Blackened brass with silver overlay on design
Ref.: Babin, Meek, Stewart, Cox

Note: Two makers of this cap badge exist.
1. Pointed leaf design with large numerals "194"; Hemsley *(Illustrated)*
2. Blunt leaf design with small numerals "194"; Tiptaft

Badge No.	Insignia	Rank	Description	Extremely Fine
194-2	Cap	ORs	Pickled brass; Hemsley	90.00
194-4		ORs	Blackened brass; Tiptaft	45.00
194-21		Officers	Blackened brass, Silver overlay on design; Hemsley	200.00
194-41	Collars	ORs	Pickled brass; Hemsley	20.00
194-61		Officers	Blackened brass, Silver overlay on design; Hemsley	95.00
194-91	Shoulders	ORs	Numeral: "194"; Caron	15.00
194-93		ORs	Title: "EDMONTON HIGHLANDERS CANADA"; Small letters; Tiptaft	30.00
194-95		ORs	Title: "EDMONTON HIGHLANDERS CANADA"; Large letters; Jackson	30.00

195TH INFANTRY BATTALION

"CITY OF REGINA BATTALION"

The Battalion was raised and mobilized in Regina, Saskatchewan under the authority of G.O. 69 July 15th, 1916. The Battalion sailed November 1st, 1916 under the command of Lieutenant-Colonel A. C. Garner with a strength of thirty-one officers and nine hundred and ninety-eight other ranks. In England the Battalion was absorbed into the 32nd Reserve Battalion. It was disbanded September 15th, 1920.

BADGE NUMBER: 195

No.-195 CITY OF REGINA OVERSEAS BATTALION/195/
SASKATCHEWAN CANADA

AUTHORIZED APRIL 14, 1916

Makers: Caron, Lees, Wheatley
Fasteners: Lugs
Composition:
Other Ranks: Browning copper
Officers:
A: Gilt on silver
B: Silver with enamel overlay on design
Ref.: Babin, Meek, Stewart, Cox

Note: Two makers of this cap badge exist. They are very difficult to distinguish from one another.

Badge No.	Insignia	Rank	Description	Extremely Fine
195-2	Cap	ORs	Browning copper; Lees	35.00
195-4		ORs	Browning copper; Wheatley	35.00
195-21		Officers	Gilt on silver; Lees	75.00
195-23		Officers	Silver with enamel overlay on design; Wheatley	195.00
195-41	Collars	ORs	Browning copper; Lees	20.00
195-43		ORs	Browning copper; Wheatley	20.00
195-61		Officers	Gilt on silver; Lees	30.00
195-63		Officers	Silver with enamel overlay on design; Wheatley	35.00
195-91	Shoulders	ORs	Numeral: "195"; Caron	14.00
195-93		ORs	Title: "CAN 195 ADA"; Lees	30.00
195-95		Officers	Silver/Enamel; Wheatley	50.00

196TH INFANTRY BATTALION

"WESTERN UNIVERSITIES C.E.F. BATTALION"

The Battalion was raised from Western Universities with mobilization headquarters at Winnipeg, Manitoba under the authority of G.O. 69 July 15th, 1916. The Battalion sailed November 1st, 1916 under the command of Lieutenant-Colonel D. S.MacKay with a strength of thirty-two officers and nine hundred and seventy-four other ranks. In England the Battalion was absorbed into the 19th Reserve Battalion. It was disbanded September 15th, 1920.

BADGE NUMBER: 196

OVERSEAS BATTALION/WESTERN UNIVERSITIES /196/CANADA

NOT AUTHORIZED

Makers: Allan, Caron, Tiptaft
Fasteners: Tangs, Pin
Composition:
Other Ranks: Browning copper or brass
Officers:
    A: Gilt on copper;
    B: Browning brass
Ref.: Babin, Meek, Stewart, Cox

Note: Two makers of this cap badge exist.
    1. Pointed leaf design; Tall type; Allan *(Illustrated)*
    2. Blunt leaf design; Small type; Tiptaft.

Badge No.	Insignia	Rank	Description	Extremely Fine
196-2	Cap	ORs	Browning copper; Allan	35.00
196-4		ORs	Browning copper; Tiptaft	35.00
196-6		ORs	Browning brass; Allan	45.00
196-21		Officers	Gilt on copper; Allan	50.00
196-41	Collars	ORs	Browning copper; Allan	16.00
196-43		ORs	Browning copper; Tiptaft	16.00
196-45		ORs	Browning brass; Allan	24.00
196-61		Officers	Browning brass, Pin; Allan	25.00
196-91	Shoulders	ORs	Numeral: "196"; Caron	14.00
196-93		ORs	Numeral: "196"; Allan	16.00
196-95		ORs	Title: "WESTERN UNIVERSITIES CANADA"; Allan	25.00

197TH INFANTRY BATTALION

"SCANDINAVIAN OVERSEAS BATTALION" /"VIKINGS OF CANADA"

The Battalion was raised in Western Canada, with mobilization headquarters at Winnipeg, Manitoba under the authority of G.O. 69 July 15th, 1916. The Battalion sailed January 26th, 1917 under the command of Lieutenant-Colonel H. G. Fonseca with a strength of nine officers and three hundred and six other ranks. In England the Battalion was absorbed into the 11th Reserve Battalion. It was disbanded September 15th, 1920.

BADGE NUMBER: 197

OVERSEAS/197/VIKINGS OF CANADA

NOT AUTHORIZED

Makers: Caron, Inglis
Fasteners: Lugs
Composition:
Other Ranks: Pickled copper or brass
Officers: Pickled copper with white metal overlay on design
Ref.: Babin, Meek, Stewart, Cox

Badge No.	Insignia	Rank	Description	Extremely Fine
197-2	Cap	ORs	Pickled copper; Inglis	35.00
197-4		ORs	Pickled brass, Inglis	40.00
197-21		Officers	Pickled copper, Wm. overlay on design; Inglis	90.00
	Ship design			
197-41	Collars	ORs	Pickled copper; Inglis	50.00
197-61		Officers	Unknown	- -
	Maple Leaf design			
197-43	Collars	ORs	Pickled copper; Inglis	16.00
197-45		ORs	Pickled brass; Inglis	16.00
197-63		Officers	Pickled copper, Wm. overlay on design; Inglis	50.00
197-91	Shoulders	ORs	Numeral: "197"; Caron	20.00
197-93		ORs	Title: "197" over "INF"; Caron	22.00

198TH INFANTRY BATTALION

"CANADIAN BUFFS"

The Battalion was raised and mobilized in Toronto, Ontario under the authority of G.O. 69 July 15th, 1916. The Battalion sailed March 28th, 1917 under the command of Lieutenant-Colonel J. A. Cooper with a strength of thirty-one officers and eight hundred and forty-one other ranks. In England the Battalion was absorbed into the 3rd Reserve Battalion. It was disbanded September 15th, 1920.

BADGE NUMBER: 198

No. - 198A   **OVERSEAS 198 BATTALION**
                        /CANADIAN BUFFS

AUTHORIZED JUNE 30, 1916

Makers: Caron, Ellis, Hemsley
Fasteners: Lugs
Composition:
Other Ranks: Pickled brass;
                 Browning copper
Officers: Gilt on silver
Ref.: Babin, Meek, Stewart, Cox

Note: Two makers of this cap badge exist.
1. Framed garter with periods; Hemsley *(Illustrated)*
2. Plain garter without periods; Ellis.
The authorized collars for this battalion are the Standard General List issue

Badge No.	Insignia	Rank	Description	Extremely Fine
198A-2	Cap	ORs	Pickled brass; Hemsley	35.00
198A-4		ORs	Browning copper; Ellis	25.00
198A-21		Officers	Gilt on silver; Hemsley	50.00
198A-41	Collars	ORs	General List	5.00
198A-61		Officers	General List	8.00
198A-91	Shoulders	ORs	Numeral: "198"; Caron	14.00
198A-93		ORs	Title: "198" over "CANADA"; Ellis	20.00

No. - 198B   **CANADIAN BUFFS**

This badge was never authorized. Permission could not be obtained for the use of the dragon from the British Regiment, the Royal East Kent.

Makers: Ellis , Gaunt
Fasteners: Lugs
Composition:
 Other Ranks: Gilt on brass
             Officers: Gilt on brass
Ref.: Babin, Cox

Note: It was proposed that the officers and men would wear the same badges.

Badge No.	Insignia	Rank	Description	Extremely Fine
198B-2	Cap	ORs	Gilt on brass; Ellis	65.00
198B-4		ORs	Gilt on brass; Gaunt	55.00
198B-21		Officers	Gilt on brass; Ellis	65.00
198B-41	Collars	ORs	Gilt on brass; Ellis	25.00
198B-43		ORs	Gilt on brass; Gaunt	25.00
198B-61		Officers	Gilt on brass; Ellis	25.00

No. - 198C　　　　　**THE BUFFS**

This badge was never authorized for use by the 198th Battalion.

Makers: Gaunt
Fasteners: Lugs, Slide
Composition:
Other Ranks: Gilt on brass
Officers: As above
Ref.: Babin, Cox

Note: This badge is identical to the badge worn by the Royal East Kent Regiment. The only difference being the finish. The Canadian badge is gilt.

Badge No.	Insignia	Rank	Description	Extremely Fine
198C-2	Cap	ORs	Gilt on brass; Gaunt	40.00
198C-21		Officers	Gilt on brass; Gaunt	45.00
198C-41	Collars	ORs	Gilt on brass; Gaunt	20.00
198C-61		Officers	Gilt on brass; Gaunt	20.00

199TH INFANTRY BATTALION

"IRISH CANADIAN RANGERS"/ "DUCHESS OF CONNAUGHT'S OWN"

BADGE NUMBER: 199

No. - 199A

QUIS SEPARABIT
/DUCHESS OF CONNAUGHT'S OWN/
199/IRISH CANADIAN RANGERS

AUTHORIZED NOVEMBER 17, 1916

Makers: Caron, Hemsley
Fasteners: Lugs
Composition:
Other Ranks: Pickled brass
Officers: Unknown
Ref.: Babin, Meek, Cox

Badge No.	Insignia	Rank	Description	Extremely Fine
199A-2	Cap	ORs	Pickled brass; Hemsley	65.00
199A-21		Officers	Unknown	- -
199A-41	Collars	ORs	Pickled brass; Hemsley	20.00
199A-61		Officers	Unknown	- -
199A-91	Shoulders	ORs	Numeral: "199"; Caron	14.00
199A-93		ORs	Title: "199" over "CANADA"; Unknown	20.00
199A-95		ORs	Title: "Crown/DCO/CANADA"; Unknown	25.00

No. - 199B   **OVERSEAS IRISH CANADIAN RANGERS**
/199/QUIS SEPARABIT

Makers: Hemsley
Fasteners: Lugs, Pin
Composition:
 Other Ranks: Pickled brass
   Officers: Sterling silver
Ref.: Babin, Stewart, Cox

Badge No.	Insignia	Rank	Description	Extremely Fine
199B-2	Cap	ORs	Pickled brass; Hemsley	75.00
199B-21		Officers	Sterling silver; Hemsley	150.00
199B-41	Collars	ORs	Pickled brass; Hemsley	30.00
199B-61		Officers	Sterling silver; Hemsley	50.00

200TH INFANTRY BATTALION

"WINNIPEG BATTALION"

The Battalion was raised and mobilized in Winnipeg, Manitoba under the authority of G.O. 69 July 15th, 1916. The Battalion sailed May 3th, 1917 under the command of Lieutenant-Colonel A. L. Bonnycastle with a strength of seventeen officers and four hundred and seventy-seven other ranks. In England the Battalion was absorbed into the 11th Reserve Battalion. It was disbanded September 15th, 1920.

BADGE NUMBER: 200

200/WINNIPEG/OVERSEAS BATTALION CANADA

AUTHORIZED APRIL 19, 1916

Makers: Birks, Unknown
Fasteners: Lugs, Pin
Composition:
Other Ranks: Pickled silver
Officers: Gilt on silver with silver overlay on numbers
Ref.: Babin, Meek, Stewart, Cox

Note: There are two makers of this badge but only the Birks is recorded here. Details of the second are not known. Shoulder numerals are not known.

Badge No.	Insignia	Rank	Description	Extremely Fine
200-2	Cap	ORs	Pickled silver; Birks	65.00
200-21		Officers	Gilt on silver, Silver numbers; Birks	60.00
200-41	Collars	ORs	Pickled silver; Birks	15.00
200-61		Officers	Gilt on silver, Silver numbers; Birks	15.00
200-91	Shoulders	ORs	Numerals "200"	Unknown

201ST INFANTRY BATTALION

"TORONTO LIGHT INFANTRY"

The Battalion was raised and mobilized in Toronto, Ontario under the authority of G.O. 69 July 15th, 1916. The Commanding Officer of the Battalion was Lieutenant-Colonel E. W. Hagarty, however, insufficient recruits resulted in the Battalion being disbanded in Canada and the enlisted men were absorbed into the 170th and 198th Infantry Battalions.

BADGE NUMBER: 201

No. - 201A

TORONTO LIGHT INFANTRY /201/CANADA OVERSEAS

NOT AUTHORIZED

Makers: Birks, Caron, Hemsley
Fasteners: Lugs
Composition:
Other Ranks: Pickled copper
Officers:
    A. Silverplate on copper
    B. Pickled copper with silver overlay on "201"
Ref.: Babin, Stewart, Cox

Badge No.	Insignia	Rank	Description	Extremely Fine
201A-2	Cap	ORs	Pickled copper, Solid; Hemsley	30.00
201A-21		Officers	Silverplate on copper; Hemsley	120.00
201A-23		Officers	Pickled copper, Silver overlay on "201"; Hemsley	150.00
201A-41	Collars	ORs	Pickled copper; Hemsley	15.00
201A-61		Officers	Pickled copper, Silver overlay on "201"; Hemsley	25.00
201A-91	Shoulders	ORs	Numeral: "201"; Caron	18.00
201A-93		ORs	Numeral: "201"; Birks	18.00

No. - 201B   **OVERSEAS BATTALION CANADA/201**

Makers: Caron for Eaton's
Fasteners: Lugs, Pin
Composition:
Other Ranks: Pickled copper with
white metal overlay
on centre
Officers: Pickled copper with
silver overlay on
centre
Ref.: Not previously listed

Note: Collars are not known.

Badge No.	Insignia	Rank	Description	Extremely Fine
201B-2	Cap	ORs	Pickled copper, Wm. overlay on centre	275.00
201B-21		Officers	Pickled copper, Silver overlay on centre	275.00

202ND INFANTRY BATTALION

"EDMONTON SPORTSMEN'S BATTALION"

The Battalion was raised and mobilized in Edmonton, Alberta under the authority of G.O. 69, July 15th, 1916. The Battalion sailed November 24th, 1916, under the command of Lieutenant-Colonel P. E. Bowen, with a strength of twenty-seven officers and seven hundred and forty-six other ranks. In England, the Battalion was absorbed into the 9th Reserve Battalion. It was disbanded September 15th, 1920.

BADGE NUMBER: 202

SPORTSMEN'S BATTALION/OVERSEAS/ 202/EDMONTON ALBERTA CANADA

AUTHORIZED MARCH 29, 1916

Makers: Jackson Bros., Tiptaft, Stanley, Aylward
Fasteners: Lugs, Pin
Composition:
Other Ranks: Pickled copper or brass; Blackened brass
Officers: Gilt on brass
Ref.: Babin, Meek, Stewart, Cox

Note: Three makers of this cap badge exist.
1. Wide rifle butt design; Small type for legends; Jackson *(Illustrated)*
2. Narrow rifle butt design; Large type for legends; Tiptaft
3. A Stanley and Aylward badge has been reported but not verified and thus not listed below.

Badge No.	Insignia	Rank	Description	Extremely Fine
202-2	Cap	ORs	Pickled copper; Jackson	40.00
202-4		ORs	Pickled brass; Jackson	40.00
202-6		ORs	Blackened brass; Tiptaft	40.00
202-21		Officers	Gilt on brass; Jackson	60.00
202-23		Officers	Gilt on brass; Tiptaft	70.00
202-41	Collars	ORs	Pickled copper; Jackson	15.00
202-43		ORs	Pickled brass; Jackson	15.00
202-45		ORs	Blackened brass; Jackson	30.00
202-61		Officers	Gilt on brass; Jackson	25.00
202-63		Officers	Gilt on brass; Tiptaft	25.00
202-91	Shoulders	ORs	Numeral: "202"; Unknown	14.00
202-93		ORs	Title: "CAN 202 ADA"; Jackson	25.00

203RD INFANTRY BATTALION

"WINNIPEG RIFLES"

The Battalion was raised and mobilized in Winnipeg, Manitoba under the authority of G.O. 69 July 15th, 1916. The Battalion sailed October 28th, 1916 under the command of Lieutenant-Colonel J. E. Hansford with a strength of thirty-two officers and nine hundred and fifty-seven other ranks. In England the Battalion was absorbed into the 18th Reserve Battalion. It was disbanded September 15th, 1920.

BADGE NUMBER: 203

/HOSTI ACIE NOMINATI

AUTHORIZED MAY 6, 1916

Makers: Birks, Caron
Fasteners: Lugs
Composition:
Other Ranks: Pickled brass
Officers:
    A: Sterling silver
    B: Pickled brass with silver overlay on "203" and "motto
Ref.: Babin, Meek, Stewart, Cox

Badge No.	Insignia	Rank	Description	Extremely Fine
203-2	Cap	ORs	Pickled brass, Void; Birks	40.00
203-4		ORs	Pickled brass, Solid; Birks	50.00
203-21		Officers	Sterling silver; Birks	160.00
203-23		Officers	Pickled brass, Silver overlay on "203" and "Motto"; Birks	125.00
203-41	Collars	ORs	Pickled brass, Void; Birks	16.00
203-43		ORs	Pickled brass, Solid; Birks	16.00
203-61		Officers	Sterling silver; Birks	25.00
203-63		Officers	Pickled brass, Silver overlay on "203" and "Motto"; Birks	25.00
203-91	Shoulders	ORs	Numeral: "203"; Caron	14.00
203-93		ORs	Numeral: "203"; Birks	14.00

204TH INFANTRY BATTALION

"TORONTO BEAVERS"

The Battalion was raised and mobilized in Toronto, Ontario under the authority of G.O. 69 July 15th, 1916. The Battalion sailed March 28th, 1917 under the command of Lieutenant-Colonel W. H. Price with a strength of twenty-seven officers and seven hundred and eighty-nine other ranks. In England the Battalion was absorbed into the 2nd Reserve Battalion. It was disbanded September 15th, 1920.

BADGE NUMBER: 204

No. - 204A

BEAVERS/204/
OVER BATTALION SEAS
/TORONTO CANADA

AUTHORIZED JUNE 28, 1916

Makers: Birks, Caron, Ellis
Fasteners: Lugs
Composition:
Other Ranks: Pickled copper; Browning copper or brass
Officers: Unknown
Ref: Babin, Meek, Stewart, Cox

Badge No.	Insignia	Rank	Description	Extremely Fine
204A-2	Cap	ORs	Browning copper; Ellis	45.00
204A-4		ORs	Browning brass; Ellis	50.00
204A-21		Officers	Pickled copper; Ellis	45.00
204A-41	Collars	ORs	Browning copper; Ellis	12.00
204A-43		ORs	Browning brass; Ellis	15.00
204A-61		Officers	Pickled copper; Ellis	12.00
204A-91	Shoulders	ORs	Numeral: "204"; Caron	14.00
204A-93		ORs	Numeral: "204"; Birks	14.00

No. - 204B   **OVERSEAS BATTALION CANADA/204**

Makers: Caron for Eaton's
Fasteners: Lugs, Pin
Composition:
Other Ranks: Pickled copper with
white metal overlay
on centre
Officers: Pickled copper with
silverplate overlay
on centre
Ref.: Not previously listed

Note: Collars not issued.

Badge No.	Insignia	Rank	Description	Extremely Fine
204B-2	Cap	ORs	Pickled copper, Wm. overlay on centre	275.00
204B-21		Officers	Pickled copper, Silverplated overlay on centre	275.00

205TH INFANTRY BATTALION

"HAMILTON TIGER BATTALION"

The Battalion was raised and mobilized in Hamilton, Ontario under the authority of G.O. 69 July 15th, 1916. On December 20th, 1916 the Battlion was redesignated a Draft Depot for the Canadian Machine Gun Corps, Military District 2, Central Ontario. On October 10th, 1917 the unit sailed for England under the command of Lieutenant-Colonel R. R. Moodie.

BADGE NUMBER: 205

HAMILTON/OVERSEAS 205 BATTALION/CANADA

AUTHORIZED APRIL 6, 1916

Makers: Hemsley, Inglis
Fasteners: Lugs
Composition:
Other Ranks: Pickled copper
or brass
Officers: Pickled copper with
silver overlay
on design
Ref.: Babin, Meek, Stewart, Cox

Badge No.	Insignia	Rank	Description	Extremely Fine
205-2	Cap	ORs	Pickled copper; Hemsley, Inglis	35.00
205-4		ORs	Pickled brass; Hemsley, Inglis	35.00
205-21		Officers	Pickled copper, Silver overlay on design; Hemsley, Inglis	60.00
205-41	Collars	ORs	Pickled copper; Hemsley, Inglis	16.00
205-43		ORs	Pickled brass; Hemsley, Inglis	16.00
205-61		Officers	Pickled copper, Silver overlay on design; Hemsley, Inglis	30.00
205-91	Shoulders	ORs	Numeral: "205"; Birks	16.00
205-93		ORs	Title: "LION HEAD" over "205"; Hemsley, Inglis	30.00

206TH INFANTRY BATTALION

"CANADIENS FRANCAIS"

The Battalion was raised in the Counties of Beauharnois, La Prairie and Terrebonne, Quebec with mobilization headquarters at Montreal under the authority of G.O. 69 July 15th, 1916. The commanding officer was Lieutenant-Colonel T. Pagnuelo. In Canada the Battalion was absorbed into the 157th Infantry Battalion.

BADGE NUMBER: 206

BON COEUR ET BON BRAS/
CANADIENS/206/FRANCAIS/D'OUTRE MER

AUTHORIZED APRIL 10, 1916

Makers: Hemsley, Inglis, Unknown
Fasteners: Lugs
Composition:
Other Ranks: Pickled copper or brass
Officers:
    A: Pickled brass with white metal overlay on "206"
    B: Pickled brass with white metal overlay on design
Ref.: Babin, Meek, Stewart, Cox

Note: Two makers of this cap badge exist.
    1. The "2" in "206" has serifs and the lion has no rib cage design; Hemsley, Inglis
    2. The "2" in "206" has no serifs and the lion has a rib cage design; Unknown
    (Illustrated)

Badge No.	Insignia	Rank	Description	Extremely Fine
206-2	Cap	ORs	Pickled copper; Unknown	40.00
206-4		ORs	Plckled brass, Void; Hemsley, Inglis	40.00
• 206-6		ORs	Pickled brass, Solid; Hemsley, Inglis	50.00
206-21		Officers	Pickled brass, Wm. overlay on "206"; Unknown	150.00
206-23		Officers	Pickled brass, Wm. overlay on design; Hemsley, Inglis	175.00
206-41	Collars	ORs	Pickled copper; Unknown	20.00
206-43		ORs	Pickled brass; Hemsley, Inglis	20.00
206-61		Officers	Pickled brass, Wm. overlay on design; Hemsley, Inglis	35.00
206-91	Shoulders	ORs	Numeral: "206"; Unknown	14.00

207TH INFANTRY BATTALION

"OTTAWA AND CARLETON OVERSEAS BATTALION"

The Battalion was raised in the County of Carleton, Ontario with mobilization headquarters at Ottawa under the authority of G.O. 69 July 15th, 1916. The Battalion sailed June 2nd, 1917 under the command of Lieutenant-Colonel C. W. McLean with a strength of twenty-seven officers and six hundred and fifty-two other ranks. In England the Battalion was absorbed into the 7th Reserve Battalion. It was disbanded September 15th, 1920.

BADGE NUMBER: 207

No. - 207A

OTTAWA CARLETON BATTALION/ OVERSEAS/207/CANADA

WITH "OVERSEAS" VARIETY

Makers: Birks
Fasteners: Lugs
Composition:
Other Ranks: Browning copper, or brass
Officers: Browning copper with silver overlay on "205"
Ref.: Babin, Cox

Badge No.	Insignia	Rank	Description	Extremely Fine
207A-2	Cap	ORs	Browning copper, Solid; Birks	50.00
207A-4		ORs	Browning copper, Void; Birks	50.00
207A-6		ORs	Browning brass, Void; Birks	50.00
207A-21		Officers	Browning copper, Silver overlay on "205", Void; Birks	100.00
207A-41	Collars	ORs	Browning copper, Solid; Birks	25.00
207A-43		ORs	Browning copper, Void; Birks	25.00
207A-45		ORs	Browning brass, Void; Birks	25,00
207A-61		Officers	Browning copper, Silver overlay on "205", Void; Birks	50.00

No. - 207B   **OTTAWA CARLETON BATTALION**
/207/CANADA

WITHOUT "OVERSEAS: VARIETY

Makers: Birks, Hemsley
Fasteners: Lugs, Pin
Composition:
Other Ranks: Pickled brass;
                   Browning copper
Officers: Pickled brass with
                silver overlay
                on "207"
Ref.: Babin, Meek, Stewart, Cox

Note: Two makers of this cap badge exist.
      1. A domed badge with a large beaver. The badge is 46 mm high; Hemsley
         (Illustrated)
      2. A flat badge with a small beaver. The badge is 43 mm high; Birks

Badge No.	Insignia	Rank	Description	Extremely Fine
207B-2	Cap	ORs	Pickled brass, Solid; Hemsley	50.00
207B-4		ORs	Pickled brass, Void; Hemsley	50.00
207B-6		ORs	Browning copper, Void; Birks	50.00
207B-21		Officers	Unknown	- -
207B-41	Collars	ORs	Pickled brass, Solid; Hemsley	25.00
207B-43		ORs	Pickled brass, Void; Hemsley	25.00
207B-45		ORs	Browning copper; Birks	25.00
207B-61		Officers	Unknown	- -
207B-91	Shoulders	ORs	Numeral: "207"; Unknown	- -

208TH INFANTRY BATTALION

"CANADIAN IRISH"

The Battalion was raised and mobilized in Toronto, Ontario under the authority of G.O. 69 July 15th, 1916. The Battalion sailed May 3rd, 1917 under the command of Lieutenant-Colonel T. H. Lennox with a strength of twenty-seven officers and six hundred and eighty-six other ranks. In England the Battalion was broken up and absorbed into the 2nd and 8th Reserve Battalions. It was disbanded September 15th, 1920.

BADGE NUMBER: 208

No. - 208A　　　　**208/OVERSEAS/CANADIAN IRISH BATTN**

Makers: Caron, Hemsley
Fasteners: Lugs
Composition:
Other Ranks: Pickled copper;
　　　　　　　　 Browning copper
Officers:
　　A: Gilt on copper
　　B: Silverplate on
　　　　 copper
Ref.: Babin, Meek, Stewart, Cox

Badge No.	Insignia	Rank	Description	Extremely Fine
208A-2	Cap	ORs	Pickled copper; Hemsley	50.00
208A-4		ORs	Browning copper; Hemsley	50.00
208A-21		Officers	Gilt on copper; Hemsley	350.00
208A-23		Officers	Silverplate on copper; Hemsley	125.00
208A-41	Collars	ORs	Pickled copper; Hemsley	25.00
208A-43		ORs	Browning copper; Hemsley	25.00
208A-61		Officers	Gilt on copper; Hemsley	50.00
208A-91	Shoulders	ORs	Numeral: "208"; Caron	14.00

No. - 208B   **OVERSEAS BATTALION CANADA/208**

Makers: Caron for Eaton's
Fasteners: Lugs, Pin
Composition:
Other Ranks: Pickled cpper with
white metal overlay
on centre
Officers: Pickled copper with
silver overlay on
centre
Ref.: Not previously listed

Note: Collars not issued.

Badge No.	Insignia	Rank	Description	Extremely Fine
208B-2	Cap	ORs	Pickled copper, Wm. overlay on centre	225.00
208B-21		Officers	Pickled copper, Silver overlay on centre	240.00

209TH INFANTRY BATTALION

The Battalion was raised and mobilized in Swift Current, Saskatchewan under the authority of G.O. 69 July 15th, 1916. The Battalion sailed November 3rd, 1916 under the command of Lieutenant-Colonel W. O. Smyth with a strength of twenty-nine officers and nine hundred and fifteen other ranks. In England the Battalion was absorbed into the 9th Reserve Battalion. It was disbanded September 15th, 1920.

BADGE NUMBER: 209

OVERSEAS 209 BATTALION
/SWIFT CURRENT/CANADA

Makers: Birks, Inglis, Tiptaft
Fasteners: Lugs
Composition:
Other Ranks: Pickled copper or brass
Officers: Pickled copper with white metal overlay on design
Ref.: Babin, Meek, Stewart

Note: Two makers of this cap badge exist.
    1. Wide short numbers with plain ribbons; Inglis *(Illustrated)*
    2. Narrow tall numbers with framed ribbons; Tiptaft.

Badge No.	Insignia	Rank	Description	Extremely Fine
209-2	Cap	ORs	Pickled copper; Inglis	50.00
209-4		ORs	Pickled brass; Inglis	45.00
209-6		ORs	Pickled brass; Tiptaft	45.00
209-21		Officers	Pickled copper, Wm. overlay on design; Inglis	100.00
209-41	Collars	ORs	Pickled copper; Inglis	35.00
209-43		ORs	Pickled brass; Inglis	30.00
209-45		ORs	Pickled brass; Tiptaft	30.00
209-61		Officers	Pickled copper, Wm. overlay on design; Inglis	50.00
209-91	Shoulders	ORs	Numeral: "209"; Birks	14.00

210TH INFANTRY BATTALION

"FRONTIERSMEN OF WESTERN CANADA"

The Battalion was raised and mobilized in Moose Jaw, Saskatchewan under the authority of G.O. 69 July 15th, 1916. The Battalion sailed April 11th, 1917 under the command of Lieutenant-Colonel W. E. Seaborn with a strength of eighteen offices and four hundred and sixty-two other ranks. In England the Battalion was absorbed into the 19th Reserve Battalion. It was disbanded September 15th, 1920.

BADGE NUMBER: 210

OVERSEAS/210/FRONTIERSMEN
/WESTERN/CANADA

Makers: Creigton's
Fasteners: Lugs, Pin
Composition:
Other Ranks: Enamelled centre on browning copper or brass
Officers:
  A: Silverplate with enamelled centre
  B: White metal with brass centre
  C: Gilt with enamelled centre
Ref.: Babin, Meek, Stewart, Cox

Note: All caps and collar badges are produced by Creigton's

Badge No.	Insignia	Rank	Description	Extremely Fine
210-2	Cap	ORs	Browning copper with enamelled centre	65.00
210-4		ORs	Browning brass with enamelled centre	60.00
210-21		Officers	Silverplate with enamelled centre	350.00
210-23		Officers	White Metal with brass centre (3 pcs construction)	500.00
210-25		Officers	Gilt enamelled centre	350.00
210-41	Collars	ORs	Browning copper with enamelled centre	50.00
210-43		ORs	Browning brass with enamelled centre	50.00
210-61		Officers	Gilt enamelled centre	50.00
210-91	Shoulders	ORs	Numeral: "210"; Unknown	14.00
210-93		ORs	Title:" CROWN/210/CANADA"	30.00

211TH INFANTRY BATTALION

"ALBERTA AMERICANS"

The Battalion was raised in the Provinces of Alberta and British Columbia with mobilization headquarters at Vancouver, British Columbia under the authority of G.O. 69 July 15th, 1916. The Battalion sailed December 20th, 1916 under the command of Lieutenant-Colonel W. M. Sage with a strength of twenty-five officers and six hundred and sixty-two other ranks. In England the Battalion was absorbed into the Canadian Railway Troops. It was disbanded September 15th, 1920.

BADGE NUMBER: 211

No. - 211A
CANADA 211 OVERSEAS
/ACTA NON VERBA

AUTHORIZED JULY 7, 1916

Makers: Birks, Caron, Lees, Tiptaft, Unknown
Fasteners: Lugs
Composition:
Other Ranks: Pickled brass; Blackened brass
Officers:
  A: Pickled brass with silver overlay on "211"
  B: Gilt on brass
  C: Browning copper with silver overlay on central design
Ref.: Babin, Meek, Stewart, Cox

Note: Two makers of this cap badge exist.
1. Blunt leaf design; Small type on motto ribbon; Lees. *(Illustrated)*
2. Pointed leaf design; Large type on motto ribbon; Tiptaft.

Badge No.	Insignia	Rank	Description	Extremely Fine
211A-2	Cap	ORs	Pickled brass; Lees	40.00
211A-4		ORs	Blackened brass; Tiptaft	75.00
211A-21		Officers	Pickled brass, Silver overlay on "211"; Lees	100.00
211A-23		Officers	Pickled brass, Silver overlay on design; Lees	275.00
211A-25		Officers	Gilt on brass; Unknown	45.00
211A-41	Collars	ORs	Pickled brass; Lees	20.00
211A-43		ORs	Blackened brass; Tiptaft	20.00
211A-61		Officers	Pickled brass, Silver overlay on "211"; Lees	40.00
211A-63		Officers	Pickled brass, Silver overlay on design; Lees	50.00

Badge No.	Insignia	Rank	Description	Extremely Fine
211A-91	Shoulders	ORs	Numeral: "211"; Caron	14.00
211A-93		ORs	Numeral: "211"; Birks	14.00
211A-95		ORs	Title: "211" over "CANADA", Birks	25.00

No. - 211B   **CANADA 211 OVERSEAS /AMERICAN LEGION**

NOT AUTHORIZED

Photograph
Not Available
At Press Time

Makers: Lees, Tiptaft, Unknown
Fasteners: Lugs, Pins
Composition:
Other Ranks: Pickled brass
Officers: Pickled brass with silver overlay on design
Ref.: Not previously listed

Badge No.	Insignia	Rank	Description	Extremely Fine
211B-2	Cap	ORs	Pickled brass; Lees	200.00
211B-4		ORs	Pickled brass; Tiptaft	200.00
211B-21		Officers	PIckled brass, Silver overlay on design	300.00
211B-41	Collars	ORs	Pickled brass; Lees	50.00
211B-43		ORs	Pickled brass; Tiptaft	50.00
211B-61		Officers	Unknown	- -

212TH INFANTRY BATTALION

"WINNIPEG AMERICANS"

The Battalion was raised in Manitoba with mobilization headquarters at Winnipeg under the authority of G.O. 69 July 15th, 1916. The commanding officer of the Battalion was Lieutenant-Colonel E. C. Pitman. The Battalion was absorbed into the 97th Infantry Battalion in Canada due to the lack of recruits.

BADGE NUMBER: 212

No. - 212A   **CANADA 212 OVERSEAS /ACTA NON VERBA**

AUTHORIZED JULY 17, 1916

Makers: Ellis, Lees
Fasteners: Lugs
Composition:
Other Ranks: Browning copper; Blackened copper
Officers: Silverplate on copper
Ref.: Babin, Meek, Stewart, Cox

Badge No.	Insignia	Rank	Description	Extremely Fine
212A-2	Cap	ORs	Browning copper; Lees, Ellis	30.00
212A-4		ORs	Blackened copper; Lees, Ellis	22.00
212A-21		Officers	Silverplate on copper; Lees, Ellis	75.00
212A-41	Collars	ORs	Browning copper; Lees, Ellis	15.00
212A-43		ORs	Blackened copper; Lees, Ellis	18.00
212A-61		Officers	Silverplate on copper; Lees, Ellis	30.00
212A-91	Shoulders	ORs	Numeral: "212"	14.00

No. - 212B

212/CANADA OVERSEAS
/AMERICAN LEGION

NOT AUTHORIZED

Makers: Hemsley
Fasteners: Lugs
Composition:
 Other Ranks: Pickled copper
  or brass
 Officers: Gilt on copper
Ref.: Babin, Cox

Badge No.	Insignia	Rank	Description	Extremely Fine
212B-2	Cap	ORs	Pickled copper; Hemsley	25.00
212B-4		ORs	Pickled brass; Hemsley	50.00
212B-21		Officers	Gilt on copper; Hemsley	75.00
212B-41	Collars	ORs	Pickled copper; Hemsley	10.00
212B-61		Officers	Gilt on copper; Hemsley	25.00

213TH INFANTRY BATTALION
"TORONTO AMERICANS"

The Battalion was raised in St. Catharines, Ontario with mobilization headquarters at Toronto under the authority of G.O. 69 July 15th, 1916. The Battalion sailed January 21st, 1917 under the command of Lieutenant-Colonel B. J. McCormick with a strength of four hundred and sixty-three officers and men. In England the Battalion was absorbed into the 4th Reserve Battalion. It was disbanded September 15th, 1920.

BADGE NUMBER: 213

No. - 213A   CANADA 213 OVERSEAS
                        /ACTA NON VERBA

AUTHORIZED JULY 7, 1916

Makers: Birks, Ellis, Lees
Fasteners: Lugs, Pin
Composition:
Other Ranks: Browning copper;
                 Antique copper
   Officers:
      A: Gilt on copper with
             enamel on design
      B: Sterling silver
Ref.: Babin, Meek, Stewart, Cox

Badge No.	Insignia	Rank	Description	Extremely Fine
213A-2	Cap	ORs	Browning copper; Lees, Ellis	35.00
213A-4		ORs	Antique copper; Lees, Ellis	35.00
213A-21		Officers	Gilt on copper with enamel on design; Lees, Ellis	240.00
213A-23		Officers	Sterling silver; Lees, Ellis	100.00
213A-41	Collars	ORs	Browning copper; Lees, Ellis	20.00
213A-43		ORs	Antique copper; Lees, Ellis	20.00
213A-61		Officers	Gilt on copper with enamel on design; Lees, Ellis	100.00
213A-63		Officers	Sterling silver; Lees. Ellis	50.00
213A-91	Shoulders	ORs	Numeral: "213"; Birks	14.00

No. - 213B CANADIAN 213 OVERSEAS/AMERICAN LEGION

NOT AUTHORIZED

Makers: Ellis, Lees
Fasteners: Lugs
Composition:
 Other Ranks: Antique copper
 Officers: Gilt and enamelled
Ref.: Not previously listed

Badge No.	Insignia	Rank	Description	Extremely Fine
213B-2	Cap	ORs	Antique copper; Lees, Ellis	35.00
213B-21		Officers	Gilt with enamel on design; Lees, Ellis	240.00
213B-41	Collars	ORs	Antique copper; Lees, Ellis	20.00
213B-61		Officers	Gilt with enamel on design; Lees, Ellis	100.00

214TH INFANTRY BATTALION

"SASKATCHEWAN BATTALION"

The Battalion was raised in Saskatchewan with mobilization headquarters at Wadena under the authority of G.O. 69 July 15th, 1916. The Battalion sailed April 18th, 1917 under the command of Lieutenant-Colonel J. H. Hearn with a strength of twenty officers and five hundred and ninety-five other ranks. In England the Battalion was absorbed into the 15th Reserve Battalion. It was disbanded September 15th, 1920.

BADGE NUMBER: 214

CANADA/OVERSEAS 214 BATTALION /SASKATCHEWAN

Makers: Dingwall
Fasteners: Lugs, Tangs, Pin
Composition:
Other Ranks: Pickled copper
Officers: Pickled copper with silver overlay on design
Ref.: Babin, Meek, Stewart, Cox

Note: Only one maker of this cap badge exists, but there are two varieties.
1. Large leaf (48 mm)
2. Small leaf (44 mm)

Badge No.	Insignia	Rank	Description	Extremely Fine
214-2	Cap	ORs	Pickled copper; Large leaf, 48 mm; Dingwall	35.00
214-4		ORs	Pickled copper; Small leaf, 44 mm; Dingwall	35.00
214-21		Officers	Pickled copper, Silver overlay on design; Large leaf; Dingwell	100.00
214-41	Collars	ORs	Pickled copper; Dingwall	12.00
214-61		Officers	Pickled copper, Silver overlay on design; Dingwall	25.00
214-91	Shoulders	ORs	Numeral: "214"; Unknown	14.00

215TH INFANTRY BATTALION

The Battalion was raised in Central Ontario with mobilization headquarters at Brantford under the authority of G.O. 69 July 15th, 1916. The Battalion sailed April 29th, 1917 under the command of Lieutenant-Colonel H. E. Snider with a strength of sixteen officers and three hundred and twenty-seven other ranks. In England the Battalion was absorbed into the 8th Reserve Battalion. It was disbanded September 15th, 1920.

BADGE NUMBER: 215

OVERSEAS 215 BATTALION/CANADA

AUTHORIZED MARCH 31, 1916

Makers: Birks
Fasteners: Lugs
Composition:
Other Ranks: Pickled copper; Browning copper
Officers:
  A: Pickled copper with silver overlay on "215"
  B: Sterling silver (1918)
Ref.: Babin, Meek, Stewart, Cox

Note: It is interesting to note that the Griffin is the personal crest of the Cockshutt family of Brantford, Ontario. It is unusual to have such a devise on a C.E.F. badge, however Lieutenant-Colonel H. Cockshutt was C.O. of the battalion on mobilization.

Badge No.	Insignia	Rank	Description	Extremely Fine
215-2	Cap	ORs	Pickled copper; Birks	80.00
215-4		ORs	Browning copper; Birks	80.00
215-21		Officers	Pickled copper, Silver overlay on "215"; Birks	120.00
215-23		Officers	Sterling silver (1918); Birks	120.00
215-41	Collars	ORs	Pickled copper; Birks	40.00
215-43		ORs	Browning copper; Birks	40.00
215-61		Officers	Pickled copper, Silver overlay on "215"; Birks	50.00
215-63		Officers	Sterling silver (1918); Birks	50.00
215-91	Shoulders	ORs	Numeral: "215"; Birks	14.00
215-93		ORs	Numeral: "215"; Caron	14.00
215-95		ORs	Title: "215" over "CANADA"; Caron	22.00

216TH INFANTRY BATTALION

"TORONTO BANTAMS"

The battalion was raised in Toronto, Ontario under the authority of G.O. 69 July 15th, 1916. The Battalion sailed April 18th, 1917 under the command of Lieutenant-Colonel F. L. Burton with a strength of thirty officers and seven hundred and eighty-three other ranks. In England the Battalion was absorbed into the 3rd Reserve Battalion. It was disbanded September 15th, 1920.

BADGE NUMBER: 216

No. - 216A   **BANTAMS OVER/216/SEAS/CANADA**

AUTHORIZED APRIL 15, 1916

Makers: Birks, Caron, Ellis, Hemsley
Fasteners: Lugs
Composition:
Other Ranks: Browning copper; Blackened copper; Brass
Officers:
   A: Sterling silver
   B: Gilt on copper with enamelled centre
Ref.: Babin, Meek, Stewart, Cox

Note: Two makers of this cap badge exist.
   1. Wide short crown; Pointed "A" in Canada; Ellis *(Illustrated)*
   2. Narrow tall crown; Flat "A" in Canada; Hemsley.

Badge No.	Insignia	Rank	Description	Extremely Fine
216A-2	Cap	ORs	Browning copper; Ellis	28.00
216A-4		ORs	Blackened copper; Ellis	28.00
216A-6		ORs	Brass; Hemsley	18.00
216A-21		Officers	Sterling silver; Ellis	50.00
216A-23		Officers	Gilt on copper enamel centre design; Ellis	100.00
216A-41	Collars	ORs	Browning copper; Ellis	12.00
216A-43		ORs	Blackened copper; Ellis	12.00
216A-45		ORs	Brass; Hemsley	12.00
216A-61		Officers	Gilt on copper, enamel centre design; Ellis	50.00
216A-63		Officers	Sterling silver; Ellis	25.00
216A-91	Shoulders	ORs	Numeral: "216"; Caron	16.00
216A-93		ORs	Numeral: "216"; Birks	16.00
216A-95		ORs	Title: "216" over "CANADA"; Unknown	30.00

No. - 216B   OVERSEAS BATTALION CANADA/216

Makers: Caron for Eaton's
Fasteners: Lugs, Pin
Composition:
Other Ranks: Pickled copper with white metal overlay on centre
Officers: Pickled copper with gilt overlay on centre
Ref.: Not previously listed

Note: Collars not issued.

Badge No.	Insignia	Rank	Description	Extremely Fine
216B-2	Cap	ORs	Pickled copper, Wm. overlay on centre	325.00
216B-21		Officers	Pickled copper, Gilt overlay on centre	350.00

217TH INFANTRY BATTALION

"QU'APPELLE BATTALION"

The Battalion was raised in Saskatchewan with mobilization headquarters at Moosomin under the authority of G.O. 69 July 15th, 1916. The Battalion sailed June 2nd, 1917 under the command of Lieutenant-Colonel A. B. Gillis with a strength of twenty-four officers and six hundred and thirty-four other ranks. In England the Battalion was absorbed into the 15th Reserve Battalion. It was disbanded September 15th, 1920.

BADGE NUMBER: 217

No. - 217   **OVERSEAS BATTALION/217/CANADA**

AUTHORIZED OCTOBER 2, 1916

Makers: Inglis
Fasteners: Lugs
Composition:
Other Ranks: Pickled copper or brass
Officers: Pickled copper with white metal overlay on design
Ref.: Babin, Meek, Stewart, Cox

Badge No.	Insignia	Rank	Description	Extremely Fine
217-2	Cap	ORs	Pickled copper; Inglis	50.00
217-4		ORs	Pickled brass; Inglis	50.00
217-21		Officers	Pickled copper, Wm. overlay on design; Inglis	75.00
217-41	Collars	ORs	Pickled copper; Inglis	10.00
217-43		ORs	Pickled brass; Inglis	10.00
217-61		Officers	Pickled copper, Wm. overlay on design; Ingis	30.00
217-91	Shoulders	ORs	Numeral: "217"	14.00
217-93		ORs	Title: "QUAPPELLE BATT./217 INF/ CANADA"; Inglis	30.00

218TH INFANTRY BATTALION

"EDMONTON IRISH"

The Battalion was raised in Edmonton, Alberta with mobilization headquarters at Victoria under the authority of G.O. 69 July 15th, 1916. The Battalion sailed February 17th, 1917 under the command of Lieutenant-Colonel J. K. Cornwall with a strength of thirty-two officers and eight hundred and eighty-three other ranks. In England the Battalion was absorbed into the 8th Brigade, Battery Troops of the Canadian Field Artillery. It was disbanded September 15th, 1920.

BADGE NUMBER: 218

OVERSEAS BATTALION ALBERTA CANADA /EDMONTON/C.E.F./218

AUTHORIZED JUNE 2, 1916

Makers: Jackson Bros.
Fasteners: Lugs
Composition:
Other Ranks: Pickled copper or brass
Officers:
    A: Sterling silver
    B: Gilt on brass
Ref.: Babin, Meek, Stewart, Cox

Note: Shoulder numerals "218" are not known.

Badge No.	Insignia	Rank	Description	Extremely Fine
218-2	Cap	ORs	Pickled copper; Jackson	45.00
218-4		ORs	Pickled brass; Jackson	50.00
218-21		Officers	Sterling silver; Jackson	100.00
218-23		Officers	Gilt on brass; Jackson	30.00
218-41	Collars	ORs	Pickled copper; Jackson	30.00
218-43		ORs	Pickled brass; Jackson	28.00
218-61		Officers	Sterling silver; Jackson	40.00
218-63		Officers	Gilt on brass; Jackson	30.00
218-91	Shoulders	ORs	Numerals; "218"	Unknown
218-93		ORs	Title: "218/CANADA"; Jackson	30.00

219TH INFANTRY BATTALION

"NOVA SCOTIA HIGHLANDERS"

The Battalion was raised in Nova Scotia with mobilization headquarters at Halifax, under the authority of G.O. 69 July 15th, 1916. The Battalion sailed October 12th, 1916 under the command of Lieutenant-Colonel W. H. Muirhead with a strength of thirty-three officers and nine hundred and ninety-seven other ranks. In England the Battalion was absorbed into the 17th Reserve Battalion. It was disbanded September 15th, 1920.

BADGE NUMBER: 219

No. - 219A   CANADA/OVERSEAS HIGHLAND BATTALLION
C.E.F./219/SIOL NA FEAR FEARAIL

AUTHORIZED APRIL 27, 1916

Makers: Birks, Hemsley, Tiptaft
Fasteners: Lugs
Composition:
Other Ranks: Pickled copper
or brass
Officers:
 A: Gilt on copper
 B: Pickled copper
with silver overlay
on circlet
 C: Pickled copper with
silver overlay on
design
Ref.: Babin, Meek, Stewart, Cox

Note: Two makers of this cap badge exist
   1. Either side of the shield is void with plain ribbons; Hemsley *(Illustrated)*
   2. Either side of the shield is solid with framed ribbons; Tiptaft.

Badge No.	Insignia	Rank	Description	Extremely Fine
219A-2	Glengarry	ORs	Pickled copper; Hemsley	40.00
219A-4		ORs	Pickled brass; Hemsley	40.00
219A-6		ORs	Pickled brass; Tiptaft	100.00
219A-21		Officers	Gilt on Copper; Unknown	550.00
219A-23		Officers	Pickled copper, Silver overlay on circlet; Hemsley	300.00
219A-25		Officers	Pickled copper, Silver overlay on design; Hemsley	300.00

Badge No.	Insignia	Rank	Description	Extremely Fine
		Maple Leaf Design		
219A-41	Collars	ORs	PIckled copper; Hemsley	100.00
219A-43		ORs	Pickled brass; Hemsley	100.00
219A-45		ORs	Pickled brass; Tiptaft	100.00
219A-61		Officers	Pickled copper, Silver overlay on design; Hemsley	150.00
		Scroll Design		
219A-47	Collars	ORs	Pickled brass; Hemsley	25.00
219A-49		ORs	Pickled brass; Tiptaft	25.00
219A-63		Officers	Pickled brass, Silver overlay on design; Hemsley	65.00
219A-91	Shoulders	ORs	Numeral: "219"; Birks	14.00

No. - 219B   OVERSEAS BATTALION CANADA/219

**Photograph
Not Available
At Press Time**

Makers: Caron for Eaton's
Fasteners: Lugs, Pin
Composition:
Other Ranks: Pickled copper with white metal overlay on design
Officers: Pickled copper with gilt overlay on design
Ref.: Not previously listed

Badge No.	Insignia	Rank	Description	Extremely Fine
219B-2	Cap	ORs	Pickled copper, Wm. overlay on design; Caron	275.00
219B-21		Officers	Pickled copper, Gilt overlay on design; Caron	300.00

220TH INFANTRY BATTALION

"YORK RANGERS"

The Battalion was raised in Toronto, Ontario with mobilization headquarters at Toronto under the authority of G.O. 69 July 15th, 1916. The Battalion sailed April 29th, 1917 under the command of Lieutenant-Colonel B. H. Brown with a strength of eighteen officers and four hundred and forty-six other ranks. In England the Battalion was absorbed into the 3rd Reserve Battalion. It was disbanded September 15th, 1920.

BADGE NUMBER: 220

12TH REGT. YORK RANGERS CELER ET AUDAX /CANADA 220 OVERSEAS

AUTHORIZED MARCH 29, 1916

Makers: Birks, Caron, Ellis, Hemsley
Fasteners: Lugs
Composition:
Other Ranks: Pickled brass
Officers:
    A: Pickled brass with silver overlay on "220"
    B: Gilt on brass
    C: Sterling silver
Ref.: Babin, Meek, Stewart, Cox

Note: Two makers of this cap badge exist. Although the design is the same for both the Ellis and Hemsley collar, the Ellis collar is 33 mm in height, while the Hemsley collar is 39 mm in height.
The design of these badges is based on the designs of the 127th battalion badges.
1. Blunt leaf design; Lion has fine mane; Ellis *(Illustration)*
2. Pointed leaf design; Lion has course main; Hemsley.

Badge No.	Insignia	Rank	Description	Extremely Fine
220-2	Cap	ORs	Pickled brass; Ellis	60.00
220-4		ORs	Pickled brass; Hemsley	60.00
220-21		Officers	Pickled brass, Silver overlay on "220"; Ellis	45.00
220-23		Officers	Gilt on brass; Hemsley	50.00
220-25		Officers	Sterling silver; Hemsley	100.00
220-41	Collars	ORs	Pickled brass; Ellis	22.00
220-43		ORs	Pickled brass; Hemsley	22.00

Badge No.	Insignia	Rank	Description	Extremely Fine
220-61	Collars	Officers	Pickled brass, Silver overlay on "220"; Ellis	30.00
220-63		Officers	Gilt on brass; Hemsley	30.00
220-65		Officers	Sterling silver; Hemsley	30.00
220-91	Shoulders	ORs	Numeral: "220"; Caron	14.00
220-93		ORs	Numeral: "220"; Birks	14.00
220-95		ORs	Title: "LION/220/CANADA"; Hemsley	30.00

221ST INFANTRY BATTALION

The Battalion was raised in Manitoba with mobilization headquarters at Winnipeg under the authority of G.O. 69 July 15th, 1916. The Battalion sailed April 18th, 1917 under the command of Lieutenant-Colonel M. McMeans with a strength of twenty-three officers and five hundred and ninety-six other ranks. In England the Battalion was absorbed into the 11th Reserve Battalion. It was disbanded September 15th, 1920.

BADGE NUMBER: 221

221/OVERSEAS BATTALION/CANADA

AUTHORIZED APRIL 15, 1916

Makers: Birks, Dingwall
Fasteners: Tangs, Lugs
Composition:
Other Ranks: Pickled copper
or brass
Officers: Pickled copper with
silver overlay on
design
Ref.: Babin, Meek, Stewart, Cox

Badge No.	Insignia	Rank	Description	Extremely Fine
221-2	Cap	ORs	Pickled copper; Dingwall	65.00
221-21		Officers	Pickled copper, Silver overlay on design; Dingwall	225.00
221-41	Collars	ORs	Pickled copper; Dingwall	22.00
221-43		ORs	Pickled brass; Dingwall	18.00
221-61		Officers	Pickled copper, Silver overlay on design; Dingwall	30.00
221-91	Shoulders	ORs	Numeral: "221"; Birks	15.00

222ND INFANTRY BATTALION

The Battalion was raised in Manitoba with mobilization headquarters at Winnipeg under the authority of G.O. 69 July 15th, 1916. The Battalion sailed November 13th, 1916 under the command of Lieutenant Colonel J. Lightfoot with a strength of thirty-two officers and nine hundred and ninety-three other ranks. In England the Battalion was absorbed into the 19th Reserve Battalion. It was disbanded September 15th, 1920.

BADGE NUMBER: 222

No. - 222A

**SINGLE MAPLE LEAF DESIGN
OVERSEAS 222 BATTALION
/NULLI SECUNDUS/CANADA**

AUTHORIZED APRIL 13, 1916

Makers: Dingwall, Tiptaft, Unknown
Fasteners: Lugs
Composition:
Other Ranks: Pickled copper; Browning copper or brass
Officers: Gilt on copper
Ref.: Babin, Meek, Stewart, Cox

Note: Three makers of this cap badge exist.
1. The lion does not have a rib cage design; Dingwall
2. The lion has five or six ribs showing; Tiptaft *(Illustrated)*
3. Of the third maker only the collars have been identified. Insufficient information is known to list the cap badges below; Unknown.

Badge No.	Insignia	Rank	Description	Extremely Fine
222A-2	Cap	ORs	Pickled copper, Void; Dingwall	40.00
222A-4		ORs	Pickled copper, Solid; Tiptaft	40.00
222A-6		ORs	Pickled copper, Void; Tiptaft	40.00
222A-8		ORs	Browning copper, Solid; Tiptaft	40.00
222A-21		Officers	Gilt on copper, Solid; Tiptaft	60.00
	Matching Cap Design			
222A-41	Collars	ORs	Unknown	- -
222A-61		Officers	Gilt on copper, Solid; Tiptaft	100.00

Badge No.	Insignia	Rank	Description	Extremely Fine
		Maple Leaf Design		
222A-43	Collars	ORs	Pickled copper; Dingwall	18.00
222A-45		ORs	Pickled copper; Tiptaft	18.00
222A-47		ORs	Browning copper; Tiptaft	20.00
222A-49		ORs	Browning brass; Unknown	30.00
222A-63		Officers	Gilt on copper; Tiptaft	30.00
222A-91	Shoulders	ORs	Numeral: "222"	Unknown

No. - 222B

MULTI MAPLE LEAF DESIGN OVERSEAS 222 BATTALION /NULLI SECUNDUS/CANADA

Makers: Unknown
Fasteners: Lugs
Composition:
 Other Ranks: Browning copper
 Officers: Unknown
Ref.: Not previously listed

Badge No.	Insignia	Rank	Description	Extremely Fine
222B-2	Cap	ORs	Browning copper	Extremely Rare
222B-21		Officers	Unknown	- -
222B-41	Collars	ORs	Unknown	- -
222B-61		Officers	Unknown	- -

223RD INFANTRY BATTALION

"CANADIAN SCANDINAVIANS"

The Battalion was raised in Manitoba with mobilization headquarters at Winnipeg under the authority of G.O. 69 July 15th, 1916. The Battalion sailed May 3rd, 1917 under the command of Lieutenant-Colonel H. Albrechsten with a strength of seventeen officers and five hundred and seven other ranks. In England the Battalion was absorbed into the 11th Reserve Battalion. It was disbanded September 15th, 1920.

BADGE NUMBER: 223

OVERSEAS BATTALION/223/
CANADIAN/SCANDINAVIANS

AUTHORIZED APRIL 25, 1916

Makers: Caron, Dingwall
Fasteners: Lugs, Tangs
Composition:
 Other Ranks: Pickled copper
 Officers: Unknown
Ref.: Babin, Meek, Stewart, Cox

Badge No.	Insignia	Rank	Description	Extremely Fine
223-2	Cap	ORs	Pickled copper; Dingwall	45.00
223-21		Officers	Unknown	- -
223-41	Collars	ORs	Pickled copper; Dingwall	20.00
223-61		Officers	Unknown	- -
223-91	Shoulders	ORs	Numeral: "223"; Caron	14.00

224TH INFANTRY BATTALION

"CANADIAN FORESTRY BATTALION"

The Battalion was raised in Eastern Ontario with mobilization headquarters at Ottawa Ontario under the authority of G.O. 69 July 15th, 1916. The Battalion sailed May 19th, 1917 under the command of Lieutenant-Colonel A. McDougall with a strength of forty-seven officers and one thousand five hundred and twenty-six other ranks. In England the Battalion was absorbed into the Canadian Forestry Corps. It was disbanded September 15th, 1920.

BADGE NUMBER: 224

CANADIAN FORESTRY BATTALION
/224/OVERSEAS

Makers: Hemsley, Tiptaft
Fasteners: Lugs
Composition:
Other Ranks: Pickled copper or brass
Officers:
    A: Silverplate
    B: Pickled copper with white metal overlay on design
Ref.: Babin, Meek, Stewart, Cox

Note: Two makers of this cap badge exist.
1. Small central crown; Thick numerals "224"; Hemsley *(Illustrated)*
2. Large central crown; Thin numerals "224"; Tiptaft.
The shoulder numeral "224" is not known.

Badge No.	Insignia	Rank	Description	Extremely Fine
224-2	Cap	ORs	Pickled copper; Hemsley	45.00
224-4		ORs	Pickled brass; Hemsley	45.00
224-6		ORs	Pickled brass; Tiptaft	45.00
224-21		Officers	Silverplate; Unknown	130.00
224-23		Officers	Pickled copper, Wm. overlay on design; Hemsley	100.00
224-41	Collars	ORs	Pickled copper; Hemsley	20.00
224-43		ORs	Pickled brass; Hemsley	20.00
224-45		ORs	Pickled brass; Tiptaft	20.00
224-61		Officers	Pickled copper, Wm. overlay on design; Hemsley	50.00
224-91	Shoulders	ORs	Numeral: "224"	Unknown
224-93		ORs	Title: "224" over "CANADA"; Hemsley	20.00

225TH INFANTRY BATTALION

"KOOTENAY BATTALION"

The Battalion was raised in British Columbia with mobilization headquarters at Fernie, B.C. under the authority of G.O. 69 July 15th, 1916. The Battalion sailed January 25th, 1917 under the command of Lieutenant-Colonel J. Mackay with a strength of twenty officers and four hundred and twenty-seven other ranks. In England the Battalion was absorbed into the 1st Reserve Battalion. It was disbanded September 15th, 1920.

BADGE NUMBER: 225

C.E.F./225/KOOTENAY BATTALION/CANADA

Makers: Allan
Fasteners: Tangs, Lugs
Composition:
Other Ranks: Browning copper
Officers: Unknown
Ref.: Babin, Meek, Stewart, Cox

Badge No.	Insignia	Rank	Description	Extremely Fine
225-2	Cap	ORs	Browning copper; Allan	40.00
225-21		Officers	Unknown	- -
225-41	Collars	ORs	Browning copper; Allan	40.00
225-61		Officers	Unknown	- -
225-91	Shoulders	ORs	Numeral "225"	18.00
225-93		ORs	Title: "225TH OVERSEAS BATT. /CANADA"; Allan	25.00

226TH INFANTRY BATTALION

"MEN OF THE NORTH"

The Battalion was raised in Manitoba with mobilization headquarters at Dauphin, Manitoba under the authority of G.O. 69 July 15th, 1916. The Battalion sailed December 15th, 1916 under the command of Lieutenant-Colonel R. A. G. Gillespie with a strength of thirty-two officers and one thousand and thirty-five other ranks. In England the Battalion was absorbed into the 14th Reserve Battalion. It was disbanded September 15th, 1920.

BADGE NUMBER: 226

MEN OF THE NORTH/
OVERSEAS BATTALION/226/CANADA

AUTHORIZED APRIL 14, 1916

Makers: Dingwall, Tiptaft, Unknown
Fasteners: Lugs, Tangs
Composition:
Other Ranks: Pickled copper or brass; Browning copper
Officers: Sterling silver
Ref.: Babin, Meek, Stewart, Cox

Note: A badge design exists with the ribbon inside the maple leaf. This badge was produced by Dingwall of Winnipeg in pickled copper with flexible lugs. The shoulder numeral "226" is not known.

Badge No.	Insignia	Rank	Description	Extremely Fine
			Internal Ribbon Design	
226A-2	Cap	ORs	Pickled copper; Dingwall	Rare
			Extended Ribbon Design	
226A-4	Cap	ORs	PIckled copper; Dingwall	40.00
226A-6		ORs	Pickled brass; Tiptaft	50.00
226A-8		ORs	Browning copper; Tiptaft	30.00
226A-21		Officers	Sterling silver; Unknown	100.00
226A-41	Collars	ORs	Pickled copper; Dingwall	15.00
226A-43		ORs	Pickled brass; Tiptaft	20.00
226A-45		ORs	Browning copper; Tiptaft	20.00
226A-61		Officers	Sterling silver; Unknown	50.00
226A-91	Shoulders	ORs	Numeral: "226"	Unknown
226A-93		ORs	Title: "INF 226 BATT NORTH WESTERN MANITOBA CANADA"; Dingwall	30.00

227TH INFANTRY BATTALION

"MEN OF THE NORTH"

The Battalion was raised in Algoma, Ontario with mobilization headquarters at Sault Ste. Marie and Camp Borden, Ontario under the authority of G.O. 69 July 15th, 1916. The Battalion sailed April 11th, 1917 under the command of Lieutenant-Colonel C. H. Lep. Jones with a strength of twenty-eight officers and seven hundred and eighty-three other ranks. In England the Battalion was absorbed by the 8th Reserve Battalion. It was disbanded September 15th, 1920.

BADGE NUMBER: 227

SUDBURY MANITOULIN ALGUMA/
227/CANADA OVERSEAS/MEN O' THE NORTH

AUTHORIZED JULY 11, 1916

Makers: Bailey, Caron, Ellis
Fasteners: Lugs
Composition:
Other Ranks: Pickled copper
or brass
Officers: Sterling silver
Ref.: Babin, Meek, Stewart, Cox

Badge No.	Insignia	Rank	Description	Extremely Fine
227-2	Cap	ORs	Pickled copper; Bailey	85.00
227-4		ORs	Pickled brass; Bailey	85.00
227-21		Officers	Sterling silver; Bailey	100.00
227-41	Collars	ORs	Pickled brass; Bailey	25.00
227-61		Officers	Sterling silver; Bailey	50.00
227-91	Shoulders	ORs	Numeral: "227"; Caron	14.00
227-93		ORs	Title: "227" over "CANADA"; Ellis	20.00

228TH INFANTRY BATTALION

"NORTHERN FUSILIERS"

The Battalion was raised in Northern Ontario with mobilization headquarters at North Bay, Ontario under the authority of G.O. 69 July 15th, 1916. The Battalion sailed February 16th, 1917 under the command of Lieutenant-Colonel A. Earchman with a strength of thirty-one officers and seven hundred and fifty-six other ranks. The Battalion served in France as the 6th Battalion, Canadian Railway Troops. It was disbanded September 15th, 1920.

BADGE NUMBER: 228

NORTHERN FUSILIERS/CANADA OVERSEAS/228

AUTHORIZED AUGUST 29, 1916

Makers: Bailey
Fasteners: Lugs
Composition:
Other Ranks: Browning copper
Officers: Sterling silver
Ref.: Babin, Meek, Stewart, Cox

Badge No.	Insignia	Rank	Description	Extremely Fine
228-2	Cap	ORs	Browning copper; Bailey	35.00
228-21		Officers	Sterling silver; Bailey	90.00
228-41	Collars	ORs	Browning copper; Bailey	25.00
228-61		Officers	Sterling silver; Bailey	40.00
228-91	Shoulders	ORs	Title: "228" on "CANADA" scroll; Bailey	25.00

229TH INFANTRY BATTALION

"SOUTH SASKATCHEWAN BATTALION"

The Battalion was raised in Saskatchewan with mobilization headquarters at Moose Jaw under the authority of G.O. 69 July 15th, 1916. The Battalion sailed April 18th, 1917 under the command of Lieutenant-Colonel H. D. Pickett with a strength of seventeen officers and four hundred and twenty-six other ranks. In England the Battalion was absorbed into the 15th Reserve Battalion. It was disbanded September 15th, 1920.

BADGE NUMBER: 229

229/OVERSEAS BATTALION/
SOUTH SASKATCHEWAN/CANADA

AUTHORIZED MAY 2, 1916

Makers: Lees, Crichton's
Fasteners: Lugs, Pin
Composition:
Other Ranks: Pickled brass;
Browning copper
Officers: Silver plate on
copper
Ref.: Babin, Meek, Stewart, Cox

Note: The shoulder numeral "229" is not known.

Badge No.	Insignia	Rank	Description	Extremely Fine
229A-2	Cap	ORs	Pickled brass; Lees, Crichton's	30.00
229A-4		ORs	Browning copper; Lees, Crichton's	30.00
229A-21		Officers	Silverplate on copper; Lees, Crichton's	150.00
Maple Leaf Design				
229A-41	Collars	ORs	Pickled brass; Lees, Crichton's	50.00
229A-43		ORs	Browning copper;Lees, Crichton's	50.00
229A-61		Officers	Silverplate on copper; Lees, Crichton's	50.00
Matching Cap Design				
229A-45	Collars	ORs	Pickled copper; Lees, Crichton's	75.00
229A-63		Officers	Unknown	- -
229A-91	Shoulders	ORs	Numeral: "229"	Unknown
229A-93		ORs	Title: "CAN 229 ADA"; Browning copper; Lees, Crichton's	25.00
229A-95		Officers	Title: "CAN 229 ADA"; Silverplate Lees, Crichton's	30.00

230TH INFANTRY BATTALION

"VOLTIGEURS CANADIEN FRANCAIS"

The Battalion was raised in Eastern Ontario with mobilization headquarters at Ottawa under the authority of G.O. 69 July 15th, 1916. The Battalion sailed January 23rd, 1917 under the command of Lieutenant-Colonel R. de Salaberry with a strength of eighteen officers and six hundred and eighty-seven other ranks. In England the Battalion was absorbed into the Canadian Forestry Corps. It was disbanded September 15th, 1920.

BADGE NUMBER: 230

No. - 230A   D'OUTREME/VOLTIGEURS CANADIENS
FRANCAIS OTTAWA/
FORCE A SUPERBE MERCY A FAIBIE

Makers: Birks
Fasteners: Lugs
Composition:
Other Ranks: Browning copper or brass
Officers:
  A: Browning copper with silver overlay on "230"
  B: Gilt on copper with silver overlay on centre design
  C: Sterling silver
Ref.: Babin, Meek, Stewart, Cox

Badge No.	Insignia	Rank	Description	Extremely Fine
230A-2	Cap	ORs	Browning copper; Birks	70.00
230A-4		ORs	Browning brass; Birks	100.00
230A-21		Officers	Browning copper, Silver overlay on "250" only; Birks	75.00
230A-23		Officers	Gilt on copper, Silver overlay on centre design; Birks	75.00
230A-25		Officers	Sterling silver; Birks	100.00
230A-41	Collars	ORs	Browning brass; Birks	50.00
230A-91	Shoulders	ORs	Numeral: "230"; Birks	16.00
230A-93		ORs	Title: "230" over "CANADA"; Birks	20.00

No. - 230B   **FORESTRY OVERSEAS BATTALION**
                          /230/CANADA

Makers: Unknown
Fasteners: Lugs
Composition:
  Other Ranks: Pickled brass
  Officers: Pickled brass with
                white metal overlay
                on design
Ref.: Babin, Cox

Badge No.	Insignia	Rank	Description	Extremely Fine
230B-2	Cap	ORs	Pickled brass; Unknown	65.00
230B-21		Officers	Pickled brass, Wm. overlay on design; Unknown	150.00
230B-41	Collars	ORs	Pickled brass; Unknown	25.00
230B-61		Officers	Pickled brass, Wm. overlay on design Unknowns	50.00

231ST INFANTRY BATTALION

"SEAFORTH HIGHLANDERS OF CANADA"

The Battalion was raised in British Columbia with mobilization headquarters at Vancouver under the authority of G.O. 69 July 15th, 1916. The Battalion sailed April 11th, 1917 under the command of Lieutenant-Colonel F. E. Leach with a strength of twenty-eight officers and six hundred and sixty-one other ranks. In England the Battalion was absorbed into the 1st Reserve Battalion. It was disbanded September 15th, 1920.

BADGE NUMBER: 231

No. - 231A   **CUIDICH'N RIGH**

Makers: Allan, Birks, Unknown
Fasteners: Lugs, Tangs
Composition:
Other Ranks:
    Cap: White metal
    Collars: Browning copper
Officers:
    Cap: Sterling silver
    Collars: Sterling silver
Ref.: Babin, Meek, Stewart, Cox

Note: Two makers of this cap badge exist.
    1. The bridge of the nose and eyebrows are not outlined; Birks *(Illustrated)*
    2. The bridge of the nose and the eyebrow form a continous line; Allan.

Badge No.	Insignia	Rank	Description	Extremely Fine
231A-2	Glengarry	ORs	White metal; Allan	125.00
231A-4		ORs	White metal; Birks	125.00
231A-21		Officers	Sterling silver (2 piece - Stag & Scroll); Unknown	400.00
231A-41	Collars	ORs	Browning copper; Allan	40.00
231A-43		ORs	Browning copper; Birks	40.00
231A-61		Officers	Sterling silver; Unknown	300.00
231A-91	Shoulders	ORs	Numeral "231"	15.00

No. - 231B   L/CUIDICH'N RIGH

Makers: Unknown
Fasteners: Lugs
Composition:
Other Ranks:
  Glengarry: White metal
  Collars: Browning copper
Officers:
  Glengarry: Sterling silver
  Collars: Sterling silver
Ref.: Babin, Cox

Leaf/Ribbon/231 Design

Leaf/Ribbon Design

Note: This cap badge is made up of four separate pieces.

Badge No.	Insignia	Rank	Description	Extremely Fine
231B-2	Glengarry	ORs	White metal; Unknown	350.00
231B-21		Officers	Sterling silver; Unknown	50.00
Leaf / Ribbon Design				
231B-41	Collars	ORs	Browning copper, Solid; Unknown	300.00
231B-43		ORs	Browning copper, Void, Unknown	300.00
231B-61		Officers	Unknown	- -
Leaf / Ribbon / 231 Design				
231B-43	Collars	ORs	Browning copper; Unknown	300.00
231B-63		Officers	Unknown	- -

232ND INFANTRY BATTALION

"SASKATCHEWAN BATTALION"

The Battalion was raised in Saskatchewan with mobilization headquarters at Battleford under the authority of G.O. 69 July 15th, 1916. The Battalion sailed April 18th, 1917 under the command of Lieutenant-Colonel R. P. Laurie with a strength of thirteen officers and two hundred and eighty-six other ranks. In England the Battalion was absorbed into the 15th Reserve Battalion. It was disbanded September 15th, 1920.

BADGE NUMBER: 232

232/SASKATCHEWAN
/OVERSEAS BATTALION/CANADA

AUTHORIZED JUNE 30, 1916

Makers: Dingwall
Fasteners: Lugs
Composition:
Other Ranks: Pickled copper or brass
Officers: Sterling silver
Ref.: Babin, Meek, Stewart, Cox

Note: Shoulder numerals are not known.

Badge No.	Insignia	Rank	Description	Extremely Fine
232-2	Cap	ORs	Pickled copper; Dingwall	25.00
232-4		ORs	Pickled brass; Dingwall	45.00
232-21		Officers	Sterling silver; Dingwall	100.00
Maple Leaf With Full Cougar Design				
232-41	Collars	ORs	Pickled copper; Dingwall	30.00
232-61		Officers	Unknown	- -
Maple Leaf With Cougar Head Design				
232-43	Collars	ORs	Pickled copper; Dingwall	18.00
232-45		ORs	Pickled brass; Dingwall	20.00
232-63		Officers	Sterling silver; Dingwall	40.00
232-91	Shoulders	ORs	Numeral: "232"	Unknown

233RD INFANTRY BATTALION

"CANADIENS FRANCAIS"

The Battalion was raised in Alberta with mobilization headquarters at Edmonton under the authority of G.O. 69 July 15th, 1916. The battalion was under the command of Lieutenant-Colonel E. Leprohon. The Battalion was absorbed by the 178th Infantry Battalion.

BADGE NUMBER: 233

No. - 233A   **BATTALION CANADIENS FRANCAIS /D'OUTRE MER/233/DU NORD OUEST**

AUTHORIZED APRIL 9, 1916

Makers: Hemsley, Tiptaft
Fasteners: Lugs, Pin
Composition:
Other Ranks: Pickled copper or brass
Officers: Pickled copper with white metal overlay on design
Ref.: Babin, Meek, Stewart, Cox

Note: Two makers of this cap badge exist.
　　　1. The pointed leaf design with plain ribbons; Hemsley *(Illustrated)*
　　　2. The blunt leaf design with framed ribbons; Tiptaft.

Badge No.	Insignia	Rank	Description	Extremely Fine
233A-2	Cap	ORs	Pickled copper; Hemsley	45.00
233A-4		ORs	Pickled brass; Hemsley	65.00
233A-6		ORs	Pickled brass; Tiptaft	65.00
233A-21		Officers	Pickled copper, Wm. overlay on design; Hemsley	100.00
233A-41	Collars	ORs	Pickled copper; Hemsley	25.00
233A-43		ORs	Pickled brass; Tiptaft	25.00
233A-61		Officers	Pickled copper, Wm. overlay on design; Hemsley	30.00
233A-91	Shoulders	ORs	Numeral: "233"; Unknown	15.00
233A-93		ORs	Title: "233 over CANADA"	22.00

No.- 233B

CANADIEN FRANCAIS/233

Makers: Caron
Fasteners: Lugs
Composition:
  Other Ranks: Browning copper
    Officers: Unknown
Ref.: Not previously listed

Badge No.	Insignia	Rank	Description	Extremely Fine
233B-2	Cap	ORs	Browning copper; Caron	50.00
233B-21		Officers	Unknown	- -
233B-41	Collars	ORs	Browning copper; Caron	25.00
233B-61		Officers	Unknown	- -

234TH INFANTRY BATTALION

"PEEL BATTALION"

The Battalion was raised in Central Ontario with mobilization headquarters at Toronto under the authority of G.O. 69 July 15th, 1916. The Battalion sailed April 18th, 1917 under the command of Lieutenant-Colonel W. Wallace with a strength of fifteen officers and two hundred and sevety-nine other ranks. In England the Battalion was absorbed into the 12th Reserve Battalion. It was disbanded September 15th, 1920.

BADGE NUMBER: 234

CANADA PEEL OVERSEAS/234

AUTHORIZED MAY 29, 1916

Makers: Birks, Caron, Ellis, Hemsley
Fasteners: Lugs, Pin
Composition:
Other Ranks: Pickled brass; Blackened copper or brass
Officers: Unknown
Ref.: Babin, Meek, Stewart, Cox

Note: Two makers of this cap badge exist.
1. Pointed leaf design with plain ribbons and large rifles; Hemsley
2. Blunt leaf design with framed ribbons and small rifles; Ellis *(Illustrated)*

Badge No.	Insignia	Rank	Description	Extremely Fine
234-2	Cap	ORs	Pickled brass; Hemsley	25.00
234-4		ORs	Blackened copper; Ellis	50.00
234-6		ORs	Blackened brass; Ellis	75.00
234-21		Officers	Unknown	- -
234-41	Collars	ORs	Pickled brass; Hemsley	15.00
234-43		ORs	Blackened copper; Ellis	25.00
234-45		ORs	Blackened brass; Ellis	25.00
234-61		Officers	Unknown	- -
234-91	Shoulders	ORs	Numeral: "234"; Caron	15.00
234-93		ORs	Numeral: "234"; Birks	15.00

235TH INFANTRY BATTALION

The Battalion was raised in Central Ontario with mobilization headquarters at Belleville under the authority of G.O. 69 July 15th, 1916. The Battalion sailed May 3rd, 1917 under the command of Lieutenant-Colonel S. B. Scobel with a strength of nineteen officers and four hundred and thirty-eight other ranks. In England the Battalion was absorbed into the 3rd Reserve Battalion. It was disbanded September 15th, 1920.

BADGE NUMBER: 235

No. - 235A   **OVERSEAS BATTALION/235/CANADA**

AUTHORIZED JULY 28, 1916

Makers: Birks, Unknown
Fasteners: Lugs, Pin
Composition:
Other Ranks: Pickled brass
Officers:
 A: Pickled brass with white metal overlay on design
 B: Silverplate on brass
Ref.: Babin, Meek, Stewart, Cox

Badge No.	Insignia	Rank	Description	Extremely Fine
235A-2	Cap	ORs	Pickled brass; Unknown	38.00
235A-21		Officers	Pickled brass, Silver overlay on design; Unknown	85.00
235A-23		Officers	Silverplate on brass; Unknown	75.00
235A-41	Collars	ORs	Pickled brass; Unknown	25.00
235A-61		Officers	Pickled brass, Silver overlay on design Unknown	40.00
235A-91	Shoulders	ORs	Numeral: "235"; Birks	15.00
235A-93		ORs	Title: "LION/235/CANADA"	30.00

No. - 235B   OVERSEAS BATTALION CANADA/235

Makers: Caron for Eaton's
Fasteners: Lugs
Composition:
Other Ranks: Pickled copper with
white metal overlay
on design
Officers: Gilt on copper with
silver overlay on
centre
Ref.: Not previously listed

Photograph
Not Available
At Press Time

Note: Collars are not known.

Badge No.	Insignia	Rank	Description	Extremely Fine
235B-2	Cap	ORs	Pickled copper, Wm. overlay on design; Caron	300.00
235B-21		Officers	Gilt on copper, Silver overlay on centre; Caron	300.00

No. - 235C   235/CANADA

INTERIM BADGE

Makers: As General List
Fasteners: Lugs
Composition:
Other Ranks: Unofficial, "235"
overlay on General
List
Officers: Unknown
Ref.: Not previously listed

Badge No.	Insignia	Rank	Description	Extremely Fine
235C-2	Cap	ORs	General list, "235" Wm. overlay	200.00
235C-21		Officers	Unknown	- -
235C-41	Collars	ORs	Unknown	- -
235C-61		Officers	Unknown	- -

236TH INFANTRY BATTALION

"NEW BRUNSWICK KILTIES"

The Battalion was raised in New Brunswick with mobilization headquarters at Fredericton under the authority of G.O. 69 July 15th, 1916. The Battalion sailed November 9th, 1917 under the command of Lieutenant-Colonel P. A. Guthrie with a strength of twenty-seven officers and one thousand and twenty-nine other ranks. In England the Battalion was absorbed into the 20th Infantry Battalion. It was disbanded September 15th, 1920.

BADGE NUMNBER: 236

No. - 236A　　THE NEW BRUNSWICK KILTIES CANADA
　　　　　　　　/SIR SAM'S OWN/SEMPER FIDELIS
　　　　　　　　/OVERSEAS 236 BATTALION
　　　　　　　　/NEMO ME IMPUNE LACESSET

Makers: Unknown 1 & 2
Fasteners: Lugs
Composition:
Other Ranks: Pickled brass
Officers: Sterling silver
Ref.: Babin, Meek, Cox

Note: Two makers of this cap badge exist.
　　　　1. Tall crown design with thick numerals "236"; Unknown-1 (Illustrated)
　　　　2. Short crown design with thin numerals "236"; Unknown-2.

Badge No.	Insignia	Rank	Description	Extremely Fine
236A-2	Glengarry	ORs	Pickled brass; Unknown (1)	75.00
236A-4		ORs	Pickled brass; Unknown (2)	75.00
236A-21		Officers	Sterling silver; Unknown (1)	500.00
236A-23		Officers	Sterling silver; Unknown (2)	500.00
			Wreath of Thistles and Maple Leaves	
236A-41	Collars	ORs	Pickled brass; Unknown (1)	65.00
236A-61		Officers	Sterling silver; Unknown (2)	75.00
			Single Maple Leaf and Thistle	
236A-43	Collars	ORs	Pickled brass; Unknown (1)	40.00
236A-63		Officers	Sterling silver; Unknown (2)	75.00
236A-91	Shoulders	ORs	Numeral: "236"; Unknown	18.00
236A-93		ORs	Title: "THISTLE 236" over "CANADA"; Unknown	30.00

No. - 236B

**MACLEAN KILTIES OF AMERICA/
SIR SAM'S OWN/SEMPER FIDELIS
/OVERSEAS 236 BATTALION
/NEMO ME IMPUNE LACESSET**

Makers: Unknown
Fasteners: Lugs
Composition:
Other Ranks: Pickled brass
Officers: Sterling silver
Ref.: Stewart, Cox

Badge No.	Insignia	Rank	Description	Extremely Fine
236B-2	Glengarry	ORs	Pickled brass; Unknown	215.00
236B-21		Officers	Sterling silver; Unknown	500.00
236B-41	Collars	ORs	Pickled brass; Unknown	40.00
236B-61		Officers	Sterling silver; Unknown	75.00

No. - 236C   **OVERSEAS BATTALION CANADA/236**

**Photograph
Not Available
At Press Time**

Makers: Caron for Eaton's
Fasteners: Lugs
Compositon:
Other Ranks: Pickled brass with white metal overlay on centre
Officers: Gilt on brass with silver overlay on centre
Ref.: Not previously listed

Note: Collars are not known.

Badge No.	Insignia	Rank	Description	Extremely Fine
236C-2	Cap	ORs	Pickled brass, Wm. overlay on centre; Caron	325.00
236C-21		Officers	Gilt on brass, Silver overlay on centre; Caron	325.00

237TH INFANTRY BATTALION

"NEW BRUNSWICK AMERICANS"

The Battalion was raised in New Brunswick with mobilization headquarters at Sussex under the authority of G.O. 69 July 15th, 1916. The Battalion was under the command of Lieutenant-Colonel Rev. C. S. Bullock. It was disbanded September 15th, 1920.

BADGE NUMBER: 237

No. - 237A   **CANADA 237 OVERSEAS
/ACTA NON VERBA**

AUTHORIZED JULY 7, 1916

Makers: Lees
Fasteners: Lugs
Composition:
Other Ranks: Pickled brass
Officers:
    A. White metal overlay on "237"
    B. White metal overlay on design
Ref.: Babin, Meek, Stewart, Cox

Badge No.	Insignia	Rank	Description	Extremely Fine
237A-2	Cap	ORs	Pickled copper; Lees	40.00
237A-4		ORs	Pickled brass; Lees	75.00
237A-21		Officers	Pickled brass, Wm. overlay on "237"; Lees	75.00
237A-23		Officers	Pickled brass, Wm. overlay on design; Lees	85.00
237A-41	Collars	ORs	Pickled brass; Lees	35.00
237A-61		Officers	Pickled brass, Wm. overlay on "237"; Lees	40.00
237A-63		Officers	Pickled brass, Wm. overlay on design; Lees	45.00
237A-91	Shoulders	ORs	Numeral: "237"; Unknown	20.00

No. - 237B   CANADA 237 OVERSEAS/ AMERICAN LEGION

NOT AUTHORIZED

Photograph
Not Available
At Press Time

Makers: Lees
Fasteners: Lugs
Composition:
Other Ranks: Pickled brass
Officers:
    A: Pickled brass with white metal overlay on "237"
    B: Sterling silver
Ref.: Not previously listed

Badge No.	Insignia	Rank	Description	Extremely Fine
237B-2	Cap	ORs	Pickled brass; Lees	400.00
237B-21		Officers	Pickled brass, Wm. overlay on "237"; Lees	500.00
237B-23		Officers	Sterling Silver; Lees	500.00
237B-41	Collars	ORs	Pickled brass; Lees	50.00
237B-61		Officers	Pickled brass, Wm. overlay on "237"; Lees	75.00

238TH INFANTRY BATTALION

"CANADIAN FORESTRY BATTALION"

The Battalion was raised in Ontario and Quebec with mobilization headquarters at Valcartier under the authority of G.O. 69 July 15th, 1916. The Battalion sailed September 11th, 1916 under the command of Lieutenant-Colonel W. R. Smith with a strength of forty-four officers and one thousand and eighty-one other ranks. In England the Battalion was absorbed into the Canadian Forestry Corps. It was disbanded September 15th, 1920.

BADGE NUMBER: 238

CANADIAN FORESTRY BATTALION
/238/OVERSEAS

AUTHORIZED JUNE 12, 1916

Makers: Hemsley, Tiptaft
Fasteners: Lugs
Composition:
Other Ranks: Pickled brass;
Blackened brass
Officers:
A: Pickled brass with white metal overlay on design
B: Pickled brass with white metal overlay on maple leaf and "238"
Ref.: Babin, Meek, Stewart, Cox

Note: Two makers of this cap badge exist. Shoulder numerals "238" are not known.
1. Wide type numerals "238" with plain overseas ribbon; Hemsley *(Illustrated)*
2. Narrow type numerals "238" with framed overseas ribbon; Tiptaft.

Badge No.	Insignia	Rank	Description	Extremely Fine
238-2	Cap	ORs	Pickled brass; Hemsley	35.00
238-4		ORs	Blackened brass; Tiptaft	35.00
238-21		Officers	Pickled brass, Wm. overlay on design; Hemsley	100.00
238-23		Officers	Pickled brass, Wm. overlay on Maple leaf and "238"; Hemsley	100.00
238-41	Collars	ORs	Pickled brass; Hemsley	25.00
238-43		ORs	Pickled brass; Tiptaft	25.00
238-61		Officers	Pickled brass, Wm. overlay on design; Hemsley	35.00
238-63		Officers	Pickled brass, Wm. overlay on Maple leaf and "238"; Hemsley	35.00
238-91	Shoulders	ORs	Numeral: "238"	Unknown

239TH OVERSEAS BATTALION

"RAILWAY CONSTRUCTION CORPS"

The Battalion was raised in Ontario and Quebec with mobilization headquarters at Valcartier under the authority of G.O. 69 July 15th, 1916. The Battalion sailed December 15th, 1916 under the command of Major V. L. MacDonald with a strength of twenty-six officers and seven hundred and thirty-eight other ranks, In France the Battalion served as the 3rd Battalion, Canadian Railway Troops. It was disbanded September 15th, 1920.

BADGE NUMBER: 239

OVERSEAS RAILWAY CONSTRUCTION CORPS
/239/CANADA

AUTHORIZED JULY 24, 1916

Makers: Birks
Fasteners: Lugs
Composition:
Other Ranks: Pickled brass; Browning copper
Officers:
  A: Browning copper with silver overlay on "239"
  B: Pickled brass with white metal overlay on design
Ref.: Babin, Meek, Stewart, Cox

Note: Shoulder numerals "239" are not known.

Badge No.	Insignia	Rank	Description	Extremely Fine
239-2	Cap	ORs	Pickled brass; Birks	85.00
239-4		ORs	Browning copper; Birks	135.00
239-21		Officers	Browning copper, Silver overlay on "239"; Birks	350.00
239-23		Officers	Pickled brass, Wm. overlay on design; Birks	400.00
239-41	Collars	ORs	Pickled brass; Birks	75.00
239-43		ORs	Browning copper; Birks	120.00
239-61		Officers	Browning copper, Silver overlay on "239"; Birks	120.00
239-63		Officers	Pickled brass, Wm. overlay on design; Birks	120.00
239-91	Shoulders	ORs	Numeral: "239"	Unknown
239-93		ORs	Title: "BEAVER/239/CANADA"	50.00

240TH INFANTRY BATTALION

"LANARK AND RENFREW BATTALION"

The Battalion was raised in Ontario, with mobilization headquarters at Renfrew, under the authority of G.O. 69, July 15th, 1916. The Battalion sailed May 3rd, 1917, under the command of Lieutenant-Colonel E. J. Watt, with a strength of fourteen officers and three hundred and seventy-five other ranks. In England, the Battalion was absorbed into the 6th Reserve Battalion. It was disbanded September 15th, 1920.

BADGE NUMBER: 240

OVERSEAS BATTALION/240/CANADA

AUTHORIZED JULY 11, 1916

Makers: Birks, Inglis
Fasteners: Lugs
Composition:
Other Ranks: Pickled copper or brass; Browning copper
Officcers: Pickled copper with white metal overlay on design
Ref.: Babin, Meek, Stewart, Cox

Badge No.	Insignia	Rank	Description	Extremely Fine
240-2	Cap	ORs	Pickled copper, Solid; Inglis	95.00
240-4		ORs	Pickled copper, Void; Inglis	145.00
240-6		ORs	Pickled brass, Solid; Inglis	95.00
240-21		Officers	Pickled copper, Wm. overlay on design; Inglis	150.00
240-41	Collars	ORs	Pickled copper; Inglis	60.00
240-43		ORs	Pickled brass; Inglis	22.00
240-61		Officers	Pickled copper, Wm. overlay on design; Inglis	100.00
240-91	Shoulders	ORs	Numeral: "240"; Birks	18.00
240-93		ORs	Title: "BEAVER/240/CANADA"; Inglis	35.00

241ST INFANTRY BATTALION

"CANADIAN SCOTTISH BORDERERS"

The Battalion was raised in Western Ontario with mobilization headquarters at Windsor under the authority of G.O. 69 July 15th, 1916. The Battalion sailed April 29th, 1917 under the command of Lieutenant-Colonel W. L. McGregor with a strength of twenty-one officers and six hundred and twenty-five other ranks. In England the Battalion was absorbed into the 12th Reserve Battalion. It was disbanded September 15th, 1920.

BADGE NUMBER: 241

CANADIAN SCOTTISH BORDERERS/241/OVERSEAS

AUTHORIZED NOVEMBER 7, 1916

Makers: Ellis, Unknown
Fasteners: Lugs
Composition:
Other Ranks: Pickled copper or brass; White metal
Officers:
    A: Sterling silver
    B: Browning copper
Ref.: Babin, Meek, Stewart, Cox

Badge No.	Insignia	Rank	Description	Extremely Fine
241-2	Glengarry	ORs	Pickled copper; Ellis	145.00
241-4		ORs	Pickled brass; Ellis	95.00
241-6		ORs	White metal; Ellis	95.00
241-21		Officers	Sterling silver; Ellis	375.00
241-23		Officers	Browning copper; Ellis	150.00
241-41	Collars	ORs	Pickled copper; Ellis	60.00
241-43		ORs	Pickled brass; Ellis	22.00
241-61		Officers	Sterling silver; Ellis	100.00
241-63		Officers	Browning copper; Ellis	45.00
241-91	Shoulders	ORs	Numeral: "241"; Unknown	20.00
241-93		ORs	Title: "R.H.C."; Unknown	18.00

242ND INFANTRY BATTALION

"CANADIAN FORESTRY BATTALION"

The Battalion was raised in Quebec with mobilization headquarters at Montreal under the authority of G.O. 69 July 15th, 1916. The Battalion sailed November 23rd, 1916 under the command of Lieutenant-Colonel J. B. White with a strength of forty-four officers and one thousand and six other ranks. In England the Battalion was absorbed into the Canadian Forestry Corps. It was disbanded September 15th, 1920.

BADGE NUMBER: 242

FORESTRY BATTALION/OVERSEAS/242/CANADA

AUTHORIZED OCTOBER 4, 1916

Makers: Caron, Unknown 1 & 2
Fasteners: Lugs
Composition:
Other Ranks: Pickled copper or brass
Officers: Pickled brass with white metal overlay on design
Ref.: Babin, Meek, Stewart, Cox

Note: Two makers of this cap badge exist.
1. Small beaver and tall crown; Unknown-1 *(Illustrated)*
2. Large beaver and short crown; Unknown-2.

Badge No.	Insignia	Rank	Description	Extremely Fine
242-2	Cap	ORs	Pickled copper; Unknown-1	40.00
242-4		ORs	Pickled brass; Unknown-2	45.00
242-21		Officers	Pickled brass, Wm. overlay on design; Unknown-1	85.00
242-41	Collars	ORs	Pickled copper; Unknown-1	12.00
242-43		ORs	Pickled brass; Unknown-2	20.00
242-61		Officers	Pickled brass, Wm. overlay on design; Unknown-1	40.00
242-91	Shoulders	ORs	Numeral: "242"; Caron	20.00

243RD INFANTRY BATTALION

The Battalion was raised in Saskatchewan with mobilization headquarters at Prince Albert under the authority of G.O. 69, July 15th, 1916. The Battalion sailed June 2nd, 1917 under the command of Lieutenant-Colonel J. E. Bradshaw with a strength of sixteen officers and three hundred and ninety-one other ranks. In England the Battalion was absorbed into the 15th Reserve Battalion. It was disbanded September 15th, 1920.

BADGE NUMBER: 243

CANADA 243 OVERSEAS

NOT AUTHORIZED

Makers: Ellis, Unknown
Fasteners: Lugs, Pin
Compositon:
Other Ranks: Browning copper;
Antiqued copper
Officers:
A: Silverplate on copper
B: Sterling silver
Ref.: Babin, Meek, Stewart, Cox

Note: Shoulder numerals "243" are not known.

Badge No.	Insignia	Rank	Description	Extremely Fine
243-2	Cap	ORs	Browning copper; Ellis	125.00
243-4		ORs	Antiqued copper; Ellis	50.00
243-21		Officers	Silverplate on copper; Ellis	145.00
243-23		Officers	Sterling silver; Ellis	350.00
243-41	Collars	ORs	Browning copper; Ellis	100.00
243-43		ORs	Antiqued copper; Ellis	100.00
243-61		Officers	Unknown	- -
243-91	Shoulders	ORs	Numeral: "243"	Unknown
243-93		ORs	Title: "243" over "CANADA"; Unknown	50.00

244TH INFANTRY BATTALION

"KITCHENER'S OWN"

The Battalion was raised in Quebec with mobilization headquarters at Montreal under the authority of G.O. 69 July 15th, 1916. The Battalion sailed March 28th, 1917 under the command of Lieutenant-Colonel E. M. McRobie with a strength of twenty-seven officers and six hundred and four other ranks. In England the Battalion was absorbed into the 23rd Reserve Battalion. It was disbanded September 15th, 1920.

BADGE NUMBER: 244

No. - 244A

KITCHENER'S OWN CANADA
/K 244 O/OVERSEAS/THOROUGH

NOT AUTHORIZED

Makers: Hemsley, Unknown
Fasteners: Lugs, Pin
Composition:
Other Ranks: Pickled copper
or brass
Officers: Pickled copper with
white metal overlay
on design
Ref.: Babin, Meek, Stewart, Cox

Badge No.	Insignia	Rank	Description	Extremely Fine
244A-2	Cap	ORs	Pickled copper, Solid; Hemsley	35.00
244A-6		ORs	Pickled brass, Void; Hemsley	90.00
244A-21		Officers	Pickled copper, Wm. overlay on design; Hemsley	100.00
244A-41	Collars	ORs	Pickled brass; Hemsley	15.00
244A-61		Officers	Pickled copper, Wm. overlay on design; Hemsley	60.00
244A-91	Shoulders	ORs	Numeral: "244"; Unknown	30.00
244A-93		ORs	Title: "SPHINX over 244"; Hemsley	35.00

No. - 244B

VICTORIA RIFLES CANADA
/244/OVERSEAS/THOROUGH

Makers: Unknown
Fasteners: Lugs
Composition:
Other Ranks: Pickled brass
Officers: Pickled brass with
white metal overlay
on design
Ref.: Not previously listed

Badge No.	Insignia	Rank	Description	Extremely Fine
244B-2	Cap	ORs	Pickled brass; Unknown	1,000.00
244B-21		Officers	Pickled brass, Wm. overlay on design; Unknown	2,500.00
244B-41	Collars	ORs	Unknown	- -
244B-61		Officers	Unknown	- -

245TH INFANTRY BATTALION

"MONTREAL GRENADIERS"/
"CANADIAN GRENADIER GUARDS"

The Battalion was raised in Quebec with mobilization headquarters at Montreal under the authority of G.O. 69 July 15th, 1916. The Battalion sailed May 3rd, 1917 under the command of Lieutenant-Colonel C. C. Ballantyne with a strength of sixteen officers and two hundred and seventy-four other ranks. In England the Battalion was absorbed into the 23rd Reserve Battalion. It was disbanded September 15th, 1920.

BADGE NUMBER: 245

No. - 245A  **GRENADE DESIGN**

Makers: Unknown
Fasteners: Lugs
Compositon:
  Other Ranks: Pickled brass; Brass
    Officers: Brass, Unknown
Ref.: Babin, Cox

Badge No.	Insignia	Rank	Description	Extremely Fine
245A-2	Cap	ORs	Brass; Unknown	20.00
245A-21		Officers	Brass; Unknown	50.00
245A-41	Collars	ORs	Pickled brass; Unknown	25.00
245A-61		Officers	Unknown	- -
245A-91	Shoulders	ORs	Numeral: "245"; Unknown	20.00
245A-93		ORs	Title: "245/GG/CANADA"; Unknown	30.00

No. - 245B   **(CYPHER) G.R.R.G./CANADA**

Makers: Unknown
Fasteners: Lugs
Composition:
Other Ranks: Pickled brass
overlay on pickled
brass grenade
Officers: Sterling silver over-
lay on pickled brass
grenade
Ref.: Babin, Meek, Stewart, Cox

Badge No.	Insignia	Rank	Description	Extremely Fine
245B-2	Cap	ORs	Pickled brass; Brass cypher overlay; Unknown	40.00
245B-21		Officers	Pickled brass, Silver cypher overlay Unknown	40.00
245B-41	Collars	ORs	Pickled brass; Unknown	25.00
245B-61		Officers	Pickled brass, Silver cypher overlay; Unknown	25.00

246TH INFANTRY BATTALION

"NOVA SCOTIA HIGHLANDERS"

The Battalion was raised in Nova Scotia with mobilization headquarters at Halifax under the authority of G.O. 48 May 1st, 1917. The Battalion sailed June 2nd, 1917 under the command of Lieutenant-Colonel N. H. Parson with a strength of fourteen officers and two hundred and thirty-three other ranks. In England the Battalion was absorbed into the 17th Reserve Battalion. It was disbanded September 15th, 1920.

BADGE NUMBER: 246

No. - 246A

CANADA/NOVA SCOTIA
HIGHLANDERS OVERSEAS
/246/SIOL NA FEAR FEARAIL

NOT AUTHORIZED

Makers: Birks, Hemsley, Tiptaft
Fasteners: Lugs
Composition:
Other Ranks: Pickled brass
Officers: Pickled brass with silver overlay on design
Ref.: Babin, Meek, Stewart, Cox

Note: Two makers of this cap badge exist.
  1. The area on both sides of the crest is void; Hemsley *(Illustrated)*
  2. The area on both sides of the crest is solid; Tiptaft.

Badge No.	Insignia	Rank	Description	Extremely Fine
246A-2	Glengarry	ORs	Pickled brass, Solid; Hemsley	225.00
246A-4		ORs	Pickled brass, Void; Hemsley	225.00
246A-6		ORs	Pickled brass; Tiptaft	225.00
246A-21		Officers	Pickled brass, Silver overlay on design; Hemsley	625.00
Maple Leaf Design				
246A-41	Collars	ORs	Pickled brass; Hemsley	100.00
246A-43		ORs	Pickled brass; Tiptaft	100.00
246A-61		Officers	Pickled brass, Silver overlay on design; Hemsley	250.00

Badge No.	Insignia	Rank	Description	Extremely Fine
			Scroll Design	
246A-45	Collars	ORs	Pickled brass; Hemsley	100.00
246A-47		ORs	Pickled brass; Tiptaft	100.00
246A-63		Officers	Pickled brass, Silver overlay on design; Hemsley	250.00
246A-91	Shoulders	ORs	Numeral: "246"; Birks	20.00
246A-93		ORs	Title: "THISTLE/246/CANADA"	35.00

No. - 246B   OVERSEAS BATTALION CANADA/246

Makers: Caron for Eaton's
Fasteners: Lugs, Pin
Composition:
Other Ranks: Pickled copper with white metal overlay on centre
Officers: Pickled copper with silver overlay on centre
Ref.: Not previously listed

Note: Collars are not known

Badge No.	Insignia	Rank	Description	Extremely Fine
246B-2	Cap	ORs	Pickled copper, Wm. overlay on centre; Caron	300.00
246B-21		Officers	Pickled copper, Silver overlay on centre; Caron	350.00

247TH INFANTRY BATTALION

"VICTORIA AND HALIBURTON BATTALION/DIE HARDS"

The Battalion was raised in Central Ontario with mobilization headquarters at Peterborough under the authority of G.O. 48 May 1st, 1917. The Battalion was under the command of Lieutenant-Colonel C. H. Ackerman. The Battalion was absorbed into the 236th Infantry Battalion. It was disbanded September 15th, 1920.

BADGE NUMBER: 247

VICTORIA AND HALIBURTON /247/OVERSEAS/CANADA

NOT AUTHORIZED

Makers: Hemsley, Unknown
Fasteners: Lugs
Composition:
Other Ranks: Pickled copper
Officers: Pickled copper with silver overlay on design
Ref.: Babin, Meek, Stewart, Cox

Note: The officer's cap is extremely rare. The only known cap, which is illustrated on the cover, was sold at a Jeffrey Hoare Auction in September, 1993 for $4,000.00.

Badge No.	Insignia	Rank	Description	Extremely Fine
247-2	Cap	ORs	Pickled copper; Hemsley	1, 000.00
247-21		Officers	Pickled copper, Silver overlay on design; Hemsley	Rare
247-91	Shoulders	ORs	Numeral: "247"; Unknown	75.00
247-93		ORs	Title: "VICTORIA & HALIBURTON"; Hemsley	150.00

248TH INFANTRY BATTALION

The Battalion was raised in Central Ontario with mobilization headquarters at Owen Sound under the authority of G.O. 48 May 1st, 1917. The Battalion sailed June 2nd, 1917 under the command of Lieutenant-Colonel J. H. Rorke with a strength of thirteen officers and two hundred and fifty-nine other ranks. In England the Battalion was absorbed into the 48th Reserve Battalion. It was disbanded September 15th, 1920.

BADGE NUMBER: 248

DE BON VOULOIR SERVIR/LE ROI /OVERSEAS/248/BATTALION/CANADA

AUTHORIZED APRIL 21, 1917

Makers: Birks, Hemsley
Fasteners: Lugs
Composition:
Other Ranks: Pickled brass
Officers: Pickled brass with silver overlay on design
Ref.: Babin, Meek, Stewart, Cox

Badge No.	Insignia	Rank	Description	Extremely Fine
248-2	Cap	ORs	Pickled brass, Solid; Hemsley	650.00
248-4		ORs	Pickled brass, Void; Hemsley	650.00
248-21		Officers	Pickled brass, Silver overlay on design Hemsley	650.00
248-41	Collars	ORs	Pickled brass, Solid; Hemsley	100.00
248-43		ORs	Pickled brass, Void; Hemsley	100.00
248-61		Officers	Pickled brass, Silver overlay on design; Hemsley	150.00
248-91	Shoulders	ORs	Numeral: "248"; Birks (1916)	75.00

249TH INFANTRY BATTALION

The Battalion was raised in Saskatchewan with mobilization headquarters at Regina under the authority of G.O. 48 May 1st, 1917. The Battalion sailed February 21st, 1918 under the command of Lieutenant-Colonel C. B. Keenlyside with a strength of fifteen officers and seven hundred and nine other ranks. In England the Battalion was absorbed into the 15th Reserve Battalion. It was disbanded September 15th, 1920.

BADGE NUMBER: 249

HEADS UP/249/
OVERSEAS BATTALION C.E.F./CANADA

NOT AUTHORIZED

Makers: Birks, Unknown
Fasteners: Lugs
Compositon:
Other Ranks: Pickled brass
Officers:
    A. Pickled brass with white metal overlay on design
    B. Pickled silver
Ref.: Babin, Meek, Stewart, Cox

Note: Cast cap badges exist, the maker is not known. It is interesting to note that this cap badge was not authorized due to the caption "Heads Up". A new design was submitted with the name "Saskatchewan" substituted for "Heads Up" and this design was authorized April 28, 1917.

Badge No.	Insignia	Rank	Description	Extremely Fine
249-2	Cap	ORs	Pickled brass, Solid; Unknown	45.00
249-4		ORs	Pickled brass, Void; Unknown	45.00
249-21		Officers	Pickled brass, Silver overlay on design; Unknown	400.00
249-23		Officers	Pickled silver; Unknown	400.00
249-41	Collars	ORs	Pickled brass, Solid; Unknown	25.00
249-43		ORs	Pickled brass, Void; Unknown	25.00
249-61		Officers	Pickled brass, Silver overlay on design; Unknown	175.00
249-63		Officers	Pickled silver; Unknown	185.00
249-91	Shoulders	ORs	Numeral: "249"; Birks	20.00

250TH INFANTRY BATTALION

"WHITE EAGLES"

The Battalion was raised in Manitoba with mobilization headquarters at Winnipeg under the authority of G.O. 48 May 1st, 1917. The Battalion was under the command of Lieutenant-Colonel W. H. Hastings. The Battalion was absorbed into the 249th Infantry Battalion. It was disbanded September 15th, 1920.

BADGE NUMBER: 250

OVERSEAS BATTALION/250/WINNIPEG/CANADA

AUTHORIZED APRIL 13, 1917

Makers: Birks, Dingwall
Fasteners: Lugs, Tangs
Composition:
Other Ranks: Pickled copper
Officers: Pickled copper with silver overlay on "250" and "Shield"
Ref.: Babin, Meek, Stewart, Cox

Badge No.	Insignia	Rank	Description	Extremely Fine
250-2	Cap	ORs	Pickled copper; Dingwall	950.00
250-21		Officers	Pickled copper. Silver overlay on "250" and "Shield"; Dingwall	475.00
250-41	Collars	ORs	Pickled copper; Dingwall	100.00
250-61		Officers	Pickled copper, Silver overlay on design; Dingwall	250.00
250-91	Shoulders	ORs	Numeral: "250"; Birks	20.00
250-93		ORs	Title: "250/CANADA"; Dingwall	

251ST INFANTRY BATTALION

"GOOD FELLOWS BATTALION"

The Battalion was raised in Manitoba with mobilization headquarters at Winnipeg under the authority of G.O. 48 May 1st, 1917. The Battalion sailed October 6th, 1917 under the command of Lieutenant-Colonel G. H. Nicholson with a strength of four officers and one hundred and seventy other ranks. In England the Battalion was absorbed into the 18th Reserve Battalion. It was disbanded September 15th, 1920.

BADGE NUMBER: 251

251/GOOD FELLOWS
/OVERSEAS C.E.F. BATTALION/CANADA

NOT AUTHORIZED

Makers: Birks, Dingwall, Stanley & Aylward, Tiptaft
Fasteners: Lugs
Compositon:
Other Ranks: Pickled brass
Officers: Sterling silver
Ref.: Babin, Meek, Stewart, Cox

Note: Two makers of this cap badge exist.
1. Short wide crown with straight "1" in "251"; Stanley & Aylward
2. Short narrow crown with a curved "1" in "251"; Tiptaft.
The sub title "Good Fellows" was requested to be eliminated from this badge design before approval would be given. With this elimination the badge design was authorized on January 30, 1917. However the corrected badge has yet to be seen.

Badge No.	Insignia	Rank	Description	Extremely Fine
251-2	Cap	ORs	Pickled brass; Stanley & Aylward	175.00
251-4		ORs	Pickled brass; Tiptaft	100.00
251-21		Officers	Sterling silver; Stanley & Aylward	300.00
	Wreath of Maple Leaves Design			
251-41	Collars	ORs	Pickled brass; Tiptaft	50.00
	Maple Leaf Design			
251-43	Collars	ORs	Pickled brass; Stanley & Aylward	50.00
251-61		Officers	Sterling silver; Stanley & Aylward	100.00
251-91	Shoulders	ORs	Numeral: "251"; Birks	18.00
251-93		ORs	Title: "251" over "CANADA"; Dingwall	20.00

252ND INFANTRY BATTALION

The Battalion was raised in Ontario with mobilization headquarters at Lindsay under the authority of G.O. 48 May 1st, 1917. The Battalion sailed June 2nd, 1917 under the command of Major G. J. Glass with a strength of six officers and one hundred and twenty-seven other ranks. In England the Battalion was absorbed into the 6th Reserve Battalion. It was disbanded September 15th, 1920.

BADGE NUMBER: 252

LINDSAY BATTALION/OVER 252 SEAS/CANADA

Makers: Birks, Hemsley
Fasteners: Lugs
Composition:
Other Ranks: Pickled brass
Officers: Unknown
Ref.: Babin, Meek, Stewart, Cox

Solid   Void

Badge No.	Insignia	Rank	Description	Extremely Fine
252-2	Cap	ORs	Pickled brass, Solid, Large Beaver; Hemsley	750.00
252-4		ORs	Pickled brass, Void, Large Beaver; Hemsley	950.00
252-6		ORs	Pickled brass, Void, Small Beaver; Hemsley	950.00
252-21		Officers	Unknown	- -
252-41	Collars	ORs	Unknown	- -
252-61		Officers	Unknown	- -
252-91	Shoulders	ORs	Numeral: "252"; Birks	40.00
252-93		ORs	Title: "252/CANADA"; Hemsley	100.00

253RD INFANTRY BATTALION

"QUEEN'S UNIVERSITY HIGHLANDERS"

The Battalion was raised in Eastern Ontario with mobilization headquarters at Kingston under the authority of G.O. 48, May 1st, 1917. The Battalion sailed April 29th, 1917 under the command of Lieutenant-Colonel P. G. C. Campbell with a strength of seventeen officers and four hundred and sixty-one other ranks. In England the Battalion was absorbed into the 5th Reserve Battalion. It was disbanded September 15th, 1920.

BADGE NUMBER: 253

No. - 253A   QUEEN'S UNIVERSITY OVERSEAS
                   HIGHLAND BATTALION/253/CANADA

AUTHORIZED JANUARY 18, 1917

Makers: Kinnear & Desterre, Hemsley
Fasteners: Lugs
Composition:
   Other Ranks: Pickled brass
      Officers: Pickled brass with white metal overlay on design
Ref.: Babin, Meek, Stewart, Cox

Note: Shoulder numerals are not known. Two makers of the cap badge exist.
1. Solid badge; Hemsley
2. Void Badge; Kinnear & Desterre *(Illustrated)*

Badge No.	Insignia	Rank	Description	Extremely Fine
253A-2	Cap	ORs	Pickled brass, Solid; Hemsley	125.00
253A-4		ORs	Pickled brass, Void; Kinnear & Desterre	125.00
253A-21		Officers	Pickled brass, Wm. overlay on design; Hemsley	175.00
253A-41	Collars	ORs	Pickled brass, Solid; Hemsley	45.00
253A-43		ORs	Pickled brass, Void; Kinnear & Desterre	45.00
253A-61		Officers	Pickled brass, Wm. overlay on design; Hemsley	125.00
253A-91	Shoulders	ORs	Numeral: "253"	Unknown
253A-93		ORs	Title: "253/QUH/CANADA"; Hemsley	40.00

No. - 253B   **OVERSEAS BATTALION CANADA/253**

**Photograph
Not Available
At Press Time**

Makers: Caron for Eaton's
Fasteners: Lugs
Compositon:
Other Ranks: Pickled copper with white metal overlay on centre
Officers: Pickled copper with silver overlay on centre
Ref.: Not previously listed

Note: Collars are not known.

Badge No.	Insignia	Rank	Description	Extremely Fine
253B-2	Cap	ORs	Pickled copper, Wm. overlay on centre; Caron	Rare
253B-21		Officers	Pickled copper, Silver overlay on centre; Caron	Rare

254TH INFANTRY BATTALION

"QUINTE'S OWN"

The Battalion was raised in Central Ontario with mobilization headquarters at Belleville under the authority of G.O. 48 May 1st, 1917. The Battalion sailed June 2nd, 1917 under the command of Lieutenant-Colonel A. P. Allen with a strength of eight officers and two hundred and forty-three other ranks. In England the Battalion was absorbed into the 6th Reserve Battalion. It was disbanded September 15th, 1920.

BADGE NUMBER: 254

OVERSEAS BATTALION
/QUINTE'S OWN/254/CANADA

AUTHORIZED JANUARY 18, 1917

Makers: Hemsley, Unknown
Fasteners: Lugs
Composition:
Other Ranks: Pickled brass
Officers:
    A: Pickled brass with silver overlay on design
    B: Sterling silver
Ref.: Babin, Meek, Stewart, Cox

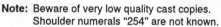

Note: Beware of very low quality cast copies. Shoulder numerals "254" are not known.

Badge No.	Insignia	Rank	Description	Extremely Fine
254-2	Cap	ORs	Pickled brass, Solid; Hemsley	Rare
254-4		ORs	Pickled brass, Void; Hemsley	120.00
254-21		Officers	Pickled brass, Silver overlay on design; Hemsley	200.00
254-23		Officers	Sterling silver; Unknown	200.00
254-41	Collars	ORs	Pickled brass, Solid; Hemsley	Rare
254-43		ORs	Pickled brass, Void; Hemsley	50.00
254-61		Officers	Pickled brass, Silver overlay on design; Hemsley	Rare
254-91	Shoulders	ORs	Numeral: "254"	Unknown

255TH INFANTRY BATTALION

"QUEEN'S OWN RIFLES"

The Battalion was raised in Central Ontario with mobilization headquarters at Toronto under the authority of G.O. 48 May 1st, 1917. The Battalion sailed June 2nd, 1917 under the command of Lieutenant-Colonel G. C. Royce with a strength of thirteen officers and two hundred and eighty-four other ranks. In England the Battalion was absorbed into the 12th Reserve Battalion. It was disbanded September 15th, 1920.

BADGE NUMBER: 255

QUEEN'S OWN RIFLES OF CANADA
/255/OVERSEAS BATTALION

AUTHORIZED JANUARY 19, 1917

Makers: Ellis, Hemsley, Tiptaft
Fasteners: Lugs
Composition:
Other Ranks: Pickled brass;
Browning brass;
Officers:
A: Sterling Silver
B: White metal
Ref.: Babin, Meek, Stewart, Cox

Note: The Ellis collar is 23 mm high while the other collars, Hemsley and Tiptaft, are 32 and 33 mm respectively. Shoulder numerals are not known.
Three makers of this cap badge exist.
1. Tall numbers with small type; Hemsley *(Illustrated)*
2. Short numbers with large type; Tiptaft
3. Not recorded; Ellis

Badge No.	Insignia	Rank	Description	Extremely Fine
255-2	Cap	ORs	Pickled brass; Hemsley	60.00
255-4		ORs	Pickled brass; Tiptaft	60.00
255-6		ORs	Browning brass; Ellis	60.00
255-21		Officers	White metal; Unknown	60.00
255-23		Officers	Sterling silver; Unknown	75.00
255-41	Collars	ORs	Pickled brass; Hemsley	40.00
255-43		ORs	Pickled brass; Tiptaft	40.00
255-45		ORs	Browning copper; Ellis	75.00
255-61		Officers	White metal; Unknown	50.00
255-63		Officers	Sterling silver; Unknown	50.00
255-91	Shoulders	ORs	Numeral: "255"	Unknown
255-93		ORs	Title: "CROWN/QOR/CANADA"	40.00

256TH INFANTRY BATTALION

The Battalion was raised in Central Ontario with mobilization headquarters at Toronto under the authority of G.O. 69 July 15th, 1916. The Battalion sailed March 28th, 1917 under the command of Lieutenant-Colonel W. A. McConnell with a strength of eighteen officers and five hundred and thirty-one other ranks. The Battalion served in France as the 10th Battalion, Canadian Railway Troops. It was disbanded September 15th, 1920.

BADGE NUMBER: 256

RAILWAY CONSTRUCTION OVERSEAS
BATTALION/256/CANADA

AUTHORIZED FEBRUARY 3, 1917

Makers: Roden, Unknown
Fasteners: Lugs
Composition:
Other Ranks: Browning copper;
Blackened copper;
Antique copper
Officers: Sterling silver
Ref.: Babin, Meek, Stewart, Cox

Badge No.	Insignia	Rank	Description	Extremely Fine
256-2	Cap	ORs	Browning copper; Roden	75.00
256-4		ORs	Blackened copper; Roden	75.00
256-6		ORs	Antiqued copper; Roden	75.00
256-21		Officers	Sterling silver; Roden	100.00
256-41	Collars	ORs	Browning copper; Roden	60.00
256-43		ORs	Blackened copper; Roden	22.00
256-45		ORs	Antiqued copper; Roden	22.00
256-61		Officers	Sterling silver; Roden	50.00
256-91	Shoulders	ORs	Numeral: "256"; Unknown	50.00
256-93		ORs	Title: "256RY over CANADA"	50.00

257TH INFANTRY BATTALION

"CANADIAN RAILWAY CONSTRUCTION BATTALION"

The Battalion was raised in Eastern Ontario with mobilization headquarters at Ottawa under the authority of G.O. 69 July 15th, 1916. The Battalion sailed February 16th, 1917 under the command of Lieutenant-Colonel L. T. Martin with a strength of twenty-nine officers and nine hundred and two other ranks. The Battalion served in France as the 7th Battalion, Canadian Railway Troops. It was disbanded September 15th, 1920.

BADGE NUMBER: 257

No. - 257A   RAILWAY CONSTRUCTION/
                OVER 257 SEAS/BATTALION/CANADA

AUTHORIZED JANUARY 18, 1917

Makers: Stanley & Aylward
Fasteners: Lugs
Composition:
Other Ranks: Pickled brass
Officers: Unknown
Ref.: Not previously listed

Note: Shoulder numerals "257" are not known.

Badge No.	Insignia	Rank	Description	Extremely Fine
257A-2	Cap	ORs	Browning brass	175.00
257A-21		Officers	Unknown	- -
257A-41	Collars	ORs	Browning brass	50.00
257A-61		Officers	Unknown	- -
257A-91	Shoulders	ORs	Numeral: "257"	Unknown

No. - 257B   CANADIAN RAILWAY CONSTRUCTION BATTALION

Makers: Stanley & Aylward
Fasteners: Lugs
Composition:
Other Ranks: Pickled brass
Officers: Unknown
Ref.: Babin, Meek, Stewart, Cox

Badge No.	Insignia	Rank	Description	Extremely Fine
257B-2	Cap	ORs	Pickled brass; Stanley & Aylward	225.00
257B-21		Officers	Unknown	- -
257B-41	Collars	ORs	Unknown	- -
257B-61		Officers	Unknown	- -

258TH INFANTRY BATTALION

The Battalion was raised in Quebec with mobilization headquarters at Quebec, Quebec under the authority of G.O. 63 June 15th, 1917. The Battalion sailed October 16th, 1917 under the command of Lieutenant-Colonel P. E. Blondin with a strength of sixteen officers and two hundred and fifteen other ranks. In England the Battalion was absorbed into the 10th Reserve Battalion. It was disbanded September 15th, 1920.

BADGE NUMBER: 258

CANADIEN FRANCAIS/LIBERTE LOYAUTE /258/HONNEUR COURAGE

NOT AUTHORIZED

Makers: Tiptaft, Unknown
Fasteners: Lugs
Composition:
Other Ranks: Pickled brass;
Blackened brass
Officers: Pickled brass with
silver overlay on
design
Ref.: Babin, Meek, Stewart, Cox

Note: Two makers of this cap badge exist.
    1. Small numerals "258" with a slanted "2"; Unknown
    2. Large numerals "258" with a straight "258"; Tiptaft' *(Illustrated)*

Badge No.	Insignia	Rank	Description	Extremely Fine
258-2	Cap	ORs	Pickled brass; Unknown	75.00
258-4		ORs	Pickled brass, Solid; Unknown	75.00
258-6		ORs	Pickled brass, Void; Unknown	75.00
258-8		ORs	Blackened brass; Tiptaft	165.00
258-21		Officers	Pickled brass, Silver overlay on design; Unknown	300.00
258-41	Collars	ORs	Pickled brass; Unknown	80.00
258-43		ORs	Blackened brass; Tiptaft	80.00
258-61		Officers	Pickled brass, Silver overlay on design; Unknown	100.00
258-91	Shoulders	ORs	Numeral: "258"; Unknown	175.00

259TH INFANTRY BATTALION

"SIBERIAN EXPEDITIONARY FORCE"

On July 12th, 1918, the Chief of the General Staff was directed to form a Brigade Headquarters, two Infantry Battalions, a Field Artillery Battery, a Machine-Gun Company and certain other troops for service in Siberia. With a British Battalion joining the Canadians in Siberia the contingent would be known as the "Canadian Siberian Expeditionary Force". An advance party of six hundred "all ranks" sailed from Vancouver, on October 11th, 1918. The force was under the command of Major-General J. H. Elmsley. The last Canadian troops left Vladivostock on June 5th, 1919. The Battalion was disbanded September 15th, 1920.

BADGE NUMBER: 259

Makers: Stanley & Aylward,
Unknown
Fasteners: Lugs
Composition:
Other Ranks: Browning copper
Officers:
  A: Sterling silver
  B: Browning copper
     with sterling silver
     maple leaf
Ref.: Babin, Meek, Stewart

Note: The officers cap is different from the OR's in that the maple leaf is larger and overlaid on the horn instead of inside.

Badge No.	Insignia	Rank	Description	Extremely Fine
259-2	Cap	ORs	Browning copper, (Small maple leaf)	375.00
259-21		Officers	Browning copper (Large maple leaf)	400.00
259-23		Officers	Sterling silver	700.00
259-25		Officers	Browning copper, Sterling silver maple leaf	700.00
259-41	Collars	ORs	Browning copper	225.00
259-61		Officers	Sterling silver	250.00
		"C" Over Numbers		
259-81	Collars	ORs	"C" bar "259"; Unknown	75.00
259-83		Officers	"C" bar "259", Sterling silver; Unknown	350.00
259-91	Shoulders	ORs	Numeral: "259"; Unknown	50.00

260TH INFANTRY BATTALION

"SIBERIAN EXPEDITIONARY FORCE"

On July 12th, 1918, the Chief of the General Staff was directed to form a Brigade Headquarters, two Infantry Battalions, a Field Artillery Battery, a Machine-Gun Company and certain other troops for service in Siberia. With a British Battalion joining the Canadians in Siberia the contingent would be known as the "Canadian Siberian Expeditionary Force". An advance party of six hundred "all ranks" sailed from Vancouver, on October 11th, 1918. The force was under the command of Major-General J. H. Elmsley. The last Canadian troops left Vladivostock on June 5th, 1919. The Battalion was disbanded September 15th, 1920.

BADGE NUMBER: 260

Makers: Stanley & Aylward
Fasteners: Lugs
Compositon:
Other Ranks: Browning copper;
Brass
Officers:
    A: Silverplated copper
    B: Sterling silver
    C: White metal
Ref.: Babin, Meek, Stewart

Note: The officers cap is different from the OR's in that the maple leaf is larger and overlaid on the horn instead of inside.

Badge No.	Insignia	Rank	Description	Extremely Fine
260-2	Cap	ORs	Browning copper, Small maple leaf	275.00
260-21		Officers	Browning copper Large maple leaf	275.00
260-23		Officers	Silverplated copper	375.00
260-25		Officers	Sterling silver	700.00
260-41	Collars	ORs	Browning copper	100.00
260-61		Officers	White metal	250.00
260-63		Officers	Sterling silver	175.00
"C" Over Numbers				
260-81	Collars	ORs	"C" bar "260"; Unknown	75.00
260-83		Officers	"C" bar "260", Sterling silver; Unknown	350.00
260-91	Shoulders	ORs	Numeral: "260"; Unknown	50.00

INDEPENDENT INFANTRY COMPANIES

(No.1) JEWISH INFANTRY COMPANY

Organized February 1, 1917, disbanded September 15, 1920.

BADGE NUMBER: 261

JRDC/PRO IMPERA/OVERSEAS/CANADA

Makers: Hemsley, Inglis
Fasteners: Lugs
Composition:
Other Ranks: Pickled copper
    or brass
Officers: Silver
Ref.: Babin 6-2, Cox 814

Badge No.	Insignia	Rank	Description	Extremely Fine
261-2	Cap	ORs	Pickled copper; Hemsley, Inglis	400.00
261-4		ORs	Pickled brass; Hemsley, Inglis	800.00
261-21		Officers	Silver; Hemsley, Inglis	800.00
261-41	Collars	ORs	Pickled copper; Hemsley, Inglis	125.00
261-61		Officers	Silver; Hemsley, Inglis	175.00
261-91	Shoulders	ORs	Unknown	- -

YUKON INFANTRY COMPANY

Organized December 22, 1915, disbanded September 15, 1920.

BADGE NUMBER: 262

DAWSON/YT/CANADA

Makers: Jacoby
Fasteners: Lugs, Pin
Composition:
Other Ranks: Brass; Copper
Officers: Gilt on copper
Ref.: Babin 6-1, Cox 813

Badge No.	Insignia	Rank	Description	Extremely Fine
262-2	Cap	ORs	Copper; Jacoby	300.00
262-4		ORs	Brass; Jacoby	300.00
262-21		Officers	Gilt on copper	650.00
262-41	Collars	ORs	Copper, Jacoby	150 00
262-61		Officers	Gilt on copper	175.00
262-91	Shoulders	ORs	Title: YUKON TERRITORY/CANADA	25.00

UNIVERSITY OVERSEAS TRAINING COMPANIES

No. 1 University Company - McGill
Mobilized May 1, 1915 At McGill University
in Montreal

There were six University Companies mobilized from the universities across Canada. Only McGill and the University of Toronto companies wore their own badges, the other four wore the General Service university badge No. 272.

All companies were mobilized at McGill and all were supplied as reinforcements for the Princess Patricia's Canadian Light Infantry.

BADGE NUMBER: 263

UNIVERSITAS COLLEGII MCGILL/AD 1821/
GRANDESCUNT AUCTA LABORE/

Makers: Lees, 1915
Fasteners: Lugs
Composition:
Other Ranks: Copper
Officers: Unknown
Ref.: Babin 3-2, Cox 957

Badge No.	Insignia	Rank	Description	Extremely Fine
270-2	Cap	ORs	Copper; Lees	75.00
270-21		Officers	Unknown	- -
270-41	Collars	ORs	Unknown	- -
270-61		Officers	Unknown	- -
270-91	Shoulders	ORs	Title: COTC	5.00

No. 2 UNIVERSITY COMPANY

UNIVERSITY OF TORONTO

Organized August 15, 1915, disbanded September 15, 1920

BADGE NUMBER: 264

C.O.T.C/UNIVERSITY OF TORONTO OVERSEAS
TRAINING COMPANY/CANADA

AUTHORIZED MAY 16, 1916

Makers: Ellis
Fasteners: Lugs, Pin
Composition:
Other Ranks: Browning copper
Officers: Gilt on copper
Ref.: Babin 3-1, Cox 965

Badge No.	Insignia	Rank	Description	Extremely Fine
271-2	Cap	ORs	Browning copper; Ellis	85.00
271-21		Officers	Gilt on copper; Ellis	100.00
271-41	Collars	ORs	Browning copper; Ellis	30.00
271-61		Officers	Gilt on copper; Ellis	35.00
271-91	Shoulders	ORs	Title: COTC; Ellis	5.00

No. 3 to 6 UNIVERSITY COMPANIES

GENERAL SERVICE BADGE

BADGE NUMBER: 265

CANADA/UNIVERSITY OVERSEAS COMPANY

Makers: Birks
Fasteners: Lugs, Pin
Composition:
Other Ranks: Browning copper;
Browning brass
Officers: Gilt on copper
Ref.: Babin 3-3, Cox 966

Badge No.	Insignia	Rank	Description	Extremely Fine
272-2	Cap	ORs	Browning copper; Birks	30.00
272-4		ORs	Browning brass; Birks	45.00
272-21		Officers	Gilt on copper	45.00
272-41	Collars	ORs	Unknown	- -
272-61		Officers	Unknown	- -
272-91	Shoulders	ORs	Unknown	- -

OVERSEAS INFANTRY DRAFTS

6TH DUKE OF CONNAUGHT'S OWN
OVERSEAS INFANTRY DRAFT

BADGE NUMBER: 266

D.C.O./VI/OVERSEAS DRAFT/
CEF/CANADA

Makers: Allan
Fasteners: Lugs, Tangs
Composition:
Other Ranks: Blackened copper
Officers: Unknown
Ref.: Babin 7-6, Cox 815

Badge No.	Insignia	Rank	Description	Extremely Fine
263-2	Cap	ORs	Blackened copper; Allan	300.00
263-21		Officers	Unknown	- -
263-41	Collars	ORs	Blackened copper; Allan	100.00
263-61		Officers	Unknown	- -
263-91	Shoulders	ORs	Title: CROWN/DCO/CANADA	25.00
263-93		ORs	Title: 6TH DUKE OF CONNAUGHT'S OWN/CANADA	25.00

11TH IRISH FUSILIERS OVERSEAS

INFANTRY DRAFT

Organized June 15, 1917, disbanded September 15, 1920

BADGE NUMBER: 267

11/IRISH REINFORCEMENTS FUSILIERS/
C.E.F./CANADA

Makers: Allan
Fasteners: Lugs, Tangs
Composition:
Other Ranks: Blackened copper
Officers: Unknown
Ref.: Babin 7-11, Cox 816

Badge No.	Insignia	Rank	Description	Extremely Fine
264-2	Cap	ORs	Blackened copper; Allan	130.00
264-21		Officers	Unknown	- -
264-41	Collars	ORs	Blackened copper; Allan	50.00
264-61		Officers	Unknown	- -
264-91	Shoulders	ORs	Title: 11TH IRISH FUSILIERS / CANADA	25.00

50TH GORDON HIGHLANDERS

OVERSEAS INFANTRY DRAFT

Organized June 15, 1917, disbanded September 15, 1920

BADGE NUMBER: 268

50/BUAIDH NO BAS

Makers: Unknown
Fasteners: Lugs
Composition:
Other Ranks: Browning copper
Officers: Silver
Ref.: Babin 7-50, Cox

Badge No.	Insignia	Rank	Description	Extremely Fine
265-2	Cap	ORs	Browning copper	1,500.00
265-21		Officers	Silver	1,500.00
265-41	Collars	ORs	Browning copper	125.00
265-61		Officers	Silver	225.00
265-91	Shoulders	ORs	Title: "50" over "Gordon"	25.00

RESERVE INFANTRY BATTALIONS

As the Canadian Expeditionary Force continued to increase in size, it became necessary to establish a Reserve Force from which replacements could be drawn to strengthen the battalions and corps of the four Canadian Divisions operating in the field. The bulk of Infantry Battalions raised for the C.E.F. went into these Reserve Battalions which were stationed in France and England. The strength of each Reserve Battalion was set at 2,000 all ranks with individual unit identities preserved. A total of twenty-six Reserve Battalions existed within the Canadian Corps.

8TH CENTRAL ONTARIO RESERVE BATTALION

BADGE NUMBER: 269

CENTRAL ONTARIO REC./8/CANADA

Makers: Tiptaft
Fasteners: Lugs
Composition:
Other Ranks: Pickled copper or brass; Browning copper
Officers: Gilt on copper
Ref.: Babin 8-8, Cox 817

Badge No.	Insignia	Rank	Description	Extremely Fine
266-2	Cap	ORs	Pickled copper; Tiptaft	30.00
266-4		ORs	Pickled brass; Tiptaft	25.00
266-6		ORs	Browning copper; Tiptaft	30.00
266-21		Officers	Gilt on copper; Tiptaft	50.00
266-41	Collars	ORs	Pickled copper; Tiptaft	10.00
266-43		ORs	Pickled brass; Tiptaft	10.00
266-61		Officers	Gilt on copper; Tiptaft	25.00
266-91	Shoulders	ORs	Unknown	- -

10TH QUEBEC RESERVE BATTALION

BADGE NUMBER: 270

JE SOUVIENS ME/X/QUE REGT./CAN RES BN

Makers: Unknown
Fasteners: Lugs
Composition:
Other Ranks: Blackened copper, white metal "X" overlay
Officers: Unknown
Ref.: Cox 818

Badge No.	Insignia	Rank	Description	Extremely Fine
267-2	Cap	ORs	Blackened copper, Wm. overlay	275.00
267-21		Officers	Unknown	- -
267-41	Collars	ORs	Unknown	- -
267-61		Officers	Unknown	- -
267-91	Shoulders	ORs	Unknown	- -

14TH WINNIPEG RESERVE

BATTALION

BADGE NUMBER: 271

CANADIAN RESERVE BATTALION
MANITOBA/14/CANADA

Makers: Tiptaft, Unknown
Fasteners: Lugs
Composition:
Other Ranks: Browning copper;
White metal
Officers: Unknown
Ref.: Babin 8-14, Cox 819

Badge No.	Insignia	Rank	Description	Extremely Fine
268-2	Glengarry	ORs	Browning copper; Unknown	85.00
268-4		ORs	White metal; Tiptaft	85.00
268-21		Officers	Unknown	- -
268-41	Collars	ORs	Browning copper; Unknown	50.00
268-43		ORs	White metal; Tiptaft	75.00
268-61		Officers	Unknown	- -
268-91	Shoulders	ORs	Unknown	- -

23RD CANADIAN RESERVE BATTALION

23rd Quebec Reserve Battalion stationed at Shoreham, England.

BADGE NUMBER: 272

RESERVE BATTALION CANADA/23

Makers: Unknown
Fasteners: Lugs
Composition:
Other Ranks: Browning copper
Officers: Bronze
Ref.: Babin 8-23, Cox 820

Badge No.	Insignia	Rank	Description	Extremely Fine
269-2	Cap	ORs	Browning copper	35.00
269-21		Officers	Bronze	150.00
269-41	Collars	ORs	Browning copper	45.00
269-61		Officers	Bronze	50.00
269-91	Shoulders	ORs	Unknown	- -